JOURNAL FOR THE STUDY OF THE OLD TESTAMENT SUPPLEMENT SERIES
272

Sheffield Academic Press

Israel in the Book of Kings

The Past as a Project of Social Identity

James Richard Linville

Journal for the Study of the Old Testament
Supplement Series 272

Well, I mean, *yes* idealism, *yes* the dignity of pure research, *yes* the pursuit of truth in all its forms, but there comes a point I'm afraid where you begin to suspect that if there's any *real* truth, it's that the entire multi-dimensional infinity of the Universe is almost certainly being run by a bunch of maniacs. And if it comes to a choice between spending yet another ten million years finding that out, and on the other hand just taking the money and running, then I for one could do with the exercise.

Frankie, a mouse.

The Hitchhikers Guide to the Galaxy by Douglas Adams:
Copyright ©Serious Productions Ltd 1979
reprinted by Pan Books

Published by Sheffield Academic Press Ltd
Mansion House
19 Kingfield Road
Sheffield S11 9AS
England

Printed on acid-free paper in Great Britain
by Bookcraft Ltd
Midsomer Norton, Bath

British Library Cataloguing in Publication Data

A catalogue record for this book is available
from the British Library

ISBN 1-85075-859-X

CONTENTS

PREFACE

In the almost four years since this project began, I have incurred a great debt to a number of people and organizations. In the first instance, my gratitude goes out to the Committee of Vice Chancellors and Principals for the Overseas Research Students Award, and to the University of Edinburgh for the Postgraduate Research Studentship.

My supervisor, Professor Graeme Auld, has invested a great deal of time and patience in me over the past several years. His guidance has helped me see my way through no small number of conundrums. My second supervisor, Dr Iain Provan, has been a valued teacher, whose always constructive criticism, especially at the early stages of my research, has made this work substantially better than what it might have been. I know that this thesis is not the sort of work that either would produce, or, perhaps, ever expected to supervise, but their support for this project was obvious from the outset. I sincerely hope that the results contained herein prove my efforts deserving of the trust they have had in me. Dr Hayman also deserves mention for sorting out numerous administrative crises I caused myself. Both he and Dr Wyatt have had a welcome role in developing and refining my line of questioning. I would also like to thank Professor Gibson and Dr Lim for their comments on my seminar papers. Dr Wyatt and Professor Robert Carroll of the University of Glasgow examined the finished product, and I am grateful for their comments, editorial skill and most of all their encouragement and votes of confidence.

Throughout my time in Edinburgh, I remained in contact with my undergraduate lecturers, Dr Francis Landy and Dr Ehud Ben Zvi, who were always willing to comment on my ideas. They have not tried to revoke my first degree, or withdraw their recommendations, so I will take it on trust that at least some of these ideas are okay; hopefully those which I actually include here.

I would also like to thank my parents and family for putting up with me and helping out with finances and, most importantly, believing in me. The few times we saw each other over the past few years were precious moments, and I'm sorry I babbled incomprehensibly about my work, and threatened to let them read copies of it, in case they might be interested...

My colleagues, Laura Yoffe, Mares Walter, Johnson Lim, Caroline Somerville, Chris Grundke, Craig Hiebert, and Stuart Weaver have provided much sympathy, not to mention company for an amazing number of cups of coffee, and the odd pint now and again. One does appreciate the occasional reality-check, but perhaps not too often, such as reality is to postgraduates, I suppose; if there is a reality, or something... but there's no point waxing all post-modern in the preface, so I'll just inscribe an undeconstructable thanks: 'thanks'.

Attempting to look studious, I was wont to frequent the library. Paul and Norma didn't seem to mind, even when I complained that they didn't get new, bright green books often enough. I'll bring back all those I borrowed when I get some proper wallpaper. Harriet and Fluffy would also like to thank Paul for looking after them during our holidays. I would also thank Harriet and Fluffy for not splooshing about too loudly when I was trying to think, but then, they're gold-fish, and they tend to do thoughtful stuff like that.

I am mostly indebted to my wife, Anna, not only for the great efforts she has put in trying to translate my sloppy Canadian into readable English, but for all the love and support she has shown me in the past few years. It seems strange that when I first came here, I did not even know her. Life without her is now unthinkable. It would seem I got more good out of Professor Gibson's Job class and Dr Wyatt's Ugaritic lessons than I had at first expected. Anna ended up with a lot of extra work. The fact that this thesis is finished is a testimony to her patience and perseverance. Any errors remaining are, of course, due to the overwhelming abundance of them in the draft she was working with. Any joy displayed by that work's author, however, is down to the overwhelming abundance of love Anna has shown him.

ABBREVIATIONS

AB	Anchor Bible
ABD	David Noel Freedman (ed.), *The Anchor Bible Dictionary* (New York: Doubleday, 1992)
AGJU	Arbeiten zur Geschichte des antiken Judentums und des Urchristentums
Anton	*Antonianum*
ARA	Annual Review of Anthropology
ASAM	Association of Social Anthropologists Monographs
ATANT	Abhandlungen zur Theologie des Alten und Neuen Testaments
ATSAT	Arbeiten zu Text und Sprache im Alten Testament
AusBR	*Australian Biblical Review*
BA	*Biblical Archaeologist*
BETL	Bibliotheca ephemeridum theologicarum lovaniensium
Bib	*Biblica*
BibSem	Biblical Seminar
BIOSCS	*Bulletin of the International Organization for Septuagint and Cognate Studies*
BL	Bible and Literature
BKAT	Biblischer Kommentar: Altes Testament
BWANT	Beiträge zur Wissenschaft vom Alten und Neuen Testament
BZ	*Biblische Zeitschrift*
BZAW	Beihefte zur *ZAW*
CBET	Contributions to Biblical Exegesis and Theology
CBQ	*Catholic Biblical Quarterly*
CBQMS	*Catholic Biblical Quarterly*, Monograph Series
ConBOT	Coniectanea biblica, Old Testament
CRBS	*Currents in Research: Biblical Studies*
CSSA	Cambridge Studies in Social Anthropology
CulAnth	*Cultural Anthropology*
DBAT	*Deilheimer Blätter zum Alten Testament*
ETL	*Ephemerides theologicae lovanienses*
FCB	The Feminist Companion to the Bible
FCI	Foundations of Contemporary Interpretations
FOTL	The Forms of the Old Testament Literature

FRLANT	Forschungen zur Religion und Literatur des Alten und Neuen Testaments
GUOST	*Glasgow University Oriental Society Transactions*
HAR	*Hebrew Annual Review*
HeyJ	*Heythrop Journal*
HSM	Harvard Semitic Monographs
HTIBS	Historic Texts and Interpreters in Biblical Scholarship
HTR	*Harvard Theological Review*
HUCA	*Hebrew Union College Annual*
ICC	International Critical Commentary
IEJ	*Israel Exploration Journal*
IntCom	Interpretation: A Bible Commentary for Teachers and Preachers
IOSOT	International Organization for the Study of the Old Testament
IOSCS	International Organization for the Study of Septuagint and Cognate Studies
ISBL	Indiana Studies in Biblical Literature
JBL	*Journal of Biblical Literature*
JR	*Journal of Religion*
JSOT	*Journal for the Study of the Old Testament*
JSOTSup	*Journal for the Study of the Old Testament*, Supplement Series
JSPSup	*Journal for the Study of the Pseudepigrapha*, Supplement Series
JTS	*Journal of Theological Studies*
KIS	Key Ideas Series
NCBC	New Century Biblical Commentary
NES	Near Eastern Studies
NIBC	New International Biblical Commentary
Numen	*Numen: International Review for the History of Religions*
OBO	Orbis biblicus et orientalis
OTL	Old Testament Library
OTS	Oudtestamentische Studiën
OWA	One World Archaeology
RB	*Revue biblique*
Rel	*Religion*
ResQ	*Restoration Quarterly*
SBL	Society of Biblical Literature
SBLDS	SBL Dissertation Series
SBLSS	SBL Semeia Studies
SCSS	Septuagint and Cognate Studies Series
Sem	*Semitica*
SemS	Semetica Studies
SHC	Studies in Hellenistic Civilization
SHCANE	Studies in the History and Culture of the Ancient Near East

SHANE	Studies in the History of the Ancient Near East
SHJ	Studies in the History of Judaism
SJLA	Studies in Judaism in Late Antiquity
SJOT	*Scandinavian Journal of the Old Testament*
SJT	*Scottish Journal of Theology*
SJT	*Scottish Journal of Theology*
SNEAC	Studies in Near Eastern Archaeology and Civilization
SPRS	Scholars Press Reprint Series
SR	*Studies in Religion/Sciences religieuses*
SRSO	Studies in Religion and Social Order
STDJ	Studies on the Texts of the Desert of Judah
TBü	Theologische Bücherei
TDOT	G.J. Botterweck and H. Ringgren (eds.), *Theological Dictionary of the Old Testament*
TRu	*Theological Rundshau*
ThWAT	G.J. Botterweck and H. Ringgren (eds.), *Theologisches Wörterbuch zum Alten Testament* (Stuttgart: W. Kohlhammer, 1970–)
TLZ	*Theologische Literaturzeitung*
TynBul	*Tyndale Bulletin*
VT	*Vetus Testamentun*
VTSup	*Vetus Testamentum*, Supplements
WBC	Word Biblical Commentary
ZAW	*Zeitschrift für die alttestamentliche Wissenschaft*
ZTK	*Zeitschrift für Theologie und Kirche*

Part I
THE BOOK OF KINGS AND HISTORICAL RESEARCH

Chapter 1

ISRAEL: THE LANGUAGE AND LITERATURE OF ATTRIBUTION

1. *Introduction*

Research into the origins of the literature now contained in the Hebrew Bible has been impacted by several re-evaluative programmes, including a wholesale questioning of the nature of the society which produced the literature. The debates surrounding the historicity of the exodus and conquest narratives have illustrated how scholars are wrestling with the question of the extent to which the ancient Israelite or early Jewish thinkers constructed a fictitious image of Israel's past to serve their own purposes. Needless to say, many of the debates are methodological, involving the inter-relationship between textual, archaeological and sociological disciplines, as well as literary theory.[1] Another important

---

1.   The bibliography on the historicity of these narratives and the pertinent archaeological evidence is growing quickly. A good assortment of opinions is expressed in D.V. Edelman (ed.), *The Fabric of History, Text, Artefact and Israel's Past* (JSOTSup, 127; Sheffield: JSOT Press, 1991). The question put by J.M. Miller in this volume expresses the situation aptly, 'Is it Possible to Write a History of Israel without Relying on the Hebrew Bible?', pp. 93-102. N.P. Lemche asks a briefer question elsewhere, 'Is it still Possible to Write a History of Ancient Israel?', *SJOT* 8 (1994), pp. 165-90. This volume also has a number of other relevant articles, including responses to Lemche. Recent contributions include a paper and response in a volume edited by Jacob Neusner: S. Mandell, 'Religion, Politics, and the Social Order: The Creation of the History of Ancient Israel', pp. 33-47, and J.F. Strange, 'Reading Archaeological and Literary Evidence: A Response to Sara Mandell', pp. 49-58, in J. Neusner (ed.), *Religion and the Political Order: Politics in Classical and Contemporary Christianity, Islam and Judaism* (SRSO, 15; Atlanta: Scholars Press, 1996). On related debates see K.W. Whitelam, 'Sociology or History: Towards a (Human) History of Ancient Palestine?', in J. Davies, G. Harvey and W.G.E. Watson (eds.), *Words Remembered, Texts Renewed: Essays in Honour of John F.A. Sawyer* (JSOTSup, 195; Sheffield: Sheffield Academic Press, 1995), pp. 148-66.

development is to see the Persian period as a creative era in which much of the biblical literature was completed. This has led to a great interest in the social-political contexts of Ezra and Nehemiah and how they supported the programmes of the returned exiles by articulating a conception of 'Israel' which excluded those who were not among the returnees.[2] For the most part, however, studies on Kings have centred on determining the compositional history of the book and the interface between biblical and extra-biblical evidence for the history of monarchic Judah and Israel. While there is very little consensus on many of these issues, the extent and nature of the 'Israel' which produced, or at least completed, Kings are still largely taken by scholars as known quantities.[3] There is an assumption of a great level of continuity between the society which produced the book and the nation(s) whose history is portrayed within it. Most often, the producer's 'Israel' is

2.   For a recent discussion on these books, see T.C. Eskenazi, 'Current Perspectives on Ezra–Nehemiah and the Persian Period', *CRBS* 1 (1993), pp. 59-86; and E.C. Meyers, 'Second Temple Studies in the Light of Recent Archaeology: Part 1: The Persian and Hellenistic Periods', *CRBS* 2 (1994), pp. 25-42. See also the anthologies: P.R. Davies (ed.), *Second Temple Studies. I. The Persian Period* (JSOTSup, 117; Sheffield: JSOT Press, 1991); T.C. Eskenazi and K.H. Richards (eds.), *Second Temple Studies. II. Temple Community in the Persian Period* (JSOTSup, 175; Sheffield: JSOT Press, 1994); E. Ulrich, J.W. Wright, R.P. Carroll and P.R. Davies (eds.), *Priests, Prophets and Scribes: Essays on the Formation and Heritage of Second Temple Judaism in Honour of Joseph Blenkinsopp* (JSOTSup, 149; Sheffield, JSOT Press, 1992). For a discussion of the sources and issues in writing a history of the period; L.L. Grabbe, *Judaism from Cyrus to Hadrian. I. The Persian and Greek Periods* (Minneapolis: Fortress Press, 1992). Other important studies: K. Hogland, *Achaemenid Imperial Administration in Syria-Palestine and the Missions of Ezra and Nehemiah* (SBLDS, 125; Atlanta: Scholars Press, 1992); D.L. Smith, *The Religion of the Landless: The Social Context of the Babylonian Exile* (Bloomington, IN: Meyer Stone, 1989); M. Smith, *Palestinian Parties and Politics that Shaped the Old Testament* (London: SCM Press, 2nd edn, 1987). A very recent example of how ideological (Marxist) criticism and anthropological analysis can combine to address these issues is W.M. Johnson, 'Ethnicity in Persian Yehud: Between Anthropological Analysis and Ideological Criticism', *SBL 1995 Seminar Papers* (Atlanta: Scholars Press, 1995), pp. 177-86.

3.   But see the brief discussion in G.N. Knoppers, *Two Nations under God: The Deuteronomistic History of Solomon and the Dual Monarchies. I. The Reign of Solomon and the Rise of Jeroboam* (2 vols.; HSM, 52; Atlanta: Scholars Press, 1993), pp. 3-4 (hereafter, '*Two Nations*, I'). The second volume, *The Reign of Jeroboam, the Fall of Israel, and the Reign of Josiah* (HSM, 53; Atlanta: Scholars Press, 1994) is abbreviated below, '*Two Nations*, II'.

considered to be the early post-monarchic Judaean component of the 'greater Israel' whose history unfolds in Kings itself, even if monarchic era texts have been adopted.[4] This close dating and the status of the book in scholarly circles as a generally reliable source of historical information may be cited as possible reasons for why the ideological character of the boundaries of 'Israel' implied within the book have not been investigated to the same degree as other features.

2. Outline, Method and Goals

The present work is intended to address this lack of attention, although, when originally conceived, it was still imagined as a kind of counterpart to H.G.M. Williamson's 1977 work, *Israel in the Books of Chronicles*, an ambition still betrayed in its title.[5] This is, however, not the first such inquiry into Kings. A great debt is owed to E.T. Mullen's far more recent study involving Kings as part of the so-called 'Deuteronomistic History'. In *Narrative History and Ethnic Boundaries*, Mullen has provided the foundations for my own study of how Kings 'constructs' an ethnic identity.[6] Like many others, Mullen was influenced to

4.   The problem of nomenclature is particularly vexing. P.R. Davies, *In Search of 'Ancient Israel'* (JSOTSup, 148; Sheffield: Sheffield Academic Press, 2nd edn, 1992), discussed below, is particularly careful about how he uses the name. For the writers of biblical literature, or at least some of them, 'Israel' was sometimes a suitable name for all this territory, as well as the designation for their own ethnic group. To allow scholarship to continue, some terms of convenience are necessary and these can allow further refinement of how political, geographical, or religio/ ethnic names were used in the relevant literature. In general, I hope context will reveal whether I am using 'Israel' to refer to the conception of particular political states (historical or fictitious), its populations, or their descendants, an ethnic or religiously defined people, however displaced or scattered, or particular geographical areas. When the context may be unclear, use of 'greater Israel' aids in specifying the collective territory of what is known from the extra-biblical record as the contemporary kingdoms of Judah and Israel, or in the conception of a single ethnic group in which the history of the two kingdoms was only a phase.

5.   H.G.M. Williamson, *Israel in the Books of Chronicles* (Cambridge: Cambridge University Press, 1977). Williamson uses the phrase 'Books of Chronicles' for 1 and 2 Chronicles, whereas I prefer a collective singular for 1 and 2 Kings. I will use 'Kingdoms' to refer to the LXX, when it is substantially at variance with MT.

6.   E.T. Mullen Jr, *Narrative History and Ethnic Boundaries: The Deuteronomistic History and the Creation of Israelite National Identity* (SBLSS; Atlanta: Scholars Press, 1993).

no small degree by John Van Seters.[7] The 'constructionist' approach could be seen itself as a development of the historical relativist positions dating back to the late nineteenth century. These held that texts reveal only their own time of composition, and cannot be relied on uncritically for providing historical information about the events narrated therein. This general perspective has influenced many a biblical scholar.[8] What has changed in the more recent formulations in biblical scholarship is the relatively radical extent to which the literary representation of Israel's history and institutions are necessarily topics for investigation as ideological constructions. As I will describe below, however, Mullen displayed but a modest appreciation of the critique of conventional scholarship inherent in his new 'constructionist' approach. Far more radical, and in many ways, more influential on my own development of the topic, has been Philip R. Davies's, *In Search of 'Ancient Israel'*, which, although not dealing at any length with Kings directly, has established a historical context for its composition that I find more suitable than that which Mullen basically adopted from existing studies of the book. It must be mentioned that Kings has been impacted to some degree by the increasingly sophisticated literary approaches that have so illuminated many other books in the Hebrew Bible, and that a number of interesting studies have been offered.[9] I

7.　J. Van Seters, *In Search of History: Historiography in the Ancient World and the Origins of Biblical History* (New Haven and London: Yale University Press, 1983).

8.　B. Halpern, *The First Historians: The Hebrew Bible and History* (San Francisco: Harper & Row, 1988), pp. 19-29, offers a discussion of Wellhausen's position in this regard, and its further development. He criticizes the scepticism of 'historical Pyronnists', pp. 3-6.

9.　A number of examples can be given, even if some of these do have some level of concern for the book as the product of a historical author: G. Savran, '1 and 2 Kings', in R. Alter and F. Kermode (eds.), *The Literary Guide to the Bible* (London: Fontana, 1987), pp. 146-64; R.L. Cohn, 'Literary Technique in the Jeroboam Narrative', *ZAW* 97 (1985), pp. 23-35; L. Eslinger, *Into the Hands of the Living God* (JSOTSup, 84; Sheffield: Almond Press, 1989); A. Frisch, 'Structure and its Significance: The Narrative of Solomon's Reign (1 Kings 1–12:24)', *JSOT* 51 (1991), pp. 3-14; R.D. Nelson, 'The Anatomy of the Book of Kings', *JSOT* 40 (1988), pp. 39-48; K.I. Parker, 'Repetition as a Structuring Device in I Kings 1–11', *JSOT* 42 (1988), pp. 19-27; J.T. Walsh, 'Methods and Meanings: Multiple Studies of I Kings 21', *JBL* 111 (1992), pp. 193-211. Recent monographs which have arrived too late to be employed here are R. Boer, *Jameson and Jeroboam* (SemS; Atlanta: Scholars Press, 1996); J.T. Walsh, *1 Kings* (Berit Olam;

hope to combine with the aforementioned interests, therefore, some appreciation of how this 'construction' of 'Israel' is a product of a story-teller's art.

It would be foolish to suggest that exploration of this multi-faceted question must proceed in the face of a paucity of historical, sociological, ideological and literary methods and theories (not to mention archaeological and theological). If anything, the student of Kings has *too many* theories to chose from. Which are most relevant is not obvious in the first instance, and one could (with no small level of justification) propose that preference for any one is itself predetermined. James Barr has pointed out that traditional historical-critical research of the Hebrew Bible (once unambiguously labelled 'literary criticism') usually proceeded from a body of practice to some level of theoretical reflection, although theory itself was usually seriously underdeveloped. On the other hand, the modern principle of synchrony within a 'literary' paradigm proceeds from a theoretical basis to determine what is relevant.[10] Even though I like to think the present work is advancing scholarship into the Hebrew Bible, I must admit that in terms of Barr's comments above, it remains, in some aspects, rather conservative. It is not fundamentally opposed to the approach taken by Williamson in his study of Chronicles, in which the book's selection of events and the wording employed is taken as indicative of the Chronicler's views on the integrity of Israel, an analysis informed by reference to what might be known of the book's historical context.[11] My study in Kings,

Collegeville, MN: Liturgical Press, 1996). Eagerly awaited is a contribution by R. Polzin on Kings, who has devoted a number of monographs to the books said to comprise the so-called 'Deuteronomistic History': *Moses and the Deuteronomist: A Literary Study of the Deuteronomistic History*. I. *Deuteronomy, Joshua, Judges* (New York: Seabury, 1980); *Samuel and the Deuteronomist*. II. *1 Samuel* (New York: Harper & Row, 1989); *David and the Deuteronomist* (Bloomington: Indiana University Press, 1993). I think it fair to say, however, that Kings has not attracted the attention in this regard to so great an extent as other books, such as Judges or Samuel.

10. J. Barr, 'The Synchronic, the Diachronic and the Historical: A Triangular Relationship?', in J.C. de Moor (ed.), *Synchronic or Diachronic?: A Debate on Method in Old Testament Exegesis* (OTS, 34; Leiden: E.J. Brill, 1995), pp. 1-14 (9-10).

11. Williamson, *Chronicles*. Included in this study is a convincing refutation of the proposal that Chronicles was composed as a unit with Ezra and Nehemiah (pp. 5-70). Likewise, I doubt the integrity of the hypothetical, so-called DtrH,

however, is informed by a range of observations from the sociological and historical disciplines, even if I deliberately avoid restricting my analysis to the application of a single, unified theory on the social production of literature. I do not wish to reduce this study to a description of how the book of Kings reveals the inner workings and 'correctness' of a particular theory. I confess to a certain insecurity concerning the glut of theoretical options, and subscribe to the belief that, when it comes to the proof of most theories, one can find what one is looking for all too easily. More importantly, however, given the still unconventional date range I accept for the book, and the tenuous character of historical reconstruction in the field of biblical scholarship, a more general approach to Kings as a whole may be defended as a means to explore possibilities within the book itself and to further inform subsequent methodological debates.

By avoiding the over-precision of a single theoretical basis, however, the study admittedly runs the risk of having its foundations in sand.[12] Yet previous work on the Hebrew Bible and in the social sciences does give some direction. The general methodological approach I defend is orientated in the direction taken by researchers in many fields who study how social objects cannot be taken 'as given' in the world, but are 'constructs' that result from negotiations between social actors in attempts to make sense of their world.[13] In pursuing such concerns, 'the

---

although I do admit to a great level of relationship between its components. My own handling of the independence of Kings, however, will be relatively brief.

12. P. Dutcher-Walls, *Narrative Art, Political Rhetoric: The Case of Athaliah and Joash* (JSOTSup, 209; Sheffield, Sheffield Academic Press, 1996), is a multidisciplinary work which has appeared too late to impact my work seriously. A single Kings narrative (2 Kgs 11–12) is subjected to separate narrative, rhetorical, ideological, and sociological analyses. Her four-fold strategy acknowledges the need for an integrated, if pluralistic approach. On the other hand, taking such an approach in any detail with a text as long as Kings in its entirety would be far beyond the scope of a single volume. On other matters, Dutcher-Walls's acceptance of a Josianic provenance for the narrative is perhaps too hasty. In my view, the process of narrowly dating a text is dependent upon the same sort of complex questions which she herself asks only *after* largely assuming a specific historical context.

13. T.H. Sarbin and J.I. Kitusse provide a brief but useful history of 'social constructionism' in their editors' prologue to a volume on the topic, 'A Prologue to *Constructing the Social*', in *Constructing the Social* (London: Sage, 1994), pp. 1-18 (2-6).

language of attribution is viewed as a topic—as opposed to a resource—for sociological inquiry'.[14] This language not only involves evaluative comments, such as some practice or idea being considered either 'good' or 'evil', 'brilliant' or 'foolish', 'ours' or 'foreign', but, as I will develop below, also the granting or withholding of value-laden proper names. The formation of whole literary works portraying the heritage of a people is, in my view, the logical extension of the 'language of attribution'. This may be labelled with some justification the 'literature of attribution', and it is under this conception that I approach the book of Kings. This topic for inquiry, however, is inherently complex. The language and literature of attribution becomes institutionalized as part of a symbolic universe that shapes reality and creates personal, group and institutional identities. There are tensions in this process. Since all social phenomena are the constructions of human activity through history, Berger and Luckmann write: 'no society is totally taken for granted and so, *a fortiori*, is no symbolic universe. Every symbolic universe is incipiently problematic. The question, then, is the *degree* to which it has become problematic'.[15] In short, I look at Kings' portrayal of Israel not only as a proposed 'solution' to the difficult issues of identity, but as an expression of the difficulty itself, and hence, another factor in the problematic symbolic universe. The lack of resolution in some areas, coupled with the impossibility of the certainty of any diachronic compositional analysis, means that the precision in date and historical context to which biblical scholarship has grown accustomed from the bulk of historically-minded research is impossible. In the rest of this chapter, and the following two chapters which comprise this opening section, I will discuss previous work on the book, and demonstrate that a fundamental reassessment of accepted conclusions and categories pertaining to the study of the book is warranted. I will also outline the 'constructionist' approach I take, offering discussions of Mullen and Davies in particular.

In the four chapters of the second section I will study the book of Kings in view of the historical context proposed in the first section. I

---

14. T. DeNora and H. Mehan, 'Genius: A Social Construction, the Case of Beethoven's Initial Recognition', in Sarbin and Kitusse (eds.), *Constructing the Social*, pp. 157-73 (157).

15. P.L. Berger and T. Luckmann, *The Social Construction of Reality: A Treatise in the Sociology of Knowledge* (Harmondsworth: Penguin Books, 1967), pp. 123-24.

will survey the book and centre on a number of episodes. I will also pay some attention to the use of the name 'Israel' and its constructs. My main goal in this section is to illustrate how the book deals with the question of a collective identity in view of the memory of the schism between Judah and the rest of Israel. This section also details what I describe as a sense of entropy depicted within the collective history; a tendency to decay that inexorably leads greater Israel to its 'exilic' existence. This entropy has many complex elements, including the depiction of Judah and Israel as two rival microcosms of the collective, neither one able to claim full legitimacy. Striking 'role reversals' between the usually apostate and unstable north, and the sometimes better-managed and stable south, probe the questions of the integrity and 'wholeness' of Judah and Israel, and the collective itself.

In the third section, I look more closely at a few episodes and themes that locate within that very history of loss an affirmation of the eternal integrity of the Israelite identity, which reconciles the destruction of monarchic Israel with a sense of the eternal nature of Israel as the people of Yahweh. Josiah's reign, 2 Kgs 22–23, sees wide-sweeping and violent purges of 'heterodox' worship in the land of greater Israel conducted in full knowledge of the impending exile, but these measures do not appease the offended deity.[16] I argue that this episode is an expression of the concept of exile as the normative interpretation of the world for the intended readers, and a model of reconciliation with the deity, which does not imply political independence. Even if the exile is a precarious existence, the reconciliation under Josiah gives the exiles a divine guardian. I also examine the theme of the exodus, and the role Egypt plays in the book. Kings often remembers that Israel, as a nation, began in the exodus from Egypt, and, at the end of Kings, a number of refugees return there (2 Kgs 25.25-26). If a 'charter' or 'constitution' for exilic Israel is to be found in Kings, however, it is not at the end of the book. The exile itself is not the positive event upon which to found such an identity. The exile is, however, the situation that needs to be validated, and strategies for surviving it need to be found. The positive

16. The usual term for Josiah's actions is 'reform', but this, to my mind, implies a level of positive steps which are not really evident in the text. Josiah is not, for example, shown as re-establishing a particular cycle of worship or festivals. Despite his reading of the scroll in public, the reaffirmation of the covenant, and the celebration of Passover (2 Kgs 23.1-3, 21-23), most of Josiah's actions are *against* one form of worship or another, and so 'purge' seems to me a rather more apt term.

reinforcement of 'Israel' is found in the early episodes of the book with the high point of the United Monarchy, the dedication of the temple. This is the mid-point of Israel's history, the end point of the exodus, and it looks ahead to the exile. It is a celebration of the unity of Israel, and the link between past and present. Related in 1 Kings 8, it provides strategies for life in exile by showing how the exile is accommodated in the very establishment of the institution that otherwise seemed to symbolize the power, prestige and autonomy of Israel's United Monarchy. This text articulates the paradox of exilic Israel; Solomon highlights how they are 'separated' from the nations, and yet builds on the theme of exile for disobedience. Ironically, Israel finds its being expressed to a great extent by geography, and yet it comprises a nation without borders. Solomon's prayer, then, is a central facet of the myth of 'exilic' Israel, which grounds the disparate elements both historically and geographically to a sacred centre.

Although I am dealing with 'processes' in terms of identity articulation and 'projects' of composition I will not make any attempt to map the historical sociological developments or individual compositional and editorial events themselves. There are too few firm starting-points that may be used to inform such a diachronic study adequately, and assessing the book in terms of identity formation may actually raise more questions relevant to such analysis. A suitably detailed social history of Kings' producers cannot be written on the strength of an analysis of Kings' claims about the past, or on the available extra-biblical evidence. The complexity of social dialogues between past and present make reading Kings as such a map impossible. Yet, something may be learned by examination of the constructs of society as they appear in Kings in the light of the general historical contexts in which it was produced, and this is what I propose to do here.

This study, therefore, remains exploratory. It is reserved in its use of specific theory, and in its appreciation of some sections of Kings it is, admittedly, subjective and speculative. I wish to integrate a reading of the book as a work of literature with an awareness that it is a historical artefact in its own right. Since we know so little of the 'who, where, when, and why' of its composition (and in terms of the intractably complex debates about genre and the many textual variants, even the 'what'), exploration of possibilities is perhaps all that may be justified in this age of radical shifts in method and the severe critiques of received knowledge. Without a clear view of the time and place of its composition, not to mention more specific issues such as the demographic, political and economic background of its production, it is unwise to subject the text to particular, detailed theories on how diverse ethnic groups identify themselves. On the other hand, my concern with Kings as a historical artefact and its composite nature pose problems as to the use of literary theories which ignore questions of authorial intent and historical contingency. Yet Kings is literature, and in reading it one imagines a world in the past, and one which was presented as the antecedents of the world of its earliest audience. It is in this literary world that the writers and early readers inscribed and encountered a manifestation of their symbolic universe, the universe which gave meaning to their lives. And it is to the meeting between these two worlds that I direct my exploration.

3. *Imagining Israel*

Since this book is directed towards 'the language of attribution' as a topic for analysis, however, some initial deliberations are in order. As will become evident in Chapter 3, I defend the same basic historical reconstruction that scholars such as Davies propose for the origins of the Hebrew Bible, that is, the Persian era reinvestments in Judah and the development of a new elite who sought to indigenize themselves in Judah.[17] One might suspect that the views of the imposed elite in Jerusalem on the extent of their own society would have extended no further than the bounds of their immediate political jurisdiction and influence. This might be reasonable if one could date the texts to early phases of this imposition, but there is no certainty in this regard. That the land and claimed histories of Judah held religio-ethnic significance to people well outside that territory during the Persian period needs little rehearsal, and so it is possible that the history of the Israelite monarchies was not produced in Judah, or was produced in Judah with an understanding that the people of 'Israel' were scattered near and far.[18] Therefore there remains no resolution to the debate as to where

---

17. Davies, *'Ancient Israel'*.

18. It is well known that the adherents of the temple of Yahu (יהו) at Elephantine at the end of the fifth century BCE considered themselves ethnically 'Jewish' or 'Judaean' and corresponded with authorities in Judah about assistance in religious and political matters, and even received instructions in such affairs, cf. the so-called 'Passover Letter', *TAD* A4.1, B. Porten, with J.J. Farber, C.J. Martin,

the book was composed. For example, Burke O. Long thinks Kings was probably written in Babylon.[19] Ernst Würthwein prefers Palestine, very possibly Mizpah.[20] Egypt is also suggested. I would tend to favour Jerusalem as the place of composition, or possibly elsewhere in Judah or Israel, but still think a very good case could be made for Egypt, for the sheer interest in the exodus, although Mesopotamia is hardly impossible.[21] The question must therefore be asked: to what degree did the authors of Kings see themselves as part of a greater, transregional 'Judaean' culture?

Because of this impasse, it is hard to label these writers 'Judaean' in the sense of *residence* or birth-place in Judah. More troublesome is the fact that certain native residents of Judah could well have been denied membership in an idealized 'Judaean' ethnicity by some of the Persian-era repatriates. Such an ostracism seems implicit in parts of Ezra and Nehemiah, if not 2 Kgs 17.24-41 itself. Already the 'language of attribution' has become the topic, not resource, of research. If 'Judaean' however, is to be taken as a 'cultural' label, that is, as is usually implicit in the term 'Jewish', some sort of cultural description is demanded. The uncertainties surrounding the rise of the set of cultural signifiers which are now regarded as 'Judaism', and the dangers of anachronistic judgments on what constituted a normative, or collective 'Judaism' in the Persian period makes the simple substitution of 'Judaean' with 'Jew' extremely difficult at best. Different things are implied by each term, and this distinction is not a false dichotomy even if, as Davies points out, neither Hebrew יהודי nor Greek ἰουδαῖος support the distinction English can make between 'Jew' and 'Judaean'. For greater clarity within English, he coins the phrase 'Juda-ism' to label the objectification of the Judaean culture which was the matrix from

G. Vittmann *et al.*, *The Elephantine Papyri in English: Three Millennia of Cross-Cultural Continuity and Change* (SNEAC, 22; Leiden: E.J. Brill, 1996), pp. 125-26.

19. B.O. Long, *2 Kings* (FOTL, 10; Grand Rapids: Eerdmans, 1991), pp. 5. See also, *1 Kings*, pp. 30-32.

20. Würthwein, *Die Bücher der Könige: 1 Könige 17–2 Kön. 25* (Göttingen: Vandenhoeck & Ruprecht, 1984), p. 503 (hereafter, *Könige*, II).

21. Suspecting Egypt are R.E. Friedman, 'From Egypt to Egypt: Dtr1 and Dtr2', in B. Halpern and J.D. Levenson (eds.), *Traditions in Transformation* (Winona Lake, IN: Eisenbrauns, 1981), pp. 167-92 (189-92) and N.P. Lemche, *The Canaanites and their Land: The Tradition of the Canaanites* (JSOTSup, 110; Sheffield: JSOT Press, 1991), p. 169.

which the more familiar range of cultural properties of 'Judaism' developed:[22]

> To put it as simply as possible, three stages can be posited: a Judean culture that has not yet been conceptualized and that therefore is not a 'Juda-ism'; 'Juda-ism', which constitutes the culture of Judea as an object of definition, and finally 'Judaism' and 'Judaisms', according to which 'Juda-ism' develops into something more than (but also different from) the 'culture' of Judea.[23]

I am largely convinced of the practicality of Davies's distinctions, even if I also recognize that the debates about this could go on indefinitely. I will amend the spelling of Davies's new term to 'Judah-ism', however, if only for greater visual contrast with 'Judaism'. It is not my purpose here to explore the actual history of the range of cultural signifiers that would characterize Judah-ism(s), although certainly Kings is more a product of that than the later Judaism.[24] In the present work, I will use 'Judaean' to refer to people, places, or institutions of the specific geographical area, and 'Judah-ism' for the broad set of cultural identifiers that linked various people (in various ways) to the land of Judah. I think it is important to coin another, related term, even though the continual multiplication of variations on the term 'Judah' runs the risk of absurdity. I will use 'Judah-ist' to refer to an adherent of Judah-ism. With this odd term, one can speak of natives or expatriates of Judah who are adherents to a Judah-ism (i.e. 'Judean Judah-ists') or non-natives (e.g. 'Egyptian Judah-ists') who share such a heritage. Moreover, one can also speak of those native to Judah as Judaeans without assuming that theirs is a religious or ethnic heritage with a peculiar affinity to what might be seen as precursory to Judaism. This, however, raises a question: What are the range of signifiers that mark Judah-ism?

At its simplest, Judah-ism should refer to some form of religious-cultural matrix that identified its members on genealogical and religious grounds with the history of Judah, and in the worship (if not exclusive

---

22. P.R. Davies, 'Scenes from the Early History of Judaism', in D.V. Edelman (ed.), *The Triumph of Elohim: From Jahwisms to Judaisms* (CBET, 13; Kampen: Kok Pharos, 1995), pp. 145-82 (151-53).

23. Davies, 'Scenes', pp. 152-53.

24. The production of Kings need not have been contemporary with its being accorded the status of 'scripture'. Indeed, even the later elevation of certain literature to the level of 'scripture' need not have been a universal characteristic of every form of Judaism, as Davies points out, 'Scenes', pp. 154-57.

worship) of the god Yahweh, imagined as being the deity with a special association with Judah.[25] This raises another very interesting, and perplexing question, however. If the origins of the literature now contained in the Hebrew Bible lie within Judah-ism, then why is there absolutely no reference in this literature to Yahweh as the 'God of Judah'? Only twice are there references to the 'God of Jerusalem' (2 Chron. 32.19, parallel to God of Israel, and Ezra 7.19, in Aramaic).[26] This contrasts sharply with the approximately 250 times Yahweh is called the 'God of Israel'.[27] It is also to be noted that the ancestor Judah, from whom all 'Judaeans' at least purportedly descend, is remembered as but one of twelve descendants of Abraham. Much of the literature of the Hebrew Bible is concerned with Judah and the rest of Abraham's descendants. For as much as there may have been a Judaean culture which did not recognize any links with the territory of the former 'northern' kingdom of Israel, or a collective under the same name, the writings in the Hebrew Bible are intimately concerned with 'Israel'.[28] The Judah-ist claims to the name are probably explicable by some perception of political

25. It is not impossible, however, that some Judaeans thought that some other deities were particularly associated with Judah, and attempted to objectify a Judaean heritage accordingly. It is, therefore, fully possible to speak of non-Yahwistic 'Judah-ism'. Yet, an association of Yahweh with at least the ruling classes of Judah seems evident, given the number of kings with Yahwistic elements in their names, and so stressing a connection between 'Yahweh' and 'Judah-ism' in the post-monarchic period should not be too troublesome. On the other hand, that Yahweh was not exclusively a deity associated with the land of Judah and Israel is asserted by T.L. Thompson, 'The Intellectual Matrix of Early Biblical Narrative: Exclusive Monotheism in Persian Period Palestine', in Edelman (ed.), *The Triumph of Elohim*, pp. 107-24 (119 n. 13). The history of monotheism is beyond my interests, yet, from the 'Judah-ist' documents found at Elephantine, it is clear that 'monotheism', as it is now understood, does not reflect their views on divinity.

26. To this observation, G. Harvey, *The True Israel: Uses of the Names Jew, Hebrew and Israel in Ancient Jewish and Early Christian Literature* (AGJU, 35; Leiden: E.J. Brill, 1996), p. 168, adds that Judaeans thought of Yahweh as their god through conceptions of Jerusalem as a city sacred to Yahweh, cf. Pss. 46.5, 6; 87.3.

27. Harvey, *True Israel*, pp. 167-77. This figure does not include other, related expressions, such as 'Holy One of Israel' (31 times).

28. The vexing question of whether the Samaritans comprised a sect of Judaism (or perhaps, Judah-ism) might be somewhat displaced, however, if it is rephrased as a question of differing ancient perceptions of what and who *Israel* is, and whether 'Judah-ism' is a necessary, or acceptable part of this. Could one speak of 'Judaism' as a 'sect' of a rather broadly imagined 'Israel-ism'?

associations between the lands of Judah and Israel dating back to Judah's monarchic period. Be that as it may, the book of Kings presents '*Judah*-ism' as necessarily implying an 'Israelite' heritage. It is my task to explore how expression is given to this and its corollary, that an 'Israelite' heritage is properly articulated within a 'Judah-ist' perspective.

For a number of scholars, understanding Persian-era Judaean society involves understanding the debates surrounding the true ideological and genealogical boundaries of 'Israel'. There is a justified emphasis on the numerous biblical texts that construct the 'ideal Israel' as the community of those who were 'exiled' but have now 'returned'.[29] Yet, Graham Harvey calls attention to the fact that the biblical literature displays little sense of a tradition of a 'true Israel', which persisted through history as the pious minority of a rebellious people and who had the only valid claim to the name 'Israel'. Rather, throughout the Hebrew Bible, 'Israel' is used of the pious and the rebellious. Even in the expression, 'God of Israel', Yahweh is posited as the deity for a nation, not a pure community:[30]

> It is the 'real Israel', good or bad, with which God is concerned. The attempt to make the people into a god-fearing nation (perhaps a 'holy nation and royal priesthood') is not made by denying the name 'Israel' to 'rebels'. 'Sinners' are condemned but remain 'Israel'.[31]

Threats and other injunctions designed to elicit obedience do not imply that the nation addressed in the narrative, or the readership itself are not 'Israel' until they obey:

> In fact, such threats only reinforce Israel's identity by giving voice again and again to God's expectations of a response. Israel is therefore 'Israel' precisely when it is in rebellion and being addressed yet again by the God who chose this particular audience.[32]

How then should the scholar relate to the concept of a special, but flawed 'Israel' standing as some kind of a representative of the highly

29. See especially, E. Ben Zvi, 'Inclusion in and Exclusion from Israel as Conveyed by the Use of the Term "Israel" in Post-Monarchic Biblical Texts', in E.W. Holloway and L.K. Handy (eds.), *The Pitcher is Broken: Memorial Essays for Gösta W. Ahlström* (JSOTSup, 190; Sheffield: Sheffield Academic Press, 1995), pp. 95-149.

30. Harvey, *True Israel*, pp. 148-88.

31. Harvey, *True Israel*, p. 187.

32. Harvey, *True Israel*, p. 188.

pluralistic religious-ethnic culture of Kings' authors? It is reasonable to assume that some of the representations in the literature stem from polemics, not only against 'non-Israelites', but also against differing perceptions of 'Israel' within the greater matrix of Judah-ism, and Yahwistic religion lacking a particular Judah-ist perspective. Such internal polemics, however, would not necessitate a complete breakdown of all integrity of this matrix, although, perhaps, this is in fact what occurred from time to time.[33] A.D. Smith, in his *Ethnic Origins of Nations*, writes that such competition between rival pasts can have integrative functions:

> For the effect of rivalry in the interpretation of history is to create a heightened consciousness of ethnicity in a given population, and even a higher level of integration through conflict among competing pressure groups and classes of the same community, by suggesting common destinies founded upon shared pasts. In the short term, rival 'histories' may divide the community or sharpen existing class conflicts; but over the long term, the effect of their propagation and inculcation is to deepen the sense of shared identity and destiny in a particular community.[34]

The nature of 'ethnicity' itself is a topic too broad to be successfully handled here, but at this point some comments are in order. Much modern thought concentrates on how 'ethnicity' is a matter of self-ascription influenced by descent, socialization, political organization, class structure, language and other factors. This highlights how the language (and for our purposes, literature) of attribution is important. Ethnic identity-formation is very much a process of differentiation and 'boundary maintenance'.[35] The cultures displayed by such groups

33. The example of the 'schism' between Judaism and 'Samaritanism' might be adduced here. F. Dexinger, 'Limits of Tolerance in Judaism: The Samaritan Example', in E.P. Sanders, A.I. Baumgarten and A. Mendelson (eds.), *Jewish and Christian Self-Definition*. II. *Aspects of Judaism in the Graeco-Roman Period* (Philadelphia: Fortress Press, 1981), pp. 88-114 (89), comments that the limits of tolerance of both parties need to be addressed.

34. A.D. Smith, *The Ethnic Origins of Nations* (Oxford: Basil Blackwell, 1986), p. 26. One may see such a process as applicable to Diaspora communities as well, as the shared memory of a common land, and communication between enclaves unites the diverse communities, despite regional variations in cultural properties and traditions (p. 46).

35. As argued by F. Barth, 'Ethnic Groups and Boundaries', in F. Barth, *Process and Form in Social Life: Selected Essays of Fredrik Barth* (London: Routledge & Kegan Paul, 1981), I, pp. 198-227, 231, originally, 'Introduction', in F. Barth

consist of 'an exaggeration of differences'.[36] This exaggeration stems from the 'inherently antithetical' nature of culture.[37] Benjamin Beit-Hallahmi writes that religion creates differences between groups, forming a basis for social identity, and so becomes an ideology, 'a system of identity maintenance'. He continues, adding that religion is so basic to identity that people do not so much 'believe' in it but accept it as part of their identity during the process of socialization.[38] This sort of differentiation takes place even during phases where one group is forced to conform to standards considered 'foreign' to itself. Even though a great homogeneity may be displayed within a complex society, it may be only a superficial veneer, masking significant differences at a deep level. Boundaries may then be symbolic, and not readily identified within the overall social structure. Anthony Cohen writes:

> Indeed the greater the pressure on communities to modify their structural forms to comply more with those elsewhere, the more are they inclined to reassert their boundaries *symbolically* by imbuing these modified forms with meaning and significance which belies their appearance. In other words, as the *structural* bases of boundary become blurred, so the symbolic bases are strengthened through 'flourishes and decorations', 'aesthetic frills' and so forth.[39]

On the other hand, flexibility in ethnic identity is to be expected. Bruce Lincoln holds that the 'virtually infinite' criteria for individual and group differentiation and association, and the resultant evocation of the sentiments of affinity or estrangement, ensure that the borders of any society can be broken. There is always a potential for disassociation and new associations. Most social sentiments are 'ambivalent mixes'. At times, sources of affinity can be suppressed with a view to establishing a clear social boundary. Conversely, sources of estrangement may be discounted when integration is preferable.[40] The corollary

(ed.), *Ethnic Groups and Boundaries* (Boston: Little, Brown & Co., 1969).

36. J.A. Boon, *Other Tribes, Other Scribes: Symbolic Anthropology in the Comparative Study of Cultures, Histories, Religions and Texts* (Cambridge: Cambridge University Press, 1982), p. 26.

37. A.P. Cohen, *The Symbolic Construction of Community* (KIS; Open University, London: Routledge, 1985), p. 115.

38. B. Beit-Hallami, 'Religion as Art and Identity', *Rel* 16 (1986), pp. 1-17 (13-14).

39. Cohen, *Symbolic Construction*, p. 44.

40. B. Lincoln, *Discourse and the Construction of Society: Comparative*

to this observation is that the culture to which any person belongs is equally fluid. This makes it hard to write definitive descriptions of the culture to which any biblical writer subscribed. Basing himself on the work of Fredrik Barth, Jonathan Friedman writes:

> From this point of view, culture is not something out there that we seek to grasp, a text or hidden code. It is a relatively instable product of the practice of meaning, of multiple and socially situated acts of attribution of meaning to the world, of multiple interpretations both within society and between members of society and anthropologists, i.e., between societies.[41]

Echoing thoughts cited above on the language of attribution, Friedman notes that his rethinking of culture redesignates it as a 'phenomenon to be accounted for, rather than one that accounts for'. Playing a major role in the 'active process of cultural constitution' is that of each member's positional identity.[42] In inquiring into the boundaries of Jewish ethnicity during the Achaemenid Period, Mark W. Hamilton observes how Jewishness varied through time and in different places. He recognizes that ethnicity is circumstantial, being a matter of choice. He considers that under the Persians, 'Jew' changed from being primarily a sociopolitical term to one with mainly religious connotations. He also bases his work on that of Fredrik Barth, who emphasizes that ethnicity expresses itself most clearly at its boundaries. He qualifies this by adding that since 'no ethnos is an island', social and ecological considerations have an impact on ethnic character. It is not enough to look at boundaries, however. Contact with outsiders, whether on good or bad terms, does not create the sense of belonging. Shared traits, even if they themselves change, are as important as the distinctions with outsiders.[43] Most importantly, Hamilton recognizes how flexible ethnic ascription may be. The Elephantine papyri show where Jewish boundaries were not. They were only partially linguistic, were probably not at

---

Studies of Myth, Ritual, and Classification (Oxford: Oxford University Press, 1989), p. 10.

41. J. Friedman, 'Notes on Culture and Identity in Imperial Worlds', in P. Bilde, T. Engberg-Pedersen, L. Hannestad and J. Zahle (eds.), *Religion and Religious Practice in the Selucid Kingdom* (SHC; Aarhus: Aarhus University Press, 1990), pp. 14-39 (23).

42. Friedman, 'Notes', p. 24.

43. M.W. Hamilton, 'Who Was a Jew? Jewish Ethnicity During the Achaemenid Period', *ResQ* 37 (1995), pp. 102-17 (102-104).

the family level, as intermarriage was possible, even if its frequency is indeterminable. The boundaries were not at the business level, for business was inter-ethnic. In matters of law, business papyri are similar in form to other Aramaean and Mesopotamian texts of the time. Moreover, inter-ethnic settlement seems the norm. Boundaries were not clearly drawn on the level of ideas as Jewish reading seemed to include Ahiqar, which contains references to non-Jewish deities. Religion and occupation seem to be the ethnic boundaries.[44] He writes that the flexibility of label depended upon the individual's place of residence. He observes that Mahseiah bar Jedeniah was called an Aramean of Syene (in the text known as Cowley 5.1, 471 BCE), while in the 460s–450s BCE he was labelled an Elephantine Jew (Cowley 6.2-4; 8.1-2; 9.2).[45] In the next decade, however, he was an Aramaean of Syene again (Cowley 13.1; 14.3; 15.2). Other examples could be given. 'Location influenced ethnic identity, but not in a rigorously predictable way. The boundary between Arameans and Jews existed but was porous.'[46]

A.D. Smith describes two main strategies of maintaining the integrity of ethnic groups. Most similar to what has already been outlined is 'ethnicism', which is ethnic renewal in the face of change. This may manifest itself in a variety of ways; from brief, dramatic outbursts, to phases lasting a generation, or cycles over centuries. Characteristic of these defensive acts, however, are their myth-making qualities and preservations of a glorious past. The other strategy is called 'ethnocentrism', which does not so much operate as a boundary-defence mechanism, since it highlights the shared traits of members. It is internal, marking common heritage and fate.[47] Regardless of the social and political factors generating ethnicity, it requires an 'idea' that a particular group of people are, indeed, a singular entity. Benedict Anderson writes that all communities, with the possible, but not certain, exception of tiny villages in which everyone knows everyone else, are 'imagined communities'; imagined because it is impossible for all the members to know all the others.[48] Thomas J. Scheff reminds his readers

---

44. Hamilton, 'Who Was a Jew?', p. 106.

45. Hamilton refers to these texts according to the classification of their modern editor, A.E. Cowley (ed.), *Aramaic Papyri of the Fifth Century B.C.* (Osnabruck: Otto Zeller, repr. 1967).

46. Hamilton, 'Who Was a Jew?', p. 108.

47. Smith, *Ethnic Origins*, pp. 48-55.

48. B. Anderson, *Imagined Communities: Reflections on the Origin and Spread*

that ethnicity is only a part of a very large and coherent system. While criticizing Anderson on some points, he still applauds his accent on group identity as an act of the imagination; that an *idea* is the basis for ethnic and cultural group formation. Scheff maintains that language and other shared traits do not constitute sufficient criteria.[49] He writes that one of the most perplexing aspects in the differentiation of cultural groups is the way people sometimes feel they have more in common with people they do not know than the people amongst whom they live. He asks, 'Why is an imagined community chosen over an actual one?'.[50] One could especially see the validity of this stress on *imagined* groups regarding Diaspora situations, where there are various communities with perhaps only occasional contact with each other, but bound by the sense of a shared heritage. As noted above, the 'Israel' imagined in the book of Kings is not a 'photograph' or a map of the writers' 'real' world, however. For one thing, it is set in that world's past. Berger and Luckmann comment on how people not only interact with contemporaries, but with ancestors and future generations, all of whom are also implicated in everyday social action. These typifications are empty projections and devoid of individualized content, but this does not prevent them entering as elements into life.[51] The imagined community, then, not only has a demographic component, but a temporal one too. The act of imagining, therefore, both engages and informs the memory, without which there is no ethnicity.[52] This results in a type of essentialism, whereby images or icons produce a world of meaning that reduce complexity of historical and social diversity to relatively few cultural images by which the world is ordered. On these images, George C. Bond and Angela Gilliam write:

of Nationalism (London: Verso, 1983), p. 15.

49. T.J. Scheff, 'Emotions and Identity: A Theory of Ethnic Nationalism', in C. Calhoun (ed.), *Social Theory and the Politics of Identity* (Oxford: Basil Blackwell, 1994), pp. 277-303 (278); so too, Smith, *Ethnic Origins*, p. 27.

50. Scheff, 'Emotions', pp. 278-79. Scheff's statements are made in the context of a critique of Anderson's *Imagined Communities* and A.D. Smith's *Ethnic Origin of Nations*. The heart of his complaint is that they emphasize cognitive elements, disregard the emotional elements and social interaction and reduce sentiment to an ephemeral status (pp. 279-81). This last point may be somewhat overstated regarding Anderson.

51. Berger and Luckmann, *Social Construction*, p. 48.

52. Smith, *Ethnic Origins*, p. 87.

They have the power to evoke the past, apprehending the present, and establishing the basis of 'imagined communities' (Anderson 1992). These imagined communities, built on clusters of key symbols that evoke a past that might have been, have a transient and ephemeral present, and a future whose distinctive signature is epiphany. In its own way, the past is the epitome of the imagined community, since it cannot exist coterminously with the present.[53]

Also important to recognize, especially as I am interested in what was probably a work directed to a Diaspora community (imagining itself as in exile), is the question of the relationship between the imagination and territory. A.D. Smith writes:

Territory is relevant to ethnicity, therefore, not because it is actually possessed, nor even for its 'objective' characteristics of climate, terrain and location, though they influence ethnic conceptions, but because of an alleged and felt symbiosis between a certain piece of earth and 'its' community. Again, poetic and symbolic qualities possess greater potency than everyday attributes; a land of dreams is far more significant than any actual terrain.[54]

In the study of 'Israel' in Kings, then, one is dealing with the memory of land, and the political control over it, as an act of the imagination directed toward or, at least, reflecting a conception of a social entity. This memory, of course, has manifested itself in the form of history-writing. This history was both influenced by the interactions of the writers in their own world, and, in turn, influenced the subsequent world. It would be wrong to suggest that this 'Imagined Israel' was a perfectly coherent whole. This extends beyond the great probability of the multiplicity of authorship. Rather it extends to the way representations of identity, and indeed, identity itself, are themselves pluriform.

What I have been calling the 'idea' of Israel or the 'imagined Israel' is illuminated by Jacob Neusner when he discusses 'Israel' as the 'social metaphor' of Judaism. By this he means 'the things to which a group of people compare themselves in accounting for their society together'.[55] This social entity may be invoked by the metaphor of a

---

53. G.C. Bond and A. Gilliam, 'Introduction', in G.C. Bond and A. Gilliam (eds.), *Social Construction of the Past: Representation as Power* (OWA, 24; London: Routledge, 1994), pp. 1-22 (17).

54. Smith, *Ethnic Origins*, p. 28.

55. J. Neusner, *The Foundations of the Theology of Judaism: An Anthology*. III. *Israel* (SHJ, 48; Atlanta: Scholars Press, 1992), p. 3.

family, Israel descended from the ancestors. 'Israel' may be a particular example of one sort of political entity or another. 'Israel' may also be a genus unto itself. 'These and other metaphors serve as the vehicles for the social thought of the Judaic systems, or Judaisms, of the ages.'[56] Neusner writes in a chapter entitled 'Imagining Society, Re-Visioning "Israel"' that among the 'works of enchantment' that religion accomplishes is the transformation of individuals and families into a corporate body, even if none of the individuals in question have ever seen or can even envisage the entirety of that corporate entity. The particular social entities, comprised of the religion's devotees, are transformed from concrete entities into abstractions that are merely represented in the 'here and now' by their contemporary exemplars: 'The social entity turns into a symbol for something more'.[57] The 'something more' for all Judaic systems, of course, is the concept of Israel, as enshrined in the Jewish Scriptures. For Neusner, the primary paradigm in the construction of this metaphoric complex is the story of Israel's exile and restoration.[58]

While Neusner's comments hold true for Judaism, which has adopted as scripture a collection of writings, including such literature as Ezra and Nehemiah, it is not so clear that the supreme paradigm of 'exile and return' is necessarily operative for all forms of 'Judah-ism' which preceded Judaism and the literature it produced. I will have opportunity to readdress this issue in Chapter 2, when I discuss the date of Kings and the notion of a normative 'exilic' period that ended at a particular point in time. As Davies reminds us, the development of Judaism and what eventually came to be its scriptures was a complex, reciprocal set of interdependencies. Judaism adopted the literature as scripture, and the literature did not determine Judaism.[59] For as much as Judaism, as a whole, was subsumed under the growing authority of a select body of texts chosen by only a part of the whole Jewish cultural sphere, some aspects of that literature itself probably came to be subsumed under the dominant themes of select narratives and other writing. In my opinion,

56. Neusner, *The Foundations*, p. 1.
57. J. Neusner, *Judaism and its Social Metaphors: Israel in the History of Jewish Thought* (Cambridge: Cambridge University Press, 1989), pp. 8-18. In Chapter 3, I will discuss a closely related issue, that of the dialectic relationship between remembered past and present.
58. Neusner, *Judaism*, pp. 14-18.
59. Davies, 'Scenes', pp. 154-57.

this is what may have happened to Kings. This book seems to know little of the 'return' as an event of paradigmatic proportions. Rather, it stresses the exile itself. But in place of this aspect of the metaphorical complex of 'Israel' are many others. Kings also builds on the metaphor of the exodus, and Israel as the 'people of Yahweh'. To a lesser degree, a patriarchal metaphor is used. To this end, one set of metaphors is used in a particular combination to tell a story which becomes yet another metaphor.

None of the individual literary 'Israels', however, can reflect the totality of the social reality imagined by the writers and readers. Each metaphor may evoke, if not to complement, at least to dispute, the relevance of others. The absence of a metaphorical identity as a redeemed community at least raises the question of whether such redemption is possible. 'Exilic Israel' has, perhaps, produced a longing for a different kind of identity. It is, perhaps, this longing that eventually facilitated the subsuming of Kings under the 'exile and restoration' model. Yet, perhaps it was a lingering sense that the longing for redemption could never be fully satisfied that preserved its 'exilicist' character, in the face of related, but alternative histories, such as that now known as Chronicles. The sum of all the literary 'Israels' cannot be taken as expressing a total, trouble-free self-image. In his study of the book of Hosea, Francis Landy notices the contradictory and unstable metaphors for God used in that book, and comments that metaphor establishes difference alongside resemblance and that the 'diversity of metaphor expresses an uncertainty of identity'.[60] Who, then, is Israel?

---

60. F. Landy, *Hosea* (Readings; Sheffield: Sheffield Academic Press, 1995), p. 18.

Chapter 2

THE NEED FOR A NEW APPROACH TO KINGS

1. *Piecemeal History*

That Kings is history-writing is virtually axiomatic in biblical scholarship. 'History', however, has become a highly value-charged term, and biblical scholars are interested in many different kinds of 'history': the actual course of events in the past, the reliability of any particular claim made in a book, the history of the composition and transmission of 'sources' incorporated into the book, and the 'history' of the book's subsequent editing. Also important is examination of the ideological perspective on 'history' held by those who had a hand in producing the book. In my view, these histories are perfectly valid topics of investigation, and many aspects of any one project would rightly require digression into an examination of facets of the others. Unfortunately, however, there is a great oversimplification of the problems relating to those historical topics seen as subservient to the 'primary' historical issues, the reconstruction of the narrated events, and the compositional and editorial history of the texts themselves. While simplification of precursory issues is to be expected in any academic endeavour, in biblical historical scholarship it is often to an excessive level. The issue of the hierarchy of historical researches is also problematic, as it often results in a conflation of different projects, with very tenuous results. Innumerable examples can be found of the text of Kings being used primarily as a 'source' of historical data (or as a source for recovering older 'sources' of such information), and this is often the route taken in commentaries. One might wonder whether the important commentaries of John Gray and James Montgomery, for example, as well as more recent ones like that of Cogan and Tadmor on 2 Kings, might be aptly subtitled as histories of Israel's monarchic period. Monarchic history seems to be as important to these scholars, if not more so, than Kings as a piece of literature from the ancient world.[1] Without implying that scholars should not be interested in more than one issue at a time, I do find that the imposed hierarchy between historical issues can lead to a situation of blurred priorities, and hence, to peculiar judgments. Gray, for instance, feels justified to 'deplore' the restricted use of Judaean annals detailing the 'rest of the acts of Josiah' (2 Kgs 23.28).[2] A literary reason for such brevity in detailing the life and death of Josiah is not sought.

For his part, De Vries maintains that a passage's true meaning is found in its original structure, setting and intention. He wishes to correct the error of beginning with the 'end product' by emphasizing the 'elemental oral and written units'.[3] De Vries's comments on 1 Kgs 3.1 are revealing. He considers the report of the marriage of Solomon to an Egyptian princess as 'virtually contemporary' with the occasion. It has 'every claim to absolute historicity', although no support for this claim is given. The report, however, 'has no paradigmatic value', as the text does not praise or blame the king, even though the deuteronomistic writer/compiler does assure the reader that, after all, Solomon did remain orthodox in his religion (v. 3). De Vries then asserts that the modern reader may well ask whether Solomon's piety was not purely formal and external, claiming that there is nothing worse than 'a punctilious piety that does not proceed from a truly loving and truly devout self'.[4] One must ask whether De Vries, in asserting the antiquity of the passage over and against its present literary context (which in its MT version does criticize Solomon for this marriage in a later passage, 1 Kgs 11.1-4), has too speedily turned his attention from the 'non-paradigmatic' historical intent of the 'original' writers to the morally reflective modern world, ignoring consideration of the world of the compilers and editors who provided us with Solomon's story in the forms we now know. The *modern reader*, De Vries implies, may question Solomon's religiosity, but the modern scholar need not ask if those who produced the post-monarchic book of Kings may have told the story as a

---

1. J. Gray, *I and II Kings* (OTL; Philadelphia: Westminster, 2nd edn, 1970); J. A. Montgomery, *A Critical and Exegetical Commentary on the Books of Kings* (ed. H.S. Gehman; ICC; Edinburgh: T. & T. Clark, 1951); M. Cogan and H. Tadmor, *II Kings* (AB, 11; New York: Doubleday, 1984).

2. Gray, *Kings*, p. 746.

3. S.J. De Vries, *1 Kings* (WBC, 12; Waco, TX: Word Books, 1985), p. xli.

4. De Vries, *1 Kings*, pp. 53-54.

deliberate, if subtle or ironic, comment on Solomon's 'punctilious piety'. I might also cite the work of Tomoo Ishida, who writes on the monarchic period, and asserts that the notion of later editors substantially supplementing ancient narratives is 'hypothetical' and leads to 'arbitrary' judgments on the historicity of the passages in question.[5] By largely assuming historicity, however, Ishida himself has made arbitrary judgments. On the one hand, De Vries, the historian of literature implies that the book as an entity is an obstacle the scholar must overcome to achieve the true goal of knowing the 'original' meaning of 'elemental units'. On the other hand, the political historian, Ishida, assumes that the texts are largely transparent, telling of little else than his object of interest. In both cases, the status of Kings as an artefact of history, and, as such, a product of someone's *artifice*, is downplayed, if not ignored.

This assumption of an original intent to be accurate is particularly pointed when there is perceived *inaccuracy* in an 'elemental' unit. Like Gray's comments on the deplorably laconic historians, this occasions equally bizarre judgments which turn attention away from features requiring literary investigation. According to 1 Kgs 10.28-29, Solomon engages in trade in chariots and horses with Egypt, Que (קוה), and other lands. The emendation of Egypt (מצרים) to *musri* (a region to the north of the Taurus range) is sometimes considered necessary because some scholars work with a premise that the report should have been factual. This premise cannot be reconciled with what seem to be illogical trading routes.[6] There is, however, no textual evidence in support of this emendation, and these attempts to reconstruct a hypothetical original reading do not come to terms with the reason why Kings reads the name as Egypt. This is an important oversight, since Israel's relations with Egypt are an important theme in Kings.[7] Moreover, the exodus is one of the primary 'social metaphors' for Israel which are articulated

5.   T. Ishida, *The Royal Dynasties in Ancient Israel* (BZAW, 142; Berlin: W. de Gruyter, 1977), p. 4.

6.   C.F. Burney, *Notes on the Hebrew Text of the Book of Kings* (Oxford: Clarendon Press, 1903), p. 151. Gray, *Kings*, pp. 268-69, thinks that both 2 Kgs 7.6 and Deut. 17.16, which mention Egypt, are dependent upon the error in 1 Kgs as well. Among recent scholars to follow the emendation in 1 Kgs is De Vries, *1 Kings*, p. 140.

7.   I will discuss this to some extent below. The importance of Egypt has already been noted by R.E. Friedman, 'From Egypt', pp. 167-92.

within the book. The presumption of *intended accuracy* and the scholarly desire to follow suit and compose for themselves accurate history has resulted in the fabrication of reliable sources, and so replaced the *reading* of a history already written, which is itself a product of specific ideological and *historical* factors.

There is in fact little, if any, internal evidence that the writers of Kings had sources of information which, by their very genre, must be accorded a great level of historicity. The frequent references in Kings to other books are often taken as references to annals or other official writings contemporary with the events and reigns they describe. Their genre and compositional dates, however, are beyond demonstration. We cannot even be sure which parts of Kings are quotations from them, if they were directly quoted at all.[8] The desire to find historically accurate sources results in an unfortunate ranking of passages in which purported 'archival records' are considered reliable, 'popular legends'

---

8.   1 Kings 11.41 refers the reader to the 'Book of the Acts of Solomon', ספר
דברי שלמה, to find out more about this king. Kings of Judah are purportedly handled in more detail in the 'Book of the Chronicles of the Kings of Judah', ספר
דברי הימים למלכי יהודה (e.g. 1 Kgs 14.29), and the Israelite kings in their own book (e.g. 1 Kgs 14.19). Most kings of Judah and Israel are said to have entries in their respective books. There is no obvious reference in any of these cases to what information was derived from them or to indicate that they were quoted directly. Even though the pattern respective of the northern and southern kings is rather consistent in Kings, there is precious little information about these books other than the names given; certainly these names do not indicate their origin or reliability. In the parallel references to Judaean kings in Chronicles, the royal biographies are given different titles, which sometimes attribute them to named people, usually prophets, cf. 1 Kgs 11.41 / 2 Chron. 9.29; 1 Kgs 14.29 / 2 Chron. 12.15; 1 Kgs 15.7 / 2 Chron. 13.22; 2 Kgs 15.6 / 2 Chron. 26.22. 2 Chron. 33.18, 19 (cf. 2 Kgs 21.17) speaks of the 'chronicles of the kings of Israel and the words of Hozai'. 2 Chron. 32.32 has Hezekiah's deeds in the visions of the prophet Isaiah in the chronicles of the kings of 'Judah and Israel' (cf. 2 Kgs 20.20). See also the references to the annals of Jehu, contained in the book of the kings of Israel, 2 Chron. 20.34 (cf. 1 Kgs 22.46). Chronicles refers to a book of the kings of 'Judah and Israel': 2 Chron. 16.11 (cf. 1 Kgs 15.23); 2 Chron. 25.26 (cf. 2 Kgs 14.18); 2 Chron. 28.26 (cf. 2 Kgs 16.19). Other rulers are said to have mentions in the book of the kings of 'Israel and Judah': 2 Chron. 27.7 (cf. 2 Kgs 15.36); 2 Chron. 35.26-27 (cf. 2 Kgs 23.28); 2 Chron. 36.8 (cf. 2 Kgs 24.5). 2 Chron. 24.27 has the book of the 'kings' (cf. 2 Kgs 12.20). If it is reasonable that the Chronicler could manipulate the titles, or record the names of alternate sources, then the same may be said of the authors of Kings.

unreliable, with 'historical narratives' occupying a debatable middle position. Burke O. Long comments that these kinds of ranking schemes lead to easy historical judgments which supplant serious literary analysis, the first task for the scholar.[9] In some cases, they are little more than subjective judgments to describe a passage as an 'authentic' monarchic document or as accurately reporting events. The signs that one is dealing with excerpts from annals are sometimes held to be the use of expressions such as אז ('then') and the ascription of events to a particular king's time.[10] Such expressions, however, have numerous counter-examples in biblical passages unlikely to have stemmed from annals or official records.[11] Moreover, styles of reporting associated with annals or inscriptions dealing with the actual deeds of a king could be copied by others not interested in recording only contemporary royal exploits.[12] One often reads how the 'sober' or seemingly factual reporting marks a passage as stemming from a source which could not contain a fictional narrative.[13] This kind of assessment is hardly to be taken

9.   B.O. Long, 'Historical Narrative and the Fictionalizing Imagination', *VT* 35 (1985), pp. 405-16 (415-16).

10.   G.H. Jones, *1 and 2 Kings* (2 vols.; NCBC; London: Marshall, Morgan & Scott, 1984), I, pp. 62-63 (hereafter, *Kings*, I), is one of the modern scholars following the influential paper by J.A. Montgomery, 'Archival Data in the Book of Kings', *JBL* 53 (1934), pp. 46-52, on the appraisal of these expressions. He also follows M. Noth, *The Deuteronomistic History* (trans. J. Doull, J. Barton, M.D. Rutter and D.R. Ap-Thomas; JSOTSup, 15; Sheffield: JSOT Press, 1981), pp. 63-68, originally, *Überlieferungsgeschichtliche Studien* (Tübingen: M. Niemeyer, 1943), who holds that the source material mentioned in Kings was based on official annals, but was not these documents themselves. Noth maintains that annals would have been written as the events unfolded, while these texts seems to have been written some time afterwards.

11.   Van Seters, *In Search of History*, pp. 300-301. Cf. B.O. Long, *1 Kings, with an Introduction to Historical Literature* (FOTL, 9; Grand Rapids: Eerdmans, 1984), p. 24.

12.   Montgomery, 'Archival', argues that in a number of places in Kings, where unexpected grammatical formulations occur in the reporting of events, a 'lapidary' reporting of a monarch's exploits was taken up in the composition of the history book, without smoothing out the style and syntax. Often these involve the use of perfects with ו, e.g. 2 Kgs 18.4 and 23.8, 10, 12. In 2 Kgs 18.36, however, where the people are the subject of such a verb, it is claimed that there was a scribal mistake, as 'the subject matter is not archival' (pp. 50-51).

13.   E.g. Gray, *Kings*, p. 268; Montgomery, *Kings*, p. 227; Jones, *Kings*, I, p. 230; T.R. Hobbs, *2 Kings* (WBC, 13; Waco TX: Word Books, 1985), p. xxxii.

seriously.[14] Davies rightly finds the practice of linking composition to the time of the events narrated to be based on a circular reasoning which reinforces the initial assumption that the society depicted in the text is a historical entity.[15] Davies's complaint goes beyond faulting the relevant scholars for mistaking the language of attribution as a resource, and not a topic of investigation. Rather, his objection centres on the uncritical acceptance of what might be labelled entire 'narratives of attribution' as a resource.

It is not within my purposes here to establish the accuracy or inaccuracy of any episode in Kings, but at this point it is illuminating to address the more restricted issue of a key component of King's language of attribution. The name 'Israel', of course, can mean a number of different things, even if its use outside of the Hebrew Bible is disregarded. Davies lists ten senses of the word which may be discerned in the Hebrew Bible:

1: The alternative name of the patriarch Jacob.
2: The name of the sacral tribal league.
3: A united kingdom with a capital at Jerusalem.
4: The 'northern' kingdom, one of the two resulting kingdoms after the dissolution of the United Monarchy.
5: An alternative name for Judah in the time-period after the fall of the northern kingdom.
6: The socio-religious community (*Gemeente/Gemeinde*) in the Persian province of Judah (*Yehud*).
7: The laity of the community, as distinct from the religious elite ('Aaron').[16]
8: The descendants of Jacob/Israel.
9: A pre-monarchic tribal grouping in Ephraim.
10: Adherents of various forms of Hebrew Bible and Old Testament religion.[17]

14. Thompson, *Early History*, p. 388, comments that plausibility and verisimilitude characterize good fiction, while knowledge of history requires evidence, not reason.

15. Davies, *'Ancient Israel'*, pp. 36-40.

16. Davies, *'Ancient Israel'*, p. 50. These seven are taken from A.R. Hulst, *Wat betekent de naam ISRAEL in het Oude Testament?* ('s-Gravenhaag, 1962).

17. For these final three, Davies, *'Ancient Israel'*, p. 50, follows J.H. Hayes, 'Israel', *Mercer Dictionary of the Bible* (Macon, GA: Mercer Press, 1989), pp. 417-20.

There have been a number of studies on the biblical use of the name 'Israel' and its constructs.[18] Often, each particular attestation is studied against its own hypothetical historical context, which quite often is considered contemporary with the events unfolding in the episodes under scrutiny. What the narrator or a character calls an entity, there-fore, is often taken as the true use of the employed term in the time-period which is being described.[19] For instance, H.-J. Zöbel and James W. Flanagan maintain that during the time of the schism between Judah and Israel, 'all Israel' was used exclusively of the north, and was a for-mal title of that kingdom. The expression 'king over all Israel' (1 Kgs 12.20) is, therefore, the formal title of an independent political author-ity (cf. 1 Kgs 12.1).[20] Some anachronistic uses of the name 'Israel' or its constructs are found, however. Often these are down to the 'Deuteronomists' who adapted 'accurate' sources into their tendentious history.[21] Reliability in the endeavours Zöbel and Flanagan have under-taken cannot be guaranteed or demonstrated. If the 'Deuteronomists' (and I will have more to say about them below) could use such an expression in a tendentious way, so too could any earlier writers.

A more open way of looking at the use of 'Israel' in the Hebrew Bible was already suggested in 1946 by G.A. Danell, although, with a publication date such as this it is not surprising that he is also interested in 'source material' and reconstructions of narrated events.[22] He cites a number of examples of the collective name being used for the larger part of the whole, whilst the smaller portion receives a different name, without suggesting that this smaller group is to be excluded from the

18. H.-J. Zöbel, 'יִשְׂרָאֵל *yisra'el*', *TDOT* VI (1990), pp. 307-420 (397-99), original in *ThWAT* (1982), III, pp. 986-1011; J.W. Flanagan, 'Judah in all Israel', in J.W. Flanagan and A.W. Robinson (eds.), *No Famine in the Land: Studies in Honor of John L. McKenzie* (Missoula, MT: Scholars Press, 1975), pp. 101-16; *idem*, 'The Deuteronomic Meaning of the Phrase "kol yisra'el"', *SR* 6 (1976-77), pp. 159-68.

19. Although some overlap in different usage is identified, cf. Zöbel, '*yisra'el*', p. 405.

20. Zöbel, '*yisra'el*', p. 405; cf. Flanagan, 'Judah'; *idem*, 'kol yisra'el'.

21. Zöbel, '*yisra'el*', p. 405, thinks 'sons of Israel' (בְּנֵי יִשְׂרָאֵל) in 1 Kgs 12.17; 14.24; 21.26 and 2 Kgs 16.3 are 'deuteronomistic' and therefore anachronistic. Flanagan, 'kol yisra'el', argues that the 'deuteronomistic' usage of the expression 'all Israel' is the fourth and final stage in the expression's history, and was anachronistically projected into the time of the exodus and conquest.

22. G.A. Danell, *Studies in the Name Israel in the Old Testament* (Uppsala: Appelbergs Boktryckeri, 1946), p. 50.

larger (e.g. Deut. 3.8-18).[23] Danell explains it as a matter of quantity, not quality. This is given as the reason why, with the dissolution of the United Monarchy, the south took its own territorial name, Judah, while 'Israel' was retained by the majority in the north.[24] Danell also rightly notices that the word 'all' (כל) is to be interpreted relatively. For instance, Josh. 8.15, 21, 24b use 'all Israel' to refer only to the main part of the army.[25] Danell also asserts that the biblical writers were flexible in their terminology, and that no firm diachronic analysis could be based on the variety of names employed.[26] Danell's observations provide a surer route into exploration of the use of the name in Kings. At the very least, he recognizes that pragmatic aspects of story-telling may have motivated the choice of names in a number of places. On the other hand, it needs to be pointed out that the choice of name in some passages is probably more significant that Danell allows. Building on Danell's work is Daniel I. Block, who provides some very thorough discussions on the expression 'sons of Israel' (בני ישראל). He finds that this expression is somewhat unusual in that it occurs predominantly in the narratives of the Hebrew Bible, but not in poetic or prophetic texts, where such a form based on בני with a geographical name is often encountered to refer to other peoples (the other exception is the 'sons of Ammon'). Block concludes that the presence of this formulation in 'historical narratives' suggests that the Israelites perceived themselves to be descended from an ancestor named 'Israel', and this idea may offer some insights into the expression's use at some places in Kings. He refrains from advising the interpreter to follow its narrative contexts, however. He offers, instead, a summarized history of the term's use, which follows the course of history as outlined in the narratives themselves, and so his own work represents less of an advance than it could.[27] What needs to be stressed here is that a multiplicity of meanings for the name 'Israel' (and constructions employing it) was open to the post-monarchic producers of Kings. In his own sweeping examination of the terms 'Hebrew', 'Jew' and 'Israel', Graham Harvey adopts a 'theory of associative fields' which emphasizes each attestation's

---

23. See, for instance, Josh. 4.12, and ch. 22; Judg. 20.14, 17.

24. Danell, *The Name Israel*, pp. 66-67, 71, 78, 92-96.

25. Danell, *The Name Israel*, p. 67.

26. Danell, *The Name Israel*, pp. 10, 90-91.

27. D.I. Block, '"Israel"–"Sons of Israel": A Study in Hebrew Eponymic Usage', *SR* 13 (1984), pp. 302-26.

immediate context, and this is the sort of approach I will adopt here.[28]

As I have implied above, interpretation of a complex narrative as a whole is not dependent upon, and in many ways, is obstructed by the atomization and independent interpretation of units in their hypothetical original contexts. The conflation of diverse academic projects results in a tendency towards conflation of the diverse conclusions: the history of composition coincides with the actual history of the monarchies; the ideology implicit in an isolated text is commensurate with the prevailing spirit of the times, the names employed in a narrative are direct evidence of the 'proper' names for the historical counterparts to which these narratives necessarily apply. A different (but certainly not exclusive) and highly popular approach rightly places more emphasis on the 'end product' than 'elemental' units.[29] But even in this regard, there is a great tendency to dissatisfaction with the ultimate 'end product(s)', and to strive to recover the 'authentic' product, the 'original' Deuteronomistic History.

2. *The Deuteronomistic History*

Scholarship directed towards Kings as a part of a longer work, the so-called 'Deuteronomistic History', has been so diverse in conclusion that it is impossible to describe it in detail here.[30] Yet this diversity is marked by some points of commonality. This central paradigm of Kings scholarship is traceable to Martin Noth's 1943 argument that Kings was the final chapter of a longer work, now represented in a somewhat expanded, but segmented form by Deuteronomy and the Former Prophets. By taking up existing traditions, and composing framework elements and speeches by central characters and narratorial

---

28. Harvey, *True Israel*, p. 8; pp. 148-88 for his study on the term 'Israel' itself.

29. To be fair to De Vries, *1 Kings*, discussed above, his study of Kings remains highly influenced by the prevalent model of this 'end product', that of the 'Deuteronomistic History', and so, like most scholars, he attempts to mix concerns for both the 'original' sources and the 'deuteronomistic' product.

30. Summaries and evaluations of work on Noth's DtrH theory and its intellectual descendants are plentiful: S.L. McKenzie and M.P. Graham (eds.), *The History of Israel's Traditions: The Heritage of Martin Noth* (JSOTSup, 182; Sheffield: Sheffield Academic Press, 1994); H.D. Preuß, 'Zum deuteronomistischen Geschichtswerk', *ThR* 58 (1993), pp. 229-64, 341-95; H. Weippert, 'Das deuteronomistische Geschichtswerk: Sein Ziel und Ende in der neueren Forschung', *ThR* 50 (1985), pp. 213-49.

essays the author composed a long and generally coherent story of Israel's acceptance of the deuteronomic law code, their conquest and occupation of the promised land, and finally, their exile. In Kings, the primary Dtr orations are Solomon's prayer in 1 Kings 8 and the narrator's discussion after reporting the fall of Samaria in 2 Kings 17, although the writer certainly composed far more than these two passages. Noth linked the composition of this Deuteronomistic History to a time only shortly after the death of the Judaean king, Jehoiachin, who, in any case would not have lived long past his release from prison (c. 561 BCE), the narration of which is the closing episode of Kings (2 Kgs 25.27-30).[31] Noth's insistence that the DtrH was very pessimistic about the future of the exiled Judaeans was the basis of the earliest critiques, although there remained disagreement about how extensive or conditional the optimism in it should be seen to be.

Early off the mark in criticizing Noth was G.A. Danell. He argues that the strongest refutation of Noth's view of deuteronomistic pessimism was the very existence of the corpus itself. It was not an epitaph for a lost nation, but was written for Israelites, an inconceivable situation had the writer thought Israel's days were finished.[32] Offering a similar and better-known critique is Hans Walter Wolff, who argues that Noth failed to provide a suitable explanation for why the ancient author took up the pen. Furthermore, Noth's explanation for the inclusion of the story of Jehoiachin's release in fact contradicted his assertion that the writer used sources selectively. On the other hand, the lack of any mention of a divine promise in the story of Jehoiachin's release argued against von Rad's interpretation which saw the book end with the suggestion of a messianic hope. Concentrating on the use of the word שוב 'return', Wolff traces a pattern of apostasy and repentance from Joshua to Kings. Solomon's prayer features this term in a number of places (1 Kgs 8.33, 35) and vv. 46-53 address the exile specifically. The purpose of the history, then, was to show that Israel, in exile, was in the second phase of the recurring cycle of apostasy, judgment, repentance and salvation.[33] Probably the maximal recognition of hope in

31. Noth, *Deuteronomistic History*.

32. Danell, *The Name Israel*, pp. 100-101.

33. H.W. Wolff, 'Das Kerygma des deuteronomistischen Geschichtswerks', *ZAW* 73 (1961), pp. 171-86 (173-74). Available in English as 'The Kerygma of the Deuteronomic Historical Work', in W.A. Brueggemann and H.W. Wolff (eds.), *The Vitality of Old Testament Traditions* (Atlanta: John Knox Press, 1975), pp. 83-100.

Kings is expressed by (the aforementioned) Gerhard von Rad, who was, nonetheless, quick to praise Noth for closing 'a regrettable and shameful gap' in Hebrew Bible study. He identifies a series of prophecy and fulfilment sequences which display the workings of the divine word through the history of Judah and Israel. He interprets the story of Jehoiachin's release as a demonstration that the line of David had not died out. This provides the implicit basis for Yahweh's rebuilding of Israel if he so willed.[34] Von Rad has convinced few others of the messianic expectation of Kings' closing episode.[35] Like Noth, Cogan and Tadmor think the notice was only inserted for reasons of updating the story of Jehoiachin.[36] There are a number of more intermediate positions which posit that the story offers some level of optimism that David has a survivor to take his throne, however much a vassal that survivor is. The hope is in the form of security in exile by accepting domination by the Babylonians themselves.[37]

Many scholars also reject Noth's conception of a single edition of the DtrH, and see an edition of it stemming from the monarchic era itself,

34. G. von Rad, 'The Deuteronomic Theology of History in I and II Kings', in *The Problem of the Hexateuch and Other Essays* (trans. E.W. Trueman Dicken; Edinburgh: Oliver & Boyd, 1966), pp. 205-21, original: 'Das deuteronomistische Geschichtstheologie in den Königsbücher', is found in *Deuteronomium Studien*. Part B. *Forschungen zur Religion und Literatur des Alten und Neuen Testaments* (Göttingen: Vandenhoeck & Ruprecht, 1947), pp. 52-64.

35. Cf. Gray, *Kings*, p. 773. In a rather strange manner, Gray links the reasons for recording the passage with the reasons why the event transpired, a glaring example of the typical synchronism identified between text and event. He suggests that the specific mention of the king's release may have been motivated by a 'primitive superstition' that closing a book on a despondent note would bring the future under a similar evil influence. A positive ending would secure brighter prospects. 'The same dread of the infectious influence of evil and curse, especially at the beginning of an enterprise, led Evil-Merodach on his accession in 561 BCE to release Jehoiachin from prison, no doubt as part of a general amnesty customary on such an occasion.'

36. Cogan and Tadmor, *II Kings*, p. 330; cf. Noth, *Deuteronomistic History*, p. 74.

37. J.D. Levenson, 'The Last Four Verses in Kings', *JBL* 103 (1984), pp. 353-61; C.T. Begg, 'The Significance of Jehoiachin's Release: A New Proposal', *JSOT* 36 (1986), pp. 49-56; Y. Hoffman, 'The Deuteronomist and the Exile', in D.P. Wright, D.N. Freedman and A. Hurvitz (eds.), *Pomegranates and Golden Bells: Studies in Biblical, Jewish, and Near Eastern Ritual, Law, and Literature in Honor of Jacob Milgrom* (Winona Lake, IN: Eisenbrauns, 1995), pp. 659-75 (667-68).

which was then updated in the so-called 'exilic' period (the most common of the various sigla for these are Dtr1 and Dtr2). Although there are a number of formulations, and some seek lengthy 'pre-deuteronomistic' antecedents to the book, it is usually observed that the style of writing changes after narrating the events of Josiah's religious programme, and that a number of important themes come to a climax in the reign of this king.[38] It is also argued that assertion of unconditional divine sanction for the davidic dynasty, (e.g. 1 Kgs 11.13; 15.4; 2 Kgs 8.19) is contradicted by other passages that make the monarchic institution conditional upon obedience (1 Kgs 2.4, 8.25 and 9.6). It is concluded that in the late monarchic period, the DtrH was composed to support Josiah's wide-sweeping 'deuteronomistic' religious reforms in Judah and Israel. This edition is seen to develop themes of the eternal covenant with David, and the wretched apostasy of the north. After the eventual fall of Judah, the history was not only sadly out of date, but, moreover, its optimistic promonarchic perspective did not accord well with the facts of the exile, and so it was updated. In Kings, this included not only the story of the fall of Judah, but the development of the theme of Manasseh's apostasy as the sin for which Josiah's reform could not atone. The eternal divine sanction was recast by adding, in a number of places, that this sanction was only conditional.[39]

---

38. Some try to find a 'prophetic document' embedded in a monarchic DtrH: A. F. Campbell, *Of Prophets and Kings: A Late Ninth-Century Document (1 Samuel–2 Kings 10)* (CBQMS, 17; Washington: Catholic Biblical Association, 1986); M.A. O'Brien, *The Deuteronomistic History Hypothesis: A Reassessment* (OBO, 92; Göttingen: Vandenhoeck & Ruprecht, 1989). S.L. McKenzie once advocated the existence of a prophetic source: 'The Prophetic Record in Kings', *HAR* 10 (1985), pp. 203-20, but now argues for a single monarchic redaction with a series of later additions, including much of the 'prophetic' material, which does not constitute thoroughgoing redaction: *The Trouble with Kings: The Composition of the Book of Kings in the Deuteronomistic History* (VTSup, 42; Leiden: E.J. Brill, 1991), pp. 10-14, 81-100.

39. Instrumental in the popularity of this theory is F.M. Cross, 'The Themes of the Book of Kings and the Structure of the Deuteronomistic History', in F.M. Cross, *Canaanite Myth and Hebrew Epic: Essays in the History of the Religion of Israel* (Cambridge, MA: Harvard University Press, 1973), pp. 274-87; the initial version of this paper is 'The Structure of the Deuteronomistic History', in J.M. Rosenthal (ed.), *Perspectives in Jewish Learning* (Chicago: College of Jewish Studies, 1967), pp. 9-24. A major work developing these ideas further is R.D. Nelson, *The Double Redaction of the Deuteronomistic History* (JSOTSup, 18; Sheffield: JSOT Press, 1981). Some have argued that the king in question in Dtr1 was

There is, however, little unambiguous evidence to support this theory. There is a noticeable lack of external evidence for the religious programme of King Josiah, the historical context most often posited for the monarchic era product. The purge narrative (2 Kgs 23.1-23; cf. 2 Chron. 34.3, 33) and that of the discovery of the law scroll (2 Kgs 22.8-20; cf. 2 Chron. 34.14-28) may be legends to validate later religious programmes.[40] The historicity of Hezekiah's reform programme (2 Kgs 18.4; 2 Chron. 29.3-31.21) is also suspect in some quarters.[41] Another, and more serious, problem in positing an abridged edition of Kings in the monarchic period is found in the premise that original editions would have displayed near-complete consistency and singularity of opinion on the validity and permanence of the davidic dynasty and other important themes. The 'coherency' approach is susceptible to the complaint that with it the scholar may be solving a self-created problem, and that success is virtually guaranteed, as any offending incoherence can be removed and ascribed to a later writer. Sometimes there are no clear criteria for determining what should be ascribed to Dtr1 or Dtr2.[42] Striking is the disagreement on some of the 'conditional

not Josiah but Hezekiah: I.W. Provan, *Hezekiah and the Books of Kings: A Contribution to the Debate about the Composition of the Deuteronomistic History* (BZAW, 172; Berlin: W. de Gruyter, 1988), but he turns from historical-critical research in his new book, I.W. Provan, *1 and 2 Kings* (NIBC; Peabody, MA: Hendrickson, 1995), p. 3. There are very many other scholars who see at least one monarchic era edition, among them R.E. Friedman, *The Exile and Biblical Narrative: The Formation of the Deuteronomistic and Priestly Works* (HSM, 22; Chico, CA: Scholars Press, 1981); Knoppers, *Two Nations*; B. Halpern and D.S. Vanderhooft, 'The Editions of Kings in the 7th–6th Centuries BCE', *HUCA* 62 (1991), pp. 179-244.

40. Bibliographical information on this will be given in Chapter 8, but here might be mentioned B.J. Diebner and C. Nauerth, 'Die Inventio des ספר התורה in 2 Kön 22: Struktur, Intention und Funktion von Auffindungslegenden', *DBAT* 18 (1984), pp. 95-118, who do, however, accord some credibility to the purge narrative, but not the discovery of the scroll.

41. L.K. Handy, 'Hezekiah's Unlikely Reform', *ZAW* 100 (1988), pp. 111-15; N. Na'aman, 'The Debated Historicity of Hezekiah's Reform in the Light of Archaeological Research', *ZAW* 107 (1995), pp 179-95. The contrary view is expressed by O. Borowski, 'Hezekiah's Reform and the Revolt against Assyria', *BA* 58 (1995), pp. 148-55.

42. For example, 2 Kgs 17.7-23. Scholars differ as to which sections should be accorded a secondary status, but at least v. 19 is usually seen as secondary. Cross, 'The Themes', p. 287, identifies only this verse as secondary, as he sees in it the

promises' of a davidic heir on the 'throne of Israel'. Frank Cross thinks that references to an heir on the throne in 1 Kgs 2.4, 8.25 and 9.5 belonged to the exilic edition, while Richard Nelson ascribes these to Deuteronomy 1, interpreting 'Israel' here to mean only the northern kingdom.[43] Many also endeavour to uncover the work of 'pre-exilic' writers by exhaustive (and exhausting) studies of Kings' formulae by which judgments on the religious practices of Judah's and Israel's monarchs are cast, or those which provide each monarch's age at accession and their death and burial information.[44] The operative premise is that each author would have been relatively consistent in giving this information, and so changes in the pattern of reporting are evidence of different authors. No confidence, however, should be given to the conclusions of such exercises, as there is little to support the basic premise of authorial consistency. Moreover, the subjectivity of some of the decisions can lead to inconsistent arguments.[45]

In my view, too much is made of the dichotomy between 'conditional' and 'unconditional' promises as markers of historical provenance. Each statement about divine support or condemnation for the

conclusion of some of the monarchic editions' themes, while Nelson, *Double Redaction*, pp. 55-63, sees the whole of 7-20 and 23b as the work of Dtr 2. More complex is the proposal of M. Brettler, 'Ideology, History, and Theology in 2 Kings XVII 7-23', *VT* 39 (1989), pp. 268-82, who sees v. 13 (except for the words 'and Judah') to v. 18a and 23 as earlier than vv. 21-22 (probably pre-exilic). Verses 7-12 are exilic, once standing as the conclusion to ch. 25, but have been misplaced. Even the inclusion of the law code of Deuteronomy in the first DtrH is disputed: see J.D. Levenson. 'Who Inserted the Book of the Torah?', *HTR* 68 (1975), pp. 203-33. See also his 'From Temple to Synagogue: 1 Kings 8', in B. Halpern and J.D. Levenson (eds.), *Traditions in Transformation* (Winona Lake, IN: Eisenbrauns, 1981), pp. 143-66.

43. Cross, 'The Themes', pp. 284-89; Nelson, *Double Redaction*, pp. 100-104.

44. Perhaps the most influential proposal is H. Weippert, 'Die "deuteronomistischen" Beurteilungen der Könige von Israel und Juda und das Problem der Redaktion der Königsbücher', *Bib* 53 (1972), pp. 301-39. Two recent ones are: Halpern, and Vanderhooft, 'Editions'; E. Eynikel, *The Reform of King Josiah and the Composition of the Deuteronomistic History* (OTS, 33; Leiden: E.J. Brill, 1996), pp. 34-135.

45. This is particularly noticeable in Nelson, *Double Redaction*, pp. 33-34, 38, who, on the one hand, attributes perceived repetition in the formulae for the final kings of Israel to an artist emphasizing cumulative sin, while a similar repetitiousness in the final Judaean reigns is attributed to the 'wooden' imitations of a second writer.

dynasty or nation needs investigation according to its own literary context, and in terms of the plot development and character motives.[46] Implicit conditions may also be read into every promise.[47] Some contend that the 'eternal' aspect of Yahweh's support for David may have represented typical royal hyperbole.[48] The post-monarchic utilization of such hyperbole to refer to a long-lost kingdom should not be taken as especially problematic, if the monarchy is seen on multiple levels. Not only is it a specific political institution, but also a symbolic embodiment of 'greater Israel' within a specific historical period. Its eternal aspects may have been celebrated in those episodes in which it was a positive force in Israel's history, and downplayed elsewhere, when such an emphasis would have been inappropriate.[49] Similar objections may be made against stratifying Kings according to 'pro-' or 'anti-monarchic' sentiments. Gerald E. Gerbrandt argues that although kingship played an extremely important role in the DtrH as a whole, it was not essentially about kingship: 'In light of this, the Deuteronomist's view of kingship cannot be presented even tentatively totally apart from his understanding of Israel, of Yahweh, and of their relationship to each other'.[50] Gerbrandt also advises his reader that the view of anti- or pro-monarchical sources in Samuel is based on a lack of awareness of the historical circumstances in the ancient Near East, in which monarchy would have been a normative form of government. The true question is 'what form of kingship was considered ideal?'[51] This is an insight which is also worth much development, even in the later dates I would think most likely for Kings. I would add, however, that the figure of an ancient, ideal king would have had tremendous symbolic value in any number of situations, and not only for hopes for a return to a monarchy in the short term. The failure of former kings does not undermine the validity of a conception of an ideal king; rather negative portrayals of some monarchs only affirm the validity of the ideal. The dichotomy

46. This is particularly emphasized by L. Eslinger in his monographs on Samuel and Kings, and I will have occasion to outline his views in a bit more detail below.

47. Hobbs, *2 Kings*, pp. xxiv-xxv.

48. Long, *1 Kings*, pp. 16-17.

49. I have broached this topic in my paper, 'Rethinking the "Exilic" Book of Kings', *JSOT* 75 (1997), pp. 21-42.

50. G.E. Gerbrandt, *Kingship According to the Deuteronomistic History* (SBLDS, 87; Atlanta: Scholars Press, 1986), p. 89.

51. Gerbrandt, *Kingship*, pp. 36-43.

between eternal or contingent, pro- or anti-monarchic passages in Kings is a feature deserving examination. It is not, however, *a priori* evidence of multiple editions. Furthermore, even if one is led to juxtapose pro- and anti-monarchic editions, the above statements do not make a pro- monarchic edition necessarily a monarchic era product. The apparent contrast between ostensibly different ideologies may well be illusory, as expressions of ideological complexes entail what, to an external observer, may seem like contradiction.[52] This necessarily complicates, if it does not make impossible, any attempt at systematizing the com- position of Kings according to an evolutionary model of specific, inter- nally consistent ideologies. The abridgment of the book at some point around the reign of Josiah requires additional arguments, but again, these are hardly conclusive.

In Van Seters's opinion, the Deuteronomist used a paratactic format, linking individual items in series.[53] Such a style challenges the premise that any 'climax' of the book, such as Josiah's reign seems to be, must occur at the very end.[54] It is dubious to maintain that an ancient author would certainly have unified a work by a climactic conclusion, and that

---

52. For instance: M.J. Aronoff, 'Myths, Symbols, and Rituals of the Emerging State', in L.J. Silberstein (ed.), *New Perspectives on Israeli History: The Early Years of the State* (New York: New York University Press, 1991), pp. 175-92 (178- 79). See too, L.E. Goodman, 'Mythic Discourse', in S. Biderman and B.-A. Scharfstein (eds.), *Myths and Fictions* (Leiden: E.J. Brill, 1993), pp. 51-112 (99); S.F. Moore, 'Epilogue: Uncertainties in Situations, Indeterminacies in Culture', in S.F. Moore and B.G. Myerhoff (eds.), *Symbol and Politics in Communal Ideology* (Ithaca, NY: Cornell University Press, 1975), pp. 210-39 (236). Moore writes: 'Ideology may be regarded as a product of what we have called the regularizing processes. Yet its instance-by-instance use permits the kind of reinterpretation, redefinition, and manipulation that is associated with processes of situational adjustment. Sometimes an ideology or part of it can be constructed precisely to cover the complex mess of social reality with an appearance of order, simplicity, harmony and plan. But sometimes, and at other levels, the ideology of a society, or of some subpart of it, is not more of a harmonious whole than the on-the-ground realities. The fact is that when we speak of the ideology of a group of persons, or of a society or some part of it, we are speaking of it as a whole. But usually, in action, in particular situations, only pieces of ideology are invoked. Since ideology is used in this way–piecemeal–inconsistencies are not necessarily apparent, as they might be when put together in an analysis.'

53. Van Seters, *In Search of History*, pp. 320-21.

54. Long, *1 Kings*, pp. 17-18.

the whole trajectory of the work would have been directed to this point. Similarly, the conclusion of a book need not show the same density and complexity of theme displayed at the outset or midpoints. Neither should the scholar depend too much on a model of addition and selective manipulation of an otherwise fixed document. Long considers such assumptions as the anachronistic imposition of modern literary preferences on ancient texts.[55] In Chapter 8, I will discuss the episode of Josiah as a climactic point in the history, but one which is anticipatory of the final destruction of Judah. There is little in the way of reliable methodology to draw conclusive judgments about early, monarchic era versions of Kings. The number of issues at stake and the ability of the same passages to be differently dated or accommodated into the basic schema reveal this. Basic issues, such as the historicity of the necessary events and the relationship of literature to them are not adequately demonstrated, and many alternative paths of investigation, such as literary artistry, and the possibility of non-literal, symbolic uses of monarchic history in Persian or Hellenistic times are mostly left unexplored as contexts and motives for composition.

If there is no convincing reason to follow the lead of Cross and Nelson, it remains that Noth's concept of a single author for all of the DtrH is not the only alternative. Many scholars argue for multiple postmonarchic editions. Walter Dietrich's work on Kings was an extension of that of Rudolf Smend's study into earlier components of the DtrH. Smend argues that a number of passages that Noth thought secondary were the work of a second deuteronomistic redactor with a strong interest in the law (labelled DtrN, nomistic). Dietrich also argued that another redaction with an interest in prophecy (DtrP) took place after the initial deuteronomistic composition, but before the additions of the nomistic reworking.[56] The work of Smend and Dietrich reflect the influence of an earlier work by Alfred Jepsen, and they, in turn, have influenced a number of others, including Ernst Würthwein and Gwilym

---

55. Long, *1 Kings*, pp. 17-20.

56. W. Dietrich, *Prophetie und Geschichte: Eine redactionsgeschichtliche Untersuchung zum deuteronomistischen Geschichtswerk* (FRLANT, 108; Göttingen: Vandenhoeck & Ruprecht, 1972); R. Smend, 'Das Gesetz und die Völker', in H.W. Wolff (ed.), *Probleme biblischer Theologie* (Munich: Chr. Kaiser Verlag, 1971), pp. 494-509. Smend accepts Dietrich's idea of DtrP in *Die Entstehung des Alten Testaments* (Stuttgart: W. Kohlhammer, 1978), pp. 120-25.

H. Jones.[57] The necessity to find redactional layers reaches an extreme level in the work of Rainer Stahl who finds not only a basic history work and a prophetic level (DtrP), but no less than three nomistic writers (DtrN1, 2, 3) and four 'theological' levels (DtrTh 1, 2, 3, 4).[58] Some scholars have tried to mediate between the position of Cross and Nelson on the one hand, and that of Dietrich on the other.[59]

Criticisms of the basic multiple post-monarchic theories are not hard to find. Some complain that these theories lack sufficient demonstration that the changes in emphasis necessitate the positing of different writers. They require a very heavy emphasis on slight variations in word choice. It is largely assumed that a single writer could not have used different terms for the same idea and that different writers could not have developed existing themes with similar language.[60] In general, the multiple post-monarchic theories appreciate the complexity of these narratives, but fail to appreciate the potential complexity of purpose and content which may have motivated any single author. To my mind, it is not a question of whether Kings was edited and re-edited in the post-monarchic period, but whether these projects were on discernible, systematic lines, each stage centring on their own unique, specific themes consistently handled with a great regularity in language. That the book may be fragmented and categorized according to such themes is not a certain indication of such a series of identifiable editions.

Some scholars, however, have re-engaged Noth's concept of a single deuteronomist writing in the exilic period. These scholars often assert that literary complexity should not be mistaken for evidence of multiple

---

57. E. Würthwein, *Die Bücher der Könige: 1 Könige 1–16* (Göttingen: Vandenhoeck & Ruprecht, 2nd edn, 1985), *Könige*, II; Jones, *Kings*.

58. R. Stahl provides a summary of his 'Aspekte der Geschichte deuteronomistischer Theologie: Zur Traditionsgeschichte der Terminologie und zur Redaktionsgeschichte der Redekomposition' (Thesis, Jena, 1982) in *TL* 108 (1983), pp. 74-75.

59. E. Cortese, 'Theories Concerning Dtr: A Possible Rapprochement', in C. Breckelmans and J. Lust (eds.), *Pentateuchal and Deuteronomistic Studies: Papers Read at the XIIIth IOSOT Congress, Leuven 1989* (Leuven: Leuven University Press, 1990), pp. 179-90. N. Lohfink, 'Kerygmata des deuteronomistischen Geschichtswerks', in J. Jeremias and L. Perlitt (eds.), *Die Botschaft und die Boten: Festschrift für Hans Walter Wolff zum 70. Geburtstag* (Neukirchen–Vluyn: Neukirchener Verlag, 1981), pp. 87-100.

60. Campbell, *Of Prophets*, pp. 6-12; Gerbrandt, *Kingship*, p. 14.

authors.[61] One of the most discussed names in this regard is Hans-Detlef Hoffmann. Hoffmann himself argues that the DtrH was the product of an exilic or early postexilic author who based the work around themes of cultic reform. The reforms of obedient kings are contrasted with those of evil monarchs. The motive was to encourage a reform in the author's own time, on the model of the ideal, Josiah. Hoffmann contends that the traditional material collected in this work has been integrated to such an extent that one cannot now separate them out, and that much of Kings is fictitious. He stresses the unity of the DtrH, despite some notable secondary additions (2 Kgs 17.34-41).[62]

Hoffmann has been criticized from a number of angles. Mark O'Brien questions why the tensions that Hoffmann sees in 2 Kgs 17.34-41 are attributed to a different author when other tensions throughout Kings are not. Neither can every feature of the book be subsumed under a concern for reform. The scheme works well up to the death of Josiah, but does not explain the final four reigns.[63] Similarly, McKenzie complains that Hoffmann has not adequately explained how Josiah's story could be the logical climax of the story of reforms.[64] In my view, however, if Hoffmann is to be criticized in this regard, it is not to the rejection of his basic thesis, but only the way in which the reform pattern is accommodated to the shape of the book as a whole. On the other hand, arguments for a single author are susceptible to numerous other objections. Later authors could easily have adopted the language of their predecessors, radically changing selected passages in ways which cannot now be appreciated. Such later development need not have produced a uniform development of new themes, but only developed those which were found in the original. It is beyond demonstration that any example of brilliant writing (and single edition theorists are often impressed with the calibre of writing) could only be the product of a solitary genius, and not a brilliant editor.

As it stands now, none of the main compositional histories on offer can claim to conclusively solve the problem of the origin of Kings. The vast number of different themes and topics, as well as the uncertain

61. J.G. McConville, 'Narrative and Meaning in the Books of Kinge', *Bib* 70 (1989), pp. 31-49; and '1 Kings VIII 46-53 and the Deuteronomic Hope', *VT* 42 (1992), pp. 67-79; Hobbs, *2 Kings*, pp. xxii-xxxiii.

62. Hoffmann, *Reform*.

63. O'Brien, *Deuteronomistic History*, p. 16.

64. McKenzie, *Trouble*, pp. 15-16.

relationship between the book and other members of the Former Prophets, suggests that any limited set of criteria will always be inadequate. On the other hand, attempting to accommodate every possible variable may be an impossible task. The present work, by concentrating on themes of ethnic-religious symbolism, only adds to the list of criteria which need to be investigated. In general, too much is dependent upon overly subjective judgments of what an ancient author would have, or could have written. In many ways, multiple-edition theorists cannot accept that single writers could compose seemingly contradictory ideological statements. On the other hand, single-edition theorists cannot categorically rule out later editors or copyists taking extreme liberties with their *Vorlage*. The very existence of shared passages, and sometimes quite extensive ones, between Samuel and Kings, on the one hand, and Chronicles, Isaiah and Jeremiah on the other, is plain evidence of the fact that quoting and rewriting earlier documents was a major factor in ancient Hebrew literary production.[65] Proof of the *unity* of authorship is therefore as troublesome as any demonstration of its multiplicity. The new proposal of Graeme Auld, based on comparisons between the different surroundings given to the synoptic passages between Kings and Chronicles may, however, provide a way forward, as it is dependent upon a comparison between extant texts. Auld contests the time-honoured proposal that Chronicles was a radical emendation of a largely complete book of Kings. He proposes instead that the origins of both books are easier to explain as independent developments from a common source-text. That source-text, a story of the dynasty of David, is mostly recoverable from the passages which both Kings and Chronicles feature. Auld does not propose a date for the development of Kings, or the number of stages it underwent to turn the story of David's house into a comprehensive history of the monarchies of Judah and Israel. He does, however, argue that Kings need not be substantially earlier than Chronicles. Most importantly, he challenges even the 'deuteronomistic' ascription of many of the key passages in Kings, as his distinction between the shared text and Kings' pluses cuts across the supposedly deuteronomistic sections (such as Solomon's prayer, 1 Kgs 8).[66] It remains to be seen whether Auld's theory will

65. Despite this, I stand by my comments above on the issue of quotations in Kings from the 'Chronicles of the Kings of Judah / Israel'.

66. A.G. Auld, *Kings without Privilege: David and Moses in the Story of the Bible's Kings* (Edinburgh: T. & T. Clark, 1994). See his own recognition of the

attain the levels of popularity of earlier proposals, and I will not devote
the present work to supporting or refuting it here. I do, however, support the challenge to the 'deuteronomistic' provenance of Kings.

3. A 'Post-Deuteronomistic' History?

While many aspects of Noth's theory have been challenged, his theory
of the DtrH has largely set the agenda to this day. In the 1994 collection
of papers in honour of the 50th anniversary of Noth's groundbreaking
work, the integrity of the DtrH was to some extent simply assumed.[67]
Objections to this certainty, however, have been voiced in some quarters. Jon Levenson questions the inclusion of Deuteronomy in the
monarchic editions, and others have suggested that even less was originally a part of it.[68] Ernst Würthwein finds an originally independent,
post-monarchic, deuteronomistic book of Kings, which underwent two
subsequent deuteronomistic redactions. Other blocks of material,
including a pre-existing, non-deuteronomistic document and new
deuteronomistic material, were then included to form a corpus which
cannot be considered a unified DtrH.[69] In advocating 'Reading Joshua
after Kings', Auld finds it more likely that it was from Samuel and
Kings that the rest of the Former Prophets and Deuteronomy itself
found their greatest influence.[70] Other objections to Noth's conception
of authorial unity have been raised. Many find it hard to reconcile the
differences between the components of the DtrH by suggesting they are
merely the products of the nature of the sources. David is portrayed

---

trouble he causes theories of the Deuteronomists, p. 150.

67. McKenzie and Graham (eds.), *History of Israel's Traditions*. In McKenzie's
own contribution, 'The Book of Kings', p. 297, he questions 'whether it is possible
to accept the unity of Deuteronomistic History without acknowledging its essential
unity of authorship'.

68. Levenson, 'Who Inserted the Book', pp. 203-33; Provan, *Hezekiah*, pp. 158-
69, argues that Samuel and Kings were the original DtrH, while the remaining
books were added in the exile.

69. E. Würthwein, 'Erwägungen zum sog. deuteronomistichen Geschichtswerk:
Eine Skizze', in E. Würthwein, *Studien zum deuteronomistischen Geschichtswerk*
(BZAW, 227; Berlin: W. de Gruyter, 1994), pp. 1-11.

70. A.G. Auld, 'Reading Joshua after Kings', in J. Davies, G. Harvey, W.G.E.
Watson (eds.), *Words Remembered, Texts Renewed: Essays in Honour of John F.A.
Sawyer* (JSOTSup, 195; Sheffield: Sheffield Academic Press, 1995), pp. 167-81.

differently in Samuel and Kings; there is repetition between Joshua and Judges.[71] Erik Eynikel writes,

> I must agree not only with Von Rad, but also with C. Westermann, whose form critical analysis leads him to conclude that we can no longer speak of a dtr history. The individual books of the dtr history are clearly unified units that do not reflect a comprehensive 'Geschichtswerk'. At best we can speak of a dtr redaction in which the historical books are parenthetically interpreted. I can agree with Westermann's reasoning in that I am also convinced that the dtr history arose in the compilation of various books that were written independently.[72]

Even if it is assumed that Noth is right in his claims about an original unity, however, it is not wise to avoid questioning how long a hypothetical DtrH would have stayed unified. A corpus spanning Deuteronomy to 2 Kings is generally thought to have been composed on a number of different scrolls.[73] One needs to ask, therefore, whether these particular scrolls were so closely associated with one another that one, or a selection of them, could not have been copied and distributed and, therefore, potentially edited independently of the rest of the corpus.

Noth felt that the deuteronomistic transitions between Judges and Samuel and Samuel and Kings were 'so smooth and clear that we can assume without further ado that Dtr. wrote it all', even though its unity needed to be 'discovered'.[74] This discovery has to penetrate a number

71. L.K. Handy, 'Historical Probability and the Narrative of Josiah's Reform in 2 Kings', in S.W. Holloway and L.K. Handy (eds.), *The Pitcher is Broken: Memorial Essays for Gösta W. Ahlström* (JSOTSup, 190; Sheffield: Sheffield Academic Press, 1995), pp. 252-75 (258-59). So, too, Davies, *'Ancient Israel'*, pp. 130-31. Also see the objections in G. Fohrer, *Introduction to the Old Testament* (trans. D.E. Green; Nashville: Abingdon Press, 1968), p. 194. German original, *Einleitung in das Alte Testament* (Heidelberg: Quelle & Meyer, 1965).

72. Eynikel, *The Reform*, p. 363. He refers to von Rad, *Theologie des Alten Testament. I. Die Theologie der geschichtlichen Überlieferungen Israels* (Munich: Chr. Kaiser Verlag, 1957), p. 334, C. Westermann, *Die Geschichtsbücher des Alten Testaments: Gab es ein deuteronomistichen Geschichtswerk?* (ThB, 87; Gütersloh: Chr. Kaiser Verlag, 1994). He sees 1 Kgs 3–2 Kgs 18 being extended to 2 Kgs 25.30 as a single block. Joshua–1 Sam. 12, 1 Sam. 13–2 Sam. + 1 Kgs 1–2 were other blocks of text. In the exile, the second Deuteronomist who updated Kings possibly also reworked the whole of the corpus (pp. 363-64).

73. It is often considered that the division between 2 Sam. and 1 Kgs, and that between 1 and 2 Kgs had been determined by scroll length; e.g. De Vries, *1 Kings*, p. xix.

74. Noth, *Deuteronomistic History*, pp. 2, 9.

of post-deuteronomistic additions.[75] The ease with which Noth actually dispensed with the 'final form' to arrive at the original, authentically deuteronomistic, form opens him to the criticism of not really challenging the question of the inclusion of Deuteronomy in the *Torah*, let alone its inclusion in the Samaritan Pentateuch.[76] More importantly, he has largely created the corpus he then studies.[77] Thus, it is a bit odd to read Dietrich's comment that Noth was going against the prevailing trends by concentrating on 'the final shape' of the text.[78] This assertion is true in so far as the 'text' is conceived of as the history-work actually produced by the Deuteronomist(s), but no DtrH as a single document now exists, and the components have been secondarily divided. Here Dietrich displays the common impression that the 'deuteronomistic' editions of the book are the 'authentic' or most historically relevant versions for discussion. Relatively few scholars of Kings' compositional history consider the 'post-deuteronomistic' stages of composition as relevant topics in themselves, except for the time spent actually arguing for their secondary status.[79] This situation is disturbing, especially in the light of the fact that many find substantial 'post-deuteronomistic' sections. Detailed examination of the 'post-deuteronomistic' priorities in dealing with the old 'deuteronomistic' book would also be a welcome sequel to many redactional studies.

The criticism here varies with the amount of later additions that

---

75. E.g. Josh. 24, Judg. 1.1–2.5; Judg. 17–21; 2 Sam. 21–24; 1 Kgs 21.20, 23; 2 Kgs 17.34b-40. A concise outline of Noth's schema of which sections of the DtrH he attributed to Dtr's taking up of source material, Dtr contributions, and later additions is found in A.F. Campbell, 'Martin Noth and the Deuteronomistic History', in McKenzie and Graham (eds.), *History of Israel's Traditions*, pp. 31-62 (58-62).

76. Handy, 'Historical Probability', p. 258.

77. Even the literary studies not concerned with historical matters embrace the notion of the comprehensive DtrH: Eslinger, *Living God*; R. Polzin, *Moses*; *idem*, *Samuel*; *idem*, *David*. Both McKenzie, 'The History', pp. 304, and Knoppers, *Two Nations*, I, p. 29, criticize these scholars for basing their studies on conclusions of explicitly historical research.

78. W. Dietrich, 'Martin Noth and the Future of the Deuteronomistic History', in McKenzie and Graham (eds.), *History of Israel's Traditions*, pp. 153-75.

79. But see, for instance, the work of A. Rofé, 'The Vineyard of Naboth: The Origin and Message of the Story', *VT* 38 (1988), pp. 89-104. Another notable exception is Auld. Auld's methodology in *Privilege* involves textual criticism and the comparison of synoptic passages, undercutting the integrity of the supposed deuteronomistic sections. Elsewhere he advises that the case of deuteronomistic origins needs re-arguing from the bottom up, 'Reading', p. 181.

scholars perceive in the book. In an unusual situation in this regard is McKenzie, who does not link any post-monarchic addition to Kings with a real redaction of the book, despite the great extent of such additions. For McKenzie, these include some of the 'northern' prophetic narratives and, of course, the concluding chapters of the book.[80] Fixing a normative end-point to in-depth interpretation, which is placed prior to an ultimate conclusion of the processes of composition and transmission, generally reflects the same quest for a pristine 'original' that marks the work of those who would atomize the text into its hypothetical elemental units.

4. *Deuteronomistic Mystery*

At its most basic, the description 'deuteronomistic' offers the scholar a quick and not entirely impractical label to mark relationships between selected phrases and passages. Problems arise, however, from the over-confidence with which these linguistic or literary features are taken as evidence of a particular political group, 'the Deuteronomists'. The accent on finding the special-interest groups responsible for the texts is, of itself, a proper goal of such research. It is not certain, however, that this knowledge can be easily obtained. Morton Smith writes that the study of the texts of the Hebrew Bible must begin with an attempt to discover the traditions presupposed by the documents. These, however, do not merely exist but must be preserved by 'parties', groups of like-minded individuals. Therefore, the study of the traditions must begin with the study of the parties.[81] I wonder, however, whether identifying the otherwise unattested party which preserved traditions is mistaking one of the goals of historical scholarship for its starting-point.[82] Despite the great range of opinion on the social place of the Deuteronomists, there is little sociological control on the interpretation of the relevant

---

80. McKenzie, *Trouble*, p. 152, lists the 'post-dtr additions' which include 1 Kgs 6.11-14; 13.1-33; 22.1-38; 2 Kgs 10.18-28; 23.25b–25.30. Strikingly, even 2 Kgs 17.7ab-17, by most standards quite deuteronomistic, is also considered post-dtr.

81. Smith, *Palestinian Parties*, pp. 4-5, 9-10.

82. Critiques of various proposals for ancient schools of thought can be found in R.F. Person, *Second Zechariah and the Deuteronomic School* (JSOTSup, 167; Sheffield: JSOT Press, 1993), pp. 260-80.

texts.[83] This is only aggravated by the sheer variety of different perceptions of *when* and *why* the Deuteronomists (however many there were)
actually worked, and *what* it was they actually produced. Yet, the
operative premise is that deuteronomistic language *must* come from
Deuteronomists, who *must* represent an identifiable political and religious entity. This general assumption, found in countless papers and
books, requires serious qualification, if not outright rejection.

Without going into details, there is a general agreement as to what
makes a phrase 'deuteronomistic'. Language and expressions in the
Former Prophets, characteristic of the legal corpus of Deuteronomy and
employed in advocating positions generally coherent with that document, may be labelled as such. Moshe Weinfeld, in his study of the
'school' behind Deuteronomy, lists a number of characteristic theological tenets on which Deuteronomy's characteristic phraseology centres:

1.   The struggle against idolatry
2.   The centralisation of the cult
3.   Exodus, covenant, and election
4.   The monotheistic creed
5.   Observance of the law and loyalty to the covenant
6.   Inheritance of the land
7.   Retribution and material motivation.

In addition to these deuteronomic tenets, the deuteronomistic historian added two more: the fulfilment of prophecy and the election of
the davidic dynasty.[84] Examples of such deuteronomistic phraseology
include accusations that the Israelites 'went after other gods' הלך +
אחרי אלהים אחרים, for example, Deut. 6.14; Judg. 2.12, 19; 1 Kgs
11.10; Jer. 7.6; or after 'the Baal' or 'the Baals' (הבעל(ים, for example,
1 Kgs 18.18; 2 Kgs 17.16. The verb כעס, 'to provoke' (object, Yahweh,
e.g. 2 Kgs 17.11; 23.19) is also common. It is frequently noted that

---

83. P. Dutcher-Walls, 'The Social Location of the Deuteronomists: A Sociological Study of Factional Politics in Late Pre-Exilic Judah', *JSOT* 52 (1991), pp. 77-
94 (79-80). Cf. McKenzie, *Trouble*, p. 6; 'Linguistic affinity does not indicate
social unity'.

84. M. Weinfeld, *Deuteronomy and the Deuteronomic School* (Oxford: Clarendon Press, 1972), p. 1. He provides a discussion of the development of the terminology on pp. 1-6, and an appendix outlining the expressions on pp. 320-65. See
also the appendices in Hoffmann, *Reform*, pp. 327-66; E. Talstra, *Solomon's
Prayer: Synchrony and Diachrony in the Composition of 1 Kings 8, 14-61* (CBET,
3; Kampen: Kok Pharos, 1993), pp. 267-74.

vocabulary alone is often not a sufficient indicator; rather, suspect passages must share certain ideological dispositions with Deuteronomy.[85] Yet if a certain coherency does mark the treatment of particular themes in some biblical books, it is not at once clear what this coherency signifies. Richard Coggins's paper, 'What Does "Deuteronomistic" Mean?' highlights how popular the term has become in describing the nature of much of the Hebrew Bible and reminds the reader of the danger of 'pan-deuteronomism'. Coggins notes that there are links in the various deuteronomistic writings, but the term should not be applied in a wilful fashion without justification. At least in some cases, these deuteronomistic features, which mark a wide variety of themes and topics, may have been the result of merely a particular stock of literary styles, motifs and expression readily employable by any reasonably well-read Hebrew author, and of this I will have more to say below.[86] Coggins's conclusion is to the point:

> We need, it seems, to be clearer than we have often been in distinguishing between what can properly be said about a particular book and its immediately related congeners; what can be said by way of describing a literary process through which other pieces of literature reached their final form; and what can be said about an ideological movement which played a major part in shaping the self-understanding of Judaism. To use the same name for them all is to invite a breakdown in understanding.[87]

A striking example of the confusion is the proposal of Lothar Perlitt, that a transitional stage between 'Hebraism' and 'Judaism' was 'Deuteronomism'.[88] Rather than evidence merely of a particular interest-group within Hebrew or Jewish society, Perlitt implies that 'deuteronomistic' language represents a major stage in religious history

85. E.g. Weinfeld, *Deuteronomy*, pp. 2-3. The scholarly reliance on linguistic and authorial-perspective criteria, particularly as they apply to Noth's initial positing of the DtrH, has been recently assessed by Talstra, *Solomon's Prayer*, pp. 22-82. He finds that the role played by an independent study of linguistic features influences the results of exegesis, and that Noth was weak in the use of linguistic analysis. The result of this investigation leads Talstra to develop a methodology which studies the prayer twice, once from a very comprehensive synchronic perspective, the second diachronically.

86. R. Coggins, 'What Does "Deuteronomistic" Mean', in Davies, Harvey and Watson (eds.), *Words Remembered, Texts Renewed*, pp. 135-48.

87. Coggins, 'What Does "Deuteronomistic" Mean', p. 146.

88. L. Perlitt, 'Hebraismus–Deuteronomismus–Judaismus', in L. Perlitt (ed.), *Deuteronomium-Studien* (Tübingen: J.B.C. Mohr, 1994), pp. 247-60 (257-60).

in its own right. It is not, however, a simple matter to apply what is properly a marker of linguistic affiliation into a marker of sociological or political organization, and in my view, it is more dubious to use it as a marker of historical periodization for something as broad and diverse as the pre-history of Judaism. Certainly, a particular interest-group may have a characteristic theology and produce literature, with a unique jargon to suit. Yet groups with contradictory positions may preserve the same literary tradition, albeit with different (perhaps unwritten) interpretations.[89] This suggests that Perlitt may be justified in his proposal, especially if Deuteronomism is seen as a rather broad mode of religious expression, but only if deuteronomistic language can be firmly dated within a specific range of dates, while other modes of expression must be dated to other times. It is far more practical to look for Deuteronomists as a particular group within a greater religious tradition, but even here, difficult questions must be asked.

There are many aspects to party formation and group identity which cannot be explored by investigating literature whose provenance is not already known. As implied by my review of the proposed DtrH compositional histories, it is sometimes largely a subjective decision as to what constitutes 'normative' deuteronomistic expression and ideology. As noted above, most scholars see multiple Deuteronomists, each with a particular version of deuteronomism to expound.[90] The evidence some find of multiple deuteronomistic editions, while not conclusive, does reveal a willingness, in some quarters, to accept that deuteronomistic language is not testimony to a purely monolithic ideology.[91] Yet I wonder if such language as is taken as evidence of Deuteronomists

89. One may think of the different simultaneous interpretations given any biblical passage in the history of Christianity. Written interpretation need not accompany the 'canonical' text itself.

90. For example, Nelson, 'Anatomy', p. 46, juxtaposes pro-davidic material in Kings with 'straight' deuteronomistic ideology. More importantly, one might point to the matter of 2 Sam. 7, in which Nathan receives an oracle that David's 'house' is to receive divine sanction forever. Noth did not include it in the Dtr compositions, as it was 'pro-monarchic', but others, who see in the Deuteronomists champions of davidic right to rule, think otherwise. Linking the chapter to the other Dtr orations seen to mark the corpus is D.J. McCarthy, 'II Samuel 7 and the Structure of the Deuteronomic History', *JBL* 84 (1965), pp. 131-38.

91. On the other hand, the school of Cross and Nelson tend to link changes in deuteronomistic thought more to historical developments surrounding the fall of the monarchy.

could not have been shared by a number of groups with diverse, even contradictory, interests. It is not apparent to me that the acceptance of a deuteronomistic view and mode of expression on one issue necessitated ancient writers restricting their contributions solely to those issues and idioms.

These observations even weigh against Patricia Dutcher-Walls's views on the subject, even though she makes some very good points. She finds that the Deuteronomists were not a particularly closed group, but were a 'coalition of elite professional groups'. Such a mixed faction is said to account better for the wide variety of interests in the relevant texts, since it reflects the diversity of interests that elite groups would hold.[92] Locating the Deuteronomists among the elite cannot be gainsaid, as it is unlikely persons not in high standing could have produced texts or had them produced on their behalf. But by accepting that elite groups would be of diverse opinion, again something to be expected, she has somewhat weakened the very notion of the Deuteronomists as the proponents of a specific ideology (except in very broad terms, that is, the ideology of the elite classes). If we are to see the Deuteronomists as a coalition, one may well imagine a shifting membership, or at least a degree of infighting, which means that 'deuteronomistic' expressions, clichés, or themes, inherited from one member-group, or developed communally, may later have been used on both sides of bitter disputes. If later dates and longer development phases for the terminology are also included as factors in these objections, then this language could have been a well-developed set of tools for various groups' internal discourses, and for restricting the scope of polemics with each other to a specific range. There is certainly no justification to any assertion that there is in Kings, or any other part of the Hebrew Bible, the *oldest* 'deuteronomistic' language ever written or spoken. Yet, if we do not have the oldest, we cannot really assert that any example we do have is characteristic of one particular, narrowly-defined ideological group.

Deuteronomistic language has its rhetorical features, but rather than provide an insight into the mind-set of the Deuteronomists, this only complicates the identification of the authors as a specific ideological group. Weinfeld, for instance, comments that a particular feature of all

---

92. Dutcher-Walls, 'Social Location', pp. 92-93. To inform her use of sociological models, however, she generally accepts that the Deuteronomists are to be located in the closing phases of the Judaean monarchy, thus largely presupposing the answers to some of the most vexing and basic questions.

deuteronomic texts, from Deuteronomy to the prose sermons of Jeremiah, is their use of rhetorical orations.[93] This, however, raises the question of whether the scholar is dealing with manifestos of a relatively singular ideology (however it developed through time), or a diverse assortment of writings, characterized by similar topics and formalized style and idiom. A lesson might be learned from Maurice Bloch's introduction as editor to the book, *Political Language and Oratory in Traditional Society*: formalized language is impoverished language, a useful tool for social control, as the set of accepted responses is limited:[94]

> One of the features of everyday speech is that it can be enriched by comparisons and cross-references to other events of an extremely wide range. When, however, we look at the language of traditional authority we find that the power of cross-references becomes more and more restricted to a body of suitable illustrations, often proverbs or scriptures.[95]

The individuality and historicity of events disappear as discussed events become like the scriptural examples. Disagreement with the norms established by the formal modes of speech becomes impossible. One cannot disagree with the order imposed by the merging of the specific into the eternal. Formalization disconnects event from speech and so increases ambiguity. Its limits mean that other tools need to be employed by leaders to communicate their own messages. In Bali, for instance, politicians are known to avoid the arena of oratory since little of a progressive nature can be accomplished by it.[96] This may be a rather extreme example, but it does suggest that the 'characteristic' deuteronomistic language could have stemmed from a *Sitz im Leben* of a politically manipulative elite, or one fearful of radical change. One can see how use of such formalized language serves expressions of the *status quo*. On the other hand, if deuteronomistic language, with its characteristic expressions and topics, is considered in some ways impoverished language, then the true message of the writer may not be revealed by the use of it *per se*, but in the manner of its usage vis-à-vis non-deuteronomistic expressions. Studies of deuteronomistic language,

93. Weinfeld, *Deuteronomy*, pp. 3-4.

94. M. Bloch, 'Introduction', in M. Bloch (ed.), *Political Language and Oratory in Traditional Society* (London: Academic Press, 1975), pp. 1-28 (7-13).

95. Bloch, 'Introduction', p. 15.

96. Bloch, 'Introduction', pp. 15-18, 26.

therefore, need to be especially conscious of literary context, and, perhaps, to make a distinction between formalized speech, whose content is more a matter of convention, and the communicative function of *ad hoc* passages. Formalized language may provide a strategy of legitimization for messages carried in non-formalized idioms, or meaning only implicit in character motives or plot. Deuteronomistic language, however it may have been intended to serve the existing power-structures, may have been appropriated or subverted in arguments for radical change. The problem is identifying which examples are 'normative' and which 'subversive'.[97] The proliferation of different theories on the number of different 'Dtr' redactions, and especially the question of whether Deuteronomy belongs in the 'original' *deuteronomistic* corpus, belies the confidence with which Nelson speaks of 'straight' deuteronomistic ideology.[98] It also makes me question what Brettler has in mind when he writes that the 'central' Dtr texts have attracted so many revisions that the editorial history of Kings can only be outlined on the basis of the 'average' Dtr material.[99]

To isolate deuteronomistic language as the product of a unique social provenance, the scholar needs to determine not only what literary role any particular passage is playing, but what literary conventions and strategies were commonly available to writers, and whether the writer was willing to obey them strictly, or willing to experiment (breaking with conventions of speech, either with or without respect, politeness, or deliberate obscenity is itself a rhetorical device).[100] Most importantly, if 'deuteronomistic' speech is seen to remain in the control of its author (instead of the author virtually incapable of any other kind of expression, as many scholars seem to suggest), then the author could variously give such dialogues to, or withhold them from, the narrator or

---

97. G.N. Knoppers, 'The Deuteronomist and the Deuteronomic Law of the King: A Reexamination of a Relationship', *ZAW* 108 (1996), pp. 329-46, writes of the deuteronomistic historian's tendentious, and sometimes subversive use of the hypothetical *Urdeuteronomium*, especially regarding royal legitimization. The subversion I have in mind is more radical than Knoppers proposes.

98. Nelson, 'Anatomy', p. 46.

99. M. Brettler, 'Interpretation and Prayer: Notes on the Composition of 1 Kgs 8.15-53', in M. Brettler and M. Fishbane (eds.), *Minḥah le-Naḥum: Biblical and other Studies Presented to Nahum M. Sarna in Honour of his 70th Birthday* (JSOTSup, 154; Sheffield: JSOT Press, 1993), pp. 17-35 (34-35).

100. See, for example, the discussion of the illusory technical terms in R.W. Cowley, 'Technical Terms in Biblical Hebrew?', *TynBul* 37 (1986), pp. 21-28.

characters at will. One of the few scholars to really address this issue in Kings is Lyle Eslinger. He notices, for instance, that in 1 Kings 8 Solomon is given 59 'Dtr' expressions, as opposed to only one anomalous example given to the narrator, noticing that 'Solomon waxes more deuteronomistic than the deuteronomist himself'. He concludes that the role of the deuteronomistic language of the narrative requires attention:[101]

> Solomon is quite able to voice the deuteronomic pieties without subscribing to them, or if he does subscribe, to be misguided in his understanding. And the narrator is even more capable of allowing Solomon to make his speech without for one minute agreeing with its propriety or unctuous piety.[102]

Eslinger also observes that, against Solomon's creative use of deuteronomistic language, Yahweh in 1 Kgs 9.3-9 uses such language *against* Solomon.[103] I will have the occasion to discuss Eslinger's work to a greater extent below, but here it suffices to point out one peculiarity in Eslinger's work, even if his accent on character motives is not to be dismissed lightly. Eslinger rarely speaks of the 'Deuteronomist', preferring to speak more of the 'narrator'. Still, he does see a connection between the narrator and the 'dtr redactor'.[104] He may be justified in this, since he still sees a unified DtrH. It does, however, seem odd for him to retain notions of a 'dtr redactor' in view of the fact that the DtrH was originally posited by Noth on the recognition that major 'Dtr orations' were outright expressions of the single author's point of view, and were the unifying principle of the corpus. Not only does Eslinger contest this in 1 Kings 8, but he considers the unexpectedly long condemnation by the narrator in 2 Kgs 17.7-23 as a sarcastic irony which mocks the very standards which by the chapter ostensibly judges Israel.[105] The nature of the 'deuteronomism' of Eslinger's conception of the author is a rather more subtle beast than that supposed by other scholars, and for these reasons, renders the term 'deuteronomistic' more problematic to apply as a label to that writer. The terms 'deuteronomistic' and 'Deuteronomists' have been stretched so far, to label so

101. Eslinger, *Living God*, p. 123 n. 3. His statistics are based on the analysis of Weinfeld, *Deuteronomy*.
102. Eslinger, *Living God*, p. 124.
103. Eslinger, *Living God*, p. 146.
104. Eslinger, *Living God*, p. 233.
105. Eslinger, *Living God*, pp. 183-219.

many different writers, writings and ideologies in different places and times, that I wonder if they are applied to the Former Prophets more from convention than from examination about what they might actually mean.

Since the present thesis calls so much of present thought concerning date and ideological interest in Kings and the Former Prophets into question, diachronic analyses based on notions of 'deuteronomistic' language and sociological and historical conclusions about presumed 'Deuteronomists' and their history-book is best avoided. This does not mean that similarities in linguistic and ideological characteristics of passages in the Hebrew Bible should not result in a categorization, or that 'deuteronomistic' is not an apt term for certain sets of these passages. It does mean, however, that the quest for a unified composition, or a religious, or political 'party' is not successfully concluded by the perceived affinity in these passages. It is not that the ideology of the Deuteronomists is beyond our grasp, but that the evidence of the ideologies of those who employed deuteronomistic language is yet too malleable within our grasp to understand their internal politics. I do not suggest here that all talk of Deuteronomists will always be a study in over-active academic fiction, yet it remains the articulation of an academic construct, not discussion of a well-evidenced socio-political entity from the past. The labels 'deuteronomistic' and 'Deuteronomist' are part of *our* language of attribution, which is as much the topic of scholarly self-critique as it is a resource for analysis. I will end my own part in this dialogue here, by noting that the language that is developed from 'conventional' historical-critical research, when imported into a fresh approach to Kings, which holds that the book stemmed from a rather different context than what is usually thought to be the case, cannot mean the same thing without forcing contradiction or limitations on the study. I do not suggest that we need an entirely new language of attribution, but, perhaps, the scholarly vocabulary is in need of some expansion to afford a more carefully-worded dialogue.

5. *The Date of 'Exilicist' Kings*

The date of Kings is most commonly determined by noting that no event after the release of Jehoiachin (c. 561 BCE) is reported (2 Kgs 25.27-30). It is, therefore, argued that the book must have been finished between this date and the 'return' of the exiles from Persian-controlled

Mesopotamia, c. 538 BCE, since such a return would have been mentioned, had it already occurred. In discussing Mullen's work above, and in an article entitled 'Rethinking the "Exilic" Book of Kings', I have argued that such a conclusion is insupportable. Determining the date of composition by isolating the first plausible social context after the earliest possible date is of dubious worth. Rather, equal weight should be given all plausible scenarios up to the latest possible date that at which there can be no doubt the book existed. My primary points were that there is no evidence that Kings was intended to be an up-to-date history, and that failure to mention events later than the mid-sixth century BCE does not indicate composition before such events could have occurred. In a new article, T.C. Römer finds more 'post-exilic' writing in Kings than many previous scholars have allowed, and suggests that the story of Jehoiachin's release is probably to be included since it has affinities with Esther and the story of Joseph in Genesis, both considered writings with a Diaspora audience. More significantly, he rightly observes that the ancient writers did not need to bring their histories up to their own times.[106] The failure to narrate the reconstruction of the temple is hardly evidence of a date prior to any proposed temple project. The so-called 'Second Temple Period' saw many conflicting temple projects.[107] There is no force to assertions that one, or any, would have been a necessary part of the story told in Kings, had that project begun. Rather, the end of the book should be taken as a literary choice by its producers and editors. As I will discuss below, in regards to Mullen's proposal, post-monarchic crises of identity may have been long term and need not be restricted to the mid-sixth century BCE.[108] I also discussed the unsuitability of a chronological scheme based on the exile as an event of bounded duration. I argued that the exile must be

106. T.C. Römer, 'Transformations in Deuteronomistic and Biblical Historiography: On "Book-Finding" and other Literary Strategies', *ZAW* 107 (1997), pp. 1-11 (10-11). He thinks that 2 Kgs 22-23 was the 'foundation myth' of the Deuteronomists, and that this episode legitimized acceptance of the end of the monarchy. Moreover, they held that the Babylonian *Golah* was the 'true Israel'. I am of a somewhat different opinion in this regard.

107. On this, see R.P. Carroll, 'So What Do We *Know* about the Temple?: The Temple in the Prophets', in T.C. Eskenazi and K.H. Richards (eds.), *Second Temple Studies. II. Temple Community in the Persian Period* (JSOTSup, 175; Sheffield: JSOT Press, 1994), pp. 34-51 (49-50).

108. Chapter 3, subsection 2, referring to Mullen, *Narrative History*, pp. 12-13, 38. I discuss this in 'Rethinking' as well.

seen as a more open interpretation of the past and present of various ancient Yahwistic groups, and that the currency of this interpretation persisted well into the Persian period.[109] The concept of the 'exile' as a definite historical period which ended at a particular date is an inadequate basis for a chronological system designed to explain the progression of Israelite, Judah-ist, and Jewish thought. If Kings strikes the reader as a product of an exile, then one has made a clearer observation of the attitude of its producers towards their world, rather than of the narrowly-defined range of dates in which these writers laboured.[110]

Among the critics of monarchic or exilic compositional dates for the bulk of biblical literature, a major point of contention has been the question of whether Persian or Hellenistic dates are most plausible.[111] Recently, Thomas M. Bolin has argued for the latter, holding that the Persian era may have marked the beginning of the compilation and composition of the literature we now study, but is not likely to have been when the bulk of the work was accomplished. Like N.P. Lemche, he contends that it is sounder, methodologically, to begin at the more recent dates, rather than the earliest possible, the reference-point accepted by the bulk of biblical scholarship as the best place to begin the process of dating texts.[112] Bolin's argument emphasizes that Ezra

109. Linville, 'Rethinking'. On the persistence of the 'Exile' as an evaluation of the current religious/political situations as late as the Hellenistic period, see, M.A. Knibb, 'The Exile in the Literature of the Intertestamental Period', *HeyJ* 17 (1976), pp. 253-72; J.M. Scott, 'Philo and the Restoration of Israel', in *SBL 1995 Seminar Papers* (Atlanta: Scholars Press, 1995), pp. 553-75 (563-66, and nn. 61-64). A number of scholars have also noted the ideologically-relative concept of the exile; Davies, *'Ancient Israel'*, pp. 43-44; N.P. Lemche, 'The Old Testament: A Hellenistic Book?', *SJOT* 7 (1993), pp. 163-93 (181-82); T.L. Thompson, *Early History of the Israelite People: From the Written and Archaeological Sources* (Studies in the History of the Ancient Near East, 4; Leiden, E.J. Brill, 1992), p. 419.

110. The same point can be made about the 'post-exilic' texts. Such a reassessment, of course, does not apply in the same way to evidence of 'pre-exilic' thought. On the other hand, some literature may have been set in an imagined 'pre-exilic' period and written with a mind to express the imagined spirit of the times.

111. Thompson, *Early History*, pp. 415-23, looks to the Persian period, as does G. Garbini, 'Hebrew Literature in the Persian Period', in Eskenazi, Richards (eds.), *Second Temple Studies*, II, pp. 180-88; Davies, *'Ancient Israel'*, pp. 94, 102-105, and *passim*, also favours Persian dates as the beginning of the process, although he sees it continuing into the Hellenistic period. Lemche, 'Hellenistic', favours Hellenistic dates.

112. T.M. Bolin, 'When the End is the Beginning. The Persian Period and the

and Nehemiah show only cursory awareness of the bulk of the Hebrew Bible traditions. He does not take into serious account the possibility of a plurality of document-producing groups, who may not have been fully aware, or accepting of, the texts and traditions articulated by their rivals.[113] In my original discussion on the topic, I expressed reservations about Hellenistic dates, feeling that they may challenge to too great an extent the existing views on the development of the Hebrew language and the relative dating of Kings and other texts. While I do not wish to abandon these reservations entirely, I must now add that regardless of how appropriate the Persian period may have been for the beginning of the literary articulation of an 'exilic' or 'post-monarchic' Israelite identity, there remains no firm argument that the basic outlines of the texts we now have were finished before the Hellenistic period. Yet the Persian period may be looked to for the beginnings of a resurgent Jerusalem and a new Israel, and so it is with some plausibility that this period saw the rise of this literature. So long as interpretation is not totally dependent upon a narrowly-defined set of motives, like the need to *fabricate* from whole cloth a new identity in face of a particular crisis (as opposed to rearticulate an existing traditional heritage), a broad date range remains acceptable. Given this open-ended historical framework, it is important to reassess the social relevance of the story being told in Kings. In this regard, the question of Kings as history-writing is re-engaged, but not in the sense that it is a source for the writing of a modern, critical history of the monarchies. Rather, it is as a history in the service of a cultural heritage.

The composition of Kings was a complex affair, and I am sceptical of any systematized solution to its intricacies. Atomization and the quest for the 'original' meaning of individual passages is hardly a suitable methodology for addressing the book as a whole. Neither is the positing of a Deuteronomistic school, and interpreting the book as their exclusive product, a solution to the problem of Kings' origins, even if the hypothetical Deuteronomists are relocated to the later time-frame I support. Without a firm reference point in history (as is granted by a dating close to the deportations, amnesty of Jehoiachin, or initial repatriation itself), how to locate the intended social relevance of the book,

Origins of the Biblical Tradition', *SJOT* 10 (1996), pp. 3-15.

113. Bolin, 'The End', p. 12. Bolin maintains that the compilation of the tradition was a task that took a long time. Davies asserts otherwise, *'Ancient Israel'*, pp. 100-101.

whose authorship is conceived in such 'anonymous' terms, remains a problem. The insolubility of the question of compositional history, however, need not result in complete despair. To avoid this, however, one needs a change of focus, with less dependence upon specific events as providing the occasion of the composition.[114] Appreciation of the text as a narrative-complex should be informed by generalizations about the most likely social and historical settings for the process of composition, with a recognition that the text does not need to reproduce exactly the social realities of the authors' present in the literary world of the past for the authors to express contemporary concerns. A range of different voices and complex literary expression must be sought in the book. To clarify some of these issues, a look at the broad, scholarly category of history-writing is needed.

114. Lamenting how many scholars' reconstructions of the development of Israelite religion depend heavily on specific events is Halpern, *First Historians*, pp. 26, 34-35 n. 27. 'More often than not, Israelite ideas are traced to single events, with the result that Israel appears sometimes to have yoked its religion solely to its military fortunes' (p. 26).

Chapter 3

IDENTIFYING WRITING AS 'HISTORY' AND
WRITING IDENTITY AS 'HISTORY'

1. *Kings as History-Writing*

A multifaceted debate surrounds what sort of writing might validly be
called 'history', and whether any part of the Hebrew Bible might fit any
of the proposed descriptions.[1] For a number of scholars, history-writing
properly refers to the products of a critical study of the evidence about
the past and the intent to represent them fairly. Some of these also
contend that, even if certain ancient writers were not bound by exactly
the same critical standards and conventions that modern historians are,
they might still properly be labelled historians.[2] Such a favourable

---

1.   This debate goes beyond the dichotomy some scholars draw between
Israelite 'history' and Canaanite 'myth', and extends to the very basic fundamental
beliefs of the scholars involved. For instance, De Vries, *1 Kings*, p. xxxi, writes:
'Secularistic nonmythical culture reduces history as effectively as does the super-
stition of mythical culture'. As for recent developments, Davies, *'Ancient Israel'*;
Thompson, *Early History*, and N.P. Lemche, *Ancient Israel: A New History of
Israelite Society* (BibSem; Sheffield: Sheffield Academic Press, 1988), have been
criticized for their own positivistic ideological delineation of scholarship by I.W.
Provan, 'Ideologies, Literary and Critical: Reflections on Recent Writing of the
History of Israel', *JBL* 114 (1995), pp. 585-606. Two responses are published in the
same volume: T.L. Thompson, 'A Neo-Albrightean School in History and Biblical
Scholarship', pp. 683-98; P.R. Davies, 'Method and Madness: Some Remarks on
Doing History with the Bible', pp. 699-705. The ideological underpinnings of
scholarship is also the topic of the new volume by K.W. Whitelam, *The Invention
of Ancient Israel: The Silencing of Palestinian History* (London: Routledge, 1996).
A lengthy review and commentary is available; N.P. Lemche, 'Clio is also among
the Muses! Keith W. Whitelam and the History of Palestine: A Review and Commentary', *SJOT* 10 (1996), pp. 88-114.

2.   De Vries, *1 Kings*, pp. xxxiii, comments that biblical historiography is
authentic, but popular, and so may contain some material of a lesser historical

comparison has been at the heart of Baruch Halpern's work, *The First Historians*. He argues that the DtrH is the product of a true historian, and sets out to demonstrate the author's critically responsible attitude both to the sources at hand and to the economical representation of the past.[3] On the other hand, some now are rethinking Kings' ascription as history-writing and its reliability for producing a scholarly history of Israel, although it is hard to imagine that any consensus will ever be reached.[4] That 'history' best labels the work of a critical writer is accepted by Thomas Thompson, but he differs from Halpern on the question of how much historical writing there is to be found in the Hebrew Bible; Thompson takes the view that there is very little.[5] There is

standard, for purposes of edification, illustration, or amusement. Yet it satisfies the criteria that historiography must derive its material from 'authenticated sources', and treat them with respect and discretion. It must 'trace an organic line of development from beginning to end', 'realistically portray cause and effect, and offer a believable and essentially reliable portrait of the persons involved'. Long, *1 Kings*, pp. 4, 8, notes that the referents of historical language must be actual events or persons in the past, although he adds that history writing does not stand apart from fictive powers of the author's imagination. Jones, *Kings*, I, p. 76, writes, 'The books of Kings are valuable as historical documents, even if they only present a selection of the material that was available. The author's dependence upon historical sources, and in some parts on prophetical traditions that have at least a historical basis, gives reliability to the historical notes in his work. Since the sources used have completely disappeared, the Deuteronomistic History has become invaluable for any reconstruction of the period of the monarchy'.

3. Halpern, *First Historians*, p. 3.

4. Of the major compositional studies on Kings, see Hoffmann, *Reform*. For other opinions in this regard, see: Y. Zakovitch, 'Story versus History', in D.C. Kron (ed.), *Proceedings of the Eighth World Congress of Jewish Studies: Panel Sessions: Bible Studies and Hebrew Language; Jerusalem August 16-21, 1981* (Jerusalem: World Union of Jewish Studies, 1983), pp. 47-60; E. Nicholson, 'Story and History in the Old Testament', in S.E. Balentine and J. Barton (eds.), *Language, Theology and the Bible: Essays in Honour of James Barr* (Oxford: Clarendon Press, 1994), pp. 135-50. Some, however, see 'history' as a literary form which may feature fictional, or artistic elements, cf. Long, 'Historical Narrative'; A. Cook, 'Fiction and History in Samuel and Kings', *JSOT* 36 (1986), pp. 27-48; Provan, *Kings*. This is not to say that scholars of this persuasion would agree on the historical reliability of any particular episode in Kings.

5. Thompson, *Early History*, pp. 376-77, 398. It is interesting how the two scholars also disagree on other terms. Halpern, *First Historians*, p. 3, notes the 'authentic antiquarian interests' of the biblical historians, while Thompson, *Early History*, pp. 376-77, understands the intents of historiographers as different from

no point rehearsing the heated debates about Kings' historicity.[6] Other aspects of this debate are also far beyond the scope of the present work, such as the implications of the new scholarly directions for modern theology.[7] I do argue, however, that to see Kings as history-writing (at

antiquarians. The latter, whose work is evidenced in redactional techniques of comprehensive tradition, display the 'antiquarian efforts of curiosity and preservation', an intentionality inimical to the field of historiography. Antiquarians tend to librarian-like pluralism, 'classifying, associating, and arranging a cultural heritage that is both greater than the compiler or any single historiographical explanation'. Thompson holds that historians are interested in the question of historicity and the critical selection and evaluation of their sources, slipping into tendentiousness because of their self-professed understanding of history. In truth, both terms, history and antiquity, are fairly flexible, with the former probably having the greater range of uses. My point here is not to isolate specific meanings for universal use, but to allow biblical writings of the past to be seen in as open a manner as possible, without imposition of too strict *a priori* classifications determining, in some detail, what a scholar may find therein.

6. The rapidly growing bibliography on the recently discovered Tel Dan inscription, and the sharp wording employed by many contributors, indicates to what great extent even the basic outlines of the biblical version of monarchic history are dependent upon few, and not easily interpreted, extra-biblical reference points. This inscription is held by some to be the first inscription evidence of David's existence outside of the Bible, because of the word(s) ביתדוד. Many would find the inscription referring to something (or some place) other than the dynasty or kingdom of an historical king David, with the letters דוד being a theophoric element or divine attribute. The inscription was originally published by A. Biran and J. Naveh, 'An Aramaic Stele Fragment from Tel Dan', *IEJ* 43 (1993), pp. 81-98. A discussion of basic positions, and statement of the difficulties of interpreting the inscription as demonstration of Kings' historical veracity can be found in N.P. Lemche and T.L. Thompson, 'Did Biran Kill David? The Bible in the Light of Archaeology', *JSOT* 64 (1994), pp. 3-22. For other viewpoints: H. Shanks, 'David Found at Dan', *BARev* 20.2 (1994), pp. 26-39; S. Ahituv, 'Suzerain or Vassal? Notes on the Aramaic Inscription from Tel Dan', *IEJ* 43 (1993), pp. 246-47.

7. The history of Israel is an important part of modern theological thought on the Hebrew Bible. Recent scholarship on the union between the history of Israel, the Bible's historiography, and questions of faith and theology include, A.R. Millard, J.K. Hoffmeier and D.W. Baker, *Faith, Tradition and History: Old Testament Historiography in its Near Eastern Context* (Winona Lake, IN: Eisenbrauns, 1994), and V.P. Long, *The Art of Biblical History* (FCI, 5; Grand Rapids: Zondervan, 1994). A number of commentaries specifically on Kings may be included in this regard to a greater or lesser degree: R.D. Nelson, *First and Second Kings* (Interpretation; Atlanta: John Knox Press, 1987); De Vries, *1 Kings;* Hobbs, *2 Kings*; Provan, *Kings*.

least in a broad sense) need not entail interpreting it according to its suitability as a source for writing a modern, critical history of the kingdoms of Judah and Israel. I have no fundamental objection to limiting the use of 'history' to such a critical endeavour, if other written representations of believed past events or realities are accorded generic titles which do not imply a hierarchy of value with 'history' at the apex. Yet, I wonder if scholarly discourse should restrict the term to its own products and to those ancient texts it prefers to liken to its own.[8] The broad range of uses for the term 'history', and the ease at which it is qualified and combined with other terms ('critical', 'sacred', 'national', not to mention, 'geological' and 'natural') suggests that it is a useful, general label, and should not be unduly restricted. Separating 'history' from 'antiquities' or 'legends' (or whatever) does not really go far in explaining the universality and importance of socially-validated stories of the past (I must stress here that social validation still underlies the acceptability of any 'critical' research about the past, not to mention the imperative to produce it).[9] Even if one can demonstrate that the intent of a biblical author was to represent fairly the actual past, this purpose is itself teleological; there is a reason why an author wants 'critical history' and not some other kind of literature. Knowledge of the past is not desirable in and of itself (either for ancient historians or modern). Regardless of the objections that may be levelled against the utility of Huizinga's definition of history for biblical research (see below), the Dutch historian's comment that history is 'purposive knowing' cannot be gainsaid.[10]

8.   An example of the use of the term 'history' to refer to non-critically researched stories believed to tell of the past is R.G. Hall, *Revealed Histories: Techniques for Ancient Jewish and Christian Historiography* (JSPSup, 6; Sheffield: Sheffield Academic Press, 1991): 'Revealed history is a rhetorical device, a *topos*. One way of convincing readers to do or believe as they should was to show how mysteries of God's working in the past make those actions or beliefs imperative or desirable in the present' (p. 116).

9.   Here one can wonder if the category 'history' relates more to the categories informing the reading than the writing itself. If a text has become a significant repository of a culture's symbolic universe, what the writer may have originally intended (e.g. to entertain, or to glorify a legendary hero, compose an extended parable for moral instruction) may be irrelevant to the later readers.

10.   J. Huizinga, 'A Definition of the Concept of History', in R. Klibansky and H.J. Paton (eds.), *Philosophy and History: Essays Presented to Ernst Cassirer* (Oxford: Clarendon Press, 1963), pp. 1-10 (7).

I will leave off, at this point, further discussion of whether the writers of Kings were historians more or less in the modern, academic sense; one may certainly find what one earnestly seeks. I will accept that, at least in broad terms, Kings may be thought of as a 'social history', even if it was composed by select members of the elite caste of that society.[11] The actual task of writing facing such a historian is, in some ways, little different from that facing the writer of 'fiction'.[12] Robert Alter writes that examination of the literary strategies behind the Bible's 'sacred history' is an aid to understanding this literature as attempts to reveal the 'imperative truth of God's works in history and of Israel's hopes and failings'.[13] Even if the biblical writers were 'creative authors', and not just 'critical historians', the biblical scholars, who themselves would be historians, still must ask what motivated the ancient authors in their labours.[14] For a number of scholars, it comes down to a question of the expression of national, or ethnic identity, which, if seen as not integral to history-writing in general, is at least the primary concern of the sort of traditions about the past preserved in the Hebrew Bible. John Van Seters conducts his investigation of historiography under Huizinga's definition of history as 'the intellectual form in which a civilisation renders account to itself of its past'.[15] He maintains that Dtr's purpose in writing was not to record events, but 'to communicate through this story of the people's past a sense of their identity—and that is the *sine qua non* of history writing'.[16] He sees the DtrH as

11. The more fundamental question of the social relevance of stories of the past surfaces in any case.

12. Thompson, *Early History*, p. 388, states that plausibility and verisimilitude are more the mark of good fiction than historical genres. On the other hand, Halpern, *First Historians* has been criticized for his avoidance of discussion of literary matters in some of his proof-texts in M. Brettler, review of *The First Historians: The Hebrew Bible and History* (San Francisco: Harper & Row, 1988), by B. Halpern, in *JRel* 70 (1990), pp. 83-84.

13. R. Alter, *The Art of Biblical Narrative* (London: George Allen & Unwin, 1981), p. 46.

14. I owe the opening thought of this sentence to M. Noth's view, *Deuteronomistic History*, p. 10, that the Deuteronomist was an 'author' and not only a 'redactor'. Of course, I am being a bit facetious, since for many scholars there is always an element of creativity in the production of any critical historiography.

15. Van Seters, *In Search of History*, p. 1, citing Huizinga, 'A Definition', p. 9.

16. Van Seters, *In Search of History*, p. 359.

providing Israel with the understanding that it was born in the exodus, and that the conditions of its tenure in the land were the laws of Moses. The exile was the result of the breach of these conditions, and, perhaps, there was a hope of repentance. In the DtrH, royal ideology was incorporated into the collective identity (cf. the title of certain kings: *nagid*, [נגיד], 'over my [Yahweh's] people Israel').[17] There is little in general to be objected to in this analysis, but it is, perhaps, unfortunate that Van Seters's comparative historiography and work on the compositional history of the DtrH occupied so much of his attention that a more thorough-going examination of how features of the finished history worked to provide such an identity for the exiles could not be afforded. It was up to another scholar, E.T. Mullen, to build on the ground prepared by Van Seters to begin such a discussion.

Support for Van Seters's close association between history and identity can be found in the work of many scholars in the social sciences. Jonathan Friedman maintains that history is essentially mythic, in that 'it is a representation of the past linked to the establishment of an identity in the present'.[18] He adds that the construction of history is a constituent of social identity, and that questions of identity generate history.[19] For Kirsten Hastrup, shared history is a more inclusive statement of identity than even a shared language. It is suggested that perhaps one could isolate the 'idea of history' as ethnicity's ultimate pre-requisite:

> Whether the history actually referred to as 'shared' in a particular ethnic identification covers a shorter or longer period in time is of less moment; what matters is that an idea of a shared history exists. Without it, an ethnicity cannot be declared, even if at another level ethnicity may still be just a way of speaking of political relations.[20]

While any attempt to declare an ethnic identity may require an 'idea' of a shared history, and even if questions of identity itself generate history, it does not follow that any particular history-text is reducible

17. Van Seters, *In Search of History*, p. 359. I will address the נגיד passages below.

18. J. Friedman, 'Myth, History, and Political Identity', *CulAnth* 7 (1992), pp. 194-210 (195)

19. Friedman, 'Myth', p. 202.

20. K. Hastrup, 'Establishing an Ethnicity: The Emergence of the "Icelanders" in the Early Middle Ages', in D. Parkin (ed.), *Semantic Anthropology* (ASAM, 22; London: Academic Press, 1982), pp. 146-60 (155).

exclusively to a declaration of ethnicity. For Thompson, who defines 'history' itself more narrowly, identity expression is only an optional part of what history might be. Other genres, such as ethnography, genealogies and constitutional narratives handle these matters specifically.[21] Even so, however, these genres involve 'writing about the past'. Thompson, of course, does not call Joshua to 2 Kings history-writing, but ethnographic aetiology, which was pivotal in creating the *ethnos* of Israel, and so both he and Van Seters have a similar view of the social function of the texts.[22]

It should be stressed, however, that social scientists also tend to stress the communal aspects of history, and Van Seters follows this. He maintains that historiography has the dual role of assessing responsibility for events in a nation's past and expressing corporate identity. Yet a caveat is issued. In the ancient Near East, concerns of identity and self-justification involved the person of the king. Unless the king was recognized as the embodiment of the state, however, such texts are not 'history'. To Van Seters, true history-writing arises when national history judges the king and not when the king writes his own account of the past.[23] On the other hand, Huizinga himself took a very broad impression of 'civilisation', ranging from simple societies to complex multinationals. Each produces its own unique form of history.[24] But can

21. Thompson, *Early History*, pp. 376-79, commenting on Van Seters, *In Search of History*.

22. Thompson, *Early History*, p. 383. It is not purely moot whether 'ethnography' should be regarded as distinct from 'history', whether one is a sub-genre of the other, or whether one term rightly names a literary form and the other an essential or optional quality of the first. On the other hand, progress in interpretation does not depend on all the intricacies of these matters being fully sorted out.

23. Van Seters, *In Search of History*, pp. 2-4, 354-55. He writes, 'insofar as any of the other Near Eastern nations express a concept of identity through their historiographic forms, it is in the person of the king as the state. In Dtr the royal ideology is incorporated into the identity of the people as a whole ('*nagid* of my people, Israel'), so that the leaders of the people must always be obedient to the Mosaic covenant' (p. 359).

24. Huizinga, 'A Definition', p. 7. See the comments in B. Halpern, review of *In Search of History: Historiography in the Ancient World and the Origins of Biblical History* (New Haven: Yale University Press, 1983), by John Van Seters in *JBL* 104 (1985), pp. 506-509 (507). For a critique of Van Seters's understanding of genre, see K.L. Younger, 'A Critical Review of John Van Seters, *In Search of History*', *JSOT* 40 (1988), pp. 110-17. He writes that genre is to Van Seters, 'a type of magic wand for interpretation' (p. 113).

the motives behind each history text be thought of in exclusively large-scale corporate terms? This suggests an important point raised in John Rogerson's critique of Van Seters. He asks if the DtrH was the result of a *civilization* rendering an account of its past, or of an *individual or a school* seeking to commend a tendentious interpretation of the past and a sense of corporate identity (such a distinction equally applies to an independent book of Kings).[25] These observations point to the relative status of any act of history-writing, and suggest a reason why a society or larger cultural group may have rival histories current at any one time, and yet remain relatively united. This is a topic to which I will return below.

It is likely that anything human beings engage in can be linked to their own perceptions of their personal and corporate identities. In expressing such identities, narrative plays a vital role, as recognized by Van Seters. Stressing this even further are Margaret R. Somers and Gloria D. Gibson, who report that philosophers of history have argued that the representation of knowledge in narrative modes (telling historical stories) were representative forms which historians imposed on chaotic experience. More recently, a wide variety of scholars have re-evaluated narrative, and are arguing that social life is itself 'storied' and 'that narrative is an *ontological condition of social life*'.[26] This research shows that action is guided by stories. Identity, regardless of how multiple or changing, results from people locating themselves or being located within a set of emplotted stories. They describe ontological narratives as stories that social actors need to make sense of their lives. They are necessary for self-identity and action. Such narratives are social and interpersonal in that they exist only in the course of structural and social interactions. People will fit stories to their own identities and will tailor reality in accordance with their stories. Interpersonal relations sustain and transform these narratives into what might be labelled 'tradition' or, in Somers's and Gibson's terms, 'public narratives'.

25. J.W. Rogerson, review of *In Search of History: Historiography in the Ancient World and the Origins of Biblical History* (New Haven: Yale University Press, 1983), by John Van Seters in *JTS* 37 (1986), pp. 451-54, referring to Van Seters at p. 320.

26. M.R. Somers and G.D. Gibson, 'Reclaiming the Epistemological "Other": Narrative and the Social Construction of Identity', in C. Calhoun (ed.), *Social Theory and the Politics of Identity* (Oxford: Basil Blackwell, 1994), pp. 37-99 (38).

These are, then, cultural and institutional.[27] The question of personal identity vis-à-vis these narratives is, for these scholars, a matter of understanding the social relationships as a variable, not an 'ideal type' or a stand-in for an unchanging sense of 'community'.[28] As I will further elaborate below, personal, group, and sub-group identity expression are complex and interrelated issues, and each individual may have several expressible identities, based on class, gender, personal experiences, and so on. This observation, of course, makes a 'normative' corporate statement of history or identity more an ideal, or a framework for individual interpretation and further articulation, although, within any society, the acceptable range of diversity may be limited.[29] This means, of course, that describing how Kings (for instance) constructs the notion of 'Israel' for its readership is not the same thing as offering a description of the writers' society directly.

The relationship between the personal motives of a writer and the reasons why a society accepted the work as an acceptable, if not definitive, version of its past would probably never be an easy matter to decide. It is all the more difficult when there is no access to the writer except from the literary product itself. The task of the biblical scholar is harder yet. There were probably multiple writers in each work, and the societies in which they lived and which accepted their work can be reconstructed only tentatively by the scholar. The multiplicity of authorship, however, does suggest that one should look at the texts as corporate statements, or at least as statements by an elite which were intended to be corporate and normative. Still, however, it does not follow that identity articulation is the dominating conscious motive behind the production of every history work. I will return to this point below. I now turn to a review of some of the other thinkers who have influenced my own approach.

27. M.R. Somers and G.D. Gibson, 'Reclaiming the Epistemological "Other"', pp. 61-62.

28. Somers and Gibson, 'Reclaiming The Epistemological "Other"', p. 66.

29. In view of Bloch's comments ('Introduction') above on the limitations of formal speech, one must consider the limiting aspects of 'formal' genres of discussion of the past which would maintain the status quo. As much as alternatives to formal speech may be developed, 'alternative histories' with their own formal characteristics may also be composed to challenge power structures legitimized by 'authorized' histories.

2. *'Narrative History' and the Expression of Israelite Identity*

Another significant step in the study of Kings has been taken by E. Theodore Mullen, and the present work is largely due to his influence. Like Van Seters, Mullen accepts the notion of a DtrH, but largely ignores questions of its history of composition. He complains that none of the major studies address the DtrH as religious text with mythological dimensions.[30] Mullen's interest in identity formation stems from an awareness that modern scholarship has failed to appreciate that the descriptions of Israel and its religion could be symbolic expressions of social boundary formation, as opposed to accurate ethnographic descriptions. He charges that this failure has led to the study of Israel against, rather than within the greater Near Eastern environment.[31] Mullen's approach takes into account the reciprocal relationship between overtly religious conceptions and notions of group identity. In his view, religion restructures selected segments of pre-existing cultural signifiers. This new structure, however, actually competes with the 'web' of culture, as it claims to be the source from which at least 'true' culture is derived.[32] One might observe that this situation is analogous to the dialectical relationship between the past, necessary for group identity, and the present which the group inhabits. As I will describe below, the past is written according to the standards of the present, and yet it is used to justify the present. Disjuncture between the past and present is not only possible but to be expected. For all of its seeming fluidity at the hands of its creators, the past is presented as immutable, and so may be used to question the vagaries of contemporary life. Alternatively, it can preserve options and legitimize innovation.

Mullen posits that the Deuteronomist in the DtrH recreated, in narrative form, a series of 'social dramas'. By using communal expressions of ritual actions, especially in the form of confessional, covenantal expressions at critical junctures within the narrative, the author created a 'common myth of descent', a history that could be shared by the group facing the tragedies of the exile.[33] These dramas, in their

---

30. Mullen, *Narrative History*, pp. 5-8.
31. Mullen, *Narrative History*, p. 60.
32. Mullen, *Narrative History*, pp. 36-37.
33. Mullen, *Narrative History*, pp. 10-16, relying on V. Turner, 'Social Dramas and Stories about Them', in W.J.T. White (ed.), *On Narrative* (Chicago: University of Chicago Press, 1981), pp. 137-64.

narrative form, have four distinct phases: 'breach, crisis, redress, and either reintegration or recognition of schism'.[34] Mullen offers a selection of these dramas which are investigated to demonstrate how they offer a vision of 'Israel' relevant to the exilic people. The central focus of this vision is that 'Israel' is a people who are the covenant people of Yahweh, and who find their true vocation in life in obedience to the divine law.[35] The writer composed a partial frame around the story of Israel in its land, the definition of Israel at the outset, and the reconstruction of that ideal towards the end. Deuteronomy provides the manifesto delimiting the group boundaries, and offers a metaphorization of 'Israel', while the story of Josiah shows the fulfilment of these demands. Although, the 'today' of Deuteronomy was recoverable through ritual at any time, the threat of destruction also loomed.[36]

According to Mullen, the story of the rise of the monarchy represented the establishment of a permanent form of leadership, and this marked a new epoch in the development of self-identity. From the 'ambiguous' start under Saul, the writer constructed a golden age, and this represented a recreation and redefinition of the basis for Israel's self-identity as a national monarchic state under a king appointed by the deity. The Deuteronomist had much invested in the symbol of the davidic dynasty, and held out much hope for the remnants of the dynasty with Jehoiachin and his heirs.[37] The DtrH is held to be propaganda for the davidic dynasty as the only legitimate dynasty in Judah. The dynasty was continuously in power except for the brief interlude under Athaliah (2 Kgs 11). This disruption was portrayed as a major crisis which was resolved by a social drama that culminated with covenantal rituals marking the return of a davidic heir. The covenant is between Yahweh, king and people and this reaffirms not only that Israel is Yahweh's people, but that young King Joash is a partner in this pact as a member of the sole legitimate dynasty. While establishing that historical breaches of dynastic succession could occur, the critical

34. Mullen, *Narrative History*, p. 39. Cf. Turner, 'Social Dramas', p. 145.

35. The chief example in Kings that Mullen, *Narrative History*, pp. 19-54, gives is that of 2 Kgs 11, the story of the overthrow of Athaliah, and the cultic re-investiture of the davidic dynasty.

36. Mullen, *Narrative History*, pp. 55-76, 84.

37. Mullen, *Narrative History*. See Chapter 6, 'The Necessity of Kingship: The Failures of the Past', pp. 163-207, and his final remarks, pp. 285-86.

ethnic and national signifiers are maintained in this story.[38] Mullen holds that the story of Josiah's reform served to recreate the ideals of a greater Israel spanning both the kingdoms of Judah and Israel. The recreation effected the postponement of the judgment. Recreation through public ritual was necessary, since Judah had, in some ways, ceased to exist when Manasseh repeated the 'abominations of the nations' (2 Kgs 21.2). The deeds of Josiah illustrate how the deuteronomic covenant blessings could be regained and social welfare ensured through the proper enactment of the covenant ceremonies. The subsequent narratives describe the failure of Josiah's successors to follow his standard, and the lack of forgiveness for the earlier deeds of Manasseh (2 Kgs 23.26-27; cf. 2 Kgs 21.2-16). The recreation effected by Josiah was only temporary. The combination of these two ideals of retribution and blessing ensure a reliable and stable universe. With the fall of Jerusalem, there is the hope of a new history on the basis of the ideal past.[39] The experiences of the past, however, showed that Israel had often failed to live up to the obligations of its own social manifesto. The restoration of Israel depended upon the exiles internalizing the vision of Israel's social manifesto, and understanding themselves in terms of its obligations:[40]

> At the base of the deuteronomistic presentation of the ideal 'Israel' lies a fundamental paradox: Yahweh had chosen 'Israel' as his special possession and, at the same time, 'Israel' was obligated to fulfil the requirements of the *tora* as contained in covenantal form in this book. The ways in which this paradox is resolved in differing situations throughout the deuteronomistic history provide an essential element in the concept of the identity of 'Israel' produced by this work.[41]

The realization that the work contains *paradox*, and not merely incompletely reconciled sources, or layering of different editorial additions, is certainly an observation which can lead to further insights. Mullen notices that the name 'Israel' itself is part of the symbolic process, and is not a natural name for an objective, clearly defined entity. The name can refer to territory, a state with a capital in Samaria, or a larger one based in Jerusalem. It may refer to a descent-group from a legendary ancestor. It is this basic ambiguity of the term that renders it

38. Mullen, *Narrative History*, pp. 19-54.
39. Mullen, *Narrative History*, pp. 77-85, 280-81.
40. Mullen, *Narrative History*, p. 285.
41. Mullen, *Narrative History*, pp. 56-57.

so powerful as a transformative symbol in a variety of situations.[42] Yet Mullen does not carry this point very far. 'Israel' as a literary concept may have been transformative to the readers, but it is, in turn, transformed and fractured within its own story. With the loss of the land and all of its institutions, what remains of Israel but the memory of a failed empire and two shattered kingdoms? If the DtrH relies on the depiction of social dramas to solve crises, why is there no social drama with the release of Jehoiachin, no mention of God's role in the amnesty? It is the quest for an identity within the *negation* of another that is the guiding mystery of the book. J.G. McConville writes:

> Kings is arguably *all about* a loss of identity, of which loss of land is finally a function. The division of the kingdom is a first manifestation of this. It is no mere 'casting off' of the north. On the contrary, the king of the northern kingdom is regularly styled 'the king of Israel', even though it is here that the most profound apostasy comes, even though he is not Davidic, and even though succession is largely by main force. Rather, separation is part of the problematic of being Israel. The question Who is Israel? hangs over these books.[43]

In my view, the writers have not only constructed an ideal Israel, but have produced an image of their own divisions to express the problematic issues for which there was no consensus or singular model. By projecting these troubling thoughts onto the ideal, grounding them in the past where the lack of resolution may at least be accommodated to the eternal order of things, they have further undermined the unity of that past world. They have 'fixed' fluidity as the norm. Ironically, dwelling on this history of estrangement may have become the vehicle for communion. It is certainly beyond scholarly demonstration, but one may be justified in speculating that it is the clash of models and the indeterminacy of the texts which allowed them to be enriched by so many different interpretations and, hence, become central to so many different religious traditions through the ages. In my own work I will illustrate how certain episodes may have founded a definition of Israel through the depiction of a ritual drama. On the other hand, some of these episodes only access the power of the myths of origin in an incoherent way, what is created in the drama is a tenuous balance between existence and chaos; identity and its negation.

Mullen's work provides much food for thought, and some criticism.

---

42. Mullen, *Narrative History*, p. 57.
43. McConville, 'Narrative and Meaning', p. 34.

He tends largely to ignore the 'social drama' of the temple dedication (1 Kgs 8), developing, instead, the contrasting themes of Yahweh's 'conditional' and 'unconditional' sanction for the davidic dynasty.[44] Mullen concentrates on the episode of the overthrow of Athaliah (admittedly useful to illustrate the centrality of the davidic dynasty) while discussing the reign of Josiah (2 Kgs 22–23) relatively briefly. He sees the people gathered before Josiah as identical to Moses' audience, both groups accepting the conditions of the covenant. With the reform, the loss of identity suffered under Manasseh is reversed and Josiah re-integrates Judah and Israel. Josiah's reform teaches the exiles how they might recreate themselves on the model of the past.[45] There is, of course, little to object to in this, except that it does not go far enough in relating Josiah's public rituals to the notion of Judah in exile. This is the final ritual constitution of Israel in the book, and it is conducted with full knowledge that Judah could not stand for much longer. Why was it important for the writer to have one final reconstitution of the people before the Babylonians vanquish Judah, and none after, around the figure of the amnestied Jehoiachin? Mullen's treatment of the exile as primarily a historical event, providing both compositional setting and motivation, reflects the sort of scholarly approaches which he himself complains do not take seriously the symbolic construction of identity. Not only is his reluctance to rethink the exile evident in his handling of Josiah, but also in his relative lack of attention to 1 Kings 8, which locates a geographical centre for exilic 'Israel' in the very land from which they were expelled. In my view, the exile is not merely the immediate cause of an identity crisis but, rather, an essential part of the identity which the writer constructs for his dispersed people. The importance of making the distinction between an ideological construction of exile and the actual physical deportations and continued state of dispersion should not be downplayed.

Mullen accepts that the DtrH was probably completed by around 550

44. In my own chapter on 1 Kgs 8, I will address the temple episode as such a 'drama'.

45. Mullen, *Narrative History*, pp. 76-85. The chapter on Athaliah's ousting is considered the best part by P.D. Miscall, review of *Narrative History and Ethnic Boundaries: The Deuteronomistic Historian and the Creation of Israelite National Identity* (SBLSS, Atlanta: Scholars Press, 1993), by E.T. Mullen Jr, in *CBQ* 57 (1995), pp. 151-52. Miscall complains that the rest of Mullen's work is 'in many ways, a recasting of older views of Dtr. and of its function and meaning'.

BCE, and regardless of the possibilities of earlier editions, is understandable as a product of this 'exilic' setting. He, therefore, accepts the frequently-found arguments criticized above. He also speculates that the DtrH or parts of the law may have been read publicly at 'one of the deuteronomistic pilgrimage festivals' (cf. Deut. 16.16-17). If the origins of these are to be dated to about 622 BCE (in Josiah's reign) then the usual figure of the DtrH's completion (560/559 BCE) would coincide with the ninth of the proposed seven year cycles.[46] This proposal can hardly be considered convincing confirmation, as it depends too much on uncertain historical conclusions. More serious, though, is his observation that at about the time Jehoiachin was released, the generation of deportees was dying off, leaving their descendants with little to tie them to their ancestral land. It is in this crisis that Mullen finds the motivation for the composition of the book.[47] While this observation needs consideration, it is going beyond the evidence to suggest that such a date marks more than a possible context for the recording of a history. It is not an argument that any *specific* history was begun or completed at this time. It is also not clear that the identity crisis facing newer generations was only of short duration. Such a dilemma is a potential problem for any minority population at the mercy of a dominant empire, and need not be held to be specific to the decades soon after an imperial conquest.

The implications of this are obvious for Mullen's thesis. He fails to establish that the texts he studies were composed in the narrow time-span of Jehoiachin's life after his release.[48] Because of this, and that no successor for Jehoiachin is named, his view that the DtrH sought to ground a hope for Israel's future around a survivor of the davidic dynasty is suspect. The potential for the continuation of the dynasty under this king is of no small importance to Mullen, since he argues that Israel reached its ultimate definition as a people under Yahweh and the divinely-legitimized dynasty of David.[49] The story of Jehoiachin's release does suggest that at least the *symbol* of monarchy has survived the conquest, but there is no need to interpret this as marking explicit

46. Mullen, *Narrative History*, pp. 7, 9-11, 38, 43.

47. Mullen, *Narrative History*, pp. 12-13, 38.

48. He took the throne at 18 years, according to 2 Kgs 24.8, reigning but 3 months. 2 Kgs 25.27 has his imprisonment last 37 years. If such figures reflect actual events at all, then Jehoiachin was about 55 at his release.

49. See his conclusion, pp. 283-86.

political ambitions for a living heir to David. The entire set of monarchic stories may have served other ends, including assertions of *cultural* and not only hoped for *political* autonomy. The memory of the monarchy as a post-monarchic cultural symbol is, in my view, a long-neglected facet of research into Kings, a neglect which is only partly understandable in view of the very early dates granted the book. In some ways, Mullen's constructionist approach makes more sense in the context of a later Kings (if not DtrH), even if it is rendered more difficult by the loss of a clear impression of the ethnographic object implied in the book. Mullen himself writes that when narrativized collections such as the DtrH reach an authoritative status within a community, they may become public symbols, providing the basis for the on-going practice of redefinition and self-understanding.[50] This I accept, but Mullen does not consider that many component passages in Deuteronomy to 2 Kings may have had their own histories as the public symbols of post-monarchic communities before their inclusion in the now extant literature. This pedigree could have been a reason why they were chosen for inclusion, even if they were modified in the process.[51] That the book ends with Jehoiachin's release says more of its suitability as an ending than the book's date of composition.[52]

Another criticism which may be raised against Mullen is his description of the time of David and Solomon as a golden age.[53] Mullen is largely influenced in this by a variety of social-scientific studies into ethnic formulation, including A.D. Smith's *Ethnic Origin of Nations*, which places great emphasis on the memory of a sacred territory and an ideal time in the construction of the constitutive myths of Diaspora

50. Mullen, *Narrative History*, p. 15.

51. This, of course, raises the issue of each redactional layer's internal consistency. If the writers and editors worked not as single-minded ideologues, but as collectors of the stories and memories of past masters, then redactional layering would be decidedly more difficult to identify than it already seems to be.

52. Jeremiah ends with the same episode, suggesting that in the mind of the ancient transmitters of this literature, it was a very suitable, meaningful conclusion, a point made to me by E. Ben Zvi.

53. Similarly, S. Mandell, 'Religion', pp. 35-38, emphasizes each redactors' 'utopian vision', the dates of which span the monarchic period. Hers is another case of an otherwise sophisticated study of biblical traditions compromised by failing to rigorously question the ideological make-up of the texts which provide the bulk of knowledge about the monarchic period itself. She also links each 'static' vision to a particular ideological group or individual.

societies.[54] Yet, David's image in Samuel and the beginning of Kings hardly makes this time an age in which religious ideals were maintained without compromise. David's adultery with Bathsheba and the convenient tragedy which claimed the life of her husband are not his only embarrassments (2 Sam. 11; cf. 2 Sam. 24), and David failed to gain permission to build the temple upon which so much Israelite ethnic focus depends (2 Sam. 7). A monarchic utopia seems more evident in Chronicles than in Samuel and Kings. Even Solomon's reign in Kings seems undermined at an early stage. The mention of high places early in his reign casts the king in a suspicious light (1 Kgs 3.2-4). More telling, however, is the reference to Pharaoh eliminating the Canaanites from Gezer to give the city to his daughter as a dowry (1 Kgs 9.16; 3 Kgdms 5.14b). The power of Solomon seems quite compromised by this claim, and it is particularly ironic since the conquest, which should have resulted in the capture of Gezer, was in fact the result of the flight from the power of an oppressive Pharaoh. One reviewer wonders if Mullen calls the reign of David a golden age for no better reason than that the sociological studies that he cites consider such ideal times as important to ethnic identity. The conquest under Joshua may fit the model of a golden age better.[55] Even Joshua's invasion, for all of its ritualistic execution, however, is compromised by sin early on, and later, by the eventual failure to eradicate all of the Canaanites (Josh. 7; 15.63; 16.10; 17.12). Neither is the period of the Judges a true ideal as the very fabric of Israel is strained to breaking point, and not all of the judges live up to the standards set for them (cf. Judg. 8.24-27; ch. 20).

The failure to find a clear golden age, however, is not a point fatal to the use of sociological research into ethnic identity to inform the study of Kings. A golden age is only a part of the valorization of the past. Smith posits two distinct types of sacred epochs: first is the time of the ancestors who communed with the gods and presided over the origins of the community. The second is an age of glory in which the community achieved its classical form and was the age of heroes.[56] One might see that the first type finds some expression in the Pentateuch. A

54. Mullen, *Narrative History*, p. 164.

55. J.A. Dearman, review of *Narrative History and Ethnic Boundaries: The Deuteronomistic Historian and the Creation of Israelite National Identity* (SBLSS; Atlanta: Scholars Press, 1993), by E.T. Mullen Jr, in *JBL* 114 (1995), pp. 301-302.

56. Smith, *Ethnic Origins*, p. 191.

muted, or better, fractured, age of glory and heroism is found in the
Former Prophets. The heroes do not serve a single form of community,
but are found as warriors/conquerors, judges, prophets and kings. With
the shifting social contexts, the authors seem quite unwilling to build
this sequence into a utopia. The heroes themselves are flawed. The
early books of the Former Prophets are permeated with an air of
entropy, despite the fact that Israel slowly builds itself an empire. Ultimately the empire itself succumbs to the forces of decay which had
plagued Israel from the beginning. It is the play between social and
political entropy and revival that carries the reader to the ultimate
destruction of Judah and Israel. But still, the Pentateuch and the Former
Prophets offer, in place of a clear 'golden age', at least an assortment of
'golden (or better, sacred) moments': the promises to the patriarchs, the
crossing of the sea, the giving of the law, the crossing of the Jordan, the
investiture of David. These moments become part of the mythic basis
of Israel which are always accessible. They rely on, and constitute
'social' metaphors. Such sacred moments are also found in Kings, and
they seem intended to reaffirm the relationship of Israel to Yahweh, to
define Israel in terms of a religious, and not exclusively monarchic,
constitution. The sacred moments in Kings do sometimes revolve
around kings, but also involve the whole of the people and their relationship with Yahweh. As Mullen points out, such defining moments
rely on the narration of religious ritual. In many ways, the two most
important ritual complexes, the dedication of the temple and the reform
of Josiah, are paradoxical when seen against their literary contexts. This
paradox, however, is a product of their importance beyond the simple
plot of the book. They act as a part of the sequence of history and as
paradigmatic events. They are, in fact, timeless moments, and are at the
heart of the myth complex telling Israel who they are.

3. In Search of the New 'Israelites'

A leading advocate of a more radical questioning of the relationship
between the social world behind the production of the literature in the
Hebrew Bible and the social world projected in it is Philip R. Davies,
although the aforementioned Thomas L. Thompson, Niels Peter
Lemche and others are also valuable contributors.[57] Davies devotes his

57. Davies, *'Ancient Israel'*; Thompson, *Early History*; N.P. Lemche, 'The Old
Testament: A Hellenistic Book?'. See also, for instance, Ben Zvi, 'Inclusion'.

brief monograph to express, in no uncertain terms, his strong objections to a lack of scholarly distinction between the Israel depicted in the Bible and the historical states in the territory claimed by the Bible as Israel. This blurring has resulted in a scholarly construct called by Davies 'Ancient Israel', inspired by the accused scholars' own labels. What was a literary construct is transformed in the work of these scholars into a perceived historical entity.[58] Davies, of course, makes much of the circularity of the arguments which see the biblical literature as being composed contemporaneously with the unfolding events it describes.[59] Davies's objections are well founded; a social entity as the subject of a literary work should not be taken *a priori* as a relatively close counterpart to an historical social entity. Changing political situations can inspire the rapid development of new traditions and stories of origins can be developed.[60] He is influenced in this regard by the work edited by Eric Hobsbawm and Terrence Ranger, *The Invention of Tradition,* which has been important in raising awareness of this issue.[61] The political contexts which Davies argues as the most likely for the development of the biblical literature do, indeed, form a likely scenario for the formation of essentially new groups (however taking up specific earlier ideas and names), and for new literary activity.

Davies argues that the Persian investment in Judah resulted in the development of a new society, based around an imported elite class, which marked a definite break with its predecessors in the region. This was accompanied by the development of an ideological superstructure which denied the society's recent origins and imperial basis and made itself out to be indigenous. This manifested itself in the form of an interpretation of the Babylonian-era deportations as an exile, and claims

58. Davies, 'Ancient Israel', pp. 22.

59. Davies, 'Ancient Israel'. See his chapters on the 'misconstrual' of literary conceptions of 'Israel' as a historical entity, 'Searching for "Ancient Israel"', pp. 22-48, and on monarchic Judah and Israel, 'A Search for Historical Israel', pp. 60-74.

60. Davies, 'Ancient Israel', p. 101.

61. E. Hobsbawm and T. Ranger (eds.), *The Invention of Tradition* (Cambridge: Cambridge University Press, 1983). The adaptability of tradition is recognized by others. R. Finnegan, *Literacy and Orality: Studies in the Technology of Communication* (Oxford: Basil Blackwell, 1988), p. 20, reports that the Gonja story of how their tribal founders divided the land between them was emended in the twentieth century. The number of founders was altered to maintain consistency between the story and a territorial reorganization.

that the descendants of these exiles were the new elite 'repatriated' by the Persians. The literati of this *golah* society created an identity based on the concrete memory of those it encountered in its new land, and probably some archival material. They accommodated these with their own claims for privilege and rites. This process did not occur suddenly, nor were its manifestations ever completely coherent. The end product, however, is the major part of biblical literature.[62] An important part of Davies's formulation is that this production was the work of the professionally literate classes, although he does maintain that it was not simply 'made to order', or that Genesis to Kings had not been reworked a number of times. The scribes not only worked at the behest of the elite, however, but partly from self-interest or even creative enjoyment. Yet, even if they were allowed some liberties with the production of such texts, in the end the products of their labours would have served the interests of the ruling classes.[63] It should be remembered, however, that the upper strata of this society was itself probably a pluralistic social grouping. The role of elites in the formation and evolution of ethnic identity is such that one scholar asserts that the cultural form, values and practices of ethnic groups are resources for *competing* elites in their conflicts over power.[64] These properties, then, become symbols for identifying members, and are called upon to create a political identity.[65] It does not matter whether the culture of the group is ancient or only recently formed, the student of ethnicity and nationality is, to a large extent, engaged in the study of politically induced cultural change.

> More precisely, it is a study of the process by which elites and counter-elites within ethnic groups select aspects of the group's culture, attach new value and meaning to them, and use them as symbols to mobilize the group, to defend its interests, and to compete with other groups.[66]

The question must be asked, however, why did the dialogue that this new elite in the Persian province of Judah engage in centre on an 'Israelite' heritage, in the first place, and not simply a 'Judaean' one?

62. Davies, *'Ancient Israel'*, p. 87.
63. Davies, *'Ancient Israel'*, pp. 106-109, 120, cf. pp. 100-101.
64. Here one recalls the discussion above concerning Dutcher-Walls, 'Social Location'.
65. P.R. Brass, *Ethnicity and Nationalism: Theory and Comparison* (New Delhi: Sage, 1991), p. 15.
66. Brass, *Ethnicity*, p. 75.

Davies considers it unlikely that Judah developed independently of monarchic Israel. It is plausible, therefore, that there were concepts of a 'greater Israel' that embraced both kingdoms. It is possible that such conceptions were even held by Judaeans. Alternatively, a migration of northerners to Judah may have followed the Assyrian invasion.[67] Different groups in various places may have had some investment in the name 'Israel' after the fall of the monarchic state in 722 BCE. This includes, most logically, those left behind in the aftermath of the conquest. On the other hand, new settlers in the region may have adapted the name for themselves, despite retention of their traditional deities (cf. 2 Kgs 17.24-41). Yet Davies is careful to point out that it is likely that the cult of Yahweh continued in Samaria, as evidence from the late fifth century BCE indicates. He considers that the name Israel may have persisted especially in this cult, as Yahweh's distinct jurisdiction. Those remaining or deported from Judah may also have had an interest in the name 'Israel', not to mention those who may have been imported into Judah by Assyria or Babylon. The exiles and refugees of both Israel and Judah, of course, must also be considered. Davies denies that the northern or repopulated groups would have been instrumental in the development of the Israel known in the Hebrew Bible, although they may well have made a contribution. Rather, because the dispersed worshippers of Yahweh in the Persian period carried the name 'Jew' or 'Judaean' (despite not being Judaean by birth or recent ancestry), and because of the centrality of Judah in the biblical literature, it is most logical to look to Judah for the rise of biblical Israel.[68]

I would, however, emphasize that the name 'Judah' would probably have been retained among refugees or deportees from the fallen monarchy in both Egypt and in Mesopotamia. It would be too much to propose that these people would always have subscribed to a concept of 'Israel' similar to that which would eventually crystallize in biblical literature. There is no telling how 'Israelite' this vision of their Judaean heritage may have been. Even if antecedents to a concept of a greater Israel could be found in the monarchic period, the association need not have been shared by all. It is hard, therefore, to suppose that the post-monarchic processes of revalorising the names 'Judah' and 'Israel' began with the Persian re-investment in Judah, and, once this began, it certainly was not the exclusive prerogative of the elite the Persians

67. Davies, *'Ancient Israel'*, pp. 69-70.
68. Davies, *'Ancient Israel'*, pp. 76-78.

were entrenching in Judah. Throughout the Near East there would have been many separate projects of identity formation and articulation, with diverse groups looking back to the homelands of Judah and Israel with various understandings of their history, and of its present occupants. The question is, did these projects, or at least some of them, enter into dialogue with each other? It would seem to me that at some point they must have.

A combination of both the active promulgation of the views of the Jerusalem authorities and a more passive assimilation between the Judah-ism of Judah and that abroad seems most plausible to me. Extreme Jerusalem-centred, and Judah-exclusive, 'Yahwism' would have been only one part of the matrix of religious and ethnic thought which led to the literature we now know. Even if the Judaean elite set the agenda for the development of this identity, their potential audiences were probably not bound by their own geo-political jurisdiction. It is most likely that the political influence of the Persian-sponsored Judaean elite was instrumental in the rise of the religious/cultural designator 'Judaism' as the primary name for this religious/ethnic group who saw themselves as the descendants of the people of Israel. Even so, the other Judah-ist enclaves may have provided the fertile ground for this elite to extend their influence beyond the borders of the imperial province. Perhaps the Jerusalem elite could, at times, expect certain positive incentives from the imperial overlords for their good behaviour, and for instilling a loyal disposition in the Judah-ists in the Diaspora as well. The power relations, and economic factors which led to the coalescing of a more or less unified sense of a Judah-ist cultural heritage across the ancient world, which would have motivated the development of the biblical historical traditions, were probably extremely complex.[69]

It is possible that imperial imposition on diverse Judah-ist or

69. P.R. Davies, 'God of Cyrus, God of Israel', in Davies, Harvey and Watson (eds.), *Words Remembered, Texts Renewed*, pp. 207-25 (220 n. 38), comments on how explaining the Jewish dispersion on grounds of forced deportation displays the pervasive nature of the biblical myth. Scholars should also look to economic and other causes for the dispersion. For other sides of the political complexities of the issue, see, for instance, Hamilton, 'Who was a Jew?'; T.M. Bolin, 'The Temple of יהו at Elephantine and Persian Religious Policy', in D.V. Edelman (ed.), *The Triumph of Elohim: From Jahwisms to Judaisms* (CBET, 13; Kampen: Kok Pharos, 1995), pp. 127-42.

'Israelite' groups caused them to recognize the resurgent Jerusalem as a significant centre to their own ideological world. This might be seen in the references to fifth century BCE instructions for the Egyptian Judahist community to celebrate particular festivals.[70] As is well known, the Judaean community in Elephantine, towards the end of the fifth century BCE, had cordial enough relations with both Jerusalem and Samaria to discuss with them their oppression at the hands of the Egyptians and to ask for support for the repair of their ruined temple.[71] Such relations imply some level of a shared horizon of identity between the Egyptian and Samarian communities and between Egypt and at least some members of Jerusalem's religious elite, which may have grown beyond mere political expediency. Those who already held some form of special regard for the old sacred places and traditions of Judah and Israel may have looked with interest to the temple of Yahweh in Jerusalem, while its masters may have profited from their international reputation. This of course, does not mean that there were no conflicts, or that Judah-ism was a unified body of practice and belief. Symbols can mean different things to different people. At the same time, however, the shared symbol can be a unifying factor in an otherwise pluralistic set of meanings.[72]

One also has to remember that even if the elite in Jerusalem were installed by imperial decree, if they engaged in making themselves indigenous, their descendants would have acted on the belief of their indigenous links to the land. One generation may have produced blatant 'fabrications' to affirm their claims to power and status. The next generation would produce literature reflecting traditions, the truth of which would be considered natural and unassailable. The acceptance of this truth, if it included recognition that enclaves of Yahweh's people persisted throughout the known world, could have complemented political and economic incentives towards building bridges between different Judah-ist groups. The 'idea' of a greater Israel, with all of its complex sentiments, could quickly become an idea not only worth writing about, but possibly worth dying for. By creating themselves as the true native population, the Jerusalemite elite's political strategy could well backfire in the face of the Persians: the 'natives' might get dangerous ideas. An

70. Porten, *Elephantine Papyri*, pp. 125-26, 'The Passover Letter', TAD A4.1

71. Porten, *Elephantine Papyri*, pp. 127-51, TAD A4.2–A4.10.

72. I will elaborate on this point to some degree below. See the comments of A.D. Smith, already cited in Chapter 1 n. 34.

independence-minded Judah, inspired by the developing stories of ancient heroes and their own Israelite empire, all motivated by belief in a god who often saved them from their enemies, was potentially a dangerous thing indeed. All the more dangerous if they cultivated links with their compatriots abroad. Although it is speculative, one might think that the danger this situation may have presented could have led to some imperial deference at certain times, to keep the Judaeans on the 'right' side. To this end, Israel's empire, however buried in the rubble of wars long since lost, was still, potentially, a political factor to reckon with. The curious way in which empire, and especially the dynasty which built it, is both celebrated and denigrated in the biblical texts reflects its ambivalent status. It is potentially a vital tool in asserting cultural integrity, and yet, that integrity must survive the loss of the empire and monarchy. On the other hand, if the Israelite empire could fall through its apostasy and hubris, how much harder could the might of the promised land's current foreign rulers be crushed?

To my mind, the development of the Judah-ist heritage which underlies the biblical literature was probably not exclusively a phenomenon internal to the land of Judah, even if the Persian-era developments there were instrumental to it. As represented by Davies, the broad 'constructionist' approach has identified, with some clarity, the general historical factors which resulted in the biblical literature. These, however, should be understood as transcending the immediate regions of that elite's jurisdiction, and include complementary and contrary responses to the specific claims of the Judaean elite. Moreover, the motives behind the greater process should not be taken as identical to the specific projects which were the writing of any particular biblical book.[73]

In my understanding, every society is engaged in a continual process of reformulating its sense(s) of its own being. Such processes, however, are marked by specific projects, such as the writing of books, which may be deliberately intended to address the current state of the process, as it appears to specific individuals. Since the process of identity re-articulation is continual, and could reasonably be seen to pervade all

73. Certainly neither Davies, *'Ancient Israel'* or Thompson, *Early History*, offer their works as the final word on the writing of any biblical book. Indeed, their observations, while sometimes taking examples from specific books, are quite general, and isolate the predominant social factors in the newer historical contexts they explore.

that humans do and think, scholars are ill-advised to explain the personal motives of an individual in terms of the direction society as a whole seems to be heading. Even if personal identities are shaped by social position, the relationship is always dialectical. In the next section of this chapter, I will discuss the personal identity vis-à-vis 'rational self-interest' a bit further. Here it suffices to call attention to what Davies calls 'a kind of social scientific quantum theory' which amounts to a philosophical paradox. It is meaningful to talk of societies and not merely groups of individuals; group actions are predictable, since group behaviour can be predicted, and regularly is, through the use of statistics. Individual behaviour, however, is unpredictable.[74] Therefore, even if imperatives can be identified to explain the course of history, this does not mean that one has found the motives guiding individual actions. It is, therefore, hard to reduce all cultural productions to the level of deliberate projects within the greater processes of social identity formation.

Here, one might wish to establish distinctions between the abstract community or ethnic-level *processes* of identity expression, and the way such processes are manifest in the continual identity *practice* of individuals. This is so even if the larger, abstract processes are only made manifest in the specific products and actions of individuals. This practice, of course, is marked by specific *projects* by which individuals, or small groups of writers or thinkers within these larger communities, undertake to inscribe their own views on the nature of their society and their place within it. Not every human production, however, should be seen as such a deliberate project. For instance, Herodotus may well have expressed himself on the identity of his own culture in writing his great historical work (and his compatriots may have variously valued or disputed his contribution in this regard), but at least his stated reason for pursuing the past was not to reformulate his own culture along lines preferable to himself. It was to explain how Greece and Persia went to war.[75]

I have already commented briefly on history-writing as a part of the narrative arts. One could certainly imagine the production of history-

74. Davies, *'Ancient Israel'*, p. 14.

75. The opening line of Herodotus, *The Histories*, sets this out: 'Herodotus of Halicarnassus, his *Researches* are here set down to preserve the memory of the past by putting on record the astonishing achievements both of our own and of other peoples; and more particularly, to show how they came into conflict' (1.1).

writing as a personal expression of an author's relationship to a culture's literary traditions. An author may have been motivated by the hope of financial gain or status to produce a version of accepted history by being a better storyteller, and not a radical ethnographer. While I applaud the new academic interest in the *process*, and do not feel that the articulation of 'Israelite' ethnicity in Kings is purely incidental to the writer's goals, I must offer my concerns about reducing Kings, or any other biblical text, to a single-minded, explicit project of heritage formation. The emphasis on identity is there in Kings, but this production has many facets to which social identity may be more implicit. Since so little is known of the time and place of its composition, it is hard to define this project outside the terms of the process of which it was a part. Even so, that process must not be taken as completely explanatory of the book. Is Kings a 'fabrication' of an ethnicity, or an articulation of a Judah-ism which already had its precursors?

4. *'Imagined Israel': Map, Mask or House of Mirrors?*

When looking at the Hebrew Bible as a whole, it is easy to find references to the 'others' within the narrative world against whom the new 'Israel' was defining itself. Ezra and Nehemiah offer the reader an apology for the *golah* and the 'holy seed' who returned from Babylonia, and who distinguish themselves from the 'people of the land' and the establishment in Samaria.[76] In the Pentateuch and Former Prophets, the Canaanites (not to mention the Philistines and other foreigners) are Israel's foils. Israel is enjoined not to follow their practices, and in Kings itself, the destruction of the kingdom is attributed to the Israelites ignoring this injunction (2 Kgs 17.8, 15; 21.2, 9, 11; cf. 1 Kgs 14.24). On the other hand, it is not so easy to determine exactly how any particular reference to the 'other' in biblical literature relates to the actual political climate of the day. Lemche suggests that the biblical portrayal of the 'Canaanites' may be part of a fifth or fourth century BCE polemic by Egyptian Jews against the *Jews* of Jerusalem.[77] The denunciations of the northern kingdom of Israel in Kings is often taken as a polemic against the nascent Samaritan sect, or an earlier (and allegedly illegitimate) 'northern' Judaism. Yet, as I will describe in my own analysis, the 'north' in Kings does not simply represent that which has so

76. Davies, *'Ancient Israel'*, pp. 118.
77. Lemche, *Canaanites*, pp. 167-68.

corrupted itself and can no longer be called 'Israel'. Rather, it remains 'Israel', as its retention of the very name indicates. The 'north' and Judah are each other's alter ego, and their independent existences, so strongly affirmed in many places in the book, are blurred in many others. Finding a simple relationship between a hypothetical political debate and its representation in traditions of the past is to be avoided. Again, one may identify a general process, but the intricacies of any particular articulation (especially a complex, and potentially composite one) make precision difficult. As I will describe below, the past is not an easily readable 'map' of the present. In some ways it may be more of a mask, hiding rebellion against an idea or group by camouflaging it in the form of an historical arch-enemy. More so, however, the past may be like a house of mirrors, making a complete understanding impossible for the plenitude of different reflections, refractions and distortions.

At this point, there seems to be something of an impasse in the course of this research. If one is to look at 'projects' of identity articulation or formation, one might expect little uncertainty, and assume that the writers engaged in such tasks would be very clear about who their society or culture was. On the other hand, the house of mirrors the biblical scholar is confronted with is built not only by multiplicity of authors, but by something even more subtle as well: the multiplicity of identities of each writer or editor.[78]

> Tension between identity—putatively singular, unitary and integral—
> and identities—plural, cross-cutting and divided—is inescapable at both
> individual and collective levels. As lived, identity is always project, not
> settled accomplishment; though various external ascriptions or recogni-
> tions may be fixed and timeless.[79]

For Craig Calhoun, this tension is not only the locus of personal struggle but potentially the source of an identity politics which does not exclusively aim at the legitimation of 'falsely essential categorical identities'. Rather, the claims of priority of larger, collective identities can have at their base deep social and moral values. It is hard, therefore, to reduce questions of identity entirely to questions of rational self-

---

78. C. Calhoun, 'Social Theory and the Politics of Identity', in C. Calhoun (ed.), *Social Theory and the Politics of Identity* (Oxford: Basil Blackwell, 1994), pp. 9-36 (27-28).

79. Calhoun, 'Social Theory', p. 27.

interest. Such self-interest is not an underlying variable or factor suitable to provide a perspective on understanding the complexity of the formation of personal identity. Self-interest is determined by the identity process itself. Identities can change, and in some ways, always do. Calhoun says, for instance, people are sometimes 'wanting better wants'.[80] This means, of course, that people do not act predictably according to their station in life. In turn, it means that it is hard to propose definitive descriptions of social movements in the societies which produced the Hebrew Bible by inference from the otherwise 'anonymous' texts. Somers and Gibson propose that social action is better explained through a narrative identity approach, which emphasizes shifting interpersonal relationships, and hence shifting identities, as the norm. They comment that:

> A narrative identity approach assumes the intelligibility of social action only if people are seen to be guided in their actions by their embeddedness in relationships and by the stories with which they identify. Actions are only rarely guided by the interests imputed to them. An interest approach assumes that people act on rational grounds, towards a preferred end or on the internalization of values. A narrative identity approach, on the other hand, sees people acting as they do so as not to violate their sense of being at that particular moment and place. Narrative identities are constituted through time, and change in time, through narrative processes.[81]

It is information about these processes which biblical scholars lack, and so direct connections between the biblical narratives and their producers cannot be made. Somers and Gibson point out that even though people must construct their narratives from the repertoire of representations and stories current in their society, the sort of narratives which predominate depends largely on the distribution of power. For this reason, the actual narrative forms employed by people to make sense of their situation will 'always be an empirical rather than a presuppositional question'.[82] Diverse groups holding different versions of history may have disputes over interpretation or application, but this need not mean that they are fundamentally destroying their society. There is no

---

80. Calhoun, 'Social Theory', pp. 27-28. His paper offers a critique of the social constructionist approaches in social sciences as 'essentialist' for their concentration on self-interest of social actors.

81. Somers and Gibson, 'Reclaiming The Epistemological "Other"', p. 67.

82. Somers and Gibson, 'Reclaiming The Epistemological "Other"', p. 73.

single interpretation of public history. Whether it is in the service of the state or the product of the people themselves, it takes on 'the rhetoric of poetics', and its veracity and ownership are the subject of claims and counter-claims. Disputes also arise over whose aesthetic principle is best suited to construct the past convincingly, that is, to provide the most hegemonic power:[83]

> Power within history lies in several domains: one is the relation of text to subject and another is the construction of individual and collective identities (for example, racial, ethnic and national). These social constructions are part of the process of inventing traditions. In the act of creating a written text subjects are transformed into transposable objects. 'We' create 'them' and in so doing, we pretend that we are creating ourselves, if only through contrasts and opposition. But in the process 'we' appropriate 'them', 'we' fix and frame the 'other' through a zealous essentialism, thereby falling prey to the dilemma of dual fabrication.[84]

This essentialism, as it pertains to the development of religion, has been noted by Mullen. He observes that, despite the competition between religion and other cultural signifiers, religion grants stability to those who are convinced by the symbolic universe it has created and 'factualized'. Among the most important aspects of the 'factualization' processes is the delineation of ethnic boundaries, identifying not only the groups to which the believers belong, but those of the unbelievers as well. Although religion depicts its classification systems as natural and immutable, the categories so established are also best seen as subject to change.[85] Such observations are made by other scholars as well. In the epilogue to a collection of papers addressing the relationship between social fact and ideology, Sally Moore writes that the matter is paradoxical. Attempting to fix social relations or symbols implicitly recognizes that mutability while struggling against it. The process of fixing this reality involves its representation as 'stable and immutable,

---

83. Bond and Gilliam, 'Introduction', p. 17.

84. Bond and Gilliam, 'Introduction', p. 13. They note that anthropology develops paradigms to study what it has itself created: 'The crisis lies in the limitations of anthropological paradigms to explain historical and ethnographic constructions'. Certainly anyone approaching the Hebrew Bible with the interests displayed in the present work is necessarily in a similar state of crisis. But then, the problem remains for anyone with an interest on the societies which produced the Bible.

85. Mullen, *Narrative History*, pp. 36-37.

or at least controllable to this end'.[86] The significance of this observation should not be down-played, and is worthy of some comment in
relation to the production of the Hebrew Bible's 'historical literature'.
Such a production is the paradoxical attempt to 'fix' social realities in
the past. To this end, it is an activity that generates paradigmatic events
and situations, perhaps through the selection, interpretation and representation of events, real or imagined, from an existing body of knowledge. As an activity engaging different writers and interpreters (which
itself implies inherent immutability), it is a form of social dialogue.

The recording of history is the recording not only of paradigmatic
situations, however, but also of change. Definitive interpretations of
change are certainly an integral part of the realities that historians are
attempting to fix. Through the course of the Former Prophets, this kind
of social change is depicted. One form of divinely-legitimized government evolves into another; the unity of Israel is destroyed and ultimately the nation is swept from its land. In Kings, one corrupt
monarchy breeds two, which, in turn, fail. Prophets are sometimes set
against the kings. One might conclude, as Mullen seems to, that this
literature is actually preserving an evolutionary social history with its
true relevance in its culmination, the release of Jehoiachin, and so
affirms a monarchic model of an ideal social reality, which, nonetheless, must be realized in exile. On the other hand, one could temper the
progressive aspects of the books with a view that they juxtapose alternative models. Each one, that of Joshua, the warrior leader, *ad hoc*
judges, Samuel as priest/prophet, and the monarchy itself is legitimized
by Israel's history of existence in their promised land, and hence,
embody ideals held in potential for those who claim to be the descendants of the Israel swept from it. At the same time, however, the literature calls the ultimate significance of each model into question, as one
is superseded by the other. Ultimately, the exile questions all of them.
The constant, immutable standard, therefore, may not be the form, but
the performance of leadership. The various kinds of leadership, each set
within its own historical framework, may be 'institutionalized alternatives' held in potential for their applicability to diverse situations.[87] The
mass of alternatives may certainly be at the disposal of the elite, but

86. Moore, 'Epilogue', p. 221.
87. P.C. Salzman, 'Culture as Enhabilmentis', in L. Holy and M. Stuchlik
(eds.), *The Structure of Folk Models* (ASA Monographs, 20; London: Academic
Press, 1981), pp. 233-56.

within any society are 'countertaxonomic discourses', for the subordinate to deconstruct the established order and effect change.[88]

The observations above certainly do not support the proposal of utterly contradictory pro-monarchic and anti-monarchic passages. They also pose obstacles for the suggestion that Kings was intended to serve a political programme centring on a claimant to David's throne. Rather, it is suggestive of complex reactions to the monarchic past, in which the age of the kings is remembered both positively and negatively. To celebrate the memory of David and Solomon and the great Israelite Empire is not the same thing as advocating the return to monarchic rule. Smith calls attention to modern nationalist movements in which past glories become symbolic of the envisioned national character. These visions are not dependent upon reproducing the past, but only less tangible aspects of it, which evoke positive emotions.[89] For all its perceived problems, the memory of monarchic independence may have been useful for building an 'Israelite' ethnicity around other political models, for which the davidic ideals are paradigmatic of behaviour, or divine sanction, not expressly prescriptive of political form.

Valerio Valeri argues that, although related to social reproduction, the past is not used simply to justify its own stereotypic reproduction. The past may represent a process of becoming, by showing tradition both preserved and successfully violated. Often several, sometimes conflicting, images of the past are maintained. The complexity of the past's relevance to the present is found in the variety of relationships between the two. A present event can stand for one or more past events as its sign or ontological substitute; metonymically, if they are linked in a syntagmatic chain, or metaphorically, if they belong to the same paradigm.[90] The relationship between past and present is therefore analogical instead of replicative. While the relevance of the past is found in

---

88. Lincoln, *Discourse*, p. 8.

89. Smith, *Ethnic Origins*, pp. 196-97, points out that the celebration of the vitality and independence of the Viking culture did not include a desire to recover old Norse culture in later Norwegian nationalist thought. The rediscovery of a glorious golden age provides status and satisfies inner needs for emotional and spiritual expression.

90. V. Valeri, 'Constitutive History: Genealogy and Narrative in the Legitimation of Hawaiian Kingship', in E. Ohnuki-Tierney (ed.), *Culture through Time: Anthropological Approaches* (Stanford: Stanford University Press, 1990), pp. 154-92 (155-57).

the present, ideologically it is the past which contains the justification of the present, as it cannot justify itself:[91]

> The relationship between past and present thus turns out to be much more complex than it appears at first. Clearly, too, the represented past is rarely characterized by timelessness, or undifferentiated duration, alone, and its constitutive power for the present depends on a combination of detemporalizing and temporalizing aspects, on a play of discontinuity and continuity in time.[92]

For those who accept the narrative as their history, this play becomes a rich field. Claude Lévi-Strauss writes that, in mythic thinking, there is no satisfaction with a single response to a problem, but, once formulated, the response 'enters a play of transformations' which generate other responses.[93] This I relate to the 'purposive knowing' (to borrow Huizinga's phrase) which is the intellectual engagement with the past. This knowledge is not attained through purely logical deduction from objective information but from the process of interpretation. For both writer and reader, this process engages the past as a complex of polyvalent symbols. Whatever objective purposes the writer may have had, the reader may gain additional knowledge from the symbolic evocation of a multitude of secondary memories, however tangential, which arise in the interpretation of each episode, character, and motif.[94] The discovery of new knowledge, then, influences the way traditions can be reinterpreted. Cohen asserts that rather than give meaning, symbols make meaning possible. This implies a relativity which allows for people in the same community using symbols differently:[95]

91. Valeri, 'Constitutive History', p. 161.
92. Valeri, 'Constitutive History', p. 164.
93. C. Lévi-Strauss, 'From Mythical Possibility to Social Existence', in C. Lévi-Strauss, *The View from Afar* (trans. J. Neugroschcel and P. Hoss; Oxford: Basil Blackwell, 1985), pp. 157-74 (172).
94. D. Sperber, *Rethinking Symbolism* (trans. A. L. Morton; CSSA; Cambridge: Cambridge University Press, 1975). Sperber considers symbolism a cognitive mechanism. Rather than see individuals endowed with universal constraints or archetypes, they have only a symbolic mechanism and learning strategy. The mechanism engages active and passive memories, but the evocation is never totally determined (pp. 136-37). 'Cultural symbolism creates a community of interest but not of opinion' (p. 137).
95. Cohen, *Symbolic Construction*, pp. 15-18.

> It is that the community itself and everything in it, conceptual as well as material, has a symbolic dimension, and, further, that this dimension does not exist as some kind of consensus of sentiment. Rather, it exists as something for people 'to think with'. The symbols of community are mental constructs: they provide people with the means to make meaning. In so doing, they also provide them with the means to express particular meaning which the community has for them.[96]

In an intriguing study of political ritual, David I. Kertzer writes that ritual can promote social solidarity without every participant sharing identical values or even the same interpretations of the ritual itself. Such symbols, he observes, can build solidarity without consensus.[97]

No facet of 'Israel', including its remembered history, was (and is) without potential symbolic value, but there is no certainty as to what range of values each individual symbol would have had in each age. Rather, engagement of symbols involves their interaction with each other, producing new knowledge. We may, with Berger and Luckmann, see this 'symbolic universe' as the matrix of all meaning, both socially objectivated and subjectively real. The entirety of the historic society and biography of the individual are events within it:[98]

> The important principle for our general considerations is that the relationship between knowledge and its social base is a dialectal one, that is, knowledge is a social product *and* knowledge is a factor in social change.[99]

Because any expression, in writing or other media, cannot exhaust the possibilities of the universe, or arrive at a definitive and fixed description, explication of the political motives underlying any symbolic expression is 'incipiently problematic', especially so if there is little knowledge of the wider symbolic and social contexts of the particular expression.[100] In turning these thoughts to the social world that produced Kings, it becomes clear that reconstructing from Kings a precise map of the society and times which produced it is fraught with difficulty. The identities behind texts are as fluid as the 'imaginings' within them. Bruce Lincoln observes that even if thought is socially

---

96. Cohen, *Symbolic Construction*, p. 19.

97. D.I. Kertzer, *Ritual, Politics and Power* (New Haven: Yale University Press, 1988), pp. 68-69.

98. Berger and Luckmann, *Social Construction*, p. 114. Emphasis original.

99. Berger and Luckmann, *Social Construction*, p. 104.

100. Berger and Luckmann, *Social Construction*, p. 124.

determined, it does not follow that thought reflects, encodes, re-presents, or helps replicate the *established structures* of society. Rather, the social determination of thought implies that all the variables within a society as a whole are represented within the full range of thought and discourse at a given moment.[101]

Even if writing, and so preservation of thought, was available only to a very limited number of people in any society in the ancient world, there is still no certainty that apparently contradictory messages are indicative of different stages in the history of the society that produced them. Lincoln writes that synthetic entities which originate from prior dialectic confrontations carry with them the tensions of their formation. This residue is potentially capable of destroying the synthesis. He returns the present discussion to a point made in the introduction: sentiment is the ultimate force which holds a society together or destroys it, and discourse is the primary instrument of its arousal, manipulation, and of making it dormant.[102] It is through the repeated evocation of the sentiments around stories of formative moments in a group's past that social identities are continually re-established. He argues that it is not because one is a member of the group that one feels pride in hearing these stories. Rather, when one feels pride, one '(re)-becomes' a member, and feels affinity for other members and estrangement from those who are not. The invocation of differing ancestors mobilizes social groups of various sizes. Likewise when one recounts different episodes from the past. He observes that in favour of Italian solidarity, Sienese and Florentine identities, themselves inscribed in narrative, can be (temporarily and imperfectly) deconstructed through recounting of common stories and heroes (e.g. Dante, Garibaldi, or World Cup Football victories).[103] The social determinants of any image of Israel in the Hebrew Bible are probably well beyond the reach of scholarship to detail, at least not without a firm grasp on the dates and places of composition, and additional information about the relevant social and political climates. This information, however, is sadly lacking. But does this entail that historically-interested investigations must be abandoned?

---

101. Lincoln, *Discourse*, pp. 6-7.
102. Lincoln, *Discourse*, p. 11.
103. Lincoln, *Discourse*, p. 23.

5. *The Task Ahead*

If one is to study Kings as an ancient text, a major change in emphasis
is necessary from the standard approaches. The goals of accuracy in
writing compositional histories, and histories of the composers, may
never be met. On the other hand, even if I avoid talk of the
Deuteronomistic History (except, of course, when I review the work of
others), the close parallels between Samuel and Kings and the uncertain
division between the two books in the various Greek versions do suggest that they are closely related. Inclusion of a discussion of select
parts of Samuel is not out of place in a discussion of Kings, regardless
of the fact that each may well have had some major independent editing.[104] On another front, a number of scholars have re-examined the
distinction usually made between the work of the ancient author/editor
and the copyist. They argue, to different extents, that textual criticism
and compositional criticism are not, in fact, fully distinct practices.[105]
For the present work, it is important that the LXX and its *Vorlage* were
parts of ancient tradition. As there are no conclusive arguments about
Kings' compositional history, and as Kings may always have been
marked by textual variety, there is no real reason to impose a hierarchy
between the MT and LXX. While textual criticism remains important, it
is also reasonable for each version to be taken as a part of the religious
heritage of Judaism as a whole. My own research will not stress a full
or detailed comparison between the LXX and MT. This is the task of
specialists in the field. In a number of more general matters, however,
some comparison is both necessary and illuminating.

A synchronic approach to Kings will be taken here, even if this
seems at odds with a historically-interested study. This discrepancy,
however, is only apparent, as 'synchronic' need not imply a disinterest

104. This will be outlined in more detail below; most of the Greek versions agree
with the MT but the LXX[L] includes the equivalent to 1 Kgs 1.1–2.11 in 2 Kgdms.

105. Auld, *Privilege*, relies heavily on comparisons between the LXX and MT.
See also, Z. Talshir, 'The Contribution of Diverging Traditions Preserved in the
Septuagint to Literary Criticism of the Bible', in L. Greenspoon and O. Munnich
(eds.), *VIIIth Congress of the IOSCS, Paris 1992* (SCSS, 41; Atlanta: Scholars
Press, 1995), pp. 21-41. On text critical issues in Kings, J. Trebolle Barrera has
been prolific, among his works see, 'The Text-Critical Use of the Septuagint in the
Books of Kings', in C. Cox (ed.), *VIIth Congress of the IOSCS, Leuven 1989*
(SCSS, 31; Atlanta: Scholars Press, 1991), pp. 285-99.

in the text as an artefact.[106] Even those scholars interested in charting the compositional and editorial stages of a biblical book must begin with the extant versions. Where my approach differs from other historical approaches is that judgment is reserved on matters of multiplicity of authorship. This basic strategy is not without precedent. For instance, Mullen has likewise taken this position.[107] I will speak of 'writers' below, but this remains a kind of short-hand for all the different combinations of composition, editing, glossing, and so on, which would have been involved in the book's production. A synchronic approach remains problematic in other ways, even if I do wish to focus on the text's expressly literary features. The actual date range I accept as possible for the book is kept relatively wide, thus begging the question of what 'time' my synchronic ('all at one time') reading seeks to illuminate. 'Synchronic' also seems to fly in the face of the recognition of the processes of composition and transmission, as well as my emphasis on the processes of ethnic self-awareness. This study, therefore, runs no small risk in positing a synchronic text in an admittedly fluid environment. In many ways this is merely substituting the academic quest for the 'original', 'authentic' or 'pristine' text for an arbitrary construct. But since we have no firm way of introducing diachronic concerns in a systematic way with any kind of precision in terms of dates and places, it is at least a necessary risk which can be minimized by keeping the artificiality of it in mind.

In view of this, little attempt will be made here to isolate specific matters of provenance in Kings' 'new' historical context, and any hypothetical scenarios offered here hardly compare to the level of specificity that my predecessors have striven for in their 'conventional' contexts in the 'pre-exilic' and 'exilic' periods. It would be foolish to turn from one road down which one has gone too far, simply to go too far, or in the wrong direction, down another, even if it can be defended as the 'right' one. Rather than producing a social and historical map of the different images and their 'imaginers', something more tentative, or (to preserve a sense of optimism) exploratory is needed. The severe critiques which can be levied against so many tenets of biblical scholarship, combined with the new vistas opened by merging biblical studies with literary and social scientific fields, implies that Kings remains rather unknown territory, and so such an exploration may be what is

106. On the 'historical' in the synchronic, see Barr, 'The Synchronic', pp. 1-14.
107. Mullen, *Narrative History*, pp. 8-9.

required. By keeping open as many variables as possible, such an initial synchronic reading may be largely indeterminate, but this indeterminacy opens multiple routes of interpretation which may raise new questions about provenance, and refine subsequent researches. The way ahead, as I see it, is to look at the 'social metaphors' of Israel employed and constructed in the book and, if only in general terms, to relate it to what may be surmised of the overall historical context.

I will posit some ideas about the social climate in which the book may have been produced, but generally these are deductions based on a comparison of the text with the 'Persian' contexts as developed from the proposal by Davies. This, of course, is not proof of this proposal. It would do no good to investigate Kings in this scenario only to conclude at the end that the facts of the book's composition have been established. The methodology of 'seek and ye shall find' is another of scholarship's all-too-popular axioms, whether one likes to admit it or not. Perhaps new research will uncover other likely scenarios, at which point new explorations of Kings will begin again. Possibly, some of these may be of the 'constructionist' variety as well. Such an approach is not the ultimate perspective on the book, but it is, at least, one which can take into account the complexity of the representation of the past, and so it can provide a route into a most intriguing piece of literature. Every society and every person is involved in a constant process of articulation of identity. Invariably, this is punctuated by specific projects; books are commissioned or written, 'traditions' are interpreted, protests are made, 'order' established. 'Members' are segregated from 'others' and, invariably, immutable boundaries are crossed and altered, only to be passionately defended once again.

For the producers of Kings, the reification of a more or less comprehensive Israelite heritage must have been as difficult as it was necessary. The conflicting goals of the Jerusalem and Samarian (and probably other) religious and administrative elites could not be swept under the table. It is easy to argue that Kings suggests Jerusalem is necessary to the spiritual wholeness of greater Israel, and yet with the schism between Judah and Israel it is this 'wholeness' which is stressed to the breaking point. It is, in my view, 'wholeness', both political and spiritual (the two are linked), that is most at issue in Kings. Yet, Jerusalem's position is distinctly ambiguous; the book leaves it as the rejected centre of an emptied land. In many ways one may see in the book a clash between strong regional identities (or multiple identities formed around two regional heritages). These find no real resolution, but moral and historical dilemmas forbid the imposition of simple, heavy-handed hierarchy. In my view, it is much harder to see Kings explicitly supporting the 'returnees' as being the whole of 'Israel', as do Ezra and Nehemiah. Kings may be inclusivist in that it accommodates the northern history and reduces Judah to the same 'exilic' state as Israel.[108] As I have noted, many have dated Kings to a time prior to the Persian era, on grounds that it did not imply an eventual return. If such arguments fail on grounds of the persistence of the notion of exile, then one might still see Kings as displaying an 'exilicist' perspective as a counter-theme to 'exile and restoration' within the broad ideological universe. This general impression will be defended below. As should be the case in any reading of Kings, however, I will not attempt to view the book as a closed world, which finds resolution in all of its themes. To borrow another phrase, the symbolic universe of Kings is incipiently problematic. This situation, however, provides the joy in reading the book and not merely the hurdles to overcome in attempts to reduce it to a single, consistent system.

108. Chronicles has a very different view of 'inclusion', which ignores the history of the north, but assimilates penitent northerners into an 'Israel' which is definitely orientated towards Jerusalem. See H.G.M. Williamson, *Chronicles*.

Part II
EMPIRE AND ENTROPY

Chapter 4

DUALITY IN THE UNITED MONARCHY

1. *Samuel and Kings*

Before turning to the study of Kings directly, I turn to the story of the United Monarchy in Samuel. Even though I question the unity of the Former Prophets as a single historical work, it is clear that Samuel and Kings have a lot to do with each other, and a number of themes initiated in Samuel are further developed in Kings. The transition between the books is relatively smooth, and many writers hold that the division between Samuel and Kings is largely artificial, and was determined only by scroll length.[1] Complicating the issue is that many scholars have recognized in 1 Kings 1 and 2 an intrinsic component of one of the underlying compositional layers of the book of Samuel, the so called 'Succession Narrative'.[2] The influence of this general thesis has led some to link the opening chapters of Kings to Samuel at the expense of their role in the opening of Kings. For De Vries, 1 Kings 1–2 is a 'severed trunk' which was cut adrift from the rest of Samuel by the interpolation of 2 Samuel 21–24. This misalignment is to be resisted by the modern reader.[3] A number of scholars, more interested in the thematic and structural features of this literature than its compositional history, link 1 Kings 1–2 to the rest of Solomon's story in Kings,

---

1.   Montgomery, *Kings*, p. 1; P.K. McCarter Jr, *II Samuel* (AB, 9; Garden City, NY: Doubleday, 1984), p. 17; Jones, *Kings*, I, p. 2.

2.   The popularity of this idea is usually traced to L. Rost, *The Succession to the Throne of David* (trans. M.D. Rutter and D.M. Gunn; HTIBS, 1; Sheffield: Almond Press, 1982), original: *Die Überlieferung von der Thronnachfolge Davids* (BWANT, 42; Stuttgart: W. Kohlhammer, 1926). The narrative strand as argued by Rost (pp. 69-73) comprises 2 Sam. 9–20 and 1 Kgs 1–2, albeit with some accretions.

3.   De Vries, *1 Kings*, p. 8.

although in this they do disagree amongst themselves.[4] This situation, however, must be judged in the light of the fact that the Greek texts are not in unanimous agreement about where the break should be made between 2 and 3 Kingdoms. The majority of them agree with the MT that the break occurs after the notice that David built an altar and that the plague against Israel was averted (MT: 2 Sam. 24.25). But a number of manuscripts, attributed to the Lucianic recension (boc₂e₂), make the division after the equivalent verse to 1 Kgs 2.11, thus including the whole of the story of David's life in the books of Samuel. Josephus begins the eighth book of his *Antiquities* at this point. For some, Lucian offers the more logical break.[5] Montgomery holds that there is evidence of yet another division in the early Greek traditions after 1 Kgs 2.46a. This evidence is the collection of what he considers supplementary material collected at the end of a book. Based on the syntax, Montgomery thinks that the next section represents a fresh beginning.[6] I will leave it to others to argue concerning the historical development of the divisions between the books. While I maintain that Kings could have been at least substantially edited independently of Samuel, and the varying portraits of David between the books suggests this as well, the connections between the two books cannot be completely ignored.

Duality within greater Israel, between Judah and Israel, is a major feature of Samuel, even if it does not mark the initial establishment of the monarchy itself. Yahweh's answer to the peoples' demand for a king is the elevating of Saul to be *nagid* (נגיד) over 'my [Yahweh's] people, Israel' (1 Sam. 9.16). This conception of 'Israel' as the deity's

---

4. Parker, 'Repetition'; Frisch, 'Structure'. See too, M. Brettler, 'The Structure of 1 Kings 1–11', *JSOT* 49, pp. 87-97. Frisch, 'Structure', p. 7, acknowledges that 1 Kgs 1–2 may have belonged to a source now spread between Samuel and Kings. Parker and Frisch have engaged in a debate on these issues; see also K.I. Parker, 'The Limits to Solomon's Reign: A Response to Amos Frisch', *JSOT* 51 (1991), pp. 15-21; A. Frisch, 'The Narrative of Solomon's Reign: A Rejoinder', *JSOT* 51 (1991), pp. 22-24. Parker addresses 1 Kgs 1–11 again in 'Solomon as Philosopher King? The Nexus of Law and Wisdom in I Kings 1–11', *JSOT* 53 (1992), pp. 75-91.

5. J.S. Thackeray, 'The Greek Translators of the Four Books of Kings', *JTS* 8 (1907), pp. 262-78 (265-66), favours Lucian's division as 'more natural'. Lucian's translation of 1 Kgs 1–2.11 lacks some of the characteristics of the translations of the 'βγ' section (2 Kgdms 11.2 to 3 Kgdms 2.11). Thackeray thinks these were removed as 'monstrosities'.

6. Montgomery, *Kings*, p. 1.

people is hardly to be taken as a general reference to the north. Later, in Kings, this very phrase may be full of irony, and raises the question to what degree the davidic rulers were the sole legitimate representatives of Yahweh in the political life of Israel. At this place in Samuel, however, the נגיד over Yahweh's people is for the benefit of all. The comprehensive jurisdiction of Saul is reinforced in 1 Sam. 10.20-25, as he is made king before all the tribes. When David is anointed in 1 Sam. 16.1-13, he is selected as the future king. His kingdom can only be understood as greater Israel, for Saul has already fallen out of favour with Yahweh, and David is destined to be his replacement.[7] Even so, separate mention of the people from Judah and Israel in 1 Samuel is not hard to find. In some cases it is the narrator who recognizes the division. In 1 Sam. 11.8 and 15.4, the armed men of Judah and Israel are numbered separately. Similarly, the army is divided on regional lines in 17.52, and in 18.16 all Judah and Israel love David. The imposition of plurality by the narrator in these verses is not really necessary to the plot itself, although they are ominous signs of later events.

The complexity of the situation between Judah and Israel in the books of Samuel really develops in 2 Samuel 2, in the ensuing power-vacuum after the deaths of Saul and Jonathan. Rather than simply become the king of greater Israel, David is anointed king over the 'House of Judah' (vv. 1-4) by the Judaeans. In vv. 8-9, Abner, Saul's commander, makes Saul's son, Ishbosheth, king over 'Israel in its entirety' ישׂראל כלה (v. 9).[8] The stage is then set with all Israel opposed to David, king of the 'House of Judah' (vv. 4, 7, 10, 11). Here one may see the northern 'majority' being granted the name 'Israel'.[9] Still, one could wonder if the change from 'all Israel', that is, Joab's intended constituency for Ishbosheth (v. 9), to simply 'Israel' in the narrator's summary of Ishbosheth's reign (v. 10), indicates that Abner sought to place Saul's heir as king of greater Israel, while the narrator accords him a reign only over the north.

The resulting power struggle in 2 Samuel 2 and 3 is not actually

---

7. Saul's fall from grace is told in 1 Sam. 15.

8. According to McCarter, *II Samuel*, p. 88, it is the equivalent of 'all Israel', (כל ישׂראל) in 2 Sam. 3.12, 21. In 2 Sam. 2.8-9, the specific territories of Gilead, Jezreel, Ephraim and Benjamin and that of the Ashurites are mentioned, with the new king himself going to Mahanaim.

9. Danell, *The Name Israel*, pp. 75-79. A 'northern' understanding is also suggested by McCarter, *II Samuel*, p. 88.

billed as a war between Judah and Israel, however, but between the 'House of Saul' and the 'House of David' (2 Sam. 3.1, 6). In 2 Samuel 2, Abner's men are called the 'servants of Ishbosheth' (v. 12), 'men of Israel' (v. 17), 'Israel' (v. 28), 'sons of Benjamin' (v. 25; cf. v. 15), 'Benjamin and the men of Abner' (v. 31), 'his (Abner's) men' (v. 29). On the other hand, David's soldiers are never called the 'sons of Judah', or any such title; they are the servants of David (vv. 15, 17, 30, 31; or 'all the people' vv. 28, 30). Danell suspects that this wording reflects David's desire to avoid implicating Judah in a civil war, using his own personal troops instead. It is not a war between two nations, but between two 'pretenders' to Saul's throne. By refraining from depicting the war as between Judah and Israel, the writers limit the implication of a civil war.[10] It is perhaps not unimportant that the book records that David's destiny of rule over greater Israel is ultimately achieved through Abner's intrigue, and the recognition of David's destiny on the part of the elders of the north, rather than brute force (3.6-21; 5.1-3). For as much as this treason results in a moral dilemma, the mutual recognition of solidarity under David smoothes the re-establishment of the United Monarchy. In Kings, a similar preference for terms describing wars between kings, instead of greater Israelite civil wars, is sometimes evident (cf. 1 Kgs 14.30; 15.6, 16, 32). A simple explanation may be that the king may represent the whole nation.[11] On the other hand, the purported royal disputes distance the cause of battles somewhat from the disunity at a civic level. If the two kingdoms are metaphorical projections of fractious, post-monarchic 'Israel', then the wars can be attributed to the kings and the (defunct) political system they represent, and not assimilated as essential to the idea of Israel as the 'people of Yahweh'. Such an interpretation is supported by 1 Kgs 12.23-24, in which Rehoboam and the people under his rule are forbidden to fight their brethren, the 'sons of Israel'. All of these battles, it should be noted, are relatively early in the history of the schism's aftermath. Later in Kings, however, Judah is defeated by Israel. This war, however, is described as the result of the arrogance and folly of Judah's king Amaziah. His rival, Jehoash, even warns him that he and Judah may fall. The defeat of *Judah*, then, is the wages of Amaziah's errors (2 Kgs 14.8-14).

10. Danell, *The Name Israel*, p. 77.

11. In 2 Kgs 16.7, Ahaz asks the Assyrian king for aid against the kings of Aram and Israel.

Unity within greater Israel returns in 2 Samuel 5, and this episode also fashions an important lens by which to interpret parts of Kings. Verses 1-5 tell of David's elevation to the kingship of Israel. At first glance, one might think that this involved only the northern tribes, since here the elders of Israel (v. 3) travel to David's Judaean capital of Hebron, suggesting that these are the same northern elders who were addressed by Abner (2 Sam. 3.17-19).[12] Yet, the initial meeting is with 'all the tribes' (2 Sam. 5.1), and 'all' the elders meet with David in v. 3, suggesting even the elders of Judah had joined in making David king. This is further reinforced by the recollection of Yahweh's words that David would shepherd the deity's people, and be נגיד of Israel (v. 2). That an event relevant for the whole of Israel is being narrated is also suggested by the covenant ceremony and David's anointing (v. 3). In my view, David has not simply added new territories to his control, nor has he become king of Israel as well as king of Judah. Rather, he has been elevated to a fundamentally new status, king of 'greater' Israel, which not only supersedes any dominion over only Judah, but is the full realization of his destiny. Even though his reign over Judah is specified in his forty years as king (vv. 4-5), the continuing narrative reports on his glowing success at winning a new capital, Jerusalem, at least one part of which is named after its conqueror, Zion becoming the 'city of David' (vv. 6-9). The reputation of the newly-crowned king spreads internationally. Hiram of Tyre acknowledges that for the sake of his people, Israel, Yahweh had exalted David's reign over Israel (vv. 11-12). On the other hand, the Philistines learn the hard way about the might of the newly reconsolidated Israel (vv. 17-25). Chapter 6 continues the consolidation of David's rule with the troublesome transportation of the ark to Jerusalem. The high point of the celebration of the reconstituted United Monarchy occurs in 2 Samuel 7 when, in a revelation to the prophet Nathan, Yahweh forbids David to build a 'house' (temple), בית, for Yahweh, promising instead to build one (dynasty) for David.

The promise of an eternal 'house' for David in 2 Samuel 7 is a watershed episode. The superfluity of a house for the deity is asserted by his recollections of his wanderings ever since the exodus (v. 6). Yahweh's people, Israel, will be shepherded by David, the נגיד, and a place for them will be appointed in which they will have peace from

12. As accepted by McCarter, *II Samuel*, p. 116.

the troubles that plagued them since the days of their judges (vv. 8-11). David's line is granted an eternal kingship, Yahweh asserting his favour will never be withdrawn from him, as it was withdrawn from Saul (vv. 12-16). David's response to the promise (vv. 18-29) asserts the eternal links between the deity and Israel (vv. 23-24). The apparent incongruity between this chapter and the destruction of the dynasty and exile of greater Israel in Kings has been discussed to some extent above. It is clear, however, that neither David nor Yahweh suggest any level of duality between Judah and Israel. In receiving his 'house' David celebrates the uniqueness of Israel, and the uniqueness of their relationship with Yahweh, demonstrated by Yahweh's actions during the exodus (vv. 23-24). This is something that will also be found in 1 Kings 8, in which Yahweh's house is consecrated. Moreover, it establishes Jerusalem as the centre of greater Israel, not just Judah, and therefore, the role of the city in the post-schism episodes in Kings is ambiguous. One could see this ambiguity as part of the matrix of thinking about 'Judah-ism' which seeks to embrace a greater conception of an 'Israelite' heritage. If the scholar is to read this against post-monarchic pluralism, or rivalry between a Judaean-focused Israelite heritage and one with an accent on Samaria, one may see an articulation of the difficulties in finding a common royal symbol to unite the two parties, and the different claims to power which the two sides could make, based on the symbol of David, whose dynasty is inextricably linked with Jerusalem and Judah. Even though Judah wins here, it is to be remembered that, earlier, the selection of Jerusalem for David's throne was made only after Israel was united. In Kings, Jerusalem's neutrality is stretched to the breaking point. The loyalty of Judah to its own son and his heirs continues to be a factor.

Duality within the monarchy soon reappears in 2 Samuel. In 2 Sam. 11.11 'Israel and Judah' appear with the ark. In ch. 15, the rebelling Absalom musters support for his coup from all Israel (vv. 2, 6, 10, 13), although it is claimed that two hundred from Jerusalem attend him at Hebron, unaware of his intent (v. 11). In the following chapters, the rebellion leads to the raised hopes of the survivors of Saul, that they will be the true beneficiaries of the situation (2 Sam. 16.3). It is David who is pitted against Israel (2 Sam. 16.3, 15, 18), including Judah (cf. 2 Sam. 17.11, 'all Israel, from Dan to Beersheba').[13] After the rebellion

13. Among those who attempt to reconstruct the history of the rebellion there is some dispute about how to view Judah's role, see McCarter, *II Samuel*, pp. 357-58,

is quashed, David returns past Gilgal, with the Judaean army and part of the Israelite one (2 Sam. 19.41). Open rivalry breaks out in 2 Sam. 19.42-44. Judah gains the upper hand, asserting that they are the king's relatives, although the northerners object that since they represent the majority of greater Israel, they have more claims on the king's favour. 2 Samuel 20 tells of the failed rebellion of Sheba, who capitalized on the ill-will generated by David. With words that will be recalled in the later division of Solomon's kingdom, he leads the northerners to give up their hopes in the davidic dynasty (2 Sam. 20.1-2; cf. 1 Kgs 12.16-17), while the Judaeans remain loyal. The wise woman of Abel shames the bloodthirsty Joab into sparing the city in which Sheba has taken refuge, who eventually becomes the only casualty of his own uprising (2 Sam. 20.14-22). Whatever animosity existed between the primary regions of greater Israel, however, wanton bloodshed in its name is portrayed as unjustifiable, not only here in 2 Samuel 20 but in 1 Kgs 12.24 as well. At the end of his campaign against Sheba, Joab is called the commander of the army of Israel (2 Sam. 20.23). With this note, then, it seems as if the two regions are now finally united, but this is not the case.

In 2 Sam. 24.1, the reader is told that Yahweh was angry with 'Israel', and that David was incited against them and he is ordered to enumerate 'Israel and Judah'. When the numbers are totalled in v. 9 the number of battle-ready Israelites is given before that of Judaean men. McCarter offers a discussion on the association of censuses and plagues made in the ancient Near East. He comments on the need for ritual purity of those enumerated, and the frequent use of censuses to draw up military conscription lists.[14] All of these elements are present here in this episode, as a plague is averted when the destructive angel turns to Jerusalem. David begs forgiveness, builds an altar and offers propitiation in the form of sacrifices, accepting full guilt (2 Sam. 24.16-25). This episode seems to intimate the eventual divisions and strife which would so characterize the narratives in Kings, and yet it is not a

386-87. McCarter argues that Judah and Israel were both involved in the rebellion. Whatever the events actually were, McCarter's arguments can be added to the statement in 2 Sam. 17.11 about the role of Judah in the story. It would be odd for Absalom, rebelling in his Judaean birthplace of Hebron, to be the favourite of a northern regional uprising. David does not flee to Judah, but away from it, while Absalom's main supporters are two important Judaeans.

14. McCarter, *II Samuel*, pp. 512-14.

simple foreshadowing. The separate enumeration of Judah and Israel in Samuel juxtaposes the armies of Israel and Judah, and the implication of rivalry between them perhaps reflects the punitive aspect of the census.[15] The duplicitous nature of Yahweh in this episode is inexplicable, and the efforts which have been expended to determine the conflation of sources, or the reworking of existing documents are at least understandable, even if they are not the final word on the chapter. There are many important themes in 2 Samuel 24, but what is most relevant here is how the theme of cultic purity involves David, who builds an altar at the Jerusalem site at which Yahweh's destroying angel was halted (vv. 18-25). The angel destroyed thousands from all Israel, 'from Dan to Beersheba' (2 Sam. 24.15). The restraint shown at Jerusalem, then, means mercy for all Israel, evidenced by v. 25 in which the plague is lifted not from Judah and Israel, but from 'Israel'. The linking of the celebration of a propitiatory ritual with a suggestion of the alleviation of rivalry seems to offer a reflection of 1 Kings 8, where Solomon, to whom the schism in 1 Kings 11–12 is ultimately linked, dedicates his new temple. Even if Samuel and Kings do not clearly associate the place of David's sacrifice with the temple site, the two episodes seem to be related. It is interesting, therefore, that in 1 Kings 8, there is no hint of a division within greater Israel (as I will illustrate in Chapter 10). What has transpired in 2 Samuel 24 is the recognition of division, particularly pointed out by the enumeration of *military* personnel, but still Yahweh punishes his people as an integral whole. This, of course, raises issues of Yahweh's morality. A similar problem arises in Kings.

In Samuel, there is the first United Monarchy, and the first period of regional autonomy, and, ultimately, a political reunification. David assumes rule over Judah in the midst of a power-vacuum, but he still seems sensitive to the heritage of a united Israel. He orders his lament over Saul and Jonathan to be taught to Judah (2 Sam. 1.18). In 2 Samuel, reintegration is attempted, but the old division is continually reaffirmed, with David perhaps not as wise as he should be in his

---

15. The question of Yahweh's culpability in his orders to David cannot be addressed here. In 1 Kgs 11-12, the schism is blamed on Solomon's excesses, yet the actual political dissolution of the United Monarchy is set in the context of a popular ultimatum delivered to Solomon's heir. One may also compare 2 Sam. 24 to Exod. 7.3; 10.1, 20, 27; 11.9-10 in which Yahweh 'hardened Pharaoh's heart' against Moses' demands to release the Israelites, so that Yahweh's power might be revealed.

response to this. David's anomalous position vis-à-vis the divisions within his kingdom in Samuel seems to encapsulate the trouble with David: is he the figurehead of Judah, or of greater Israel? To whom is David himself to be more loyal to, his own Judaean kin, or the other tribes who form the majority? If it is David who aggravates regional tensions, is one to be loyal to him or to the collective? In Kings, these questions are raised anew, but with more complex twists as David himself is no longer alive, and new kings of the north are raised by the god who once promised David an eternal reign; the same god who eventually was willing to give up both kingdoms. Kings, then, takes up a theme familiar to the reader of the earlier components of the Former Prophets. The entropy, or the forces of decay and corruption seemingly intrinsic to 'Israel' are followed through to their bitter, exilic end. This end, however, is not absolute. Whereas Samuel ends by looking ahead to the United Monarchy, and Judges painfully awaits a king (cf. Judg. 17.6; 18.1; 19.1; 21.25), Kings, in the very midst of its tale of destruction, establishes a seemingly fragile but tenacious grip on the future. By recalling the myths of Israels origins, and assimilating these to the story of the monarchy, the divisions and disputes of greater Israel are accommodated and explained. Divergent view points can each find a voice in a complex past. The story told by Kings, then, becomes a new myth of origin in which exile is the created order; Israel has its place, and in the internalization of the ideals upon which the squandered opportunities of the past were based, it also has the certainty of communion with the divine, and the transcendence of the political limitations placed on a dispersed people.

2. The United Monarchy in Kings

The theme of the initial episode in Kings is no novelty to the reader of Samuel: rivalry for the throne. In 1 Kings 1, Bathsheba, Solomon's mother, and Nathan, the prophet, are faced with Adonijah's claim on the throne of the aged David. Although the story itself deals mainly with how Solomon came to reign, it has some interesting features, which suggest that Solomon might not be as careful with the fragile union between Israel and Judah as he might have been. This is implicit in a number of instances where choice of wording suggests some level of internal favouritism.

The references to 'Israel' in 1 Kings 1–2 are best taken as indicating greater Israel.[16] By themselves, the two references to 'all Israel' in 1 Kgs 1.20 (spoken by Bathsheba) and 2.15 (Adonijah) seem innocent enough, but when seen against the words given other characters, however, they do offer some means of comparing the priorities of the speakers, Solomon in particular. The first fracture in the appearance of a unified greater Israel is evident in the initial stages of Adonijah's attempt on the throne. In Adonijah's mustering of his support, he is reported to have called on 'the sons of the king, and all the men of Judah, servants of the king' (1 Kgs 1.9). Nothing is said of representatives of the other tribes. Adonijah banks on the belief that Judah is the key to control all Israel.[17] The narrator's words seem to imply a certain level of nepotism and tribal favouritism within David's administration, and this will only be heightened in Solomon's time. This can also be seen, partially, in the differences in words given to Solomon and his father on a few select issues. The first concerns references to Yahweh. The expression יהוה אלהי ישראל, 'Yahweh, the God of Israel', appears twice in the first two chapters (numerous times subsequently).[18] In 1 Kgs 1.29-30 David swears by the life of Yahweh that he will fulfil an earlier vow he made in the name of the God of Israel (v. 30) that Solomon should succeed him. It is interesting that the epithet is used in association with the original vow of succession. In a similar fashion in

---

16. Cf. MT's 'the borders of Israel' גבול ישראל. LXX[L] at 3 Kgdms 1.3 has 'in all Israel', considered more probable by De Vries, *1 Kings*, p. 4, although little is gained by preferring one or the other. In 2 Kgs 10.32 and 14.25, גבול ישראל seems to refer to the territory of the northern kingdom only. The paucity of these references make it hard to consider the term as any sort of 'technical' theological designation, and the context grants the most important nuances, although these two passages, and particularly the latter, are still deserving of investigation (see below). The term 'Land of Israel' is also used sparingly; 2 Kgs 5.2, 4; 6.23.

17. He does have the support of Joab, the army commander (1 Kgs 1.7, 19), and other officers (1.25). In contrast, in Absalom's assumption of royal functions, Absalom offers judgment for those of any tribe of Israel (2 Sam. 15.2), and seeks support from every tribe (v. 10), duping a number of Judaeans to offer initial support (v. 11). Ironically, Absalom seeks to establish himself in Hebron, the city where David reigned over Judah and was also offered Israel (2 Sam. 5.1-5). In the reported speech of Bathsheba and Nathan (1 Kgs 1.17-21, 24-27), David is told that Adonijah had mustered some named and unnamed officials and the 'sons of the king', although he is not told of the 'men of Judah' who the narrator reports are implicated in the rebellion (v. 9).

18. There is probably no reason to suspect that the absence or presence of any divine epithet is solely due to a consistent pattern of usage by different writers.

1 Kgs 1.47, a messenger reports on what the courtiers said to David. They spoke of 'God' אלהיך (K), אלהים (Q) magnifying Solomon. When David's response is recalled, however, the divine name with the epithet appears (1 Kgs 1.48). What this seems to imply is that David is concerned that what is at issue is not simply rights to the throne as personal authority, even if, in v. 48, he speaks of 'his (own) throne'.[19] By invoking 'the God of Israel' he suggests that the king's throne does not symbolize personal ownership of Israel.[20] David has his throne, but Israel belongs to Yahweh. For his part, however, Solomon says nothing of the 'God of Israel' in these chapters (cf. 1 Kgs 2.23-24, 26, 32, 43).[21] This lack is perhaps most conspicuous in 1 Kgs 2.24 where Solomon recalls that Yahweh had placed him on the throne of David, recalling David's vow in 1.48. The simpler divine name put in Solomon's mouth makes him appear less aware than David of the national or ethnic focus of Yahweh's dealing with monarchs. A similar impression is gained in comparing David's labelling of Abner and Amasa as the commanders of the forces of Israel in 1 Kgs 2.5 with Solomon's later words on the subject. When Solomon carries out the advice of David concerning Joab, who is held responsible for the deaths of the two commanders, he refers to Abner as the commander of Israel, and Amasa as the commander of Judah (1 Kgs 2.32). Solomon seems not to care about healing the old division, and fittingly, he shall be responsible for the ultimate collapse of the United Monarchy.

If David's own position on the fundamental unity of greater Israel was somewhat compromised in Samuel, it is a situation seemingly compounded in David's commands about Solomon. In 1 Kgs 1.34, David orders Solomon to be anointed 'king over Israel', מלך על־ישראל, while in the next verse, Solomon is appointed *nagid*, נגיד, over Judah and Israel.[22] David seems to use 'Israel' in two different senses,

---

19. David does speak of Yahweh as Solomon's god in 1 Kgs 2.3, however, but legitimacy is no longer in question. Rather, with the expression 'your God', David reinforces Solomon's obligations. David refrains from labelling Yahweh the 'God of Israel' in 2.4 when he recalls the vow the deity made concerning David's continued tenure on the 'Throne of Israel', but here the association between Yahweh and Israel is already apparent.

20. In 1 Kgs 1–2, the throne is usually referred to as being David's or Solomon's, as I will detail below.

21. Although he will in 1 Kgs 8, as I will describe below.

22. LXX[L] in v. 34 adds 'and Judah' which is considered by De Vries, *1 Kings*, p. 5, to be a gloss. He also considers that the reference to 'Judah' in v. 35 is

the first in a comprehensive sense, the second with the more restricted denotation of the northern territories. It is, however, a reflection of the history of separate thrones as related in Samuel and later in Kings that the term 'king' is used to mark Solomon's dominion over greater Israel. The verse seems all the more ironic as Solomon is the final king of the United Monarchy. On the other hand, 1 Kgs 1.35 is the only verse in Samuel–Kings which speaks of a נגיד of both Judah and Israel. The other references to נגיד indicate persons of great symbolic importance in transitions from one phase to another in Israelite monarchic history. For as much as Solomon is an important king, his succession to David's throne does not mark the sharp break with the past that the rise of the other נגידים seems to represent. 1 Kgs 1.35, however, may still be interpreted in view of the earlier נגיד references. In Samuel, Saul and then David receive two titles, they are both king and נגיד (1 Sam. 8.22; 9.16; 10.1; 2 Sam. 5.1-5). The נגיד in Samuel was the divine response to a demand or requirement for a new leader. 1 Kgs 1.35 seems to be recalling this situation and conflating it with the question of unity within the United Monarchy. The title 'king' has already been claimed on behalf of Solomon in 1.34 and in reference to a unified kingdom. In v. 35 David closes off consideration of a division within the United Monarchy under the auspices of potential leaders claiming the title which marked Saul and David as the human representatives of a new phase in Israel's history as a theocracy. Both components, Judah and Israel, are included in the jurisdiction of a single נגיד. No new phase in history, other than a simple succession of kings, can be legitimized, at least in David's mind.

The story of Solomon's judgment in 1 Kgs 3.16-28 concludes with the notice that 'all Israel' saw that Solomon displayed divine wisdom. There are many nuances and ambiguities in this episode, and it has

secondary as it is represented inconsistently. In MT and LXX[B], it follows Israel, while it precedes 'Israel' in LXX[L]. De Vries argues that such references to Judah make little sense in a United Monarchy context, but does not address the Samuel stories, or relate this to the later stories of the division of the kingdom. There is, of course, little to gain in interpreting the story as a product from the time of the United Monarchy, and so the authors' knowledge of the existence of separate kingdoms must be assumed as probable at virtually every compositional stage. It is probable that LXX[L] v. 34 is an addition, but the changed order in v. 35 is less than settled. That LXX[L] would have Israel and Judah in v. 34 and Judah and Israel in v. 35 indicates that, perhaps, little should be made of the changed order.

been the centre of much research, certainly not the least interesting being the number of feminist readings. Some scholars, such as K.A. Deurloo and Carole Fontaine, find in this story a metaphor for the history of Israel, or an intimation of the ultimate division of the kingdom. The proposed butchering of the child is taken as suggestive of the schism.[23] If the proposed analogy is pursued, a number of questions present themselves. Are the roles of the women purely incidental, necessary for the logical setting of the story, or do they represent rival conceptions of how Solomon should rule the whole of Israel? Solomon's eventual solution recognizes the propriety of the claimant who affirms the rights of the child to life. Ironically, it is through the surrender of her claim that these 'proper' rights are established in the first place. No such solution preserves the integrity of Israel at the schism, however. There is no outraged mother to plead Israel's case as the angry Yahweh divides the nation between the house of David and the new dynasty of Jeroboam (cf. 1 Kgs 11). By what miracle does Israel yet live?[24] That miracle, as I will describe in the next chapter, is found in the evocation of Israel's earlier history, especially the exodus myth. Israel is, in a manner of speaking, not slain by the deity's sword of judgment, but is twice reborn.

Perhaps the most difficult passages concerning regionalism within the United Monarchy episodes of Kings, however, are found in chs. 4 and 5. These chapters are marked by severe textual differences, including many uncertain readings, and different placements of passages, and, in the LXX, repetitions in the supplements to ch. 2. Among the features of these chapters, most interesting are, again, the mention of Judah and Israel as separate regions, and the expression 'all Israel'. As noted already, 'all Israel' in 1 Kgs 1.20 and 2.15 are not problematic in

23. K.A. Deurloo, 'The King's Wisdom in Judgment: Narration as Example (I Kings iii)', in A.S. van der Woude (ed.), *New Avenues in the Study of the Old Testament* (OTS, 25; Leiden: E.J. Brill, 1989), pp. 11-21 (20). C.R. Fontaine, 'The Bearing of Wisdom on the Shape of 2 Samuel 11–12 and 1 Kings 3', in A. Brenner (ed.), *A Feminist Companion to Samuel and Kings* (FCB, 5; Sheffield: Sheffield Academic Press, 1994), pp. 143-60 (159), originally published in *JSOT* 34 (1986), pp. 61-77. See her own response to the reprinted article in the same volume, 'A Response to the "Bearing of Wisdom"', pp. 161-67 (165).

24. I am cautioned against drawing the analogy between the judgment and the schism too closely, or taking interpretation along these lines too far by Francis Landy (personal communication). My statements here are far more modest than I originally planned.

their reference to greater Israel. Similarly, Solomon's reputation for justice spreads across 'all Israel' in 1 Kgs 3.28, here also to be taken in its most comprehensive scope. In 1 Kgs 11.16, a similar understanding should be adopted as well, since the talk is of Joab's command over 'all Israel' during the occupation of Edom in the time of David. 1 Kgs 11.42 is a closing note about the length of Solomon's reign 'in Jerusalem'. In the MT, he is said to have reigned over 'all Israel' while reference to this is not found in the LXX (cf. 2 Sam. 5.5 and 1 Kgs 2.11). This should not be taken as too weighty a deviation, although MT's insistence that Solomon was the king over 'all Israel' may have been a reflection of the use of 'Israel' in v. 38, which specifies that Jeroboam was to rule all but one tribe. Thus, the MT offers a poignant reminder that Solomon ruled a united nation, but all that is now changing. This may be part of the MT's sharper criticisms of Solomon (see below), but probably little could be built upon it. The first verse of the MT ch. 4 holds that Solomon became king over 'all Israel', while the Greek has only 'Israel'. Little might be made of this, as the MT only seems to reinforce a comprehensive utilization of the name, which is hardly denied in the Greek. On the other hand, the MT's reinforcement is rendered rather ironic as the chapter progresses.

Most of the work on 1 Kgs 4 has followed the approaches criticized in Chapter 2 in attempting to arrive at the 'original' form of the text and gain an accurate view of Solomon's administration, which is at issue therein. Verses 2-6 list Solomon's primary administrators and officers, שׂרים, including upper administrative and record-keeping posts, the army command, the priesthood, an advisor (רעה המלך) and an administrator over other officials (על־הנצבים). These posts are relevant to greater Israel, and not simply the northern territories. The true difficulties begin with 1 Kgs 4.7, which reports that Solomon had twelve officials who were over 'all Israel', נצבים על־כל־ישׂראל, and were to provide for the royal house, each responsible for a month's provision. Verses 8-19 purport to give their names and districts, although the textual variants are numerous, some jurisdictions overlap, and there are other repetitions.[25] The first major problem is that, if 'all

25. P.S. Ash, 'Solomon's? District? List', *JSOT* 67 (1995), pp. 67-86. He contests the usual methodology employed to solve the numerous riddles of the passage, which attempt to recover an original form accurately portraying Solomon's administration. He raises serious questions about the historical veracity of vv. 7-19 in illuminating the reign of Solomon and instead argues convincingly that such an

Israel' in v. 7 means greater Israel, then the absence of a clear mention of an official over Judah in the following Hebrew list (vv. 8-19) is rather conspicuous (I will turn to the LXX below). The list closes with a problematic reference to a single, anonymous, official 'who was in the land' (נציב אחד אשר בארץ). Many take this to be a reference to a Judaean, even though its reading as such makes for thirteen officials, when twelve are demanded by v. 7. In any case, the official is left without any name, a unique occurrence in the list. Recently, Paul Ash has provided a convincing case that it is secondary.[26] Whatever the original list, however, the question demanded by the approach taken here is whether one should see the passage as specifying Judah or not.

The enigmatic passage may refer back to the officer Geber (v. 19a), stressing that he was the only governor of his district, but there are, perhaps, better alternatives.[27] Some favour seeing v. 19 as the corruption of a passage which originally read that one officer was over all those named in the list. A variety of explanations and emendations have been proposed. Simon De Vries suggests that the relative particle אשר in v. 19bβ arose after the loss of the construct 'land of Judah', and served to explain that there was one supernumerary over 'all the land'.[28] Some hold that originally the clause referred back to Azariah, who, in v. 5, is mentioned as being over the officers, נצבים. C.F. Burney accepts Klostermann's view, and would reconstruct על־ [כל־] אחד נציב after הנצבים.[29] Rudolph prefers reconstructing שׂר נצבים, especially in the light of the presence of אשר in the MT.[30] In the equivalent LXX passage (which does read 'land of Judah'), however, there is no counterpart to the relative particle. Yet some support for

early document, in any case, can never be recovered. He suggests instead that the list evolved with changing social perceptions of the past, and this is something I will develop here, but in a way not pursued by Ash. He also provides bibliographical data on treatments of this passage.

26. Ash, 'Solomon's List', pp. 76-77 nn. 42-44. The lack of a personal name or patronym marks it as unique in the list. Jones, *Kings*, I, pp. 141-45, for example, thinks that the original list referred to twelve divisions of Israel, with Judah standing outside the system. De Vries, *1 Kings*, p. 71, thinks the original *eleven* officials excluded one for Judah (Gilead in v. 19 being an earlier gloss).

27. Cf. Jones, *Kings*, I, p. 145.

28. De Vries, *1 Kings*, p. 72.

29. Burney, *Notes*, pp. 46-47.

30. W. Rudolph, 'Zum Text der Königsbucher', *ZAW* 61 (1951), pp. 201-15 (202).

Rudolph might be found in the LXX in spite of the fact that in 4.5, neither the Hebrew or Greek give a title to Azariah, who is 'over the officers' (that he is a שׂר is implied from v. 2). In 3 Kgdms 2.46h, which has some parallels to 4.1-6, Ornia is said to be 'chief over the officers' suggesting שׂר על נעבים.[31] The possibility that the verse was meant to reflect the role of Azariah cannot be ignored, and textual corruption and/or manipulation is a very strong possibility. Whether an older edition of Kings read similarly is a problem which may never be solved. In the MT, however, it does seem as though Judah is to be left without its own officer (נצ'ב) responsible for providing for Solomon. There are, however, possible solutions to this problem.

It is possible to take 'in the land' (בארץ) in 1 Kgs 4.19 as a reference to Judah, with 'the land' being used in a familiar, domestic sense, meaning the 'homeland'. A similar use may be found in 1 Kgs 9.18.[32] While not totally convincing, with only one other example in Kings, such a proposal has the value of needing no emendation. On the other hand, the LXX reads 'Land of Judah'. If the *Vorlage* did not contain 'Judah', the translators may have tried to offer an interpretation of a difficult reading.[33] Alternatively, there is some justification, although it is not completely convincing, that the *Vorlage* did read 'land of Judah'. Some scholars would adjust the verse division recorded in the MT between 4.19 and 20. Verse 20 opens with 'Judah and Israel', and so the suggestion is that 'Judah' should be connected to v. 19, rendering 'land of Judah', and leaving only 'Israel' to prosper under Solomon.[34] I do not favour this because of the presence of 'Judah and Israel' in MT's 1 Kgs 5.5, which seems to frame 4.20-5.5. Counterparts to both 4.20 and 5.5 appear in the LXX miscellanies (3 Kgdms 2.46a, g,

31. E. Tov, 'The LXX Additions (Miscellanies) in 1 Kings 2 (3 Reigns 2)', *Textus* 11 (1984), pp. 90-117 (101).

32. Gray, *Kings*, pp. 135, 140; Montgomery, *Kings*, pp. 122-23. Montgomery gives extra-biblical examples.

33. The strength of the argument rests with 1 Kgs 9.18, 'in the wilderness, in the land' (במדבר בארץ) as specifically referring to 'Judah'. M. Noth, *Könige: I Könige 1–16* (BKAT, 9.1; Neukirchen-Vluyn: Neukirchener Verlag, 1968), p. 202, notes that even the ancient translators had problems with the verse, and that the Syriac read it as 'in the wilderness land', בארץ מדבר, while, as far as it is attested in the Greek, the two geographical terms are linked with και. Noth concludes that the MT suffered some kind of omission after בארץ.

34. E.g. Noth, *Könige*, pp. 57-58; Würthwein, *Könige*, I, p. 42; De Vries, *1 Kings*, p. 72. Such is also implied also by Ash, 'Solomon's List', p. 76.

respectively), and both read 'Judah and Israel'. This suggests that 4.20 should not lose its reference to 'Judah'.[35] It is quite possible that 'Judah' once appeared in both 19 and 20, and that one was lost due to a scribal error.[36] The position that 'Land of Judah' should be reconstructed is usually supported by reference to the LXX.[37] On the other hand, the Greek counterpart does not occur at the end of the list as in the MT, but is second last, behind Issachar. The LXX does not even follow the list of officials with a counterpart to MT's 4.20. The central problem with reconstructing the MT on the grounds of the Greek (and the converse), however, is that attempting to derive a *single, original* list ignores the possibility of tendentious manipulation in both versions. It is also dependent upon the familiar premises that the passage's primary referent, and the scholar's chief concern, is the historical Solomon's reign, and that the original list had to display logical coherence. Even Ash, who argues against recovering an 'original' document, largely ignores his own conclusion that the list underwent modifications reflecting changing social circumstances. He writes: 'the best text to follow in text-critical and redaction-critical analysis' is the MT.[38] What, one may ask, were the social circumstances that led to the different versions? Does the lack of a Judaean officer (at least explicitly) in the MT say something about those who developed this reading (other than their sloppiness in textual transmission and confusing attempts at correction)? I think so.

Whatever the list once read in the MT precursors, its list of twelve officials is complete without Judah, while showing signs of duplication elsewhere.[39] Without a name, or a specified district, the thirteenth official is truly the 'odd man out'. This is at least suggestive that someone may have preferred having some other twelfth district instead of Judah, but chose not to change 'all Israel' in v. 7.[40] This may be why

35. This is against the position of Noth, *Könige*, p. 58, that the unusual order of 'Judah and Israel' in 5.5 is, in turn, dependent upon the errant linking of the two names in 4.19/20.

36. De Vries, *1 Kings*, p. 72.

37. De Vries, *1 Kings*, p. 72; Jones, *Kings*, I, p. 145.

38. See Ash, 'Solomon's List', p. 76 n. 41, on the influence of changing circumstance; see pp. 84-85.

39. Ash, 'Solomon's List', pp. 75-79, discusses the repetitions which may be attributed to glosses.

40. One should not expect to reduce the scope of the problem to arriving at arithmetic exactitude. In 1 Kgs 11.29-40, Ahijah's sign of the robe torn into twelve

'in the land' is left with no specific geographical name in v. 19, even if 'land of Judah' was once found here. But if Judah was excluded (or never intended), what is the force of 'all Israel' in v. 7, and what does this say about the portrayal of Solomon's administration? As I have noted above, the MT displays features which may be taken as increasing the reader's awareness of Solomon's lack of sensitivity concerning fractures in greater Israel. In my view, a similar thing is taking place here. In the beginning of the chapter, we read of Solomon's administrators, all of whom might be taken to be based in Judah, although running affairs throughout greater Israel. In vv. 7-19, however, the obligations of those responsible for providing for the court are officials 'over all Israel' and their provision seems to come from many districts, but *not* Judah. It is with no small level of irony, then, that in 4.20 the reader is informed of *Judah's and Israel's* prosperity, with Judah even warranting mention ahead of Israel. The MT then reports (5.1-6) that Solomon attained vast amounts of provision and tribute from his great empire, and how 'Judah and Israel' lived in safety all his days, adding a note about the size of the king's cavalry force. This passage seems to interrupt a longer unit (1 Kgs 4.7-19; 5.7-8), since 5.7-8 takes up the theme of the officers' delivery of their yearly contributions.[41] The mention of foreign tribute raises the question of why Solomon needed district officials to provide for him in the first place.[42] This question does not completely undermine the image of a happy and rich kingdom, but, along with the exclusion of Judah in the district list, it does imply that perhaps the utopia is somewhat tarnished. The people are happy and prosperous, but is it only temporary? *Judah and Israel* prosper, but is some of Judah's prosperity at the expense of Israel's, and will it come back to haunt Solomon? I suspect that the authors are subtly introducing, at an early

pieces is to signify to Jeroboam that he will rule ten tribes of Israel while one is retained for the heirs of David, leaving one piece, and one tribe, unaccounted for. The creative arithmetic here should be a warning against simply aiming for consistency in a 'recovered' reading of 1 Kgs 4.6-19.

41. That this passage is an interruption is held by many scholars: e.g. Jones, *Kings*, I, pp. 145-46. Yet equivalents to vv. 2-3, listing the amount of supplies, are also found close by in the LXX, following that texts' version of vv. 7-8. A somewhat shorter version of v. 4 is also found here.

42. Ironically, Solomon's supply of Tyrian wood for the temple is at the cost of providing the food for Hiram's house (1 Kgs 5.24-25).

stage, gaps in Solomon's moral character, setting the stage for the division of the kingdom. Another phase is soon in place in 5.27-31, with the transfer of workers from 'all Israel' to Lebanon, to provide timber and stone for the temple. Here the impact of 4.7-19 is particularly hard-felt. Does 'all Israel' here include Judah?[43] In the MT, one has the suggestion that, perhaps, this is not the case.[44]

By contrast, the LXX offers a somewhat different perspective in its version of the list of twelve officials, and different sequencing of those passages which follow the MT's list. I have already pointed out that 4.19 is not followed by the reference to Judah and Israel (MT 4.20). Instead, the LXX continues with the equivalent of MT's 5.7, which is the logical continuation of 4.7-19, as it sums up the work of the officials. The immediate juxtaposition between the riches and provision received from internal and external sources is gone, and the report of the loyalty of Solomon's men does not offer such a strong intimation about the eventual demands of the davidic kings. The LXX[BL] also seems to offer him a better reputation in 4.7-19. Judah is clearly included within the twelve-region system and is not even placed last in the list. The Greek even attempts to find a name for the Judaean official by offering a transliteration of the term 'officer' נציב in v. 18.[45] Furthermore, if Judah is included in the 'all Israel' of v. 7, then there is little to suggest that it did not belong in the 'all Israel' of the forced labour in 5.27.

The next major passage of interest to the present study is that of the dedication of the temple in 1 Kings 8. This episode is best handled in an independent chapter, but something may be said of it here. A major component in 1 Kings 8 is the union of all the components of Israel. In the light of what has already been said above, however, it is interesting

43. The labour force is called the מס in both 5.27 and 4.7. The forced labour of the non-Israelites, in 9.20-22 is called מס־עבד, while Jeroboam's workers of the house of Joseph are labelled a סבל (1 Kgs 11.28).

44. See the similar comments of J.T. Walsh, 'The Characterization of Solomon in First Kings 1–5', *CBQ* 57 (1995), pp. 471-93 (489-90). On Solomon's chariotry, Walsh writes, 'The necessity of such an armed force suggests that the people's security was less the result of Solomon's glorious administration of the empire than of brute strength'.

45. Ash, 'Solomon's List', pp. 76-77, compares נציב in v. 9 (cf. 1 Chron. 11.16; 18.13; 2 Chron. 8.10; 17.2) with the *niphal* participle of the root in 1 Kgs 4.5, 7; 5.7, 30; 9.23. The root is also found at 1 Sam. 10.5 and 13.3, where it is also transliterated in the Greek.

how the MT in the first five verses offers more extensive descriptions of the congregation of Israel than does the LXX. I link this to the suggestions, elsewhere, of the differences in the portrayal of Solomon's insensitivity to internal divisions. If this has given the reader cause to doubt the king, the situation could, potentially, come to a head at the dedication of the temple. Yet little spoils Solomon's greatest hour, not even his own ambition. Solomon is successful in defining Israel as a united and durable nation in their relationship to their deity, through a focus on the new temple. Probably the most important referents to Israel in the chapter, however, are those which call Israel the 'people of Yahweh', 1 Kgs 8.16, 30, 33, 34, 36, 38, 41, 43, 52, 56, 59, 66. These numerous references are made more significant when seen against the number of times when Yahweh is called the 'God of Israel': 1 Kgs 8.15, 17, 20, 23, 25, and in the LXX alone, vv. 26, 28. Both of these expressions highlight the sacral connection between greater Israel and Yahweh, and, as I will describe below, their use in later episodes seems well chosen to make comments on the relationship between Judah and Israel, and on the conception of a greater Israel. Ironically, the next attestations of 'God of Israel' are in 1 Kgs 11.9, 31, in the context of the condemnation of Solomon and the announcement of the division of the kingdom.[46] The repeated association between Israel and Yahweh in Solomon's temple dedication suggests the importance of the event to the construction of an Israelite identity as the people of Yahweh. As I will describe in a later chapter, this is reinforced by a number of other features of the text. This emphasis overshadows the portrayal of Solomon's high regard for his own role and that of the dynasty. As I will argue, this creative moment in Israel's history sees Solomon, at least temporarily, transformed, and so able to provide the necessary leadership figure. But at this sacred moment Solomon is engaged in affairs far larger than himself, as the whole history of Israel converges on this single moment and place. Soon, however, the story will return to matters in which Solomon's humanity is at issue in affairs less monumental, and linked strongly to the sequence of events which led to the exile.

The next episode of note, and one which looks ahead to Solomon's and Israel's failure, is Solomon's second vision, in which the destruction of the temple is predicted, should Solomon disobey Yahweh

---

46. It is used after this a number of times as well, including the condemnation of Jeroboam, 1 Kgs 14.7.

(1 Kgs 9.1-9). As in 1 Kings 8, the opening verses of ch. 9 bring together some concern for the dynasty and the destiny of Israel. The section deals with the promise to Solomon that he will not lack an heir if he minds his ways (vv. 4, 5). In the MT, the heir will sit upon the 'throne of Israel', as in 1 Kgs 2.4, and 8.25. Some contend that these promises only refer to rule over the north, and exclude Judah. This notion will be handled in a short section on the 'throne of Israel' at the end of this chapter. To anticipate my conclusions, the 'throne of Israel' represents sovereignty over greater Israel. 'Israel', in the warnings of vv. 6-9, is hardly to be seen as referring only to the northern component, since Israel is mentioned in conjunction with the 'house', that is, the Jerusalem temple. Furthermore, the land from which Israel is to be expelled is referred to as the land granted to them by Yahweh (v. 7), recalling the exodus. Such recollections clearly mark the rejection of the temple as an event central to the history of greater Israel. The second vision prepares the way, not so much for the division of the kingdom, but the fall of both Israel and Judah. An important feature in this vision is the shift from singular references to Solomon in vv. 3-5, to plural references to Solomon and his sons in v. 6. In v. 9, it seems as if it is not only the actions of Solomon and his descendants which are at issue, but the actions of all Israel (such a shift has attracted a number of theories of multiple authorship, as could be expected, although some find it a unity).[47] Provan reads this passage in the light of the petitions for mercy in 1 Kgs 8.22-53, and sees in it the inevitability of disaster, understanding אם־שׁוב as '*when* (instead of '*if*') you turn aside' (1 Kgs 9.6; cf. 8.46, כי).[48] The inevitability of transgression, of course, is most explicitly stated by Solomon in 1 Kgs. 8.46, claiming that there is no one who does not sin. As ch. 9 opens, then, Solomon is no longer the one who completes the exodus, installing the *Torah*, first delivered to Moses, in the house of Yahweh.

47. Knoppers, *Two Nations*, I, p. 109 nn. 35, 36, offers a brief, but good synopsis of opinions. He argues for three stages of composition (pp. 109-10), and argues that the most likely referent to 'they' in v. 9 is Israel. It is worth noting that v. 9 is the predicted answer to hypothetical questions about why the nation and temple were destroyed. Even so, the strategy of the question and answer sequence must be to explain the preceding, and so, even if Solomon and his 'sons' in v. 6 does not seem to refer to Israel directly, we are entitled to read the whole passage as implying that Israel is being warned here, and not just Solomon and his heirs.

48. Provan, *Kings*, p. 83.

He is, in a manner of speaking, like the Israelites on the plains of Moab, hearing the curses which will befall them, should they dishonour their god in the land he is intending to give them. And, like the Israelites as a whole, Solomon will eventually prove deaf to the warning and so blind to the consequences of his actions.

Of Solomon's sins, the condemnation of 1 Kgs 11.1-8 is unequivocal, but according to v. 4, the unfortunate influence of Solomon's foreign wives led the king astray only in his old age. Many scholars, therefore, see a two-phase representation of Solomon's reign. The first phase celebrates the wealth, wisdom and power of the king, the second tells of the apostasy of his old age. One argument is that the positive portrayal includes ch. 10, with the negative section beginning in ch. 11. Yet, some holding this view consider the opening of Kings, with its story of the rise of Solomon, to be negative.[49] Others find the beginning of the decline in ch. 9, although there is further disagreement at which point in the chapter the criticisms really begin. Such arguments often involve complex structural analyses, with diverse opinions as to how chs. 1 and 2 fit, as a unit, with the rest.[50] Arguments can be made, however, that rather sharp criticisms of Solomon are found throughout his story.

Eslinger even finds a great deal of evidence leading to the conclusion that Solomon's prayers themselves are part of the writer's negative presentation of him. The dedication is the king's subtly-crafted rhetoric intended to cajole Yahweh into granting him an unconditional promise, such as David received. I will have the opportunity, in the final chapter, to address this matter in more detail, although I will qualify Eslinger's findings to no small degree.[51] More moderate impressions of the

---

49. See Porten, 'The Structure', pp. 93-128; Nelson, *Double Redaction*, p. 113; Long, *1 Kings*, pp. 121-22; D. Jobling, '"Forced Labor": Solomon's Golden Age and the Question of Literary Representation', *Sem* 54 (1991), pp. 59-76; Knoppers, *Two Nations*, I, pp. 63-168.

50. Parker, 'Repetition', pp. 23-25 argues for 9.1 as the start of the negative views, with chs. 1–2 as a frame story with 11.14-43 (cf. Noth, *Deuteronomistic History*, pp. 60-61); Brettler, 'The Structure', sees chs. 1–2 as a more negative introduction to the 'blessed' phase of Solomon's reign (1 Kgs 3.3–9.25). A. Frisch, 'Structure', pp. 6-12, begins the critical section at 9.10, with the first two chapters integrated into a great chiastic structure extending to 12.24. Frisch and Parker argue not only from the content of the chapter, but from different understandings of the structure of the Solomon narratives.

51. Eslinger, *Living God*, pp. 123-81. He devotes several pages to the greater

general negative portrayal of Solomon, however, are expressed, and these have established what, I think, is a justified reading: implicit in the story of Solomon's wealth, prestige and wisdom are the seeds of his own downfall.[52] In fact, Solomon's self-condemning irony in 1 Kgs 8.46, in which he states that there is no one without sin, casts its shadow not only on Solomon, but 'on every positive evaluation of Solomon's successors, and stretches all the way to Josiah'.[53] Yet, latent in Solomon's selfish rhetoric are undercurrents which destabilize his goals, and allow the reader to find the seeds of hope in his own futile attempts at self-glorification.

Differences between the MT and LXX in 1 Kings 1–11 may have been motivated by differing goals in portraying the character of Solomon. Some contend, with some justification, that the MT is harsher on Solomon than the LXX is (Eslinger's comments pertain especially to the MT but, to some extent, may still apply to the Greek). This includes different sequencing, the description of Solomon's religious and secular buildings, including a palace for his Egyptian queen (1 Kgs 7.1-12), among other variants.[54] Even so, the Greek does not offer a whitewash of Solomon, since he is condemned in 1 Kgs 11.1-13, as he is in the MT.[55] The differing assessments of Solomon, however, may be related to what has already been discovered: that the MT implies that Solomon was less sensitive to division within his kingdom than the LXX suggests. It also suggests that the LXX prefers to look at Solomon's reign, or at least part of it, as somewhat more of a positive period in history than does the MT, and therefore, more of a positive symbol of all that was glorious about the ancient kingdom. In the MT there is no true golden age that Solomon, only late in life, squandered.

literary context of 1 Kgs 8 (pp. 125-55), and describes how Solomon is struggling with Yahweh to possess royal power on his own terms, and how the amoral deity leads Solomon into greater temptation while increasing the severity of the consequences.

52. Walsh, 'Characterization', p. 471; Provan, *Kings*, pp. 91, 97-102.

53. McConville, 'Narrative and Meaning', p. 36.

54. See Auld, *Privilege*, pp. 24-26, also D.W. Gooding, 'Pedantic Timetabling in the 3rd Book of Reigns', *VT* 15 (1965), pp. 153-66 (154-57). In finding the Greek order secondary to the Hebrew, Gooding has a different view from Auld, who feels that the MT rearranged things to further condemn Solomon.

55. The most important variant is the absence of any reference to Solomon's Egyptian wife in a somewhat differently formulated presentation of his illicit marriages in 1 Kgs 11.1-3.

Instead there is an empire built on foundations of sand. Such different memories of Solomon may reveal something of the respective producers' different perceptions, but fuller discussion of this will have to wait.[56] If, however, the collapse of the United Monarchy is to be blamed ultimately on Solomon, this is not the only result of his apostasy. 1 Kings 9.1-9 includes the threat of the destruction of the whole of greater Israel with the warning to Solomon. The convergence of the sins of Solomon and of Israel, as a whole, can be seen later in Kings. In 2 Kgs 23.13, Josiah destroys the cultic installations set up by Solomon. During the destruction of the temple, Solomon is mentioned again (2 Kgs 24.13; 25.16). The implication of this convergence is to link not only the division of the kingdom to Solomon, but the beginning of the slide into exile.

Of the nature of Solomon's sin, 1 Kings 11 is quite explicit. Solomon was led astray by his foreign wives, whom, we are told, he should never have married in the first place (vv. 1, 4; cf. Deut. 7.3-4; Josh. 23.12). The dangerous situation is traced to an early stage in the king's reign, even if it is not manifest until Solomon's old age. The marriage to an Egyptian princess is related in the early chapters of the book (MT, 1 Kgs 3.1; LXX, 2.35c, 5.14). Mullen rightly notes that the condemnation for intermarriage bases itself on the demands for ethnic distinctiveness, in the service of an ideal construct of Israel. He prefers, however, to juxtapose this against the preservation of davidic rule over at least some part of greater Israel.[57] The biblical injunctions against intermarriage are a major topic of research in sociological studies of the Persian period. It is sometimes concluded that the ban had an economic base, and that many of the women so ostracized were probably not really 'foreign', but were merely victims of changing perceptions of group identity.[58] It is significant, however, that in Kings the people, as a whole, are not condemned for this infraction, quite unlike other biblical

---

56. In a later chapter on the role of Egypt in Kings, I will address this issue again.

57. Mullen, *Narrative History*, p. 259.

58. For example, see H.C. Washington, 'The Strange Woman (אשה זרה / נכריה) of Proverbs 1–9 and Post Exilic Judaean Society', in Eskenazi and Richard (eds.), *Second Temple Studies*, II, pp. 217-42, and, in the same volume, D.L. Smith-Christopher, 'The Mixed Marriage Crisis in Ezra 9–10 and Nehemiah 13: A Study of the Sociology of the Post-Exilic Judaean Community', pp. 243-65, and T.C. Eskenazi and E.P. Judd, 'Marriage to a Stranger in Ezra 9–10', pp. 267-85.

books, such as Judg. 3.1-5 and Ezra 9–10. In Kings, Solomon, and later
Ahab, are condemned for intermarriage. Such illicit unions not only
mark Solomon's reign, but 'taint' the whole of the subsequent davidic
dynasty in Kings: Solomon's heir is the son of an Ammonite woman,
1 Kgs 14.21, 31 (LXX, v. 21 only). One should note that, according to
Ruth 4.18-19, David himself had a Moabite grandmother.[59] In the
Greek, Jeroboam also marries an Egyptian (3 Kgdms 12.24e). As I will
describe below, the Greek denies Jeroboam the title *nagid*, נגיד. If this
is viewed in the light of the Greek's claims that he married an
Egyptian, then one might infer that Solomon's marriages (or at least
marriage to the Egyptian princess) were the reason why it is David who
declares Solomon נגיד, and not Yahweh or someone speaking on behalf
of Yahweh.

Not all foreign dealings are explicitly condemned, although some
may be seen as at least suspicious, especially in his acquisition of
wealth. Hiram of Tyre, of course, helps in the construction of the
temple (1 Kgs 5.15; LXX 5.1), but he also blesses Yahweh, and so his
'foreignness' is not without some mediation (1 Kgs 5.21; LXX 5.7).
Similarly, in 1 Kgs 10.1-10, the visit of the Queen of Sheba is celebrated, and she too blesses Yahweh (1 Kgs 10.9), although one might
link her gift of gold to the later intimations of Solomon's excesses,
especially in view of the injunctions in Deut. 17.17, which mention
polygamy and the quest for wealth. Yet, the contrast between the
anonymous consorts of the king and the portrayal of the Queen of
Sheba (1 Kgs 10.1-13) is consistent with Solomon's ambivalent portrayal. Solomon demonstrates divine wisdom in the presence of the
queen, the foreign woman he did not marry.[60] Thus, it is with some
irony that one reads her words in the Greek and Syriac commenting on
the happiness of Solomon's wives (3 Kgdms 10.8). In the Hebrew, it is
Solomon's men she speaks of.[61]

59. The repetition in 1 Kgs 14, in the MT, may be taken as emphasizing the
point, and this may be taken along with the greater emphasis it places on
Solomon's foreign wives, linking the marriage to the Egyptian with the other
improper unions it denounces in ch. 11.

60. A. Reinhartz, 'Anonymous Women and the Collapse of the Monarchy: A
Study in Narrative Technique', in Brenner (ed.), *A Feminist Companion to Samuel
and Kings*, pp. 43-65 (51).

61. Hebrew has אנשׁיך instead of נשׁיך. De Vries, *1 Kings*, p. 136, thinks the MT

The projection of the sin of intermarriage onto the monarchy makes the actions of the kings paradigmatic for greater Israel as a whole. Why such a projection is made, and how this affects the portrayal of women in the book of Kings, cannot be dealt with in full here. It is, however, a topic which has generated some very interesting work, and is deserving of far more.[62] It is curious how the end or destiny of so many of the Kings of Judah and Israel hinges on the actions of a woman (often nameless). One of the most serious errors of David was his adultery with Bathsheba (2 Sam. 11–12.23).[63] In 1 Kings 1–2, however, Bathsheba manipulates David, and the aged king's feebleness is all the more obvious in the presence of the beautiful Abishag. It is also the desire for Abishag that proves to be Adonijah's undoing (1 Kgs 2.13-25). Jeroboam learns of his doom when his wife inquires into the fate of their son (MT: 1 Kgs 14.1-14; LXX: 3 Kgdms 12.24g-na). Ahab's Sidonian wife, Jezebel, is the cause of at least part of his poor reputation (1 Kgs 16.31). A descendant of this union, Athaliah, becomes the illegitimate queen of Judah (2 Kgs 11) and, in so doing, almost destroys the house of David. These episodes, along with the condemnation of Solomon, make the final prophetic oracle in the book all the more mysterious. The prophetess Huldah delivers to the zealous reformer, Josiah, the news that, despite all his piety, the kingdom is still doomed (2 Kgs 22.15-20).

3. *The King and the* Nagid

One of the most important links between Samuel and Kings, and one which spans most of the monarchic story in these books, is the occasional reference to certain monarchs as *nagid*, נגיד, a feature already discussed to some extent above. The title clearly marks the bearer as a figure of some authority, and, in Samuel and Kings, this authority is linked quite closely to the concept of monarchy. Scholars have differed in the reconstructions of the term's history of use vis-à-vis these books' history of composition. Questions of the military, royal, and sacral connotations of the title are main issues in these debates. There is,

is a 'tendentious alteration' based on 1 Kgs 11.1. 2 Chron. 9.7 (Greek and Hebrew) reads with the MT Kings.

62. See, for instance, Brenner (ed.), *A Feminist Companion to Samuel and Kings*.

63. Although he is saved from committing murder by Abigail in 1 Sam. 25.

however, little point in offering a full discussion of these debates here.[64] The relatively brief examination of the eleven uses of the term in Samuel and Kings which can be afforded here, however, is still revealing.

Unlike Chronicles and other biblical texts, which use the title in a wide range of priestly, administrative and other connotations, Samuel and Kings use the title exclusively of persons who are, or are destined to become, kings. For example, it is used in reference to foreign leaders (Ezek. 28.2; Ps. 76.13); eschatological figures (Dan 9.25, 26; 11.22) including David (Isa. 55.4); officials of priestly rank (Jer. 20.1; Neh. 11.11; 1 Chron. 9.11, 20; 2 Chron. 31.12, 13; 35.8); military officers (1 Chron. 12.28; 13.1; 27.4); and others (1 Chron. 26.24; 2 Chron. 28.7). Chronicles has half of the 44 uses of the title and shares with Samuel some of the attestations in which David is granted the title. Chronicles, however, does not feature those which speak of Saul in that role (cf. 1 Chron. 11.2 / 2 Sam. 5.2; 1 Chron. 17.7 / 2 Sam. 7.8). On the other hand, Chronicles has some unique references associating the נגיד with the tribe of Judah (1 Chron. 5.2; 28.4). Although some scholars accentuate the varieties of meanings for נגיד in Samuel and Kings, what strikes me is the relative consistency of use, which suggests that an important theological theme is being developed in these books. Yahweh tells Samuel to anoint Saul נגיד over Yahweh's people in 1 Sam. 9.16. This is accomplished in 1 Sam. 10.1. Through Samuel, Yahweh

---

64. Some bibliography can be given: M. Brettler, *God is King: Understanding an Israelite Metaphor* (JSOTSup, 79; Sheffield: JSOT Press, 1989), pp. 33-35; J.J. Glück, 'Nagid-Shepherd', *VT* 13 (1963), pp. 144-50; B. Halpern, *The Constitution of the Monarchy in Israel* (Chico, CA: Scholars Press, 1981), pp. 1-11; E. Lipiński, 'NAGID, der Kronprinz', *VT* 24 (1974), pp. 497-99; G.C. Macholz, 'NAGID–der Statthalter, "praefectus"', *DBAT* 1 (1975), pp. 59-72; T.N.D. Mettinger, *King and Messiah: The Civil and Sacral Legitimation of the Israelite Kings* (Lund: Gleerup, 1976), pp. 151-84; W. Richter, 'Die *nagid*-Formel: Ein Beitrag zur Erhellung des *nagid*-Problems', *BZ* 9 (1965), pp. 71-84; U. Rütersworden, *Die Beamten der israelitischen Königzeit* (BWANT; Stuttgart: W. Kohlhammer, 1985), pp. 101-105; L. Schmidt, *Menschlicher Erfolg und Jahwes Initiative: Studien zu Tradition, Interpretation und Historie in Überlieferungen von Gideon, Saul und David* (Neukirchener–Vluyn: Neukirchener Verlag, 1970), pp. 91, 141-71; S. Shaviv, 'Nabi and Nagid in I Samuel IX 1-X 16', *VT* 34 (1984), pp. 108-13. Most attend to etymology and the term's supposed changing meanings across the different redactional strata. Halpern, *Constitution*, p. 257 n. 2, complains that interpretations based on hypothetical etymology are flawed.

predicts a replacement for Saul in 1 Sam. 13.14. Abigail reminds David that Yahweh made him נגיד (1 Sam. 25.30). In 2 Sam. 5.2, the elders of Israel recall the divine selection of David, and Yahweh instructs Nathan to speak to David about this in 2 Sam. 7.8. David recalls Yahweh's preference for him as נגיד, when Michal criticizes him (2 Sam. 6.21). David orders Solomon be made נגיד in 1 Kgs 1.35. Jeroboam and Baasha are condemned by prophets for failing in their capacity as *nagidim* (pl.) נגידים (1 Kgs 14.7; 16.2). Isaiah is instructed to speak to Hezekiah, the נגיד (2 Kgs 20.5).[65] Beyond the royal connections, it is important to note that in every case but the last, the actual selection of the title-bearer is indicated. In each of these cases, it is Yahweh who selects the נגיד, except in 1 Kgs 1.35. This, and the fact that the concept of the נגיד is intimately related to the issue of the monarchy, it is understandable that different proposals have been made for understanding the title as meaning something in the neighbourhood of 'the one designated to be king', whether through divine or human choice.

For some, the title's simplest meaning is roughly equivalent to 'crown prince', or designated heir. Support for this proposal, therefore, throws great weight on 1 Kgs 1.35, in which David elevates Solomon to the status of נגיד when indicating that he should succeed him. Moreover, in 2 Chron. 11.22, Abijah is granted the title when he is designated heir to the throne.[66] Given the wide variety of uses of the term in Chronicles, however, there is little to suggest that the meaning of 'heir' should impose too strongly on other routes to interpretation in Samuel and Kings. In these books, only in 1 Kgs 1.35 is a true heir to the throne identified. Hezekiah is already king when the title is mentioned on his behalf. David was the founder of a new dynasty, as were Jeroboam and Baasha. More could be made of נגיד as 'the designated

---

65. 1 Sam. 10.1 is longer in the Greek, including two references to the selection of Saul, and emphasizing his role as a military leader. In the longer text of 1 Kgs 8.16, preserved in a Qumran fragment, another reference to Yahweh's failure to select a נגיד may be found, as I will discuss briefly below. LXX omits a reference in regard to Jeroboam.

66. Lipiński, 'NAGID', pp. 497-99. Mettinger, *King*, pp. 151-84. Halpern, *Constitution*, pp. 9-11, likewise favours such an interpretation but also holds that it originally carried sacral legitimation for the heir to the throne as well. He argues that the necessity of such legitimization was lessened as succession became more routine.

one', but the implications of this designation have more to do with the bearer's relationship to a theocratic interpretation of the rule over Israel than the mundane monarchic political form. A number of scholars have commented on how the title designates someone in a position of authority in the divine administration over Israel. R.A. Carlson maintains that the introduction of Saul as נגיד marks a shift in the DtrH from the period of the judges to that of the monarchy, and that it was employed as a deuteronomic definition of the ideal national leader. This is evidenced especially in 1 Sam. 13.14; 2 Sam. 5.2; 7.8; 1 Kgs 14.7; 16.2 and 2 Kgs 20.5. The deuteronomistic employment of the term stemmed from its fewer overtones in comparison with 'king', especially in deuteronomic context (e.g. cf. Deut. 17.4-20; 1 Sam. 8.12).[67] Carlson has made a valuable insight but it cannot be taken too far. The pious and zealous Josiah is 'king', and never נגיד (cf. 2 Kgs 22.1–23.25). The reason may lie in the expectations placed in the נגיד. As I will illustrate below, Yahweh is depicted as having a specific range of duties for the נגידים, which, given the impending doom hanging over Josiah's Judah, was no longer relevant.

That role initially seems to be that of a military saviour for Israel, as this is the thrust of Yahweh's choice of Saul (1 Sam. 9.16; 10.1). A similar military role is implied for David, although the emphasis soon shifts. David is the commander, and Israel will have peace under the watchful eye of their 'shepherd' in 2 Sam. 5.2; 7.8-11 (cf. 1 Sam. 25.28). This image is already foreshadowed in 1 Sam. 9.3, as Saul goes out to seek lost livestock, only to have his fateful encounter with Samuel. David himself is introduced as a shepherd boy (1 Sam. 16.11). The image of the נגיד as a guardian, or, perhaps better, a steward, compares favourably with the non-royal, administrative applications of the title in Chronicles and elsewhere. One could expect that, in general, a נגיד not only has authority over, but was also accountable for the care of those in the official's jurisdiction. The נגיד in Samuel and Kings is not an absolute ruler; he is answerable to Yahweh. This observation provides a clue to interpretation, anticipated by Eslinger. In his literary study of 1 Samuel 1–12, he argues that 1 Sam. 9.16 is part of a

---

67. R.A. Carlson, *David, the Chosen King: A Traditio-Historical Approach to the Second Book of Samuel* (Stockholm: Almqvist & Wiksell, 1964), pp. 52-54. Others see נגיד as a preferable title to 'king': Montgomery, *Kings*, p. 78, comments that it is an 'anti-monarchic' term, yet he translates it as 'prince'; cf. Gray, *Kings*, pp. 91.

rhetorical strategy ensuring that the king demanded by the people is actually portrayed as no more than a vassal of Yahweh. In 2 Sam. 5.2, King Saul is to be replaced by David who is both king and נגיד. The monarchy becomes a cover for a theocracy.[68] As much as the title is linked to the monarchy, it is also linked to a sacral conception of Israel.

It is significant that, in most places, the נגיד is said to have (or it is implied that he has) some jurisdiction over 'Yahweh's people': 1 Sam. 9.16, 10.1 (MT, 'inheritance', נחלה; in LXX, Saul is the 'archon', ἄρχων, of the 'people of Yahweh'); 1 Sam. 13.14; 2 Sam. 6.21; 2 Sam. 7.8; 1 Kgs 14.7; 16.2; 2 Kgs 20.5 (in this last reference, the collocation 'Israel' is not found). Abigail speaks of David as נגיד over 'Israel' (1 Sam. 25.30). She might have in mind a political territory, but since she speaks volumes about the obligations of David to the people, her use of נגיד should then be seen as pertaining to David's leadership amongst the people. In 2 Sam. 5.2, the elders of Israel recall that David is to be the shepherd of 'Yahweh's people, Israel', and be נגיד over 'Israel'. Here the parallelism suggests that David is imagined as the נגיד of the deity's people. More problematic is 1 Kgs 1.35, which has been discussed already. This reference is also unique in that Yahweh is given no role.

If the term נגיד in Samuel and Kings does not actually mean 'heir', it still conveys a sense of succession in the steward-ship of Israel. Most נגידים are the founders of new dynasties (Saul, David, Jeroboam, Baasha). Saul, of course, ushered in the monarchic period, while David replaced him. This sequencing marks the continuation of theocratic fiat over human rulers, their accountability, and the succession of phases in history. The exception, of course is Solomon in 1 Kgs 1.35, whose *nagid*-ship is never accorded divine legitimacy, either by the narrator, Yahweh himself, a prophet, or any other character. Was he a legitimate title-bearer? Albrecht Alt thought that David had usurped Yahweh's prerogative in naming the נגיד.[69] One may well read it in this light, as

68. L. Eslinger, *Kingship of God in Crisis: A Close Reading of 1 Samuel 1–12* (BL, 10; Sheffield, Almond Press, 1985), pp. 307-309.

69. A. Alt, 'The Formation of the Israelite State in Palestine', in A. Alt, *Essays on Old Testament History and Religion* (trans. R.A. Wilson; BibSem; Sheffield: Sheffield Academic Press, 1989), pp. 171-237 (233), original: 'Die Staatenbildung der Israeliten in Palästina', in A. Alt, *Reformationsprogramm der Universität Leipzig, 1930*, reprinted in A. Alt, *Kleine Schriften zur Geschichte des Volkes Israel* (3 vols.; Munich: Beck, 1953), II, pp. 1-65. Alt, of course, tends to think in

David seems to be portrayed falling back into his old rashness, but he is not so bold as to claim the right to place Solomon over 'Yahweh's people'. If Saul had failed to live up to the demands of his role, and Solomon eventually disgraced the house of David, 'conditions of employment' are also clearly identifiable in the next two occurrences of the title, both in prophetic oracles. In 1 Kgs 14.7, in which Yahweh's word to Jeroboam's wife speaks of the end of the house of Jeroboam, Jeroboam is asked if he has not been raised up to be made נגיד over Yahweh's people, Israel (there is no equivalent verse in LXX, but this will be discussed later). In 1 Kgs 16.2 Baasha is likewise condemned. This latter verse explicitly refers back to the fate of Jeroboam. Oddly, however, it is only somewhat after the fact, that their status as נגידים is revealed, in the context of prophecies of their downfall for their sins. Neither prophecy speaks of the subject as 'king' of Israel, although in Jeroboam's case reference is made to his receipt of the kingdom, ממלכה, (1 Kgs 14.8, MT only), and of a future, unnamed king (Baasha, 1 Kgs 14.14, MT only) who will destroy his household. It is, therefore, rather surprising to read that these terrible sinners were actually intended to represent Yahweh before Israel. In view of the fact that both Jeroboam and Baasha are kings of the northern territories, it is easy to interpret 'Yahweh's people, Israel' in these places as referring exclusively to the north. On the other hand, not only is there a precedent for reading the collective in the other נגיד references in Samuel and 2 Kgs 20.5 (where only 'Yahweh's people' appear), but the expression is often used to refer to the whole of the Israelite people, particularly in the context of Solomon's prayer (see the chapter on 1 Kgs 8 below). Were Jeroboam and Baasha the stewards of Judah as well?

The two prophetic words about Jeroboam and Baasha share some other interesting features with earlier titular grants, which lead me to think that the text is stressing the integrity of greater Israel, and the abiding relationship of both Judah and Israel with Yahweh. Both northern kings are reminded that Yahweh had elevated them from humble surroundings to become the נגיד. Although not specified in the words which installed him as נגיד, Saul too was of humble birth, at least by his own estimation (1 Sam. 9.21). David's promotion from shepherd to נגיד is spoken of in Nathan's oracle in 2 Samuel 7. Again, it is Solomon

terms of the historical David; his insight, however, is easily translatable into a more literary-orientated reading.

who is the exception, as he is not promoted from humble beginnings, although, not being the eldest of David's sons, he was not the logical choice for a king. Hezekiah is also an odd man out, as he was of royal birth and his succession seems not out of the ordinary (2 Kgs 16.20). Yet, his title is mentioned only in the context of his healing by Yahweh, and the revelation that he is destined to save Jerusalem from Assyria. The accent on the promotion in the other cases, however, suggests that the נגיד was raised to fulfil a certain role on behalf of Yahweh. This role seems to be that of Yahweh's representative in response to a religio-political crisis. As Eslinger noticed, Saul became נגיד when the people decided that they would prefer a king in place of the potential judge-ship of Samuel's corrupt sons (1 Sam. 8.1-6, 19; 9.16). David became נגיד as a replacement for Saul. Jeroboam was raised up in place of a davidic king, and Baasha was his replacement. The offences which earned Jeroboam and Baasha the scorn of their biographers are not those of acting as the rebel or revolutionary against a legitimate king. Jeroboam receives a divine oracle announcing his rise to the kingship of the north (1 Kgs 11.29-39), while Baasha's bloody insurrection is given divine approval (1 Kgs 15.27-30). They are condemned for cultic offences and it is in the context of their denunciation that their status as נגידים is specified.

If the נגיד was to be the divinely-appointed answer to threats to the theocracy, or moments of transition in its history, does the transfer of the *nagid*-ship to the north reveal a loss of legitimacy or status for Judah? Is it a symbol for divine disfavour of the goings-on in Judah that Yahweh had gone to the extreme of granting Jeroboam the title once held by David, and then even passed it on to another northerner after the disgraces of Jeroboam's dynasty? But after the fall of Samaria the Assyrian threats to Jerusalem set the stage for Hezekiah to assume the title once lost to the house of David. Yet it remains *nagid*-ship over 'Yahweh's people'. Oddly, however, the name 'Israel' is not mentioned here. While it is possible to interpret this as a suggestion that 'Israel', in the previous two נגיד references, identified only the north, there is nothing specific in 2 Kgs 20.5, or its immediate context, which suggests that only Judah is discussed in this place.[70] With the

---

70. It is curious that Isaiah's version of the verse (Isa. 38.5) does not use the title. This suggests that the reference in Kings is an addition to whatever the source material was for the shared narrative. On the assumption that the passage is original to Kings, that נגיד is hardly found in Isaiah (only 55.4) is not convincing evidence

granting of the title to Hezekiah, David, the greatest נגיד, is recalled. Does this association usher in a new age? That Judah had lost and then regained the symbolic leadership of Yahweh's people seems implicit with the inclusion of the title in the Hezekiah oracle; yet the hopes that Hezekiah could change forever the downward spiral are dashed. He foolishly opens the treasuries to foreign inspection and cannot fully appreciate the symbolic significance of his actions (2 Kgs 20.12-19). He is succeeded by the evil Manasseh, whose offences sealed the fate of Judah's monarchy. No new נגיד is raised, charged with salvaging the situation: Josiah, the most pious king, and, therefore, the best chance to fulfil the intended role of the נגיד, has come too late. It is as if the Assyrian and Babylonian conquerors have replaced the נגיד as Yahweh's appointed stewards, but not even the governor, Gedaliah, is accorded the title (cf. 2 Kgs 25.22-26). Perhaps the writers awaited a new נגיד to usher in a new independent monarchy or some other political form within the constraints of the imperial system; perhaps their book was composed to preserve the lessons of history for anyone who would be Yahweh's new steward.

In the preceding, I have largely avoided reference to the Greek translations, but I now turn to this issue. In Greek, נגיד is translated by two terms. Saul is anointed ἄρχων in 1 Kgdms 9.16; 10.1. 1 Kgdms 13.14 also uses ἄρχων to translate נגיד, when it refers to a replacement for Saul, implicitly referring to David. Elsewhere, however, ἡγούμενος is used (1 Kgdms 25.30; 2 Kgdms 5.2; 6.21; 7.8; 3 Kgdms 1.35; 16.2; 4 Kgdms 20.5. There is no Greek equivalent to 1 Kgs 14.7). I am quite uncertain whether any wide-ranging interpretation of the LXX's portrayal of the various rulers could be developed based on the shifting vocabulary alone, but one may conclude that Saul, as archon (ἄρχων) is not considered of the same status as those who receive the title ruler, ἡγούμενος.[71] There is no tradition of Saul being נגיד in Chronicles, and so perhaps the translators sought to reflect this in their handling of

that it was removed when the section was included in Isaiah. On the other hand, the ten other uses of the term in Samuel and Kings suggest that its occurrence in 2 Kgs 20.5 should not be viewed as completely coincidental.

71. Both Greek terms are used in reference to Israelite and foreign military commanders or other officials in Samuel and Kings, with ἄρχων being in the majority. For instance, ἄρχων can translate שר (2 Sam. 10.3; 1 Kgs 1.25; 2 Kgs 25.23); סרן, (1 Sam. 6.4). On the other hand, ἡγούμενος is used to translate שר (1 Sam. 22.2, 2 Sam. 3.38) or, in feminine form, גבירה (1 Kgs 15.13).

Samuel and Kings. Moreover, it is Saul as ἄρχων who is raised to answer the demand for a king, so that Israel might be 'like the other nations' and be defended from their enemies (1 Kgdms 8.5, 9.16). 1 Kingdoms 10.1 utilizes the term ἄρχων twice and repeats the identification of the military role of Saul (MT here uses נגיד but once and omits mention of his intended military function). Thus, one may ask if the greater emphasis on the military role of Saul in the Greek is a negative comment on possible military ambitions for a hypothetical new monarchy. Saul is replaced not for failing to save Israel, but for his disobedience to Yahweh's commandments (1 Sam. 13.13-14). Although Samuel here speaks of a new ἄρχων, when it is clear that his successor is David, the term used is ἡγούμενος (1 Kgdms 25.30; 2 Kgdms 5.2). The introduction of the ἡγούμενος replaces the *archony* of Saul, and so a greater break with the earlier kingdom is made. Did the translators foresee a pious 'davidic' ruler who did not need to 'liberate' Israel, and so avoid making it like the foreign monarchic nations, or reliving the excesses of the past?

Some of the most severe textual discrepancies in Kings occur in the context of the biography of Jeroboam, and the story of the schism. In the shared Greek and Hebrew account at 1 Kgs 12.16, as well as in 2 Chron. 10.16, the rebelling people dismiss the davidic dynasty with words to the effect: 'Now, see to your house, David'. In the unique, second Greek account, the people declare that David's heir is neither ἄρχων or ἡγούμενος (3 Kgdms 12.24t). It is interesting that the exclusive LXX story does not refer to the rejection of David's grandson as *king*. This may be a strategy by which the rebels are portrayed as rejecting both symbols of human agents of direct theocracy. But what is the significance of his rejection as ἄρχων and ἡγούμενος? On the one hand, Rehoboam is rejected for the role of military saviour to which Saul was especially anointed (1 Kgdms 9.16; 10.1). At the division of the kingdom (in both Greek versions), Rehoboam attempts not to save Israel, but to win it by force (1 Kgs 12.21-24; 3 Kgdms 12.24x-z). It is also possible to see in the LXX that, by rejecting Rehoboam as ἄρχων, the people have also rejected him as an imperial overlord, since this term was used of Solomon's reign. In 3 Kgdms 2.46b and k Solomon is ἄρχων of an empire stretching from Egypt to the Euphrates (cf. MT's

1 Kgs 5.1).[72] In 3 Kgdms 2.46f, ἄρχων is also used to describe Solomon as ruler (cf.1 Kgs 5.4).[73]

The long passage unique to the LXX at 3 Kgdms 12.24 includes an oracle against Jeroboam and his sick boy, and this actually precedes the LXX's second, exclusive account of the confrontation at Shechem (3 Kgdms 12.24l-m). This is opposed to the MT order, which places it after his rise to the throne (1 Kgs 14.1-18). It is significantly shorter than the version in the MT and does not include the rhetorical question about Jeroboam's elevation to the role of נגיד, or his failure to live up to the standards of David. The condemnation of Jeroboam as a wayward ἄρχων or ἡγούμενος would, however, make little sense being placed *before* the story of his rise to power. The lack of a prediction of his future evil ways to justify the oracle of his doom, along with the withholding of an equivalent to the title נגיד, indicates that the LXX does not portray his apostasy as a bitter betrayal. Jeroboam is doomed before he begins, a tragic figure in whom there was never any hope at all. He is little more than a pawn to divide the kingdom, and to lead the north into the apostasy which eventually led to its destruction.[74] Baasha, on the other hand, is ἡγούμενος, as the LXX retains the story of his rebellion against Jeroboam and the oracle denouncing his own furthering of Jeroboam's sins (3 Kgs 16.2). This feature highlights Baasha as a potential solution to the problem created by the doomed Jeroboam, while still highlighting how the *nagid*-ship has moved north.

In the MT, there is a succession of holders of the title which follows the fortunes of the United Monarchy. It is then transferred to the northern kingdom, but ultimately it is the davidic Hezekiah who is the final נגיד and establishes the primacy of this royal line. With the pattern already established, however, there seems no guarantee that the davidic line could retain the title unconditionally. Even so, the history of the dynasty preserves models of how the ideal נגיד should behave, and so the immortality of the dynasty as a symbol is ensured. The LXX seems to offer a similar but hardly identical picture. The title נגיד is translated

72. This Hebrew verse is the only one in MT Kings in which מושל is found.

73. The verb in MT employed here, רדה 'to rule' or 'have dominion', is used only sparingly, cf. 1 Kgs 5.30; 9.23.

74. Jeroboam in the LXX is rather more of a tragic figure. Josiah, on the other hand, is more evenly portrayed between MT and LXX. He, too, was doomed by a prophetic announcement before he began his programme of forced religious conversion.

by relatively common terms which, elsewhere in Samuel and Kings, are used to refer to officials or officers. On the other hand, the divine grant of titles sets Saul apart from David. The lack of a title for Jeroboam radically alters the retrospective impression of his rule. He was not the proposed solution to the problem of the davidic dynasty: he was merely a means to an end. That the davidic kings had shown themselves superior, if not perfect holders of this title, is clear. Yet the periodization and shift of the office north prevents the conclusion that legitimacy is exclusively a Judaean prerogative. Israel had its own stewards of the theocracy as well, and even if they failed, Israel was still deemed worthy at a time when Judah was not. This strategy seems to uphold Judah's status, while allowing a sense of common history for greater Israel to be articulated.

To sum up, the נגיד represents the solution Yahweh proposes to a leadership crisis: Israel's problems with foreign powers, Samuel's corrupt sons, the wayward Saul, the severe taskmasters who were David's successors, and the threat against Jerusalem in the wake of the fall of Samaria. By presenting the king as Yahweh's steward, the role of the monarchy is contextualized historically. The monarchy is not seen to be the ultimate answer to the problems of Israelite politics, and its loss is not fatal to Israel as Yahweh's people. Rather, hope may be had in those who fulfil the obligations of the נגיד who represents Yahweh on earth. It is interesting that the title occurs mostly in the context of the origins of the monarchy and its early history, and that few of these figures live up to their roles.

4. *The Throne of Israel*

Another important, if enigmatic, theological concept which figures largely in the opening chapters of Kings is that of the 'throne of Israel', כסא ישראל. Within the narratives of Solomon's reign, references to thrones occur quite frequently. In 1 Kings 1–2, the throne is the property of individuals, which only fits the plot of the succession of royal rule: the throne of David: 1 Kgs 1.13, 17, 20, 24, 27, 30, 37, 47, 48; 2.12, 24, 33, 45, or the throne of Solomon, 1 Kgs 1.37, 47. What is at issue here is not so much the throne as a physical item but the power it represents.[75] There is little explicit reference to the jurisdiction placed

75. In some cases, the term כסא refers more specifically to the physical chair granted to a royal figure: Solomon is to be seated on his father's throne. Elsewhere,

under that power, but there is nothing to suggest that control over anything other than greater Israel is at stake. It is noteworthy that David recognizes the relationship of Yahweh to Israel (cf. 'God of Israel' 1 Kgs 1.30, 48), even though it was he who took it upon himself to declare who shall inherit the kingdom. Although portraying power as personal property in the context of a dispute over succession does not seriously trivialize the monarchy, it does associate the throne with the human realm.[76] When David begins his instructions to his son, however, a rather different nuance is found, which furthers explication of the power relations between the monarchy, its jurisdiction, and Yahweh. Here, in 1 Kgs 2.3, Yahweh is *Solomon's* god and, in v. 4, the throne is the 'throne of Israel'. David sees that Solomon's obedience is the key to success, and so implies that his line has no claim on the throne as a matter of personal property. Any claim to the throne is contingent. This reference, along with the rather similar 1 Kgs 8.25 and 9.5, has been a matter of some debate, as some hold that what is contingent is rule over the north, and not over greater Israel.

That the 'throne of Israel' in these verses pertains only to the north is argued by Friedman and Nelson, both of whom attribute the verses to the hypothetical monarchic era DtrH. Friedman notices that the promises of a davidic occupant on the 'throne of Israel' are all conditional (1 Kgs 2.4, 8.25, 9.4-5), while the 'eternal' dynastic promises do not speak of this throne (cf. 1 Kgs 11.36, 15.4; 2 Kgs 8.19).[77] Nelson

---

Solomon and his mother each have their own thrones in 1 Kgs 2.19. In 1 Kgs 22.10, the kings of Judah and Israel are seated upon their thrones. The furnishings of an abode for an itinerant prophet may also include a 'throne', here perhaps better understood as merely 'chair' (2 Kgs 4.10). On the other hand, Yahweh is seen in a vision upon a throne (1 Kgs 22.19). The throne and its surrounds built by Solomon is described in 1 Kgs 7.7; 10.18-19. Even though the priest Eli sits on (and falls off) a כסא in 1 Sam. 1.9; 4.13, 18, there are strong royal connotations. Polzin, *Samuel*, pp. 23, 60-61, 64, writes that Eli is portrayed as a royal figure, whose fate is an analogy of the eventual collapse of the monarchy. F.A. Spina, 'Eli's Seat: The Transition from Priest to Prophet', *JSOT* 62 (1994), pp. 67-75, reads the text as criticizing the priest for improperly using a symbol of the monarchy. At 1 Kgs 1.46 the 'royal throne', כסא המלוכה, is mentioned. Cf. Deut. 17.18; 2 Sam. 7.13 כסא ממלכתו and 1 Kgs 9.5 כסא ממלכתך. Joash is placed on the throne of the kings in 2 Kgs 11.19, כסא המלכים.

76. In contrast, Chronicles sometimes refers to the throne as Yahweh's; 1 Chron. 28.5; 29.23.

77. Friedman, *Exile*, pp. 12-13.

observes that the conditional promises are concentrated in Solomon's narratives, and are not interspersed throughout the whole of Kings, which is considered odd if they were meant to be programmatic. Rather, the conditions only apply to Solomon, even if 1 Kgs 2.4 and 8.25 include reference to his 'sons'. This is considered the result of the historian taking up earlier sources. In 1 Kgs 9.4-5, Solomon alone is addressed (vv. 6-9, which do speak of Solomon's heirs, are excised as belonging to Dtr2). In these promises, the historian links long-term dynastic stability to the actions of an individual; a similar situation to that found in 1 Kgs 11.38 in regard to Jeroboam. Nelson concludes that the conditional 'throne' oracles applied only to Solomon and that the obedience of the latter kings of Judah is not at all at issue. He concludes that in the monarchic DtrH, the davidic dynasty was considered eternal over Judah, and conditional over Israel. Nelson also points to the use of the expression in regard to the reign of the Israelite king Jehu (2 Kgs 10.30; 15.12).[78]

Such arguments are not at all convincing. Regardless of the evidence for seeing 1 Kgs 9.6-9 as later than the promise in v. 5, it does seem somewhat *ad hoc* to suggest that the references to David's descendants in the two other 'throne' promises were 'forced' upon the writer by pre-existing documents, and that they refer only to David's own children, and not to succeeding generations.[79] Even though Jeroboam is granted the chance of a 'sure house', בית־נאמן, like David's (1 Kgs 11.38), he is not offered the 'throne of Israel'. This is peculiar if the conditions placed on Solomon pertained solely to the rule over the lands that Jeroboam eventually won. I also find it suspect that Nelson finds support for his 'northern' interpretation of Solomon's throne promises in those attestations of the expression set in Jehu's reign but accords no value to others set in the reign of Solomon. Nelson rightly considers 1 Kgs 8.20 and 10.9 as referring to the united throne, but he considers these two occurrences 'entirely neutral'. Provan has criticized Nelson in this regard.[80] Little more needs to be said of 1 Kgs 10.9, in

---

78. Nelson, *Double Redaction*, pp. 100-104. For his summary of Dtr2 additions, which do not include 8.20 or 10.9, see p. 120. Nelson has found some support from J.S. Rogers, 'Narrative Stock and Deuteronomistic Elaboration in 1 Kings 2', *CBQ* 50 (1988), pp. 398-413 (406).

79. See 1 Kgs 13.2 for Josiah as a 'son' born to the 'House of David'.

80. Nelson, *Double Redaction*, pp. 103-104; Provan, *Hezekiah*, pp. 107-108.

which the Queen of Sheba praises Yahweh, who, she says, enthroned Solomon out of love for Israel. The greater context of 1 Kings 8, and even 2.4, however are worth elaborating on, as they cause Nelson's position no end of difficulties.

As I will describe below, 1 Kings 8 does not recognize a dualism within Israel. In Solomon's speech of 1 Kgs 8.15-21, Solomon twice speaks of the exodus (vv. 16, 21), and twice of 'Israel' as the people of Yahweh (v. 16). He calls Yahweh the 'God of Israel' thrice (vv. 15, 17, 20). The 'throne of Israel' in v. 20, therefore, is certainly to be seen as a reference to dominion over greater Israel. In the king's next oration (vv. 23-53), a similar emphasis on the collective is made. The audience of the speech is the whole community קהל of Israel (v. 22). In the speech's introduction, Yahweh is 'God of Israel' in vv. 23, 25, 26. The entire chapter, in fact, is presented as ceremonies in front of the various leaders and collected populations of greater Israel (1 Kgs 8.1-5). As Provan notes, it is not at all likely that a single 'divisive' use of the name Israel would appear in the dedication ceremony at v. 25 without some sort of explanation, especially if an identical construction is employed with a comprehensive meaning only shortly before.[81] In fact, Nelson himself has anticipated such an objection by arguing that if Judah was intended in 1 Kgs 2.4, then the writer would have specified this by some means.[82] The required information is provided by context. One need only point to the reference to the law of Moses in 1 Kgs 2.3, which recalls Judah and Israel's shared heritage. More telling, however, is David's insistence that the two commanders killed by Joab were leaders of 'Israel' (v. 5). David's own reign is counted solely as being over Israel (v. 11). Pertaining to 9.5, even if we allow Nelson the right to disregard vv. 6-9 as later additions, the vision includes reference to the dedicatory speeches Solomon made in the previous chapter (9.3).[83] I conclude that the 'throne promises' in 1 Kings refer to

81. Provan, *Hezekiah*, p. 107.
82. Nelson, *Double Redaction*, p. 104.
83. The question of 1 Kgs 9.5 is made particularly difficult by the textual variants, but whatever the 'original' might be, it still seems to me that greater Israel is at issue. Instead of a promise of someone on the throne of Israel, the LXX offers a promise that there will always be a man 'ruling' in Israel, which reflects the wording in 2 Chron. 7.18 (מושל בישראל). The Greek expression used in LXX Kings and Chronicles is ἀνὴρ ἡγούμενος ἐν Ισραηλ, which suggests that this may be an allusion to someone fulfilling the sort of role that the נגיד / ἡγούμενος would fulfill. If

greater Israel, as do all of Kings' references to the 'throne of Israel'.

The specific use of the expression 'throne of Israel' in the texts referring to Jehu's reign (2 Kgs 10.30; 15.12) should bear little weight on the interpretation of the promises made in 1 Kings. The simplest way to construe these references is, of course, with 'Israel' as the northern kingdom. Rather, the implications of 1 Kings might be read into 2 Kings. Like Solomon, Jehu's tenure on the throne is not without its own conditions, even though the notion of an eternal dynasty is not made to Jehu. Ironically, the rise of Jehu sees the temporary suspension of the davidic dynasty in Judah (2 Kgs 11). This suggests to me that 'throne of Israel' in Jehu's reign has a potential double meaning. Logically, it specifies rule over the north but, like the נגידים, is symbolically relevant for greater Israel.[84]

While there are no other references to the 'throne of Israel', there are other occurrences of the term כסא in Kings, although some are not particularly noteworthy. 1 Kings 16.11 tells of Zimri's ambitions for a throne, while 2 Kgs 10.3 has Jehu issue a challenge to his opponents to find someone to fill the now empty throne of the Ahab's dynasty. 2 Kings 13.13 has Jeroboam II inherit the throne of Joash. These verses construe 'throne' as a personal possession. Kings closes with the deposed Jehoiachin regaining a throne in the court of the Babylonian king (2 Kgs 25.27-28), although no jurisdiction is attached to it, and he is called 'king of Judah'. 2 Kings 11.19 relates how Joash, ascended the 'throne of the kings' the וישב על־כסא המלכים, and so reinstated the dynasty. The importance of this episode cannot be underestimated, as it involves the eradication of northern-inspired heterodox worship, and the rule of a female descendant of Omri of Israel (2 Kgs 8.26). The expression 'throne of the kings' highlights the restorative symbol of Joash's gaining of power. It is not his throne, or only his fathers', but is

this is the case, then it is the only reference to the ἡγούμενος in Kings as a potential, ongoing factor in history, and the only one which suggests that Solomon had some legitimacy in this role. On the textual side, some think that the MT's 1 Kgs 9.5 was emended on the basis of the reading of 2.4 and that the 3 Kgdms reading is original; DeVries, *1 Kings*, p. 119; Auld, *Privilege*, p. 63. Japhet, *Chronicles*, p. 617 thinks it possible the LXX of 1 Kgs 9.5 reflects the original, but she also points to the influence of Mic. 5.1 on this and 2 Chron. 7.18. The basic formula of these promises is not restricted to Kings and Chronicles cf. Jer. 33.17.

84. Jehu's own episode will be discussed further below.

the property of a (legitimate) dynasty as a whole.[85] It should be clear from this survey, however, that not only are the 'throne' promises concentrated in the reign of Solomon, but so, too, are most references to thrones in general. Solomon not only wins the power behind David's throne, but actually builds his own chair to prove it, in a rather grand style (1 Kgs 7.7; 10.18-20). What this concentration establishes is the association of Solomon with power, prestige and the trappings of kingship, while introducing comments on the true nature of royal rule in Israel. Occupying the 'throne of Israel' is a matter of obligation, not privilege, and the example of Solomon, who failed to appreciate this, is probably to be seen as applicable to anyone who would aspire to a similar leadership role. Thus, the limits placed on Jehu are understandable. Unlike the title נגיד, however, no subsequent Judaean king attains the throne of Israel. With the fall of Jehu, the north's zealous if flawed reformer, this symbol of the ideal of the monarchic power has suddenly disappeared. This absence marks the rest of northern, and, indeed, Judaean monarchic history. Even in the story of Judah's own Josiah, there is little value placed on his membership of the celebrated dynasty of David.[86]

---

85. This is noted by Long, *2 Kings*, p. 152; Mullen, *Narrative History*, p. 51.
86. I will address this issue in Chapter 8.

Chapter 5

THE DIVISION OF THE KINGDOM

1. *Introduction*

The story of the division of the kingdom and its immediate aftermath is related in 1 Kings 11–14, although the Hebrew and Greek differ greatly. Chapter 11 describes the divine plan to tear the greater part of the kingdom from Solomon's heir (vv. 9-12). In 1 Kgs 11.14-25, two foreign adversaries are said to have troubled Solomon's reign, and, in vv. 26-31, Jeroboam is introduced as the one designated by Yahweh to receive control over the bulk of the Israelite kingdom. The confrontation between Israel on the one hand, and Solomon's heir, Rehoboam, on the other, is related in ch. 12. Rehoboam is rejected as king and Jeroboam is crowned, but Judah remains loyal to Solomon's heir, and so the United Monarchy is effectively at an end. To solidify his rule over Israel, Jeroboam institutes religious programmes intended to offer an alternative to the Jerusalem cult, and this is explicitly condemned (1 Kgs 12.30-33; cf. 13.33-34). An encounter between Jeroboam and a Judaean Man of God at Bethel is related in ch. 13. The Bethel altar is torn down as a sign that one day in the future, a certain Josiah, a descendant of the house of David, will desecrate it further with the bones of the heterodox priesthood instituted by Jeroboam (1 Kgs 13.1-4). In the next chapter of the MT Jeroboam receives an oracle of doom for his family and the destruction of Israel (1 Kgs 14.1-18) when his wife seeks a prophetic word about their ill son. The LXX includes a second version of the rise of Jeroboam and the Shechem rebellion, which are presented together in a lengthy section, 3 Kgdms 12.24a-z. This section also includes the Greek's only counterpart to the story of the oracle concerning Jeroboam's child (3 Kgdms 12.24g-n). This places it before his confrontation with Rehoboam at Shechem (24o). There are significant variants in the synoptic passages as well (1 Kgs 11.26–12.24). Among these, the most important differences have to do with the question of the timing of Jeroboam's return from Egypt and the assembly at Shechem (1 Kgs 11.43–12.3; cf. 2 Chron. 10.1-3).[1] The end of Jeroboam's dynasty, in both Greek and Hebrew, does not come until the rebellion of Baasha against Jeroboam's son Nadab (15.27-30). There are very many issues of import in these chapters, but not all can be dealt with here.[2] Of the divergence between the MT and LXX much has been written and much more needs to be said before all avenues are fully explored, but the extent of the problem precludes a detailed discussion here.[3]

While the problem of the origins of the variants cannot be simply ignored, the plurality of traditions attest the basic story's importance as a living body of tradition. On the other hand, it is possible at least to

---

1.   On the textual situation here, see T.M. Willis, 'The Text of 1 Kgs 11.43–12.3', *CBQ* 53 (1991), pp. 37-44.

2.   Similarly, there is a great deal going on in 1 Kgs 13 beyond the oracle to Jeroboam, but I cannot adequately treat these here. For recent work on the chapter and bibliography, see J.T. Walsh, 'The Contexts of 1 Kings XIII', *VT* 39 (1989), pp. 354-70, (354 n. 1); D.W. Van Winkle, '1 Kings XII–XIII 34: Jeroboam's Cultic Innovations and the Man of God from Judah', *VT* 46 (1996), pp. 101-14. Also, for a recent view on the adversaries of Solomon (1 Kgs 11.14-25) consult D. V. Edelman, 'Solomon's Adversaries Hadad, Rezon and Jeroboam: A Trio of "Bad Guy" Characters Illustrating the Theology of Immediate Retribution', in S.W. Holloway and L.K. Handy (eds.), *The Pitcher is Broken: Memorial Essays for Gösta W. Ahlström* (JSOTSup, 190; Sheffield: Sheffield Academic Press, 1995), pp. 166-91.

3.   On the relationship of the different versions, the reader should also consult the recent discussions by Z. Talshir, 'Is the Alternative Tradition of the Division of the Kingdom (3 Kgdms 12.2a-z) Non-Deuteronomistic?', in G.J. Brooke and B. Lindars (eds.), *Septuagint, Scrolls and Cognate Writings: Papers Presented to the International Symposium on the Septuagint and its Relations to the Dead Sea Scrolls and Other Writings, Manchester, 1990* (SCSS, 33; Atlanta: Scholars Press, 1992), pp. 599-621; and especially her monograph, *The Alternative Story of the Division of the Kingdom (3 Kingdoms 12:24 q-z)* (Jerusalem: Simor, 1993). See also Knoppers, *Two Nations*, I, pp. 169-223, and the well-known article by D.W. Gooding, 'The Septuagint's Rival Versions of Jeroboam's Rise to Power', *VT* 17 (1967), pp. 173-89. Other recent studies on these chapters include, Cohn, 'Literary Technique'; A. Frisch, 'Shemaiah the Prophet versus King Rehoboam: Two Opposed Interpretations of the Schism (I Kings xii 21-4)', *VT* 38 (1988), pp. 466-68; J. Holder, 'The Presuppositions, Accusations, and Threats of 1 Kings 14.1-18', *JBL* 107 (1988), pp. 27-38; S.L. McKenzie, 'The Source for Jeroboam's Role at Shechem (I Kgs 11:43-12:3, 12, 20)', *JBL* 106 (1987), pp. 297-300; *idem, Trouble*, pp. 21-59; J. Trebolle Barrera, 'Redaction, Recension, and Midrash in the Books of Kings', *BIOSCS* 15 (1982), pp. 12-35.

some extent to continue with a synchronic, holistic reading. This, of course, is much easier in the Hebrew than the Greek, since that version has only a single story of Jeroboam. For most scholars, the real comparison is between the MT and the second LXX account.[4] A full *literary* study of the Greek would require handling both accounts, and this results in great difficulty in determining the overall portrayal of events and characters. The two accounts do share a single ending, however, with Jeroboam's heterodox cult established in the new northern kingdom, and Rehoboam being left to rule Judah. However Jeroboam's rise is presented, his legacy in each book is one of shame; no version prevents his developing into the arch-villain of the north, although there is a massive difference in how each version retrospectively views the potential of his early career.[5] The plot of the LXX may then be interpreted in terms of its outcome, and so compared to the MT.[6] Rather than

4. Some find the second LXX version critical of Jeroboam while the MT offers a more favourable impression: R.P. Gordon, 'The Second Septuagint Account of Jeroboam: History or Midrash?', *VT* 25 (1975), pp. 368-93. Gooding, 'Septuagint's Rival Version', is of the opinion that in the first LXX version Jeroboam is almost 'saintly', on the model of David, whilst those who developed the second account tried to vilify him. Talshir, *The Alternative Story*, pp. 277-91, has a high regard for the artistry of the author of the second LXX account. By denigrating Jeroboam, however, the author has not exonerated Rehoboam. Knoppers, *Two Nations*, I, pp. 170-79, writes that the MT portrayal evinces multiple concerns, although it tends to offer an initially positive impression of Jeroboam as the divinely designated king. He takes the view that the second LXX account does not vilify Jeroboam, pointing out that in many ways his more active role marks him more as a protagonist with a number of desirable characteristics. Explicit, severe criticisms of him could have been included but were not. See McKenzie, *Trouble*, p. 28, on the absence of Dtr language in the LXX. Others hold that the MT and the second LXX version treat Jeroboam as of roughly the same moral character, despite the major differences in plot: M. Aberbach and L. Smolar, 'Jeroboam's Rise to Power', *JBL* 88 (1969), pp. 69-72.

5. For some, Jeroboam's portrayal is as the archetypal evil leader, found in other Near Eastern literature. See C.D. Evans, 'Naram-Sin and Jeroboam: The Archetypal *Unheilsherrscher* in Mesopotamia and Biblical Historiography', in W. Hallo, J. Moyer and L. Perdue (eds.), *Scripture in Context*. II. *More Essays on the Comparative Method* (Bloomington: Indiana University Press, 1983), pp. 97-125; Holder, 'The Presuppositions'. For a contrary view, see H.J.L. Jensen, 'The Fall of the King', *SJOT* 1 (1991), pp. 121-47 (129-31).

6. In a full narrative analysis this is quite unsatisfactory, as every nuance of the text, however repetitious or inconsistent, requires investigation, as well as translation technique, and so is a major undertaking requiring specialist skills.

concentrate on Jeroboam, however, I will look at these episodes from the point of view of their handling of the themes of the schism as developed from, and developing, social metaphors, by which the readership may imagine their 'Israel'.

2. *The Torn Robe*

In 1 Kgs 11.9-13 Solomon's punishment from Yahweh is announced. Yahweh will tear the kingdom away from Solomon (קרע אקרע את־ הממלכה) and give it to his 'servant'. The punishment, however, will only come in the days of Solomon's son and will not affect the entire kingdom; one tribe will remain for David's heir, for the sake of David and Jerusalem. A similar picture is given when Jeroboam meets the prophet Ahijah (1 Kgs 11.29-39). The prophet tears his robe, and in giving Jeroboam ten pieces of it, gives him a sign that ten parts of the kingdom will be his.[7] The prophetic word that the kingdom will be divided and the sign of the torn robe displays two interrelated themes. Not only will the kingdom be 'torn' from David, but it will be 'torn apart'. The first plays on the recollection of David's receipt of the kingdom from Saul in 1 Sam. 15.27-28, but the second is more determined by the schism itself, although it clearly has its intimations in 2 Samuel as well. Yet these two themes together do not fully exhaust the symbolic action. It is significant that the robe is torn into twelve fragments, and not only two. The *distribution* of the fragments becomes the 'tearing' the prophet mentions, not the actual rending of the garment. Moreover, each tribe is given some level of independent existence within the symbolic action.[8] Here Israel is imagined according to its most ancient guise, as the family of tribes descended from Jacob.[9] This highlights the poignancy of the predicted schism, and yet, affirms that integrity is not uniformity. Since a 'torn' robe can represent the totality

---

7. The missing tribe is variously interpreted, but often it is thought to be Benjamin, absorbed into Judah (cf. 1 Kgs 12.21), e.g. De Vries, *1 Kings*, p. 151; Provan, *Kings*, p. 98. LXX, however, has two pieces reserved for the davidic dynasty.

8. Except, of course, the tribe represented by the 'missing' piece.

9. Here I mean 'ancient' in the terms of the greater story of Israel preserved in the traditions now represented, not ancient in terms of the patriarchal story being the oldest story of origin the people of Israel had. It may be ancient in this sense too, but this can hardly be demonstrated.

of Israel, then the distribution of its pieces need not signify this 'ancient Israel's' dissolution.

There is an interesting textual variant in the prophetic words to Jeroboam worthy of note. In the Hebrew of 1 Kgs 11.34 Yahweh is reported as stating that not all of the kingdom will be taken from Solomon, since he has been made a ruler, נשיא, for life, while the LXX reads that Yahweh will oppose, διότι ἀντιτασσόμενος ἀντιτάξομαι, Solomon throughout his life.[10] Solomon's retention of a title in the Hebrew here is significant; but equally so that this title is not נגיד, as this is usually reserved in both Samuel and Kings for those granted particular obligations and status over 'Yahweh's people, Israel'. Even when Solomon is granted this title by David in 1 Kgs 1.35, it is not without suspicion. Despite occurring numerous times throughout the Hebrew Bible, נשיא, appears in Kings only here and in 1 Kgs 8.1, in which it refers to non-royal leaders of Israel meeting for the temple dedication (the LXX lacks a counterpart). As נשיא, Solomon becomes more like one of the leaders of the patriarchal houses (נשיאי האבות לבני ישראל) who congregate to witness the dedication of the temple and so play a subservient role to Solomon himself. The Greek reading seems unusually sharp in its condemnation, although this is mediated to some degree by a less harsh treatment elsewhere. If the LXX denies Solomon the title נשיא, however, it also denies Jeroboam the title נגיד. In either version the political jurisdiction of the davidic dynasty is now restricted to the south.

The implications of Solomon's actions are highlighted by the narrator's use of the now familiar epithet, 'God of Israel' (1 Kgs 11.9), when naming Yahweh as the deity Solomon had offended.[11] The divine epithet is also used in the introductory formula of Ahijah's prophecy (1 Kgs 11.31). The use of the epithet reinforces the difficulty of the situation of Judah; since it is excised from the rest of Israel, at least politically, does it remain in communion with the 'God of Israel'? In a number of places in ch. 11 reference is made to Jerusalem, the chosen city identified with Yahweh's name (cf. vv. 13, 32, 36). It is reported that for the sake of David and Jerusalem, a single tribe is reserved for

10. Knoppers, *Two Nations*, I, pp. 187-90, offers a good discussion of the confused textual situation here, preferring in his own translation to follow the Greek, although his reconstructed Hebrew is a new proposal, שׂטן אשׂטנו.

11. In this verse, the king's two visions are recalled (1 Kgs 3.5-15; 9.2-9). In the latter, national destruction is predicted for sin, but the schism is not intimated.

Solomon's heir. The schism, then, is not the dissolution of Israel, but the removal of the davidic dynasty from rule over it, while preserving the promise to David and the special status granted Jerusalem because of the temple. This builds on earlier passages. In 1 Kgs 8.16, Jerusalem is implicitly the chosen city of all those in the tribal territories of Israel (cf. 8.44, 48).[12] In the verses following, Solomon recapitulates the association between the davidic dynasty and Jerusalem, it was he and his father who planned and built the temple to Yahweh. The inseparability of the dynasty and city is portrayed as fundamental to the constitution of greater Israel, not only Judah. As pointed out above, in 2 Samuel 5–7 it was only after the consolidation of David's rule over greater Israel that David took Jerusalem to be the capital of his domain, and received the promise of an eternal house. The allocation of Judah to the davidic dynasty in 1 Kings 11 becomes a symbolic preservation of an ancient *status quo* in which the temple celebrated the inalienable relationship between greater Israel, its deity and the dynasty. Although Judah may have a special status because of David, the city itself is not solely a Judaean capital, but the centre of all Israel. The implication of this preservation is that thought concerning Judah's relative independence, or Jerusalem's status, is directed towards the reaffirmation of the intrinsic integrity of Israel.

This may be illustrated by reference to 1 Kgs 11.36, in which one tribe is granted to David as an eternal נִיר, or 'dominion' before Yahweh 'in Jerusalem'.[13] There are some other, related occurrences of the term in Kings, but these seem to display somewhat different nuances, and each should be interpreted in their own context. This rare term is also found in 1 Kgs 15.4, where Abijam receives the נִיר for David's sake, this being the reason why Judah was not destroyed in Abijam's apostate

12. In LXX[B] and the parallel 2 Chron. 6.6 Jerusalem is mentioned explicitly in this context.

13. E. Ben Zvi, 'Once the Lamp has been Kindled...: A Reconsideration of the Meaning of the MT *Nîr* in 1 Kgs 11:36; 15:4; 2 Kgs 8:19; 2 Chron. 21.7', *AusBR* 39 (1991), pp. 19-30, points to the lack of consensus in ancient translations. In the Vulgate, *lucerna* is used consistently, which supports the typical modern understanding of the term as a 'lamp'. On the other hand, the Targum renders it as *malkû* (rulership, kingdom). In the Greek, different terms are used in each case: 1 Kgs 11.36, θέσις (deposit); 1 Kgs 15.4, κατάλειμμα (remnant); 2 Kgs 8.19, λύχνος (lamp). Ben Zvi understands נִיר as meaning 'fertile field' or 'fief/dominion', while a root meaning of 'yoke' or (metaphorically) 'dominion' is less likely. He advises that 'lamp', the usual translation, be abandoned altogether.

reign. It is found again in 2 Kgs 8.19 in similar circumstances involving Jehoram. These verses, of course, are central to theories of a 'pro-monarchic' strand in Kings, as they seem to imply eternal divine sanction for the davidic dynasty.[14] On the other hand, these verses seem to find their greatest relevance in the conflict between Judah and Israel, and not in the eternal survival of Judah's dynasty itself. In 1 Kgs 11.36, the isolation of Judah from the rest of Israel is clearly at issue. David's heirs will have their ניר, one tribe, before Yahweh *in Jerusalem*, the city Yahweh chose. I take this to imply that Judah, as a davidic property, will be represented in the divinely chosen city where *all* the tribes of Israel are at least ostensibly represented. Far from being cast out, the dynasty and its dominions are still fully within the sacral conception of Israel. Indeed, this promise is made in the context of a prophet speaking in the name of the 'God of Israel' (1 Kgs 11.31) to Jeroboam, predicting that he will take control of 'Israel' (v. 37). Thus, Jeroboam is given no leverage to claim that Judah is no part of greater Israel, or that the city does not have a role to play for the whole of the Israelite people. By extension, it affirms a Judah-ist interpretation of 'Israel' and gives no credence to a Judah *without* Israel.

In the second ניר reference, 1 Kgs 15.4, this implication does not seem present, even if the MT and LXX[L] refer to the ניר being 'in Jerusalem', and that the establishment of the city is mentioned later in the verse in connection with the ניר.[15] There is no mention of Yahweh's choice of the city, and the issue of the symbolic value of the city to greater Israel is not really at issue. The divine grace shown to Abijam is the primary topic. Yet, the reference to the exceptional grace shown to a king less righteous than David (despite the presence of a seemingly snide comment that David was not perfect himself, 1 Kgs 15.5) is followed by a comment on the persistent state of war between Abijam and Jeroboam (v. 6). Verses 9-24 tell of Abijam's son and successor, Asa. These two contrast, however, in that Asa was considered a 'good' king, following in the ways of David (v. 11). Like his father, however, he wars with Israel, and this leads to some compromises. Even though Asa is remembered for offering votive gifts at the temple, he uses the temple and palace treasures to buy the support of Aram to break an Israelite blockade (vv. 18-21). Asa seems not to know the source of his

14. See, for instance, Nelson, *Double Redaction*, pp. 99, 108-109.
15. De Vries, *1 Kings*, p. 186, prefers to omit 'in Jerusalem' with the LXX[B].

true help. Asa does not seem to be aware that he rules the divinely supported נִיר, mentioned in the context of his father's reign (who himself was at war with Israel). The war between the kingdoms still does not revoke divine sanction for the davidic dynasty, but the absence of any condemnation of Asa's trust in Aram, in preference to Yahweh, is curious. One reads, however, that Asa was crippled in his old age, and so, perhaps, the silence is made good through insinuation. Ironically, the king whom Asa fought was Baasha, a נָגִיד of Yahweh's people, who destroyed Jeroboam's dynasty, and founded yet another doomed royal line (2 Kgs 15.33–16.14). The first נִיר reference establishes a theme of import for a retrospective view of history. The second seems more intimately concerned with how the two kingdoms fared in the course of that history.

The claim in 2 Kgs 8.19 that Judah was immune to destruction in Jehoram's reign because of the promised נִיר to David and his descendants should likewise be seen in its immediate context. Here there is no specific mention of Jerusalem. As with the previous attestation, the king in question is likened to the northern kings (v. 18). By this connection, not to mention the fact that Jehoram is actually the son-in-law of Ahab, the fate of Judah hangs as much in the balance as does Israel's. Earlier in the chapter, Elisha predicts that Hazael will seize the throne of Aram and brutalize the 'people of Israel' (vv. 7-15). Already in the life of Elijah this was planned, as was the rise of Jehu (1 Kgs 19.15-18). Following the נִיר reference in 2 Kings 8, the rebellions of the Edomites and Libnah are reported (vv. 20-22). Jehu's story unfolds in the next chapter, at which point in time Israel and Judah are at war with Aram again. 2 Kings 8.19, then, seems to allow Judah a way out of the trap being set for Israel, even though it is implied that it deserves to be included. The aftermath of Jehu's rise, however, shows that while the davidic dynasty is (at least temporarily) protected from destruction at the hands of foreign armies, it can be persecuted from within Judah itself. The release of Jehoiachin at the end of Kings seems to imply that there is a davidic king who survived the destruction and was at least nominally over Judah. Symbolically, at least, the נִיר can still exist. This נִיר, however, is not the totality of what Judah is; it remains a part of Israel.

These issues raise the question of the permanence of the punishment of the davidic dynasty. While the prophet in 1 Kings 11 promises Jeroboam dominion over all he may desire, should he obey Yahweh

(vv. 37-38), he adds in v. 39 that the descendants of David will be punished, but not forever.[16] It is possible to take this to mean that the division will not last forever and that one day the house of David will take control of greater Israel once more; but this is not really implied directly in Kings. It is possible to see the reign of Hezekiah as the beginning of the end of the afflictions of the division, as Hezekiah's reign sees the final collapse of the north (2 Kgs 18.9-12), and Hezekiah is considered by Yahweh to be נגיד over Yahweh's people (2 Kgs 20.5). Josiah's reign might also be seen to reflect this development, as Josiah eliminates the remnants of Israel's illegitimate cult (23.15-20). He also eliminates some of the offensive remnants of Solomon's apostasy (2 Kgs 23.13-14).[17] Neither of these kings' reigns, however, really mark the end of the troubles of the davidic dynasty. Hezekiah's lack of judgment results in a prediction of the exile (2 Kgs 20.16-19) and Josiah's actions are taken under the certainty of it (2 Kgs 22.15-20). If at least part of the punishment due the dynasty is the division of the kingdom, its conclusion does not really come with Hezekiah or Josiah, as neither is accorded kingship over greater Israel; both remain kings of Judah. One may also look to the release of Jehoiachin (2 Kgs 25.27-30), but again, the problem of division is not really addressed, as Jehoiachin is only the 'King of Judah' and, in any case, remains a vassal. Kings gives no indication of when the time of punishment for the house of David may be over. That the end is yet to come is also implied by 1 Kgs 9.6-9, which looks ahead to the exile, and not schism. The end of the punishment, at which point David's enduring 'house' will presumably be restored in some fashion, seems still in the future, although the end of Kings seems to be a guarantee that the future, perhaps, does hold such promise. Whether any rebuilt davidic 'house' will rule over greater Israel, be it an exclusively Judaean political entity, or only some kind of abstract ideal, does not appear to be answered explicitly.

The prophecy of Ahijah to Jeroboam includes the promise that if Jeroboam follows the example of David, then Yahweh will build for Jeroboam a 'sure house' בית־נאמן, as was built for David (1 Kgs 11.38;

---

16. This verse is not found in LXX[B].

17. The report about the removal of Solomon's legacy immediately precedes the report about Josiah's activities in the north. The connection is probably not coincidental.

cf. 2 Sam. 7.16).[18] Jeroboam, then, is at least potentially a new David.
As Knoppers points out, the promise to Jeroboam has attached to it the
same obligation that Solomon was supposed to fulfil. On the other
hand, Jeroboam's prospects, if he is successful, resemble those of
David. Knoppers argues that the deuteronomistic writer does not
(except for 1 Kgs 11.33) define the divine statutes and commands Jeroboam and Solomon are to obey; but they should be seen as pertaining to
cultic matters, as Solomon's sins involve heterodox worship of foreign
gods at various shrines. Jeroboam, therefore, was supposed to remain
faithful to the proper religion of the Jerusalem temple.[19] The implication that Jeroboam was to remain loyal to the Jerusalem temple puts
an odd condition on his rule and on the independence of his kingdom.
The central shrine for his people is to be found in a place outside of the
kingdom. With this understanding, then, matters of separate political
domains are presented as less important than cultic unity. It is easy to
see how such a message could have been relevant to post-monarchic
times, when political geography was determined by imperial organization, but Yahwistic religion was spread across such boundaries. One
could only wonder whether the producers of Kings were implying that,
had Jeroboam remained faithful to Jerusalem's temple, there would
have been two 'houses' worthy of their fond memory, that of David
and, perhaps, even more so, that of Jeroboam. Yet, there is always the
danger that by establishing two dynastic founders as figureheads, a
level of plurality could be entrenched that would undermine unity far
more than could the mere memory of there being two distinct
kingdoms. A Judah-ist history had to sacrifice one of the houses, and
this could never be the house that once ruled greater Israel from Jerusalem. Jeroboam had to be proven a failure on the very issue of faith-
fulness to the temple cult whose institution was a high point in the
history of a united people in their promised land.

The rise of the failed house, however, was an opportunity to call into
question the very identity of greater Israel; an ironically purposeful
questioning, which, in the end, asserted a common heritage and
accommodated the reality of a pluralistic Israel. If the descriptions of

18. In 1 Sam. 2.35 a בית נאמן is on offer for a 'true priest' כהן נאמן who will
take the place of Eli.

19. Knoppers, *Two Nations*, I, pp. 199-203. He offers a comparison between
the wording of the conditions to Solomon and Jeroboam (p. 200); cf. 1 Kgs 2.3;
11.33, 38.

Solomon's sins and the prophetic legitimacy granted Jeroboam expressed doubts about the need or desirability for a new political union between Judah and the territories of the former Samarian kingdom, the schism itself is not portrayed as forcing an ethnic or religious distinction between Judah and Israel. The division of the kingdom is not intended to portray the birth of two fundamentally opposed peoples, but to show how a single people were sadly divided against themselves. Unity of the claimed normative religion, and singularity of ethnicity are implied in many places in the following narratives. There is little resolution to many questions raised about the prophecy of the division. We do not know clearly when the punishment of David's house will end or if greater Israel will ever be united in its own land again or under a single leader again. The story of the schism and the subsequent histories of the two monarchies are not the simple fulfilments of the prophecy. Rather, there is a complex exploration of the notion of 'tearing' Israel apart and the narrative ultimately attempts to resist the full force and violence of the prophecy which it is at pains to show fulfilled.

3. *The Confrontation at Shechem*

The importance of the schism to Israel's history is such that the narration of a simple coup amongst the elite will not do; a gathering of Israel is necessary. The convocation of 'all Israel' in 1 Kgs 12.1 seems to set the stage for what might be seen as a social drama. The breach, crisis, redress, and reintegration / schism pattern of social drama, however, operates only superficially within the narrative world of the characters.[20] If one expects an orderly series of rituals, which make Rehoboam and Jeroboam legitimate monarchs of the two regions, such expectations are dashed. Descriptions of formal, religious rituals, marking the completion of the drama, are not found; rather, there is a breakdown in order, decisions seem to be made by a mob, not a congregation. Yet key elements in the episode recall the exodus and other phases in Israel's past. This makes of the schism a kind of re-creation, a sort of ritualized history, and in this re-creation of the past, the innovation of the schism can be accommodated. In accessing the primary myth of origin of greater Israel as a distinct people, the episode is structured like a house of mirrors, making the schism a perverse parody of the birth of

20. Mullen, *Narrative History*, pp. 10-16, 38-40.

the nation as a whole. Thus, the reader confronts the history of a fractured greater Israel; each component appears resolute in their independence, but in numerous episodes, each becomes a microcosm of the whole.

1 Kings 11 prepares the reader to look for the rejection of Rehoboam because of the religious conduct of his father, but these expectations are not rewarded in ch. 12. At issue in 1 Kgs 12.1-15 is the harsh service imposed by Solomon, and the refusal of Rehoboam to lighten the people's labours. If the reader acknowledges the seemingly discriminatory policies of Solomon into this narrative, however, there is still little evidence to suggest that there is any animosity between Judah and Israel. For many scholars, 'all Israel' in 1 Kgs 12.1, 16 means only 'all of the northern tribes', and they see in the confrontation the initial stages of a schism in the United Monarchy.[21] In my view, however, the 'all Israel' which confronts Rehoboam should be taken as the whole of the Israelite people, including Judah.[22] Provan proposes such a reading, and holds that the rejection of the house of David and enthronement of Jeroboam was a decision taken on behalf of the whole of the Israelite people. Judah, however, made an independent choice. The political ideal, as determined by the corporate body, was not to be realized in practice, according to the will of Yahweh. He argues that if a clear distinction between Judah and Israel at v. 17 was intended, it is not fully clear why it does not refer only to 'Judah' instead of 'sons of Israel dwelling in the cities of Judah'.[23] It is equally unclear why v. 20 refers to 'all Israel', instead of 'Israel' to avoid ambiguity. Provan also stresses the great symbolic value of Shechem to the whole of Israel.[24]

In Kings, no reason is given why the expected succession of Rehoboam had to be staged at Shechem, or why such a convocation was necessary at all. In any case, in the MT, Rehoboam has received some form of legitimization as king upon the death of his father (1 Kgs 11.43), but in both Hebrew and Greek, he still goes to Shechem so 'all

---

21. For instance, Jones, *Kings*, I, pp. 246, 249-50; Knoppers, *Two Nations*, I, pp. 218-21; Würthwein, *Könige*, I, p. 153. Noth, *Könige*, p. 272; Montgomery, *Kings*, p. 252; Gray, *Kings*, p. 304; Long, *1 Kings*, p. 136.

22. A strong case for this has been presented by Provan, *Kings*, pp. 103-105. See also De Vries, *1 Kings*, pp. 157-58.

23. Jones, *Kings*, I, p. 253, suggests that the 'sons of Israel dwelling in Judah' is a reference to relocated persons of northern, perhaps Benjaminite descent.

24. Provan, *Kings*, pp. 105-106.

Israel' could make him king (1 Kgs 12.1).[25] Shechem is a place of great importance in the history of greater Israel. As the writers recognize the schism as an important event, its setting in such a place is not wholly unexpected. As Provan points out, the site of Shechem has numerous implications for the whole of the Israelite nation's sense of self-identity; and, therefore, Rehoboam's coronation there, before the whole of the nation, and not only the northern tribes, should not be surprising. It was the site of the covenant renewal of Joshua 24 and where Joseph's bones are buried (Josh. 24.32). Since Shechem also figures in the attempt of the first Israelite to attain a kingly role, which, in any case, failed rather miserably, it is the ideal setting to ask the king to consider the identity of Israel and how his kingship will be conducted (Judg. 8.22-23; ch. 9).[26] The historical importance of Shechem suggests that far more is happening in 1 Kings 12 than simply the dividing up of political boundaries. As in the case of David, in 2 Samuel 5 where he became king over all Israel, the story has come to a point of transition. Rehoboam, however, seems unaware of just how radically this meeting will transform the world, or that he is involved in the reversal of David's rise to the kingship of greater Israel. From now on, David's dynasty produces only kings of Judah. In staging the coronation at Shechem, Rehoboam seems led into a trap. He is far away from Jerusalem, the capture of which celebrated David's rise to rule over all of Israel.

His expectations of becoming king are not met. Rather, he is given an ultimatum which he rejects: the people will be worked even harder than in the past (1 Kgs 12.1-14). Only here does the narrator report that this is the working out of the prophecy (v. 15). It is important to note, however, that in v. 16, when 'all Israel' express their outrage at Rehoboam's stubbornness, it is not 'Judah' who is rejected, but 'David', the 'son of Jesse', and the 'house of David'. The choice of the expression allows that the collective, and not just the northern territories, have rejected the rule of the davidic dynasty. The verse, however, ends with

---

25. The first LXX version of the schism does not mention Rehoboam's succession in its briefer version of the transition from the death of Solomon to the Shechem rebellion (1 Kgs 11.43–12.2). It does refer to 'all Israel' intending to make Rehoboam king in Shechem. In the second account, there is no mention of the succession, and no mention that Rehoboam was intending to become king at Shechem. He travels there after Rehoboam has gathered the tribes (3 Kgdms 12.24n).

26. Provan, *Kings*, pp. 103-104.

only 'Israel' going away to their tents. Because the change from 'all Israel' to 'Israel' occurs in a single verse, and the final clause is a fitting conclusion to the corporate declaration, it should not be taken as an indication, at this point, of a division between the north and Judah. It is only in v. 17 that the MT reveals that Rehoboam ruled over the 'sons of Israel' who were dwelling in Judaean cities (בני ישראל הישבים בערי יהודה).[27] This verse reaffirms Judah's membership in Israel, and so the reader may wonder if Judah 'went to their tents' with the rest of the nation in disgust over Rehoboam, but having little they could practically do about it. Verse 17 does not indicate that Rehoboam was chosen as king by Judah, merely that he reigned. This may imply some level of popular support, but little could be made of this. In v. 18, 'all Israel' stone Solomon's taskmaster, Adoram, to death, and Rehoboam flees to Jerusalem. It is possible that 'all Israel' may here simply specify the north, according to Danell's observations about the 'majority' rights to a collective name and the relative status of all (כל).[28] On the other hand, no mention of the flight of the Judaeans is made, and, perhaps, they are best implicated in the murder of Adoram too. A 'majority' reading makes some sense of v. 19, in which 'Israel' is said to be in rebellion against the House of David 'unto this day'. Here 'all' is dropped. On the other hand, if the Judaeans are seen as acting against Adoram, one should expect them to be included, to some degree, in the rebellion of v. 19. That the rebellion lasts 'unto this day' seems to imply that only the north was in rebellion, since, from the perspective of hindsight, Judah retained the davidic dynasty.[29] Yet, I am not so certain that

---

27. The MT reads וימלך. De Vries, *1 Kings*, p. 17, reads the verb as causative: the Judaeans and Israelites in Judah 'caused Rehoboam to reign', giving no explanation, perhaps taking his cue from the odd word order, where the people are mentioned first, followed by the verb, and then the reference to Rehoboam. Burney, *Notes*, p. 139, finds 'Rehoboam' the subject of an admittedly rare construction, but he finds other examples: 1 Kgs 9.21; 15.13; 2 Kgs 16.14.

28. Danell, *The Name Israel*, pp. 66-67, 71, 78, 92-96.

29. If one understands the episode as suggesting it was Judah that broke with a corporate decision, then it is Judah which was actually the agent of the predicted division, and not the northern tribes. Such a reversal makes not only 1 Kgs 12.19 difficult, but 2 Kgs 17.21, which says that Israel 'tore away' from the house of David. I will discuss this verse below. Brettler, 'Ideology', p. 279, points out that the verb 'to rebel' פשע is usually used in terms of a vassal opposing its overlord, and therefore, in 1 Kgs 12, Israel is depicted as rebellious, and illegitimate. While this may be so in many cases, it seems unlikely, however, that such a connotation

Judah is completely excused here. While the verse may recall only the north's continued 'rebellion', its use of the term may have more of a corporate than simply majority character. 'All Israel' rebelled, and 'unto this day' some are still in rebellion. In v. 20, however, it is reported that when 'all Israel' hears of Jeroboam's return, they call and make him king. Only here is it added that the tribe of Judah followed the House of David. Opposing the house of David, for want of better treatment, may be one thing, but submitting to *King* Jeroboam, who had no real connection with Judah except that he was Solomon's taskmaster, may be understood as quite another. Judah has broken ranks with the collective.

In the majority of LXX texts, there is no equivalent to v. 17, while in the LXX[L], it is actually longer, reading that Rehoboam reigned over the Judaeans and the Israelites dwelling in Judah.[30] In the majority of LXX texts, however, the absence of v. 17 gives the story a different nuance, in that there is no hint of a division within greater Israel before v. 19 (unless it is implicit in v. 16), and so seems a little more consistent. This version makes no mention of Jeroboam during the rebellion itself before v. 20, and so is somewhat more consistent. 'All Israel' make Jeroboam king, although he becomes king only over 'Israel'.[31] The LXX[L], however, seems to view the matter rather like the MT in v. 17, with the exception that it does not label the Judaeans as 'sons of Israel' but reserves this expression for the northerners, the Judaeans being mentioned separately. This allows the reader greater freedom in separating Judah from the 'Israel' mentioned in the following verses. Even so, on the strength of the 'all Israel' references at the start of the chapter, I would argue that v. 20, in all versions, should still be taken as a summary and continuation of the preceding episode, involving the

can be isolated here. The bulk of 1 Kgs 12 is devoted to describing how the rejection of Rehoboam is the will of Yahweh. It is to be remembered that it was because of the harsh service that the confrontation with the king came about. The initial act of this rebellion is hardly to be interpreted as illegitimate in the eyes of the writers, even though they might have thought that the animosity between Judah and the north had gone on too long, or that it was time to try to restore 'davidic' leadership over the Israelite people. Frustration at a continuing unsatisfactory situation could have motivated the strong words.

30. There is disagreement as to the original reading, cf. De Vries, *1 Kings*, p. 155; Burney, *Notes*, p. 176.

31. The Greek manuscripts also differ amongst themselves as to whether 'all Israel' should be read in v. 18.

corporate decision to make Jeroboam king of greater Israel. The only thing that stands in their way is Judah opting out of whatever pact united Israel in this matter.

The second LXX account (3 Kgdms 12.24n-z) opens with Jeroboam himself assembling the tribes of Israel at Shechem. This is followed by a version of the prophecy of the robe. In its very short form, Jeroboam is to receive ten pieces, although this sign does not receive much elaboration. In 3 Kgdms 12 (MT as well), Jeroboam is destined to become king by the prophet Ahijah. In the second version at v. 24o, however, there is some variance in the words of the prophet Shemaiah. The Lucianic manuscripts say that Jeroboam will reign, βασιλεύσεις, but the other Greek texts do not include this word.[32] Jeroboam is certainly not offered the extreme privilege of a 'sure house' like David. Indeed, he had already received the oracle of the death of his son, and the failure of his own line. Even though it may appear as though Jeroboam is being set up as someone doomed to fail, there is no real indication at this point that his rebellion at first only involves the northern tribes. The second account does use some different wording from the first. In v. 24t, 'all the people' declare the davidic line illegitimate, although 'Israel' is called to their tents in protest at Rehoboam's stubbornness. The following narrative is quite short, there is no mention of the fate of Adoram, and no discussion of the rebellion of 'Israel'. This version, however, is also interpretable according to the proposal of Provan, a unified protest before Rehoboam results in a collective rejection of rule, even though Judah and Benjamin are, perhaps, portrayed as rather more willing to follow Rehoboam than they may have been in the other versions of the story. They are depicted following Rehoboam into Jerusalem after he had 'strengthened himself' and returned to Jerusalem.

The textual situation in 1 Kings 12 is complex, and each version may have been altered by a number of different writers and editors to bring out different themes and implications. The variety of the possible uses of the name 'Israel' and constructs employing it ensure that a certain

---

32. Lucian is read as original here by McKenzie, *Trouble*, p. 26. Talshir, *Alternative Story*, pp. 107, 230, disagrees, explaining that in Lucian, τάδε λέγει κύριος is taken as an introductory formula, thus the expected verb was added. She feels that this was merely an attempt to avoid awkward syntax. Talshir observes that Jeroboam is accorded no royal title and that it seems as if the author of the alternative story was reluctant to admit explicitly that Jeroboam was destined to become king.

ambiguity should be expected, and that an ultimate solution may not be possible. It remains that Judah, in general, appears fickle, and this aspect of the troublesome schism may have served to make an important point. Judah was not completely blind to the oppressions which they and their northern brothers suffered. Yet, in the end, they remained loyal to their own royal family. Such a portrayal may also have served to limit the prospects of non-Judaean leaders for the post-monarchic Yahwistic communities, especially those in Judah itself. Judah (and Benjamin) are given an example of loyalty to follow. Even so, it is an admission that not all was right with the house of David, and that the situation had deteriorated so badly that even internal protest was justifiable. Leaders are given a warning that they have no right to impose unjust policies on their people. On the other hand, the schism episode may legitimize limits on the authority of Judah over the north, at least in political, if not cultic affairs.

4. *The Myth of Israel's Double Birth*

The interwoven history in Kings which follows the schism implies that neither Israel or Judah can really exist without the other and maintain a sensible hold onto the past that made them the people of Yahweh. The perversity of the situation is intimated in the twisted recollections of that common history which are contained in the story of the division. While this ensures that greater Israel is reaffirmed in the midst of its political dissolution, it becomes a parody of itself, and, as such, its new identity(ies) can hardly be stable. Within the narrative world, one expects these events to lead to no good; seen as 'social metaphors', these new 'Israels' are at once mutually referential and exclusive. They preserve the 'ideal' only by the fascinating and engaging way that it taxes that ideal's integrity.

One can compare the schism to some of the troubles experienced by David in 2 Samuel in maintaining control over greater Israel. In particular, Jeroboam attains what Sheba failed to secure. The words of the people in 1 Kgs 12.16 closely recall Sheba's own words which incited the ill-fated rebellion in David's day (cf. 2 Sam. 20.1). On the other hand, even though Sheba's uprising seems a direct result of animosity between Judah and Israel (2 Sam. 19.41–20.2), and involved only the northerners, there is no need to see an identical situation here. If this story was known to the writers of Kings, they have recalled the past, but not exactly. In my view, it is the collective which originally confronts Rehoboam and rebels against the house of David. The true schism occurs later. Where once there was a suppressed rebellion of only part of greater Israel, there is now a radical transformation: the duality in Israel is realized with Yahweh's approval. As noted above, the site of Shechem also has its significance in the past. The story seems to play off that told in Judges 8–9: Gideon's ironically-named son, Abimelech, sets himself up as ruler in Shechem. He is the first Israelite to be declared a king, and he comes to a grisly end.[33] The most important reflections of Israel's early history, however, are the many different themes adopted from the story of the descent into Egypt, the exodus and wilderness traditions. Jeroboam, the Ephriamite, is of the House of Joseph, and it is over the labour force of Joseph that Solomon places him (1 Kgs 11.26-28). Joseph, of course, was the first Israelite to become established in Egypt after his brothers sold him into slavery (Gen. 37). Jeroboam himself flees to Egypt (1 Kgs 11.40). Judah and its royal house also relive the role of Joseph in Egypt, as once did Joseph's own descendant, Jeroboam. In Samuel and Kings, the davidic dynasty receives the lordship over Israel, and is rejected when it takes its power for granted, perhaps as another refraction of the traditions behind the story of Joseph, and his vision of dominion over his brothers (Gen. 37). In time, it is Judah which outlasts its siblings, and, with its hold on the temple, it is Judah which holds the key to preserve the nation, as much as Joseph once preserved his own brothers.

The Egyptian king does not try to stop Jeroboam's return, unlike the earlier Pharaoh who tried to prevent the Israelites undertaking their exodus (1 Kgs 12.2-3; Exod. 5–10.27). The real confrontation in Kings is between Jeroboam, the new Moses, and Rehoboam, in the role of the exodus Pharaoh. He, like his Egyptian predecessor, becomes obstinate by the will of Yahweh (1 Kgs 12.14-15; cf. Exod. 5.1-21). Both Rehoboam and the pharaoh who Moses confronted increase the hardship of the people (1 Kgs 12.11; Exod. 5.1-21).[34] Israel's identity has become confused; they are no longer free, but exploited. In Provan's words, all Israel 'turned away from him (Rehoboam) and left his "Egypt" for a

---

33. He is made 'king' in Judg. 9.6. Even more so than the cases of certain monarchs in the book of Kings, a woman is cast as a significant player in his downfall. Abimelech has to ask a man to kill him to save him from the disgrace of being fatally wounded by a woman (Judg. 9.52-54).

34. Provan, *Kings*, pp. 103-105.

better country'.[35] That the kingdom had become Egypt is shown not only in the marriage of Solomon to the Egyptian princess, but in her father's dowry gift, the city of Gezer, a town within the borders of Israel (1 Kgs 9.16; 3 Kgdms 5.14b). Ironically, it is a Pharaoh who destroys the Canaanites there, something the Israelites should have done long ago. The real power behind Solomon was Egypt, perhaps evidenced by his arms dealings there (1 Kgs 10.28-29). This is something quite explicitly banned in Deut. 17.16, likening it to a return to Egypt. For the exodus generation, however, going back to Egypt was the preferable course of action (e.g. Num. 11.5, 18-20; 14.3-4; 20.5; Deut. 1.27). Not only does monarchic Israel figuratively go back to Egypt, but Egypt itself invades the land of promise. In 1 Kgs 14.25-28 Pharaoh Shishak plunders the temple and takes the gold shields of Solomon. This follows the report that religious apostasy is hardly restricted to the north (vv. 22-24). For Judah, history is not so much affirming as haunting, with no logical paradigm for their own situation. They are in Egyptian sanctuary and slavery, and yet they are in Canaan. The Judaean sins exceed those of their ancestors, and they copy the practices of their predecessors in the conquered land (1 Kgs 14.22-24), calling into question their own distinctiveness.[36] They remain in the land of promise and hold the chosen city of Yahweh, but by their actions have become Canaanites.

The north, however, finds itself in the wilderness, estranged as it is from Jerusalem, the new centre of the promised land. Jeroboam's foolish attempt at consolidation around the golden calves only proves how lost they are. To consolidate his rule, Jeroboam institutes his own cult, little more than a copy of the Jerusalem practices (1 Kgs 12.26-33). In 1 Kgs 6.1 and in 1 Kgs 8.9, 16, 21, 53, the exodus is recalled in connection with the Jerusalem temple, and so it is not incidental that Jeroboam includes in the cult some new features, two golden calves, which recall the shame of the wilderness. He claims that these are the deities

35. Provan, *Kings*, p. 106.

36. I will discuss in more detail below the numerous references to the 'conquest' tradition and the Canaanites. In Kings, recollection of the conquest, or the winning of the land is usually in the context of charges that the people were acting like the Canaanites. This is a clear indication that the writers were trying to define their favoured religious praxis as true 'Israelite' behaviour, while those that thought otherwise were only mimicking 'foreigners'. Also note that Rehoboam's mother is Ammonite (1 Kgs 15.21, 30; LXX, v. 21 only).

responsible for the deliverance from Egypt (vv. 28-29; cf. Exod. 32; Deut. 9.16-21). Here he recalls the declaration made by Aaron about his own golden calf (Exod. 32.4, 8), which so infuriated Yahweh. Both Aaron and Jeroboam address 'Israel' on the issue of the identity of the deities represented by the calves. In the Exodus passage, it is easy to see the name 'Israel' referring to the collective. Even though Jeroboam has gained control of only the north, his similar claims in 1 Kgs 12.28 should be taken not only as an address to his own kingdom, but also as a type scene, in which *all* of Israel is invited to follow the 'new' gods of the exodus.[37] This is reinforced later at v. 33, in which Jeroboam's festivals are for the benefit of the 'sons of Israel', a term earlier used to refer to the exodus community (cf., for example, 1 Kgs 6.1). The memory of the defining event in the history of the whole of the people of Israel has become corrupted. Yet, any call of Jeroboam to reunite greater Israel around himself is too late; greater Israel is now divided. The northern tribes will not repeat the pilgrimage of the original temple dedication, which, in 1 Kings 8, is celebrated as the final stage in the exodus itself (cf. Chapters 9 and 10 below); they now go to Bethel and Dan (v. 29), to celebrate only what shamed their ancestors. Thus, not only has Jeroboam broken faith with Yahweh, whose presence is represented by the temple, he has divided the people. Moreover, he has given his people a myth of origin which is only a twisted reflection of their relationship with the divine, which gives them their identity as a people.

The new Moses has become Aaron, and there is no one to return to the mountain to retrieve the law anew. In the confused refractions of the founding myths, greater Israel is not so much divided politically and religiously as it is dismembered and strewn across mythic time and space. The 'essence' of greater Israel is not fully attributable to Judah or Israel. Kings must tell the story of both kingdoms; the north is not left by the wayside or treated only incidentally (cf. Chronicles). In my view, this myth of the schism may be taken as reflective of the plurality and power struggles of the post-monarchic period. Yet the story of each independent kingdom also becomes a metaphor for the whole of greater Israel. This is, perhaps, easier to see regarding Judah, but it is also apparent, and perhaps more interestingly, in regard to Israel. This may be found not only in the reflections of the schism as Israel's exodus (or

37. Contra Zöbel, '*yisrael*'.

exile?) from itself, but in the consequent evaluations of the Jeroboam dynasty. Jeroboam's name resonates through the rest of the story of the north in both its Hebrew and Greek guises; most subsequent Israelite kings follow in his footsteps. Oddly, his name does not appear in the context of Judaean episodes. When a Judaean king, such as Manasseh (2 Kgs 21.3), is compared to a named northern king, it is Ahab (see also 2 Kgs 8.16-18, 27). Ahab, who reportedly was not happy with the modest extent of Jeroboam's sin (1 Kgs 16.31-33), is hardly remembered with much fondness. Yet, he is at least granted the dignity of having his biography include a repentance. The absence of such a repentance narrative on the part of Manasseh is all the more damning of him. The dwelling on Jeroboam's sin in the northern episodes, however, serves to trace the fall of that kingdom back to Jeroboam's twisted exodus, and the double birth of a nation divided against itself. In this light, the fall of Israel is assimilated to a greater movement in the history, the very reversal of the exodus itself—the exile of greater Israel.

The myth of the schism is strangely perverse; it produces two liminal 'Israels', neither one complete, and neither one expendable, and yet it fulfils the divine will expressed in the prophecies of the previous chapter. On the one hand, the two 'Israels' remain linked to each other and the common past through their 're-births' according to the time-honoured traditions of origin. The way in which these origins are reaccessed, however, only highlights the perversion of the twin birth. Ultimate reconstitution of a singular whole within the land seems not in the offing anywhere in Kings. More important is the explanation of plurality and exile, and the implication of the conclusion of the book, that some kind of reconstitution is found in exile, and in the potential for a new exodus which this represents.

Chapter 6

THE TWO KINGDOMS

1. *Alternative Israels*

After the division, Kings interweaves the stories of Judah and Israel. Typically, the reign of one or a few kings of Israel or Judah is narrated, followed by the events occurring in the other realm at about the same time. The reigns of the kings are synchronized, with the ascension of a king from one state dated by the regnal year of the contemporary monarch of the other kingdom.[1] That the story of the two kingdoms was considered necessary to tell indicates that the conception of a greater Israel is operative here, but the relationship between the two realms is not always clear. These two identities both clash and complement each other: while Judah usually seems to win the favour of the authors, the presence of the north is not merely an embodiment of evil. Rather, it is the manifestation of the 'other' side of greater Israel, in which Judah cannot but participate. Israel is necessary to Judah, for it offers not only negative lessons, but preserves a way of imagining Israel not dependent upon, and even in contrast to, the davidic dynasty.

In these episodes, Judah and Israel are sometimes enemies, sometimes allies. One of the final images of the story of the schism in 1 Kings 12 is the declaration that Rehoboam should abort his attempt to recapture the north, because the schism was an act of Yahweh (1 Kgs 12.21-24). Here, Rehoboam had mustered the forces of Judah and Ben-

---

1.   These synchronisms are notoriously inconsistent. Proposals of co-regencies are among the means of solving the historical problems, although ultimately the chronologies may be artificial. Among the many studies is J. Hughes, *Secrets of the Times: Myth and History in Biblical Chronology* (JSOTSup, 66; Sheffield: JSOT Press, 1990). Recently, G. Galil, *The Chronology of the Kings of Israel and Judah* (SHCANE, 9; Leiden: E.J. Brill, 1996), has defended anew the affirmation that accurate historical information can be deduced from the texts. His critique of such positions as that of Hughes can be found on pp. 1-11.

jamin to fight the 'House of Israel'. A prolonged state of war between Judaean and Israelite kings, however, is revealed in 1 Kgs 14.30, 15.6, 16, 32. On the other hand, in 1 Kings 22 Jehoshaphat of Judah and Ahab of Israel find common cause to reclaim Ramoth-gilead from Aram. A similar combined operation involving Jehoshaphat with Israel's Jehoram is related in 2 Kings 3. This involves Edom as an ally against Moab. Both times, however, the allies are defeated. Subsequent events see blood spilt between Judah and Israel. Jehu's bloody rebellion (2 Kgs 9–10) eliminates not only the house of Ahab, but indirectly forces the house of David into hiding. Athaliah (daughter of Omri, 2 Kgs 8.26, or of Ahab; cf. v. 18) seizes the Judaean throne after Jehu murders her son, Ahaziah. This situation inverts the norm, with a king of at least qualified good reputation in Israel (2 Kgs 10.26-31) and an apostate ruler in Judah (and a female one at that, paralleling the story of Jezebel, whose own life is lost in Jehu's coup, 2 Kgs 9.30-37). While the situation in Judah is soon reversed with a davidic king returning to the throne (2 Kgs 11), Judah and Israel's behaviour are soon brought into comparison over how they handle Aramean aggression. The pious davidic king, Joash, bribes the Aramean king to withdraw (2 Kgs 12.18-19). Israelite Jehoahaz pleads with Yahweh, who sends Israel a deliverer (2 Kgs 13.4-5) from the Aramean threat. Ultimately, however, the apostate Israelites do not change their ways. Israel is left almost undefended (2 Kgs 14.6-7). Something of a recovery is made under Jehoash, although Elijah's final prophetic sign indicates that victory was not as complete as it could have been (2 Kgs 13.14-19). The security of Israel during the reign of Jehoahaz is also attributable to the covenant with Abraham, Isaac and Jacob; and Jehoahaz' son Jehoash recovers some of the lost territory (2 Kgs 13.22-25).[2] Although Azariah recovers some territory for Judah, Israel shows even new vigour under Jeroboam II, with some rather extraordinary assistance: it is reported that Yahweh had resolved not to blot the name of Israel out, and so he saved them, ויושיעם, from their bitter plight through Jeroboam (2 Kgs 14.25-27).

Marking the affiliation of the north to Yahweh in such 'unconditional' terms as these offers a counterpart to the 'unconditional'

2. The other reference to Abraham and Isaac is also in a northern context: 1 Kgs 18.36. Jacob's renaming as 'Israel' is mentioned in 1 Kgs 18.31 and 2 Kgs 17.34. The former is a 'northern' reference, while the latter is set in the aftermath of the Assyrian resettlement of Israel.

sanction for David, whose dynasty now rules only Judah. As others do, I maintain that Kings does offer condemnation of the north in the terms of its frequent and violent dynastic changes, while in general maintaining the primacy of the symbol of continuity represented by the davidic line.[3] Yet, the patriarchal covenant, and the other statements of Yahweh's abiding concern suggest that the 'davidic model' is but one of several institutionalized alternatives for imagining Israel. This can be further illustrated by pointing out other facets of the theological complex of Yahwism which are also lacking in the north. The narrator does not explicitly remind the reader of the exodus in relating northern episodes, and neither does any character. Moreover, even the Jerusalem temple is ignored.[4] This is compounded by the absence of mention of Moses in the northern episodes, even if the choice of words describing Jehoahaz' plea and the granting of a deliverer, מוֹשִׁיעַ (v. 5) evokes images of him (2 Kgs 13.3-5).[5] Perhaps מוֹשִׁיעַ is even a word play on Moses, מֹשֶׁה (alternative explanations for the identity of the מוֹשִׁיעַ will be given below).[6] Auld points out that northern loyalty to the standards mediated through Moses is not an issue, nor is it even worth denying.[7] It is clear from 1 Kgs 6.1 and ch. 8, however, that the *Torah* of Moses and the exodus are assimilated to the temple, and so refraining from these themes in regard to the north seems more a strategy of inclusion than exclusion. On the other hand, the presence of great prophets like Elisha and Elijah reinforces the sense of Israel as Yahweh's people, and their 'legitimate' religious heritage. This strategy also includes lesser

---

3.   A recent study developing the counter theme to this in Jehu's reign is E.T. Mullen, Jr, 'The Royal Dynastic Grant to Jehu and the Structure of the Book of Kings', *JBL* 107 (1988), pp. 193-206. There have been a number of studies which suggest that Kings confuses (accidentally or deliberately) issues of dynastic succession in both Judah or Israel. Mullen, *Narrative History*, pp. 22-23, thinks the claims of an (almost) unbroken dynasty of David spanning nearly 400 years invites close scrutiny. On Jehu as a member of the family of Omri, see T.J. Schneider, 'Rethinking Jehu', *Bib* 77 (1996), pp. 100-107. On the possibility that behind the Israelite Joram and the Judaean king of the same name was a *single* monarch, see J. Strange, 'Joram, King of Israel and Judah', *VT* 25 (1975), pp. 191-201.

4.   But see 2 Kgs 14.11-14, in which Jehoash of Israel sacks the temple, and carries off hostages.

5.   Long, *2 Kings*, pp. 165-66; Hobbs, *2 Kings*, pp. 167-68.

6.   Long, *2 Kings*, p. 166.

7.   Auld, *Privilege*, p. 143. In 2 Kgs 18.12, however, northern disobedience to the *Torah* is claimed, but this is set in the reign of Hezekiah.

prophetic figures, such as Ahijah (1 Kgs 11.29-39; 14.4-16); Jehu (1 Kgs 16.1-4) Micaiah (1 Kgs 22.7-28); and Jonah (2 Kgs 14.25); and others who remain anonymous (1 Kgs 13). The 'prophetic' model, however, not only stands in opposition to the apostate northern monarchy, but also the southern temple cult. The memory of these prophets in the northern territory preserves a Yahwistic heritage for the north, in spite of Judah's exclusive hold on the temple during the time of the two monarchies.[8] Yahwistic Israel can be imagined as something other than the congregation of the temple cult, and this idea is strong enough to be set within the time period of the first temple itself.[9] Different models of the core of Israel's 'proper' religion persist: that of the patriarchal covenants, Mosaic law, davidic theology, temple worship, or leadership based on revelation through those accorded the status of 'prophet'.[10] Even if the models preserved in the 'north' are seen as subordinate to the high status of Judah and the temple, they still persist, and total suppression of their symbolic value to Jerusalem should perhaps not be forced. At the schism, Israel was twice reborn. What is preserved in Judah is but one part of the parent's legacy. The other part is the heirloom of the northern sibling. At the end of this chapter, however, I will show how the clash of monarchic models, that is, the 'House of David' and the 'House of Jehu', results in a carnivalesque chaos, in which even Judaean claims to primacy, because of David, are challenged. This has no greater evidence than the reference to Jehoahaz and the deliverer, מוֹשִׁיעַ. However it evokes images of Moses, the identity of this deliverer, however, is a matter of some debate. Some, stressing historical scenarios behind the texts, propose that another foreign enemy of Aram is intimated, although this proposal has its critics.[11] Seeing Elisha as the saviour of Israel is more likely, especially with the

8. Some scholars hold that the social role of prophets was problematic to some of the writers of Kings: see E. Ben Zvi, 'Prophets and Prophecy in the Compositional and Redactional Notes in I–II Kings', *ZAW* 105 (1993), pp. 331-51.

9. On the other hand, Judah has its prophets too, Isaiah and Huldah, both of whom are interested in the security of Jerusalem, if not in the temple itself.

10. A recent opinion, however, holds that in the DtrH the prophets are almost always portrayed in a way that does not usurp royal power, although cracks in this ideological facade appear: W.J. Bergen, 'The Prophetic Alternative: Elisha and the Israelite Monarchy', in R.B. Coote (ed.), *Elijah and Elisha in Socioliterary Perspective* (SemS; Atlanta: Scholars Press, 1992), pp. 127-37.

11. Gray, *Kings*, pp. 594-95, gives an overview of some of the proposals.

similarity of the names, מוׁשיע / אליׁשע.[12] I find this word play more plausible than one with Moses. On the other hand, the prophet is strangely absent from the text of the salvation. Quite extraordinarily, Jehoahaz appeals to Yahweh directly, and Yahweh heads him (2 Kgs 13.3-5). That deliverer, however much it seems at first to be a prophetic figure, ultimately is strongly intimated to be none other than Jeroboam himself, who saved the nation because of the divine promise (2 Kgs 14.25-27). In an odd twist, a king of the north has actually fulfilled what the first legitimate Israelite king, Saul, was originally intended to do when Samuel was told to anoint him נגיד (1 Sam. 9.16, והוׁשיע את־ עמי and 2 Kgs 14.5-27, ויוׁשיעם).

2. *Rights to a Name*

The general patterns in the use of certain names employed in the episodes set in the time of the two kingdoms are noteworthy. The south is almost always 'Judah'. The simple name 'Israel' is used of the populations or territory of the northern state, as would be expected. This can be easily explained in terms of 'majority' rights to the collective name, as Danell suggests, and is understandable in terms of the actual historical names of the kingdoms, not to mention a desire to produce a non-ambiguous narrative. In a number of places, the northern populations are labelled with expressions which were used to refer to greater Israel in the time before the division and during the schism, but these cause little concern. Here the expression 'all Israel' may simply mean 'all of the (northern) kingdom of Israel', or at least, its army (e.g. 1 Kgs 15.27, 33; 16.16, 17; 20.15; 2 Kgs 3.6).[13] In a number of cases, the name 'Israel', or expressions employing it, ostensibly point to the north through the immediate context, but can actually be construed as having a much wider significance. Here the narrative seems to play on the dual meaning of the term. It not only assures the north a place within the people of the 'God of *Israel*', but also makes their experiences paradigmatic for *all* Israel.

Terms that express sacral connotations for greater Israel are generally withheld from the north, although there are some exceptions. References to 'Yahweh's people, Israel' appear rarely after the division: for

---

12. Hobbs, *2 Kings*, pp. 167-68, rules out seeing some historical enemy of Aram implied in the text. He, like Gray, *Kings*, pp. 595-96, holds that Elisha is indicated, following the example of the prophetic archetype, Moses.

13. There are textual variants in 1 Kgs 16.16 and 2 Kgs 3.6.

example, in the context of the summaries of Jeroboam's and Baasha's poor performance as *nagidim* (pl.), נגידים (1 Kgs 14.7; 16.2). Jehu does not become נגיד in Kings, although his jurisdiction as king is described in somewhat similar terms. In 2 Kgs 9.6 Jehu is anointed king for the 'people of Yahweh, Israel'. Jehu's reign as king is interesting in other ways, as I will describe below. The sacral connotations of his dominion are put to good use in the structure of the book, as well as his occupation of the highly symbolic 'throne of Israel'. Judah, however, is also given an opportunity to reaffirm its status as the 'people of Yahweh' in 2 Kgs 11.17, upon the reinstatement of the davidic dynasty.

The epithet 'God of Israel' appears frequently in a variety of contexts. Some seem quite formulaic, especially those used to introduce the word of the deity, particularly in prophetic announcements (i.e. 'thus says Yahweh...' 1 Kgs 11.31; 14.7; 2 Kgs 9.6; 21.12; 22.15, 18), or oaths in the divine name (1 Kgs 17.1, 14; cf. 1 Kgs 1.30).[14] The formulae for prophetic pronouncements do not always include the divine epithet, however, as 1 Kgs 12.24, 13.21, and 2 Kgs 7.1 reveal, nor do oaths (1 Kgs 18.15). The failure of the formulae to employ the longer divine title consistently makes any inference based on the pattern of its occurrence less than conclusive, but in the post-schism episodes something noteworthy does occur. The epithet is found in narratives concerning the northern state, but not Judah, until the north has been eliminated. 1 Kings 14.13 reports that Jeroboam's son pleased the God of Israel. On the other hand, Baasha eliminated Jeroboam's heirs because he provoked (כעס) this deity (1 Kgs 15.30). The motif of the provocation of Israel's god reappears (1 Kgs 16.13, 26, 33; 22.54).[15] Elsewhere, the divine title 'God of Israel' is used in Elijah's utterances (1 Kgs 17.1, 14) and Elisha's, concerning Jehu (2 Kgs 9.6). Later, the narrator reports that Jehu disobeyed the law of the 'God of Israel' (2 Kgs 10.31), and that Jeroboam II reclaimed land according to his word (2 Kgs 14.25). To this might be added 1 Kgs 18.36, which has Elijah pray to the god of Abraham, Isaac, and Israel, asking that the deity prove himself 'God in Israel' (MT), or the 'God of Israel' (LXX).[16]

---

14. Cf. 2 Kgs 14.25 and the fulfilment of the word of the 'God of Israel'.

15. 'Yahweh' is the object of the provocation (identified through the name itself, the use of a pronoun, or simply the context) in 1 Kgs 14.9, 15; 16.2, 7; 21.22; 2 Kgs 17.11, 17; 21.6, 15; 23.19, 26.

16. אלהים בישראל; κύριος ὁ θεὸς Ισραηλ. Cf. the variants in 1 Kgs 20.23, 28; 2 Kgs 22.19.

Only after the fall of Israel is reported (1 Kgs 17.1-6) does the epithet figure in passages in the narratives of the southern history (discussed below).

Other expressions used in the northern episodes are worthy of note. The Hebrew of 1 Kgs 14.13 and 18 tell of 'all Israel' mourning Jeroboam's son. Since the northern kingdom had by this time already been established, one should, perhaps, see the expression in these places as referring to only the whole of the north. On the other hand, in the light of the discussions in the chapters on the schism, and the נגיד, it is also possible to see 'all Israel' as referring, again, to the collective (allowing for some dissent amongst Judaeans). This is further reinforced by the way in which the episode echoes the sad story of David and Bathsheba's first child (2 Sam. 12.1-24); a king under judgment loses his child. There are significant differences though; the death of David's child is not obviously symbolic of the destruction of a dynasty. Rather, the death saves the nation from having an 'illegitimate' claimant to the throne. Yet, in the MT, Jeroboam had at least the potential to become a new David. The death of the child symbolizes Jeroboam's failure and reconfirms the davidic line as the primary royal symbol of greater Israel. Certainly in 1 Kgs 12.28-33, the question of whether the alternative cult of Jeroboam, devised for the 'sons of Israel' (בני ישראל) (v. 33), was intended for only the northerners, or was open to all, is an ambiguity which helps tie the northern apostasy to a tendency towards the religious impropriety portrayed as endemic to greater Israel in biblical literature as a whole. The apparent double meanings of both expressions, בני ישראל and 'all Israel' (כל ישראל), are found in a number of other places in the story of the north.

1 Kings 18–19 tells of Elijah's confrontation with the prophets of Baal on mount Carmel, the alleviation of a drought, and the prophet's encounter with Yahweh at the Mountain of God at Horeb. There are many features in this narrative complex which access other traditions of relevance to greater Israel, even though the famine is said to affect only Samaria severely (1 Kgs 18.2) and the primary royal opponents are Ahab and Jezebel of Israel. The prophet and the king initially dispute who the real 'troubler of Israel' (עכר ישראל) is, but Ahab still summons 'all Israel' and the non-Yahwistic prophets to Mount Carmel (1 Kgs 18.17-20).[17] At Carmel, Elijah demands they choose between

---

17. In v. 20, MT has 'all the sons of Israel' to LXX's 'all Israel'.

Baal and Yahweh (1 Kgs 18.21).[18] The pan-Israelite implications of the narrative are brought home, not only by the confrontation between Yahweh and other gods, but by the symbolism of the altar repaired by Elijah. It is of twelve stones, representing the tribes of Israel (1 Kgs 18.30-31). The narrator is quick to point out that the tribes are those descended from Jacob, who was renamed Israel. This reflection on the ancestry of the northern tribes links the narrative to the history of greater Israel. This is done again in v. 36, when the prophet evokes the god of 'Abraham, Isaac and Israel', the deity who is 'God in Israel'. As the story continues into ch. 19 Elijah flees, first to Beersheba in Judah (no mention of a Judaean king is made), and then, in a scene somewhat reminiscent of the wilderness wanderings, strikes out towards the Mountain of God, arriving there after forty days.[19] Rather than receive the law, as did Moses, Elijah receives divine instructions to anoint a new king of Aram, and Jehu as the new king of Israel, and is warned of a blood-bath in which only a remnant of Israel will be left: 7000 people who have not bowed down to Baal (1 Kgs 19.15-18). The encounter between the prophet and Yahweh also highlights the comprehensive conception of Israel. Twice Elijah complains that the 'sons of Israel' (בני ישראל), have abandoned the covenant with Yahweh (1 Kgs 19.10, 14). Even though בני ישראל here is logically the northern tribes, the scene of the prophet at the Mountain of God makes of it a moment of import for all. Even a Judaean reader may find his or her own history given voice in the prophet's complaint.

Else K. Holt finds that Israel's flirtation with polytheism presents a social crisis in the narrative. She argues that the prophets of Baal were the scapegoats for Jezebel in a kind of 'anti-sacrifice'. Jezebel becomes the scapegoat for Ahab, who, with his own actions of repentance, or at least remorse, can be likened to Josiah (MT 1 Kgs 21.27-29; LXX, ch. 20).[20] The fact that the ultimate scapegoat in this episode is the foreign Jezebel relativizes any dispute within greater Israel.[21] The cults

18. Cf. the speech of Joshua in which he asks the people to decide who they will serve; Josh. 24.15.

19. B.P. Robinson, 'Elijah at Horeb, 1 Kings 19.1-18: A Coherent Narrative?', *RB* 98 (1991), pp. 513-36, argues that Elijah tries to assimilate the role of Moses to himself, to his own discredit.

20. E.K. Holt, '"... urged on by his wife Jezebel": A Literary Reading of 1 Kgs 18 in Context', *SJOT* 9 (1995), pp. 83-96.

21. It is eventually internalized with Manasseh, but note that he is a Judaean.

of Baal and Asherah are 'foreign', and have no proper place within greater Israel as a whole. Even though the confrontation is set in the north, Baal and Asherah are hardly considered strangers to Judah (e.g. 2 Kgs 21.3-7). The northern story, then, carries lessons for greater Israel. This is further reinforced by the blurring of the distinction between Judah and Israel in the following narratives. Kings of the two realms campaign together; Judaean kings follow the example of their northern counterparts, and, indeed, marry into the family of Ahab (1 Kgs 22; 2 Kgs 3.4-27; 8.18, 27-29).[22] In 2 Kgs 8.12, a collective sense of בני ישראל seems to lie under the surface again. Here an Aramean general is told he will severely oppress the בני ישראל. The close relations between Judah and Israel at this point in the narrative suggest that the expression may have nuances of a collective meaning, even if Judah is granted some divine grace (2 Kgs 8.19).[23] 2 Kings 13.3-5 tells of divine anger with 'Israel', here most likely only the north, since the sins of Jehoahaz are at issue in v. 2. Yet the king pleads with Yahweh, and so 'Israel' is granted a deliverer and the בני ישראל dwell in their homes, as before. The switch in the names for Israel is curious. On the one hand, it may be purely incidental. On the other, it may be explained as a strategy whereby the localized events of the northern apostasy, pleading and deliverance are then translated into a general lesson on how Yahweh can reinstate the whole of Israel, imagined as a 'descent group', securely in their homes.

Back-tracking a little, 1 Kings 20 (LXX, ch. 21) is another example of an ostensibly northern episode with a comprehensive application. In 1 Kgs 20.15 the king of Israel musters 7000 men, the בני ישראל, under governors, to face an Aramean threat.[24] It is 'Israel', however, who is victorious (v. 20). Once the enemy had analysed their defeat, and try to fight 'Israel' once more (vv. 26-27), the sadly outnumbered בני ישראל

22. Certainly the 'camp of Israel' in 2 Kgs 3.24 refers to that of the combined forces, even the Edomites. The 'Israel' that flees is also best taken as the collective.

23. Or perhaps the collective implications are actually reinforced through the exception made for Judah. In 2 Kgs 8.18, 27, sins of the Judaean kings are likened to those of the apostate northern dynasty which the Judaean monarchs had married into. Judah goes to war alongside Israel against Aram, although Judaean casualties are not enumerated (2 Kgs 8.28-29). Aram eventually attacks Judah in the reign of pious king Joash, but the assault is aborted when Joram offers the Arameans the palace and temple treasures (2 Kgs 18–19).

24. This figure recalls the pious remnant predicted in 1 Kgs 19.18.

prepare for battle once more. A second Israelite victory is predicted by a Man of God, saying that Yahweh would not let go unanswered the Aramean perception of him as a god of the mountains who is ineffectual on any other terrain (1 Kgs 20.28). In v. 29, the בני ישראל defeat their enemies.[25] The Aramean attack is turned in a fashion reminiscent of the way in which Israel originally gained a foothold in Canaan. In 1 Kgs 20.29-30, battle is not joined until the seventh day, and the remnant of the enemy die when the wall of Aphek falls on them.[26] This story recalls the seven-day vigil before the ritual assault on Jericho brought the walls of that city down (Josh. 6, esp. vv. 15, 20). Whereas none but the family of Rahab were spared in Joshua 6, the king of Israel, in 1 Kings 20, negotiates with his defeated foe, only to receive a prophetic sign that this mercy is done only at the cost of his own life (vv. 30-43; compare Saul's sparing of Agag in 1 Sam. 15.17-24). Another refraction of the conquest tradition can be found. Ahab, the 'troubler', עכר, of Israel in 1 Kgs 18.18 may be likened to Achan in Josh. 7.25 who 'troubled', עכר, Israel by taking banned property from the spoils of Jericho.[27] The army that confronted Aram is labelled the 'sons of Israel' (1 Kgs 20.15, 27, 29). There is little impediment to understanding these references simply as 'sons of the northern kingdom', that is, the army, but given the other associations with pre-monarchic, or at least, pre-schism, episodes in history, the choice of name seems to facilitate the evocation of the concept of a greater descent group which comprise Yahweh's chosen people. Less subtly, one may see a comprehensive sense intended in the narration of the final days of Ahab as well, which see another battle with Aram (1 Kgs 22.1-38). Both the kings of Israel and Judah consult prophets to determine whether they should commit to such an endeavour. Micaiah says that he sees 'all Israel' scattered over the hills (v. 17). Even though Ahab takes this reference as a personal omen of misfortune, it is clear

25. LXX[BL] has only 'Israel' in the second v. 27 attestation and in v. 29. De Vries, *1 Kings*, p. 244, attributes this to a desire to match 'Aram' with an equivalent gentilic reference to Israel.

26. In v. 29, בני ישראל is found in the MT, whereas the LXX has simply 'Israel'.

27. Provan, *Kings*, pp. 153-54. Holt, 'Jezebel', p. 89 notes that the execution of Achan takes place outside of the Israelite camp, likewise the slaughter or 'anti-sacrifice' of the 'foreign' prophets is some distance from the altar Elijah built (1 Kgs 18.40). This protects the sacred centre from desecration. Note, also, the death of Ahab in the disputed territory of Ramoth-gilead in 1 Kgs 22.35, 37.

that the union of both kingdoms of greater Israel make the prophet's words applicable to the collective as well. So, too, in 2 Kgs 9.14 where 'all Israel' fight with Aram over Ramoth-gilead; again Judah and Israel are allies (cf. 2 Kgs 8.28). Jehu is anointed 'king over Israel' in 2 Kgs 9.6, and so 'all Israel' in v. 14 may be taken as referring to the collective.

Even though בני ישראל (as well as 'all Israel') may be used only of the inhabitants of the northern kingdom in the episodes of the two monarchies, its occurrence in contexts of a pan-Israelite significance suggests that the writers may have deliberately evoked memories of the United Monarchy, or even earlier periods in the socially-validated history of their readers, including the patriarchal age.[28] As I have mentioned already, the expression is sometimes used in the United Monarchy episodes to refer to the exodus generation. There are also a number of references in which בני ישראל is used to identify the conquest generation. Often this is in the context of complaints about intermarriage, or for following the practices of the Canaanites, displaced long ago. The most famous offender so far in this survey of Kings has, of course, been Solomon (1 Kgs 11.2-8). In 1 Kgs 14.24, however, the Judaeans, under Rehoboam, repeat the abominations of the displaced nations:

עשׂו ככל התועבת הגוים אשר הוריש יהוה מפני בני ישראל

Similarly constructed (but not identical) judgments are made elsewhere: 1 Kgs 21.26 (LXX ch. 20; Ahab); 2 Kgs 16.3 (Ahaz); 2 Kgs 17.8, 11 (Israel as a whole); and 2 Kgs 21.2, 9 (Manasseh). In each of these cases, the foreigners are driven out or destroyed before the בני ישראל, who are named explicitly, or implied from an earlier verse (cf. 2 Kgs 17.11). The assimilation of monarchic era sin with recollections of the conquest affirms the understanding of בני ישראל as a term of comprehensive relevance, and so supports the suggestion that the northern episodes above might be read, not only as episodes within the history of the regional kingdoms, but of the greater history of Israel as a whole. Noteworthy is the fact that most of the conquest references are actually set in comprehensive contexts; the United Monarchy (1 Kgs 11.2), the

---

28. There are very few references in Kings to the patriarchs known from Genesis. 1 Kgs 18.36 has Elijah evoke Yahweh as the 'God of Abraham, Isaac and Israel' to demonstrate that there is a 'god in Israel'. 2 Kgs 13.23 refers to the covenant with Abraham, Isaac and Jacob when Yahweh delivers 'Israel'. Jacob's renaming as 'Israel' is mentioned in 1 Kgs 18.31 and 2 Kgs 17.34.

sins of the whole of Israel (those in 2 Kgs 17), or of the Judaean kings
and their people (1 Kgs 14.24; 2 Kgs 16.3; 21.2, 9).

I have now introduced the Judaean episodes and a closer look at
these is in order. Except for these references, and a few places in the
schism narrative itself (1 Kgs 12.24; cf. 1 Kgs 12.17, MT only), Judah's
connection with greater Israel is not asserted directly through the names
ישׂראל, or בני ישׂראל in the narratives set in the Judaean episodes of the
period of regional independence. Judah does vow to be the 'People of
Yahweh' in 2 Kgs 11.17, but nowhere is Yahweh the 'God of Israel' in
regard to the southern episodes, at least not until the fall of Samaria is
reported. The name 'Israel' and expressions employing it actually occur
with a degree of frequency after the fall of the north is related in
2 Kings 17, although in many cases it does refer back to the defunct
northern kingdom (2 Kgs 18.1, 9, 10, 11; 21.3; 23.15, 19, 22, 27). A
smaller number, however, refer to the collective. 2 Kings 18.1-12
repeats the story of the fall of Samaria, setting it in the framework of
the reign of Judah's Hezekiah. It offers more than a single synchronism
between Hezekiah and the events in the north (2 Kgs 18.1, 9, 10). The
references to the northern kingdom in these verses stand out against the
assertion of Hezekiah's obedience to the 'God of Israel' (1 Kgs 18.5).
Moreover, he obeyed the commandments given to Moses (v. 6).
Disobeying these spelt the doom of the northern kingdom (v. 12). The
concept of a patriarchal covenant had already been established as the
operative factor in the north's continued communion with Yahweh
(2 Kgs 13.23). In the second part of 2 Kgs 18.12, however, the covenant is not construed as the promises to the patriarchs but as the *Torah*
delivered by Moses. This re-establishes a hierarchy within the range of
institutionalized alternatives which the northern history embodied. It
does not, however, render null and void the models of 'Israel' operative
within that history (which, in fact, make it a history of Yahweh's
people, *Israel*, and not 'ex-Israelites').

The comparison between Jerusalem's salvation in the time of
Hezekiah, the obedient servant of the 'God of Israel' (1 Kgs 18.5), and
the exile of the state of Israel, casts a sense of absence and estrangement over the following history of Judah. Yet, there is a sense of resur-
gence. Hezekiah rebels against Assyria and battles the Philistines
(2 Kgs 18.7-8). His story mostly concerns his defiance of Assyria and
the way in which Yahweh saved him and the city. Its intricacies cannot
be investigated here, but many aspects of it are significant to the present

purposes. First, Hezekiah succeeds Ahaz, who not only failed to follow the example of David, but did the sort of things that the kings of Israel and even the Canaanites did (2 Kgs 16.2-3). Ahaz also incorporated Aramean elements into the Jerusalem cult (2 Kgs 16.10-18). Hezekiah's predecessor, then, has seriously compromised not only the orthodoxy of the temple religion, but has also transgressed the bounds of Israel itself, and reduced the Jerusalem cult to that of a foreign religion. With Ahaz dead, and Israel destined for Assyrian exile, Hezekiah can repair the damage, for Judah at least. This Hezekiah does in grand style, following the example of David, and eliminating improper worship (2 Kgs 18.3-6). On the other hand, Hezekiah was restoring Judah as a remnant of greater Israel, and not as a completely distinct nation in its own right. This can be illustrated, to some extent, by the recollections of the past, and the wording employed in a few key passages. In 2 Kgs 18.4 Hezekiah breaks the bronze serpent, Nahustan, made by Moses, to which the בני ישראל had been burning incense (cf. Num. 21.6-9). Danell finds it surprising that the expression 'sons of Judah' is not found here, and takes the employed expression as evidence that the sacral congregation in Jerusalem had always been named 'Israel'.[29] Rather, the wording of this statement and the association of the serpent with Moses suggest that the text is implicating all Israel in this sin, or at least affirming the identity of Judah as part of greater Israel, which highlights the error of idolatry as a failing to which anyone of greater Israel is susceptible.

Only after the fall of Israel is reported (1 Kgs 17.1-6) does the epithet 'God of Israel' appear in Judah's story. In Hezekiah's story there are a few examples; 2 Kgs 18.5 and 19.15, 20. One may also associate these with the reference to the Holy One of Israel (קדוש ישראל)' in 2 Kgs 19.22. The anonymous prophets who spoke of divine judgment against Judah are quoted as speaking in the name of the God of Israel (2 Kgs 21.12). Huldah uses the epithet too (2 Kgs 22.15, 18). Its reintroduction in the 'Judah alone' episodes helps keep the name 'Israel' alive, asserts the divinely-ordained connection between Judah and greater Israel and helps prevent the view that Judah could now be conceived as the sole people of Yahweh. It also allows anyone ascribed a 'northern' heritage to look to the Judaean history for lessons not taught in the exclusively northern stories (the reverse of this is also applicable).

---

29. Danell, *The Name Israel*, pp. 98-99.

Despite these passages, however, there is a hint in 2 Kings 18–20 of a 'Judah alone' perspective, particularly in 2 Kgs 19.30-31, which speaks of a remnant of survivors from Judah. References are made to Yahweh's defence of Jerusalem (19.34; 20.6). The defence of the city is said to be for the sake of Yahweh himself, and for David. What is significant about these verses, however, is that they do not offer a hope of permanent salvation for the dynasty or kingdom of Judah. Indeed, the exile of Judah is foreseen in 20.12-19. Taken together, the salvation of the city and the prophecy of the exile preserve the image of David, even when there is no assurance of the eternity of his dominion. The sacral link between David, Yahweh, and 'his people' is expressed in 2 Kgs 20.1-6, in which Hezekiah successfully prays to be healed of his illness. Yahweh wishes to be known to Hezekiah as 'the god of your father, David', calling Hezekiah the נגיד of Yahweh's people, and promising to deliver Jerusalem for his own sake and for David's. It is significant, however, that what is promised here is the deliverance of the city, and not the kingdom. It is the city that contains the temple, and the city that Yahweh chose. It is not an entity defined exclusively in terms of post-schism political terms, but of pre-schism religious ones. The invocation of the name David is as relevant to greater Israel as it is to mere Judah. After the reign of Hezekiah, however, there is but little more to be heard of David. Ahaz was the final king of Judah to be buried in the 'city of David' (2 Kgs 16.20). It is recalled in 2 Kgs 21.7 that Yahweh told David and Solomon that Jerusalem was the place where Yahweh's name will be. Josiah is said to have followed the righteous example of David in 2 Kgs 22.2. With the impending collapse, the symbol of the dynasty's vitality, David, is withdrawn from the reader's view.

If little is made of David after the reign of Hezekiah, somewhat more is made of greater Israel and, especially, its pre-schism history. In 2 Kgs 21.2 and 9, Manasseh's sins are likened to those of the foreigners displaced and destroyed before the בני ישראל. His actions are compared to those of Ahab, and his defilement of Jerusalem is portrayed as offending the city Yahweh chose for his name (v. 4). The Asherah is rebuilt in the place which Yahweh chose out of all the tribes of Israel (v. 7). The establishment of the temple is said to have marked the end of Israel's wanderings out of its land (v. 8), if only they would obey the law of Moses. This verse is not only an ironic reflection on the fate of the north, but casts in stone the fate of Judah. In the next verse, lack of obedience is recorded, and, again, it reflects pre-schism, and even pre-monarchic, Israel. The Judaeans have followed the example of those destroyed before the children of Israel (a similar sentiment is expressed in v. 11, pertaining solely to Manasseh).[30] Already, however, the northern components of Israel have not so much wandered as been carried out of their land. The symbols of their apostasy, the heterodox paraphernalia of Ahab's practices, now stand in Jerusalem itself. It is hardly surprising, then, that the judgments passed on the house of Ahab and Samaria as a whole, also will be passed on Judah and Jerusalem (2 Kgs 21.12-15). Neither is it surprising that the offended deity is identified as the 'God of Israel' (v. 12). This god decides to act, and Jerusalem will be judged as sharply as was Samaria (vv. 12-13). In v. 14, Yahweh says that he will reject the remnant of his heritage, ונטשתי את שארית נחלתי. This rejection recalls the assertion of Solomon in 1 Kgs 8.51-53, that the Israel of the exodus was Yahweh's inheritance. It is to the exodus that the writer of 2 Kgs 21.15 then turns, claiming that not only were the Judaeans of Manasseh's time sinning, but that Yahweh's heritage had been sinning *ever since* the exodus. Thus, the apostasy of Manasseh's reign is not portrayed entirely as an independent episode simply in a causal chain of events, but as a major representative case of the repeated errors of the whole history of Israel. With this, Manasseh is not so much everyone's villain (not just Judah's), but he is, in a manner of speaking, *everyone*, seemingly the embodiment of Solomon's perhaps naïve, perhaps manipulative admission that there is no one who does not sin (1 Kgs 8.46).

The cumulative weight of this apostasy seems to be lifted in the reign of Josiah (2 Kgs 22.1–23.30) who eliminates the heterodox worship from both Judah and Israel. Yet this is not to be; Judah is doomed (2 Kgs 22.15-17; 23.26-27). The prophetess Huldah twice refers to the 'God of Israel' in making her pronouncements (22.15, 18). The purge conducted by King Josiah also has a pan-Israelite aspect, as the king eradicates the heterodox worship from the north (2 Kgs 23.15-20). Moreover, Josiah does away with the last remnants of Solomon's

---

30. This is the final such recollection of the conquest, and only here is the verb השמיד, 'destroyed', used. Elsewhere, הוריש 'dispossessed' is used, 1 Kgs 14.24; 21.26; 2 Kgs 16.3; 17.8; 21.2. Cf. the 'exiled' הגלה nations in 2 Kgs 17.11. The stronger verb used in the final instance adds an ironic note to the comparison. The nations were destroyed, and not merely displaced, and therefore, the Israelites had no excuse for prolonging their practices.

apostasy (2 Kgs 23.13). Here, Solomon is remembered as a 'King of Israel' (see, too, 2 Kgs 24.13). Pre-monarchic and post-schism times are evoked together in 2 Kgs 23.22, when Josiah's Passover is compared to those celebrated by the judges of Israel and the kings of Israel and the kings of Judah. Yet again, however, the ultimate fate of Judah is to become like her northern sibling (2 Kgs 23.27). Here, rejection of the chosen city is declared. The choice of the city from among the tribes (שבטם) of Israel was first mentioned in the temple dedication (1 Kgs 8.16, cf. vv. 44, 48). In the condemnation of Solomon, the choice of the city is associated with the special status of David (1 Kgs 11.13, 32, 36). The selection of Jerusalem does not reappear until the reign of Manasseh (2 Kgs 21.7), in which the selection is, again, said to be from all the tribes of Israel. The references to the choice of the city follow a pattern: the dedication of the temple, the establishment of a davidic kingdom in Judah at notice of the impending schism, and the ultimate destruction of that kingdom. In the final stage, both 2 Kgs 21.7 and 23.27 integrate the fate of Judah with that of Israel, and so the selection of Jerusalem does not ultimately separate the city from greater Israel, but marks it as the centre of it. In the latter, David and Solomon, who ruled greater Israel, are both mentioned by name. In 2 Kgs 23.27, the rejection of Jerusalem is mentioned immediately after the equating of the fate of Judah with that of Israel. Ironically, then, it is in exile that Israel recovers its fundamental unity. It is another reference to Solomon as the 'King of Israel' which is Kings' final use of the name 'Israel' (2 Kgs 24.13). Instead of the clearly positive or negative aspects of Solomon's reign, this verse recalls the anomalous; the golden treasures of the great king are plundered by Babylon. The riches lavished upon the temple, which spoke of the power and independence of a great people and underscored the intimate relationship of Israel to her God, are gone. Israel has been dispersed abroad. Ironically, it was from afar that Solomon obtained so much of his wealth (1 Kgs 5.1; 9.14, 26-28; 10.10-17, 21-25).

3. *Carnival Time in Israel*

In the preceding, I have deliberately ignored the reign of Jehu, so that it might be dealt with in greater length here. In my view, one encounters a similar situation here to that of the Shechem episode. Rather than create a social drama in which the characters orchestrate a smooth restoration of order, the narrative world itself is ritualized, but in a chaotic way. It is a carnivalesque inversion of established order, which questions the very stability of the symbolic universe that gives the drama its social relevance. Yet it implies the possibility that the constraints of history can be transcended, if only symbolically, to grant a sense of new birth. The carnivalesque flavour of 2 Kings 9–10 has been insightfully demonstrated by Francisco García-Treto, and a brief summary of his argument is in order. García-Treto considers it superficial to find in these chapters a simple anti-Samaritan polemic. He proposes that it is a meditation on the fall of the 'House of David', accomplished through a carnivalesque characterization of it in the 'House of Ahab', which Jehu destroys.[31] García-Treto finds many elements of the carnival in Jehu's rebellion. These include a radically altered system of social interaction, where previous hierarchies are either ignored or inverted, the mixture of the 'sacred' with the 'profane', obscenity and excessive violence. Most importantly, there is the crowning, and subsequent decrowning, of a 'carnival king'. Jehu's anointing is his 'crowning' (2 Kgs 9.1-14) and the denunciation of him constitutes his 'decrowning' (10.29-31). These are seen as a set of brackets around the rest of the story.[32]

Unlike Saul or David, who were anointed by Samuel, Jehu is not anointed by the primary prophetic figure of the time. Elijah's successor, Elisha, appoints one of the 'sons of the prophets', בני נביאים, to do it (2 Kgs 9.1).[33] García-Treto finds in this the suspension of typical social roles, which is so characteristic of carnival. It also shows the carnivalesque *mésalliance* between the Israelite general and the apprentice who anointed him. There is an almost comical aspect to the order that the prophet's underling should flee as soon as he anoints the new king (2 Kgs 9.3). The junior, however, actually disobeys his master, by adding to the anointing formula statements that Jehu should strike

31. F.O. García-Treto, 'The Fall of the House: A Carnivalesque Reading of 2 Kings 9 and 10', *JSOT* 46 (1990), pp. 47-65. On 'house' as a *Leitwort* (occurring 18 times in these chapters) see pp. 48-50. His theoretical position on carnival relies on the work of M. Bakhtin, especially, *Problems of Dostoevsky's Poetics* (ed. and trans. C. Emerson; Minneapolis: University of Minneapolis Press, 1984).

32. García-Treto, 'Carnivalesque Reading', pp. 50-53.

33. Elijah was once commanded to perform this ritual (1 Kgs 19.16). Hobbs, *2 Kings*, pp. 25-27, discusses the expression בני נביאים which occurs a number of times in Kings. He concludes that the expression often refers to lay supporters of Elisha. The person mentioned in 2 Kgs 9.1 reappears in v. 4 as נער 'lad' (which may indicate status or age).

down the house of Ahab (2 Kgs 9.7-10). When he does flee, then, it is
as if a '"sorcerer's apprentice" had unwittingly pronounced a spell he
cannot control'. The rather odd behaviour of the unlikely king-maker is
highlighted by his being labelled a 'madman', מְשֻׁגָּע (v. 11).[34] The rapid
movement of Jehu against King Joram is characterized by the fiery
chariot-driving of Jehu (v. 20, שִׁגָּעוֹן). The narrator's language adds
momentum to the mounting sense of chaos, as more of Joram's men
fall into line behind Jehu and join the carnival procession (2 Kgs 9.16-
20, 32-33).[35] The characters' own language adds to the scene. In the
anointing ceremony the element of profanity is introduced by the reference to the 'cutting off' of everyone who 'urinates on a wall' מַשְׁתִּין
בְּקִיר. This profanity is characteristic of the carnivalesque.[36] When Jehu
meets his enemy, Joram, he insults him for his mother's 'whoring'
(2 Kgs 9.22). Jezebel's corpse, he says, is to be unrecognizable 'dung
on the field' (2 Kgs 9.37). Yet, she, too, is 'crowned' or, perhaps,
'anointed' by her own attention to her eyes and hair (2 Kgs 9.30). She
appears as a queen, not a whore or witch. In Jehu's recognition of her
royal status (2 Kgs 9.34) and abuse after her death, however, she is
decrowned. Jehu's immediate response to the overthrow is to eat and
drink, while the dogs and birds leave little to find of the former queen;
her blood is translated into urine as it splatters on the wall, אֶל־הַקִּיר
(v. 33). The new king's procession leads eventually to Samaria, where
Jehu convenes 'all the people' to witness his 'service' of Baal. Here
Baal is installed in ritual homage, although the true sacrifice is his own
worshippers. As Jezebel was reduced to dung, so the house of Baal has
become a latrine (2 Kgs 10.27).[37]

García-Treto observes that there is an ambiguity in the 'house' theme
in these chapters, and wonders whether the House of Ahab and House
of Baal mask references to the House of David and the first temple. The
text may not only comment on the north, but may subject all human
authority to ridicule. Most significantly, the oracle against Jerusalem, in
2 Kgs 21.11-15, includes reference to the punishment of Ahab, as Manasseh had followed Ahab's example (2 Kgs 21.3). García-Treto does

34. García-Treto, 'Carnivalesque Reading', pp. 55-56.
35. García-Treto, 'Carnivalesque Reading', pp. 56-67.
36. The threat to eliminate all males, מַשְׁתִּין בְּקִיר, is also found in 1 Sam. 25.22,
34. In Kings, the houses of Jeroboam, Baasha and Ahab are so threatened, 1 Kgs
14.10; 16.11; 21.21; 2 Kgs 9.8.
37. García-Treto, 'Carnivalesque Reading', pp. 57-60.

not carry this line of questioning very far. He closes by noting, however, that in carnival, the old world dies, and the possibility of new life
arises.[38] García-Treto's cursory questioning opens the door to a potential reading of Judaean history which, unfortunately, cannot be fully
explored here, but some comments are in order. First of all, I think it
necessary to observe that Jehu not only destroyed the House of Ahab,
but established his own dynasty. This leads to the question of whether
Jehu's coup is imagined as prefiguring the *destruction* of the davidic
dynasty, or whether Jehu's dynasty is not the carnivalesque alter ego of
David's royal line.

For as much as Jehu took power at the expense of Ahab's dynasty,
so, too did David at the expense of Saul, although with less bloodshed.
Jehu is the only northern king to do 'what is right' in the eyes of Yahweh, which intimates that perhaps he would fulfil the model of David,
although these hopes are immediately dashed(cf. 2 Kgs 10.28-31). Perhaps the most telling feature, however, is the establishment of Jehu's
line on the 'throne of Israel' (2 Kgs 10.30; 15.12). Moreover, like Saul,
David and Solomon, Jehu is anointed.[39] What is especially interesting
about Jehu's anointing, however, is that it is done in the name of the
'God of Israel', and it makes him king of 'Yahweh's people' (2 Kgs
9.6).[40] The use of the sacral description of Israel, reminiscent of Jeroboam's and Baasha's (and others') role as נגידים, suggests that Jehu's
dynasty may be seen for its symbolic importance to greater Israel. As
Jeroboam, at least to some extent, displaced the house of David as the
symbolic head of greater Israel, and Baasha eliminated the house of
Jeroboam, so, too, is Jehu Yahweh's 'solution' to the house of Ahab
(2 Kgs 10.30). In his predecessors' cases, however, their status as נגידים
imposed on their role as monarch. Jehu's anointing, then, is a part of
the inversion of the normal order: here a king is called in to do the job
of the נגיד.

---

38. García-Treto, 'Carnivalesque Reading', pp. 60-61.

39. In 1 Sam. 15.1, Saul is anointed king over Yahweh's people, and, in 1 Sam.
15.17, as king over Israel. He was also anointed נגיד over Yahweh's people and
inheritance נחלה; 1 Sam. 9.16; 10.1. David's anointing is not to a role that is
specified in the ritual itself, performed by Samuel (cf. 1 Sam. 16.3, 12, 13), but the
people do anoint him 'king over Israel' in 2 Sam. 5.3. David orders Solomon to be
anointed 'king over Israel' by a priest and prophet in 1 Kgs 1.34.

40. In the initial command to Elijah to anoint Jehu, the wording is למלך על־
ישראל (1 Kgs 19.16).

As Jehu's story unfolds, one is led to wonder if he will attempt to claim the whole territory of greater Israel as his own. Mullen observes that, because Ahaziah was condemned for walking in the ways of Ahab (2 Kgs 8.27) and belonged to Ahab's family by marriage, he was condemned to death under Jehu's orders, at least according to Jehu himself (cf. 2 Kgs 9.27-28).[41] The murder of Ahaziah, however, results in seizure of the Judaean throne, not by Jehu, but by Athaliah (2 Kgs 11.1), Ahaziah's mother (2 Kgs 8.26-27; 11.1). She begins to murder the rest of the 'royal seed' (כל־זרע הממלכה), missing only the boy Joash, who is hidden from her (2 Kgs 11.1-3). Thus, the davidic dynasty is suspended, and in hiding. Although all the elements of carnival are not present in 2 Kings 11, one may see in Athaliah's story the crowning and decrowning of a 'carnival queen'. The odd situation of Athaliah ruling in Judah leaves only the bloody reformer, Jehu, as the sole legitimate holder of royal power in greater Israel. Athaliah, herself, is not accorded the status of a true monarch of Judah in Kings. She is given no regnal formulae on a par with the kings, only being said to have reigned (מלכת) for the six years the boy was hidden (2 Kgs 11.3). Her reign stands outside the course of 'real' history, traced by the formulae describing the birth, death and other information about the men who ruled Judah and Israel.[42] Moreover, Baal was worshipped during her reign (2 Kgs 11.18). If we are to read in Jehu's story a desire to rule both kingdoms, his failure to capitalize on the murder of Ahaziah not only limits his success in eradicating Baal from greater Israel, but indirectly also preserves the house of David, whose last survivor returns to power and finishes the job Jehu had set for himself (2 Kgs 11).

The question of the legitimacy of the Jehu dynasty has been attended to by Mullen, who maintains that the longevity of the dynasties of Omri and Jehu constituted problems for the deuteronomistic writer. The dynasty of Omri could be explained by the eventual pious response of Ahab to the prophecy of Elijah (1 Kgs 21.20-29). For Jehu, however, the writer introduced the idea of the limited grant.[43] This allowed the

---

41. Mullen, 'Dynastic Grant', p. 199. In 2 Kgs 8.18, the 'daughter of Ahab', who married Ahaziah's father, Joram, is logically Athaliah, but cf. 8.26, where she is the 'daughter of Omri'.

42. Nelson, 'Anatomy', p. 44.

43. Of the four subsequent generations who maintained the 'sin of Jeroboam' (10.31; 13.2, 11; 14.24; 15.9), note the discrepancy with the decalogue, Exod. 20.5;

preservation of the system of condemnation for the northern kings, alongside the accounting for the dynasty's long hold on the north. In Mullen's appraisal, the kings of Jehu's dynasty 'represent nothing exceptional'. Each does evil, after the pattern of Jeroboam, and each king has Yahweh to thank for their remaining on the throne. This notion allowed Dtr some opportunity to explore issues arising in the history of Judah, which, since the reporting of the death of Solomon, had not been the major focus.[44] Yet, while the young Joash is in hiding, Jehu carries the torch for greater Israel. For eliminating the House of Ahab and Baal-worship from Israel, he is awarded his dynastic grant. This tenure on the throne of Israel, which David and Solomon once possessed, however, is equally 'conditional' and Jehu's early compromises ensure that his dynasty is limited. Jehu fails to subvert the 'sin of Jeroboam': unlike Jeroboam, however, he was never offered a chance to earn a 'sure house' on a par with David (cf. 2 Kgs 10.30-31; 1 Kgs 11.38). His limited grant is recalled in 2 Kgs 15.12, when Zechariah is finally murdered by Shallum. In maintaining the 'sin of Jeroboam', Jehu, the 'carnival king', has compromised the carnival by failing to subvert all that he could; Jeroboam's golden calves remain sacred in a world where virtually all other markers of established order, dynasty, hierarchical authority and subservience are rendered base or irrelevant.

On the other hand, the period of Jehu's dynasty, for as much as it is remembered for its apostasy, is also remembered for how close the divine is portrayed to the people of the northern kingdom. In this, the comparison between the house of Jehu and that of David needs to be explored a bit further. In 2 Kgs 10.32 it is reported that Yahweh allowed part of Israel to fall to Hazael. Similarly, 2 Kgs 13.3 reports more Aramean successes due to royal sin. Yet, the next verse reports that Jehoahaz entreated Yahweh, and the deity granted mercy to Israel.[45] In vv. 4-5, it is reported that Yahweh sent an unnamed deliverer and that life returned to normal for the children of Israel. Hobbs recognizes, in v. 4, allusions to the exodus. Jehoahaz seeks (חלה) the presence of Yahweh (cf. Exod. 32.11), and the deity responds favourably: כי ראה את־לחץ ישראל (v. 4; cf. Exod. 3.9; Deut. 26.7), and grants

---

Deut. 5.9, whereby the third and fourth generations will still be punished for the sin of worshipping an image.

44. Mullen, 'Dynastic Grant', pp. 193-94.

45. The harshness of Aramean rule is predicted in 2 Kgs 8.12.

Israel a saviour, מוֹשִׁיעַ (v. 5).[46] Even if the proposed word-play between מוֹשִׁיעַ and מֹשֶׁה are best downplayed, the allusions to the exodus are still intriguing.[47] That the Israelites were able to live in their own homes as before may also be likened to the recollection of the exodus in Deut. 26.7-9.[48] The people of Israel did not change their heterodox ways (2 Kgs 13.6), and Jehoahaz is left with but a token army, implicitly suggesting that Israel still remained open to threat (2 Kgs 13.7). The failure of his descendant, Jehoash, to secure the ultimate defeat of Aram is also related in the chapter. Still, three victories are won and captured towns are recovered (2 Kgs 13.14-24). Most importantly, the victories are accredited to Yahweh's compassion and his memory of the covenant with 'Abraham, Isaac, and Jacob' (v. 23). It is reported that Yahweh would not destroy Israel, nor banish them, 'until now' (MT only: עַד־עָתָּה).[49] The sense of security that this gives is reinforced in ch. 14. Jeroboam II restores territory to Israel, and this is seen as a divine response to the sufferings of Israel, who are defenceless (vv. 26-27). It is added that Yahweh resolved not to eliminate the name 'Israel' from under heaven (v. 27). The preservation of Israel is, therefore, linked to divine fiat, not any status accorded the Jehu dynasty. Jeroboam II may actually be the saviour of ch. 13, or at least recall the saviour's role, but his success is certainly not due to any particular favour he has won; he, too, repeats the sins of the first Jeroboam (2 Kgs 14.24). Yet the Jehu dynasty has seen a remarkable turn-around in the fortunes of Israel. Unlike Judah's persistence, however, this recovery is due not to a divine promise to the dynasty, but to a more basic association between Israel and Yahweh, an association that transcends monarchic history completely and so grants the north even more legitimacy.

As Mullen points out, however, the Athaliah incident is only the first dynastic crisis in Judah which coincides, at least in part, with the stability in the north under Jehu's line. After the restoration of the davidic

46. Hobbs, *2 Kings*, p. 167.

47. On the word play, see Long, *2 Kings*, p. 166.

48. Hobbs, *2 Kings*, pp. 167-68, stresses the association between Elisha and the prophetic archetype, Moses.

49. LXX omits a counterpart. Hobbs, *2 Kings*, p. 171, takes the verse as indicating reasons for the delay in the destruction of Israel. Long, *2 Kings*, p. 167, notes that, in its context, this reference is not unintelligible even if the writer knew of the destruction of the Israelite kingdom. Provan, *Kings*, p. 232, finds it a post-exilic assertion of divine acceptance of Israel.

line with Joash (2 Kgs 11), there is little long-term peace, even though
Joash and his successor, Amaziah, generally 'did what was right'
(2 Kgs 12.3-4; 14.3-6). Joash repairs the temple but then sends its
wealth to Aram as a bribe (2 Kgs 12.5-19). He is killed by his servants,
and replaced by Amaziah (12.21-22). Amaziah foolishly goes to war
with Israel, loses, and suffers the indignation of being captured (2 Kgs
14.1-14). Moreover, Jerusalem's wall is breached, the temple and palace plundered, and people taken hostage. He, too, eventually dies in a
coup (2 Kgs 14.19-21). Only with Azariah does dynastic stability
return, though this king suffers by being struck with leprosy (2 Kgs
15.1-7). On the other hand, the dynasty of Jehu is relatively stable, even
if only Jehu gets a qualified good report. All the kings of Jehu's line,
except the last, seem to die peacefully (Jehu, 2 Kgs 10.35; Jehoahaz,
13.9; Jehoash, 13.13; Jeroboam II, 14.29). Zechariah, however, is killed
in the coup of Shallum (15.10-12).[50] The reversal of roles between
Judah and Israel is instructive, as it challenges the dynastic ideal of the
house of David. A royal banner in the colours of the apostate north flies
over Jerusalem, and a woman has seized the throne. The murders of the
davidic heirs and the lucky escape of one young child hearken back to
the troubles of 2 Samuel, only now regicide has become a reality and
the threats all the more dangerous. There can be no doubt that the carnival has come to Jerusalem as well.

The placing of temporal boundaries on the celebration of the northern
chaos, with the fixed duration of Jehu's dynastic grant, allows the representation of disorder there to be all the more enthusiastically pursued
within its own allotted time-frame. In the south, however, the more
open-ended nature of the history of the davidic dynasty offers no such
containment, and Jehu's celebration of upheaval mirrors more than
contemporary events in Judah. The strange twists that 2 Kings displays
in the aftermath of Jehu's revolt serve to render all hierarchical structures ordering this history suspect. Jehu is not a parody of David or any
of his successors. Jehu's dynasty is not a playful misrepresentation of
the royal line of Judah, displaced on the 'expendable' northern kingdom, intended solely to uphold the 'true' model. Rather, the transformations are more total: Jehu's dynasty becomes David's, and Judah
becomes Israel. Jehu's closest counterpart in Judah is Josiah: both are
the most praised kings of their respective kingdoms, and both purge

---

50. Mullen, 'Dynastic Grant', pp. 200, 206.

their respective cults. Four kings succeed Jehu before the end of the dynasty. Four kings succeed Josiah.[51] Other parallels are less direct. Shot by Jehu's archers, Ahaziah is carried to Megiddo. Dying there, he is taken by chariot to Jerusalem (2 Kgs 9.27-29). Pharaoh Necho kills Josiah at Megiddo, and his corpse is brought back to Jerusalem (2 Kgs 23.29-30).[52] As was the case in the schism episode, the time of Jehu's dynasty is a 'house of mirrors', in which greater Israel is imagined in a number of different, contrasting ways. The carnival has swept everything up in its spell, and leaves the reader wondering if any order is ever possible again. The carnival is not a simple parody, as García-Treto and Julia Kristeva observe;[53] rather,

> The laughter of the carnival is not simply parodic; it is no more comic than tragic; it is both at once, one might say that it is *serious*. This is the only way that it can avoid becoming either the scene of law or the scene of its parody, in order to become the scene of its *other*.[54]

Kristeva writes that the carnival engages a 'dream logic', which transgresses the linguistic codes and social morality that establish character, personality and subject development in narrative. Yet, this transgression only succeeds because it accepts another law.[55] She distinguishes between carnival as a dialogic *'transgression giving itself a law'* from 'libertine' and 'relativizing' literary forms based on the principle of a law which anticipates its own transgression.[56] One could see the latter in the preservation of institutionalized alternatives. On the other hand, carnival is more radical. It is not clear to me, however, that it produces 'another law'.

My reservations stem from Ingvild Salid Gilhus's objection to Bakhtin's position that carnival occurs outside the world of the church

---

51. Jehu's successors: Jehoahaz, Joash, Jeroboam, Zechariah. Josiah's successors: Jehoahaz, Jehoiakim, Jehoiachin, Zedekiah.

52. 2 Chron. 35.23 has Josiah shot by archers, but he dies in Jerusalem.

53. García-Treto, 'Carnivalesque Reading', p. 52. He cites Kristeva from the first English appearance of *Desire in Language* (New York: Columbia University Press, 1980), p. 80. The version available to me is 'Word, Dialogue and Novel', in J. Kristeva, *The Kristeva Reader* (ed. T. Moi; New York: Columbia University Press, 1986), French original in *Séméiotiké* (1969).

54. Kristeva, 'Word', p. 50.

55. Kristeva, 'Word', p. 41.

56. Kristeva, 'Word', pp. 42-43, italics in original.

and religiosity and that it belongs to a different sphere.[57] Instead, it is maintained that there are 'universal forms and contents in carnivalesque religion'. Their meanings are produced in the interplay between these features within the specific religious systems in which they are found.[58] Based on Victor Turner's model of symbols, Gilhus observes how ludic and liminal situations, playing on the sensory rather than ideological meanings of symbols, produce a new, but unstable ideological pole. This occurs because the changed symbols are conceived against the background of the old order.[59] Carnivals such as the mediaeval Christian carnival, the 'Feast of Fools', never gave rise to an alternative, permanent ideology. It is possible to consider that the carnival served a didactic purpose in dismantling and then reassembling the symbolic order, in order to make its participants more aware of it, and therefore, actually served the ideological system it inverted. Yet, there is little evidence that the feast transformed the participants. Gilhus explains the carnival as a playful exercise 'just for fun', and not explicable in its entirety as a strategy to reduce tension or to fulfil a didactic purpose.[60] The ludicrous aspects of carnival, with all its suspension of conventional values, blurs the relations between the elements of the cosmology. The ludicrous intervenes between chaos and cosmos. It is, therefore, creative, but temporary.[61]

Even if carnival is a radical suspension of order, it is hard to see how 'another law' can establish itself beyond the 'decrowning' of the carnival king. Jehu's version of divine law is supplanted by the imposition of the narrator's judgment on him. As the old order reasserts itself, however falteringly (esp. in Judah, cf. 2 Kgs 11–12), the carnival is, itself, replaced by the resumption of the dominating principles of history in the book. Once again, there is the entropic slide into exile which began with the sins of Solomon and Jeroboam's misbegotten rebirth of the nation. On the other hand, the fact that Jehu's episode is not simply

---

57. I.S. Gilhus, 'Carnival in Religion. The Feast of Fools in France', *Num* 37 (1990), p. 47 n. 4, referring to M. Bakhtin, *Rabelais and his World* (Cambridge, MA: MIT Press, 1968), p. 7.

58. Gilhus, 'Carnival', pp. 24-52 (24).

59. Gilhus relies on V. Turner, 'Symbolic Studies', *ARA* 4 (1975), p. 156, for this point.

60. Gilhus, 'Carnival', pp. 25, 51 n. 96

61. I.S. Gilhus, 'Religion, Laughter and the Ludicrous', *Rel* 21 (1991), pp. 257-77 (257-58).

one more step along this trajectory, but reflects and inverts numerous other episodes, suggests that it requires investigation, in some levels, as a reflection on the whole course of history. In this light, the reassertion of order and even the dominating position of narrator to pass judgment are all relativized. If there is 'another law' it is, perhaps, found under the surface of both the old order and the carnival; that is the divine fiat to preserve Israel, as in the time of the apostate Jehu dynasty, or to sweep it away, despite the piety of Josiah. The 'fun' of Jehu's story is its serious laughter at the expense of the monarchic history, and human experience itself.

Chapter 7

THE REJECTION OF ISRAEL AND THE FALSE SONS OF JACOB

1. *United they Fall*

One of the most important sets of reflections on the integrity of greater
Israel is found in 2 Kings 17. Scholars have found a number of historical problems in interpreting the first six verses and have proposed a
number of diachronic solutions; these, of course, need not be dealt with
here.[1] A number of scholars have been troubled by the fact that the text
dates the fall of Samaria to the ninth year of King Hoshea, even though
he was actually deposed three years earlier (vv. 4-6).[2] This is not as
problematic as many suggest, if one looks at the passage as an ironic
statement on the plight of the imprisoned king, or as a mere reflection
of a desire to maintain consistency. More importantly, the delayed
destruction of Samaria parallels, in some ways, the protracted fall of
Judah in 2 Kgs 23.34–25.21, as I will describe in Chapter 9. The real
matter at hand is 2 Kgs 17.7-23, as this is the explication of the events
just described, although its scope is certainly wider. Hoffmann sees a
formal pattern of argument employed to justify the destruction of the
north.[3] His structural analysis can be adopted with some small

---

1.   The historical issues deal with the number of Assyrian assaults, the king(s)
involved, and the meaning of אֶל־סוֹא מֶלֶךְ־מִצְרַיִם, which might refer to an Egyptian
king, or a place. Cf. Cogan and Tadmor, *II Kings*, pp. 196-200. Proposals for
source allocation in these verses are sometimes highly contradictory. Some would
have vv. 3-4 stem from a northern annal, and vv. 5-6 from a Judaean one, cf. Jones,
Kings, II, pp. 542, 560; also Noth, *Deuteronomistic History*, p. 78; Gray, *Kings*, pp.
638-39. S. Talmon, 'Polemics and Apology in Biblical Historiography: 2 Kings
17.24-41', in R.E. Friedman (ed.), *The Creation of Sacred Literature* (NES, 22;
Berkeley: University of California Press, 1981), pp. 57-68 (59-60), ascribes vv. 3-4
to a Judaean, and vv. 5-6 to an Israelite.
2.   Cogan and Tadmor, *II Kings*, p. 196; Gray, *Kings*, pp. 639-40.
3.   Hoffmann, *Reform*, pp. 127-28.

qualification, but I would also maintain that the section as a whole is concerned with the guilt of both Israel and Judah. His analysis may be schematized (with a slightly different numerical system) as follows.

    1. Primary argument: vv. 7-18 (19f.)

    A. Establishing of the facts of the matter.

        1.   First phase of the argument

        a.   Thesis (verdict), with the use of a keyword, in 'sin' (חטא): v. 7

        b.   Evidence, list of cultic sins: vv. (8) 9-12

        c.   Prophetic intervention (appeal to repent): v. 13, but to no avail, v. 14.

        2.   Second phase of the argument.

        a.   Renewal of the basic thesis, with a new key expression, 'his covenant' (את בריתו): v. 15.

        b.   Evidence, second list of cultic sins: vv. 16-17.

    B. Consequences

        a.   Anger of Yahweh, and rejection of Israel: v. 18

        b.   Extension of judgment to Judah: vv. 19-20

    2. Primary argument: vv. 21-23

    A. Establishment of the facts of the matter

        a.   Thesis with keyword: in 'sin' (חטא)

        b.   Evidence, the sin of Jeroboam: v. 22

        c.   Prophetic intervention, announcement: v. 23.

    B. Consequences, Ultimate destruction of Israel: v. 23

I am more inclined to associate the 'prophetic intervention' in the initial primary argument as a transition to the second phase, rather than only as a part of the first phase. This is because it introduces a new subject to which the following verses refer, while still building on the preceding verses. The two-phase opening argument first deals with the 'sons of Israel', and then, in the second phase, with 'Israel and Judah'. Both phases, however, deal with the collective of greater Israel. A number of scholars have suggested that the reference to 'Judah' in v. 13 is a gloss, and that the whole unit, vv. 7-17, properly refers only to the sins of Israel.[4] This view is quite mistaken. There is no textual evidence that v. 13's reference to Judah is secondary, and efforts to excise it are, therefore, based on assumptions about the passage's referent which are made prior to close examination.[5] Other arguments that support this

---

    4.   E.g. Cogan and Tadmor, *II Kings*, pp. 196, 204; Montgomery, *Kings*, pp. 468-69. On the other hand, Jones, *Kings*, II, p. 549, thinks that the verse indicates that Judah and Israel were only warned, not that they were both punished.

    5.   The textual situation is noted by P.A. Viviano, '2 Kings 17: A Rhetorical

assumption are also similarly weak. Its only basis is that the passage occurs after the fall of Israel, but before the fall of Judah. This, however, is not conclusive evidence, as the passage continues into v. 20, which does look ahead to the fall of Judah. There is no reason why an explanation for an event cannot precede the actual detailed description of its occurrence, especially since another event, here the fall of Israel, anticipates it.

The opening phrase of v. 7, ויהי כי־חטאו, is somewhat difficult. The combination ויהי כי־ is rare, and some are of the opinion that it links v. 7 necessarily to v. 6 (and hence, the fate of the north directly); that is, 'This happened because'.[6] Others see v. 7 as less directly connected to the preceding. Montgomery considers the clause v. 7a not completed until v. 18, commenting that a long delay before an apodosis is not unheard of (cf. Jer. 16.10-13). He reads the unit as: 'And it came to pass, because the Bnê Israel sinned, *etc.* (v. 18) [that] Yahweh was very angry' (ויתאנף).[7] This allows, but does not necessitate, seeing the long intervening text as referring to the collective and not specifically the north. Nelson and Provan have similar views to Montgomery about vv. 7 and 18.[8] They maintain, however, that in the present text the sins of the collective are described throughout the unit.[9] This position can be defended by addressing vv. 7-17 in two steps, according to the general structure discussed above, with the second section beginning at v. 13.

The initial change of focus, from the northern kingdom in v. 6 to greater Israel in v. 7, is effected by the ambiguity of 'sons of Israel' (בני ישראל) in v. 7aα, which could well refer only to the north. In vv. 7aβ-9, however, that possibility is minimized, since reference is made to the god who brought them up out of Egypt. In v. 8, the בני ישראל followed the practice of the nations dispossessed before them. The subject of the main clause is implied from v. 7, בני ישראל, while, in a subordinate clause, Yahweh is said to have displaced the nations before the בני ישראל. In the next verse, the בני ישראל reportedly

and Form-Critical Analysis', *CBQ* 49 (1987), pp. 548-59 (551).

6.   Cf. Hobbs, *2 Kings*, p. 231; Jones, *Kings*, II, p. 548.

7.   Montgomery, *Kings*, p. 468; cf. Cogan and Tadmor, *II Kings*, p. 204. Nelson, *Double Redaction*, p. 55, observes that without v. 18, ויהי כי could be construed as a retrospective causal clause, but this would be anomalous.

8.   Provan, *Hezekiah*, pp. 71-72; Nelson, *Double Redaction*, pp. 55-56. Provan explains the intervening text as an addition, while Nelson rules this out.

9.   Provan, *Hezekiah*, pp. 71-72; Nelson, *Double Redaction*, p. 126.

ascribed lies to Yahweh (v. 9).[10] They made illicit offerings, like the nations dispossessed before them (v. 11). Throughout vv. 7-12, the accused can be none other than the בני ישראל, who, according to v. 8, and v. 11, are assimilated to the Israel of the exodus and conquest. Thus, the whole of the Israelite experience since the delivery from Egypt is put under judgment. It is unlikely that the sins enumerated in vv. 7-12 refer only to the north. In this light, ומלכי ישראל אשר עשו, which ends v. 8, is all the more enigmatic.[11] Some take it to mean that the Israelites followed the practices of the northern kings, as well as that of the foreign nations, also referred to in the verse.[12] Others, however, read it as saying that the Israelites followed the poor example of the kings 'whom they made'.[13] Given the emphasis on the collective in the immediate context, I suspect that the practices of the kings of greater Israel may be in view here. Certainly, Solomon followed in the footsteps of the foreign nations (cf. 1 Kgs 11.4-5) despite the warnings (1 Kgs 9.6). In the condemnation of Manasseh, the repetition of foreign practices is mentioned again (2 Kgs 21.2, 9, 11).

The sins described in 2 Kgs 17.7-11 reflect the actions of both Judah and Israel as well as the United Monarchy, as a number of scholars have noted. Worship of the 'other gods' (2 Kgs 17.7) is found in connection with Solomon (1 Kgs 9.6; 11.4, 10). Jeroboam followed and made other gods, according to 1 Kgs 14.9. The covenant, which is binding on all Israel since it is described as issued to the 'sons of Jacob', includes a ban on the worship of such deities (2 Kgs 17.35, 37, 38). The Asherah idols (2 Kgs 17.10) are a problem for both kingdoms: in Judah, 1 Kgs 14.23; 15.13; 2 Kgs 18.4; 21.3, 7; 23.6, 14; in the north, 1 Kgs 14.15; 16.33; 18.19; 2 Kgs 13.6; 23.15. Some argue that the burden of guilt for some of the listed infractions falls more heavily on Judah than Israel.[14] Provan finds that the worship at the heterodox

---

10.   The term ויחפאו in v. 9 is variously interpreted, as it is used only here in the Hebrew Bible. The meaning offered here follows the proposal by Cogan and Tadmor, *II Kings*, p. 205, based on context (cf. Montgomery, *Kings*, p. 468). But Jones, *Kings*, II, p. 549, accepts the evidence of the LXX, Rashi and David Kimchi, and considers the verb to mean to 'do things in secret'.

11.   Some suggest it is a gloss, Burney, *Notes*, p. 332.

12.   Cogan and Tadmor, *II Kings*, p. 204; Jones, *Kings*, II, p. 549; cf. Hobbs, *2 Kings*, pp. 223, 231-32.

13.   Montgomery, *Kings*, p. 468.

14.   Viviano, '2 Kings 17', p. 552.

shrines and the burning of incense, which so provoked Yahweh, are more easily associated with reports of Judaean practices than Israelite, and maintains that the editor had in mind the collective guilt of the people (key words, high places [במות], burned incense [קטר], provoked [כעס]).[15] Verses 7-12, then, are best seen as enumerating the errant ways of the 'sons of Israel' as a whole. Only v. 8 implies that these are specifically monarchic era sins. Rather, the sins seem to exceed the temporal bounds of the monarchy.

The second phase, vv. 13-17, takes the opportunity to point out that 'Israel' and 'Judah' were warned by the prophets, and reminded of the commandments given to the ancestors. Here there is an obvious collective sense, but the discussion itself revolves more specifically around monarchic era greater Israel. Against the image of the apostate kingdoms, however, is the body of pious and concerned prophets, and the ancestral law (v. 13). The following verses do not name those who acted so inappropriately, and so the accused must be seen to be 'Israel' and Judah'. This is until the consequences of these actions are specified in v. 18, where it is stated that Yahweh rejected 'Israel', although Judah remained. The failure of Judah, however, is specified in v. 19, and the rejection of 'all the seed of Israel', כל־זרע ישראל, is specified in v. 20. Verses 13-17, then, should be easily seen to refer to collective sins. If the first phase looked back at the exodus and conquest, the second embraces the bulk of monarchic history. Yet, the monarchy is not the primary issue here. Judah and Israel are reminded of an ancestral obligation (vv. 13, 14). Moreover, their sins are but the repetition of those of their ancestors, as much as Jeroboam's calves recalled the sins of the wilderness (v. 14). It is not at all surprising, then, that when the punishment due to Judah is compared to that of Israel, it is recalled that the ancestors of Israel had been sinning since the exodus (2 Kgs 21.15).

Although the participation of the north is easy to see in 2 Kgs 17.14, vv. 13-17 also enumerate certain sins described elsewhere in Kings as committed only by Judaeans:

A: 2 Kgs 17.16: 'Worship of the Host of Heaven'; cf. 2 Kgs 21.3, 5 (Manasseh); 23.4, 5, 12 (practice eradicated by Josiah).
B: 2 Kgs 17.17: 'Augery and Divination'. The term קסם occurs in Kings only here. The context of its attestation in Deut 18.10, however, has affinities with 2 Kgs 21.6, where נחש is found.

---

15. Provan, *Hezekiah*, pp. 72-73.

C: 2 Kgs 17.17: 'Passing children through fire'; cf. 2 Kgs 16.3 (Ahaz); 21.6 (Manasseh).

Some who hold that the passage properly refers only to the north explain this situation as the ascription of Judaean sins to Israel.[16] For his part, Brettler suspects that narratives of the Israelite practice of child sacrifice, divination, and the worship of the 'host of heaven' did not survive.[17] All of this, however, sounds like special pleading. Brettler's alternative explanation is that the list of Manasseh's sins were used to supplement the list of northern misdeeds. The motive for this would have been to improve the image of Manasseh, by showing him under the influence of the north. Attempts at improving this king's image are obvious in 2 Chron. 33.12-13, in the pseudepigraphical Prayer of Manasseh, and in Josephus's *Antiquities* 10.41-5.[18] On the other hand, Brettler's comparison of Manasseh and Ahab in Kings is actually less than complementary to his case. Immediately after noting that Ahab had provoked Yahweh (1 Kgs 21.26), Ahab himself is said to have expressed remorse, and to have earned some measure of mercy from Yahweh (1 Kgs 21.27-29). Manasseh, in Kings, is granted no such repentance; Ahab's story makes Manasseh look all the worse. It is hardly likely that there is any attempt in the book to minimize his poor reputation. I find no reason why 2 Kgs 17.7-12 is not best seen as addressing the guilt of the collective 'sons of Israel' and that vv. 13-17 then focuses on the two monarchies. Verses 18-20 simply narrate the fall of one, and then the other, and ends with a comment on the collective punishment. Verses 21-23 merely recapitulate the northern history, reintroducing the reader to the chronological point where the story left of at the end of 2 Kgs 17.6.

16. Cf. Knoppers, *Two Nations*, II, pp. 64 n. 36, 197, who cites Cogan and Tadmor, *II Kings*, pp. 206-14, and Burney, *Notes*, p. 231, as demonstrating that vv. 11-17 'ascribe for the first time many of Judah's sins to Israel'. Knoppers also cites Viviano, '2 Kings 17', p. 552, in this regard. She, however, is of the opinion that, 'In the guise of accounting for the fall of the North, 2 Kings 17 actually highlights Judah's failings' (p. 552). She refuses to excise 'Judah' from v. 13, or see v. 19 as a later insertion (pp. 551-52). Rather than simply dwell on the fall of the north, the author 'is most emphatically addressing himself to Judah's situation' (p. 556).

17. Brettler, 'Ideology', p. 275.

18. Brettler, 'Ideology', p. 276.

Discussion of Brettler's aforementioned work, however, would be incomplete without mentioning that he holds that 2 Kgs 17.7-18 is not a unified text. He observes that vv. 7b-11aα closely match 1 Kgs 14.23, which discusses the sins of Judaeans. It is maintained, however, that this makes the identity of the 'sons of Israel' (בני ישׂראל) in 2 Kgs 17.7-12 difficult. He proposes that vv. 7-12 are a misplaced fragment that originally spoke of the reasons for the fall of Judah and was first located in 2 Kings 25. When or how it was moved is uncertain, but it seems motivated by an incorrect equation of בני ישׂראל with 'Israel', that is, the northern kingdom. On the other hand, vv. 13-18 represent a text originally about the north.[19] I am reluctant to accept with the same certainty as Brettler that the changes in terminology between the two separate units go beyond stylistic shifts. In the very least, whatever בני ישׂראל in vv. 7-9 refers to is not completely irreconcilable with the reference to 'Israel' in v. 13. It is only problematic to Brettler because he excises from v. 13 the reference to Judah.[20] If בני ישׂראל in the first section is taken as a collective reference, then the reference to both Israel and Judah in v. 13 presents no problem. I also fail to see the rigid distinction between the divergent ways of referring to foreign nations. Rather, they refer to different nations: on the one hand, the conquest-era nations dispossessed or exiled (2 Kgs 17.8, 11) and, on the other, those still existing which surround greater Israel (2 Kgs 17.15). Indeed, Solomon did as his contemporary foreign neighbours (1 Kgs 11.1-5), as his wives led him astray. Again, the problem Brettler sees disappears if one recognizes vv. 7-12 as statements about the collective, while 13-18 (with 'Judah' left in) discusses greater Israel in terms of the two kingdoms, and refers to nations contemporary with those states.[21] The premise that narratorial explanation can only properly occur *after* the full narration of the events in question has led Brettler into complex editorial theories which are not at all necessary or easily supported. Such a premise influences the work of others as well.

---

19. Brettler, 'Ideology', pp. 269-70 n. 15. He also holds that vv. 18b-20 are an update about Judah; vv. 21-22 a condemnation of the north, and v. 23, part of vv. 13-18a, concerns Israel.

20. Brettler, 'Ideology', pp. 271-72.

21. This does not mean that the two units were composed together, but merely that the inconsistencies between them do not require seeing two fundamentally different subjects of discussion; the sins of Judah in the first unit, and the sins of Israel in vv. 13-17.

The meaning of the phrase כל־זרע ישראל is another important topic. In 2 Kgs 17.20, it is stated that Yahweh cast off 'all the seed of Israel'. Pauline A. Viviano holds that since the exile of Judah has yet to be narrated, v. 20 is out of place chronologically, and so the unity of the greater section is problematic. She reads v. 20 as resumptive of 18, while v. 19 should be viewed as a footnote. If so, however, כל־זרע ישראל refers only to the north. It serves as a summary of the real point; Judah is intact but sinful.[22] I doubt whether v. 19 is best read as a 'footnote'. Rather, it seems to be the final conclusion of the narration of the collapse of greater Israel, which seems to me the main thrust of the section.[23] One might be inclined to equate the 'plunderers', שׁסים, of v. 20 (a term that does not appear elsewhere in Kings) with the marauding bands, גדודים, that plagued the history of the northern kingdom (2 Kgs 5.2; 6.23; 13.20, 21). On the other hand, גדודים, is also used of the enemies of Solomon, and of Judah (1 Kgs 11.24; 2 Kgs 24.2).[24] The term שׁסים in Judg. 2.14, 16 refers to the punishers of Israel, in a context which has a number of other similarities to 2 Kings 17.[25] 1 Samuel 14.48 has Saul save Israel from her plunderers.[26] In these three attestations, the שׁסים should be seen to oppose the collective. While these other books were probably edited or composed at least semi-independently from Kings, the possible reference back to these traditions suggests that 2 Kgs 17.20 should perhaps be read as naming the collective.[27] This is reinforced by Judah's explicit or implied membership

22. Viviano, '2 Kings 17', pp. 252-53.

23. Some maintain, as I do, that it refers to the collective, e.g. Gray, *Kings*, p. 649; Long, *2 Kings*, p. 183. On the other hand, Jones, *Kings*, II, pp. 551-52, is counted among those who feel it is restricted to the north.

24. Nelson, *Double Redaction*, p. 56, thinks v. 20 was inserted by a second redactor, that it anticipates the fall of Judah, and alludes particularly to 2 Kgs 24.2. Nelson does not discuss the references to the גדודים opposing Israel (2 Kgs 5.2; 6.23; 13.20, 21).

25. Nelson, *Double Redaction*, pp. 43-68, and Eslinger, *Living God*, pp. 202-204, attend to this issue, albeit with very different approaches.

26. Cf. the Philistines' actions in 1 Sam. 23.1.

27. Even if one would place Kings as earlier than Judges, the development of Judg. 2.11-14 on the basis of 2 Kgs 17.7-20 at least suggests how Kings was interpreted.

in the ישׂראל זרע in every other attestation of the expression, according to Nelson.[28]

On the other hand, I agree with Viviano when she says that vv. 21-22, which re-introduce the schism and the sin of Jeroboam, lead the reader back to the history proper, and are somewhat anti-climactic. They provide a transition to the story that follows.[29] In 2 Kgs 17.21-23, however, discussion returns to the northern kingdom alone. This short section summarizes the history of that realm, and offers the specific explanation for its downfall. It still follows roughly the same lines of argument that Hoffmann identified in the longer, two-phase argument (which I maintain, against his position, concerns greater Israel). The recollection of the schism in these verses, however, seems at odds with the great legitimacy offered to Jeroboam in 1 Kings 11. The key clause is in 2 Kgs 17.21: כי־קרע ישׂראל מעל בית דוד. The subject of this clause is a matter of some debate. Brettler refutes the popular position that the verb קרע 'to tear' has Yahweh as its subject, as implied from the previous verse.[30] He contends that the subject of קרע should be Israel. Instead of the usual translation, 'When he (Yahweh) had torn Israel from the house of David', Brettler reads it as Israel breaking away from the house of David. Brettler holds that the verse understands the rise of the non-davidic monarchy as illegitimate from its inception, and links their exile to their quest for independence. This is in contradiction to the prophecy of Ahijah, which does grant divine sanction to the division. Brettler recognizes that every other passage referring to the 'tearing' of the kingdom has Yahweh as the unambiguously-stated subject, while the object is never 'Israel', but 'the kingdom', either ממלכה alone (1 Sam. 28.17; 1 Kgs 11.11, 31; 14.8), or once 'kingdom of Israel' (ממלכות ישׂראל) (1 Sam. 15.28). These verses all mark the object with את, while this particle does not precede 'Israel' in 2 Kgs 17.21. Brettler, however, is reluctant to emend קרע *qal* to *niphal*, and adduces evidence from the Targum and Peshitta readings that the *qal* verb could have a middle voice, that is, 'to tear themselves away',

28. So Nelson, *Double Redaction*, p. 56. Cf. Isa. 45.25; Jer. 31.36, 37; Ps. 22.23; Neh. 9.2; 1 Chron. 16.13.

29. Viviano, '2 Kings 17', pp. 553-54.

30. For 'Yahweh' as the subject, see Montgomery, *Kings*, p. 470; Cross, 'Themes', p. 281; Hobbs, *2 Kings*, p. 236.

admitting that the *niphal* would normally be expected to be employed for this.[31]

On the one hand, the LXX[L], Targum and Vulgate do presuppose the verb נקרעו.[32] On the other hand, LXX[B] reads ὅτι πλὴν Ισραηλ ἐπάν-ωθεν, omitting an equivalent to the root קרע.[33] The major Greek texts may be understood as implying that Israel revolted from the House of David. Hobbs, however, finds no reason for the Greek, and other versions, to emend the text to avoid making Yahweh the subject of the action.[34] The tendency to read the MT as implying that Yahweh tore Israel from the house of David, is based on the claims of 1 Kgs 11.31, which has Yahweh resolved to do just that. Yet, the textual variants seem unwilling to imply that Yahweh is the subject of the action here, even if the reasons are unclear. Even though I have some sympathy with Brettler's argument, I cannot agree that the verse portrays the separation of Israel from the house of David in a manner completely irreconcilable with the earlier narrative. The story of the division in 1 Kings 11 and 12 must look ahead to the whole of the history of the independent monarchies, while 2 Kgs 17.21 only recapitulates the fact of the division in the briefest of terms, and needs to illustrate only those aspects of the event which are necessary to explain why Israel was exiled. But, this does not so much deny legitimacy to the origins of the northern state, as merely introduce the culpable originator of their sins. There is no sense that, had they not 'torn themselves away' from Judah, their exile would not have happened. The more immediate cause of the exile is Jeroboam's influence. Verse 21 does give a different emphasis to the motif of 'tearing' greater Israel asunder by avoiding mention of Yahweh's role in Israel's independence, but, rather than illustrate the illegitimacy of the Israelites' action, it may only highlight the rashness with which it was carried out. They were 'torn' or perhaps 'liberated' (by their own actions or Yahweh's) only to fall into the errors of an apostate ruler.

---

31. Brettler, 'Ideology', pp. 277-79. Knoppers, *Two Nations*, II, p. 66 n. 39, however, finds that the discrepancy between the singular קרע and the plural וימליכו suggests that the former verb has Yahweh as its subject.

32. Noted by Gray, *Kings*, p. 650; Montgomery, *Kings*, pp. 478-79. Cf. Jones, *Kings*, II, p. 552, who reads, 'When Israel was torn…'.

33. I.e. ῥήγνυμι: cf. 3 Kgdms 11.11 διαρρήσσων διαρρήξω τὴν βασιλείαν; 3 Kgdms 11.31 ῥήσσω τὴν βασιλείαν.

34. Hobbs, *2 Kings*, p. 223.

By following the general outline of that used in vv. 7-20 for greater Israel, the brief discussion of the history of the northern kingdom in 2 Kgs 17.21-23 marks the history of the north as a phase of the greater course of history.[35] The use of בני ישראל in v. 22 seems restricted to the northerners, as 'Israel' is used in the surrounding verses with this meaning. Even so, it does recall the opening phases of the discussion of greater Israel in vv. 7-11 and repeats the keyword 'sin', חטא (vv. 7, 21, 22). Verse 23 recalls the prophetic warning of v. 13. Israel is exiled to Assyria, a note which returns the reader to the events of v. 6. The discussion has, therefore, come full circle. This digression, by linking the fate of the north to that of greater Israel as a whole, has made Samaria's fate paradigmatic for that soon to befall Judah.

2. The False Sons of Jacob

Having returned to the course of history left off at 1 Kgs 17.6, the text turns to discuss the aftermath of Israel's fall, but does not follow the fate of the deported Israelites. Rather, vv. 24-34 tell of the Assyrian resettlement of the northern territory. The settlers, however, suffer from lions sent by Yahweh in retribution for their impiety. The Assyrians repatriate an Israelite priest to Bethel to teach the settlers Yahwistic religion. The settlers, however, merely merge reverence for Yahweh with that of their traditional deities. 2 Kings 17.34-41 criticizes the syncretic worship and establishes the grounds of proper worship for those of Israelite heritage. The combined block of text has received a wide variety of diachronic and historical analyses.[36] It is sometimes considered that at least vv. 24-34, if not the entirety of vv. 24-41, are a commentary on the rise of the Samaritan religion in the northern territories, especially as the Vulgate and LXX[B] appear to have taken this interpretation.[37] Many scholars have cautioned against this approach, however, recommending that שמרנים in v. 29 be read as 'Samarians' in distinction to 'Samaritans', to acknowledge the later origins of the

---

35. If vv. 7-18 are largely an insertion, however, then one is inclined to think it was designed to mimic the features of the shorter vv. 21-23.

36. E.g. C. Frevel, 'Vom Schreiben Gottes Literarkritik, Komposition und Auslegung von 2 Kön 17, 34-40', *Bib* 72 (1991), pp. 23-48. Even Hoffmann, *Reform*, pp. 137-39, who otherwise is reluctant to admit to composite composition, admits that vv. 34-41 are from a second Deuteronomist.

37. E.g. J. Macdonald, 'The Structure of II Kings xvii', *GUOST* 23 (1969), pp. 29-41 (39); Hoffmann, *Reform*, p. 138.

'Samaritan' religion.[38] There is little to support the view that since שמרנים is an unusual gentilic in classical Hebrew, it should be read as an anachronism based on the name of the Assyrian province of *Samerina*.[39] The term was current any time after the Assyrian conquest.[40] It follows from this, then, that while the later 'Samaritans' may have had some kind of continuity (beyond mere geographical proximity) with earlier 'Samarians', it cannot be demonstrated that Kings actually refers to them. Moreover, the 'nations' imported into Israel by Assyria are not those called Samarians in v. 29. Instead, 'each nation' גוי גוי 'make' their own gods and install them in the 'house of the high places' built by the Samarians and in the cities in which each nation was dwelling. The Samarians, therefore, seem to be the exiled Israelites.[41] If this is so, then there is a problem associating the name 'Samarians' in Kings with any purported 'non-Israelite' group. On the other hand, polemic against some form of 'foreign' influence in northern Israel is evident in 2 Kgs 17.24-41, and this does require some investigation.

Often 2 Kgs 17.24-41 is divided into two, with the break in the middle of v. 34. It is sometimes noted that v. 33a has the settlers 'fear' ירא Yahweh, while v. 34b says they did not (cf. v. 25). The relationship between the units is a matter of dispute. The second unit is sometimes considered a late addendum clarifying the critique of the settlers.[42] According to Jones, for instance, vv. 34b-40 correct the impression given in the previous section, stating unambiguously that the syncretic worship of the settlers is not in any way true worship of Yahweh.[43] On

---

38. Ben Zvi, 'Inclusion', p. 139 n. 108; Long, *2 Kings*, p. 180.

39. Gray, *Kings*, p. 652. Macdonald, 'Structure', p. 37, considers the gentilic construction more like Akkadian, and that vv. 29-33, on other grounds, are quite late.

40. Cogan and Tadmor, 2 *Kings*, p. 211; Nelson, *Double Redaction*, pp. 63-64. Nelson still considers v. 24 to reflect the 'correct term', בני ישׂראל, and uses this as evidence that v. 24 is earlier than 29.34a. Hobbs, *2 Kings*, p. 238, takes שמרנים to be a parody on שׁמרים, 'guardians, keepers'.

41. Rashi and David Kimchi thought this as well, according to Dexinger, 'Limits', p. 91.

42. Montgomery, *Kings*, p. 477; Gray, *Kings*, pp. 655-56.

43. Jones, *Kings*, II, p. 555. See also Friedman, *Exile*, pp. 24-25, who delineates vv. 35-40a as an insertion. Macdonald, 'Structure', pp. 32-38, finds vv. 34-40 secondary, with v. 41 as later still, basing some of his analysis on the study of the verb forms employed. This general view is also shared by Nelson, *Double Redaction*,

the other hand, some see the two units as unrelated. Cogan asks how the foreigners in Unit 1, vv. 24-34a, can be considered the 'sons of Jacob', bound by the *Torah* in vv. 34, 35, 37.[44] He considers that the brackets formed by the phrase 'until this day' (vv. 24, 34) mark Unit 1 as an addition. Unit 2 falls within the greater context of vv. 7-23, and discusses the northerners' sins. The settlers themselves appear again only in v. 41, and so Unit 2 is then reduced to 34b-40.[45] Ben Zvi juxtaposes the two units, observing that, according to 2 Kgs 17.24-33, the entire Israelite population was removed by Assyria prior to the resettlement. After the collapse of Israel, then, the population is portrayed as unrelated to ethnic Israel. He considers, however, that vv. 34-41 concern the population of northern Israel as ethnic Israelites. The discrepancy is accounted for by positing that the image portrayed in vv. 24-33 was understood by the writers and audience of the final or redacted text as hyperbolic, possessing a subjective truth, or as a polemical claim contrary to their own reconstruction of the past, which is then put forward in the subsequent section.[46]

Like many other sections of Kings, it would seem that one is dealing with a composite text. The discrepancies between the two units do not render the whole section as unreadable, even if there remain some difficulties especially in vv. 40-41. I base my views on observations made by W. Rudolph. He observes that the position that Units 1 and 2 are incompatible because they imply that the settlers were Israelites depends upon linking 'them' (אתם) in 2 Kgs 17.35 with the anonymous subject of v. 34b (implicitly the settlers). Rather, אתם actually refers back to the 'sons of Jacob' in v. 34b. The train of thought is as follows: the Samarian colonists are not worshippers of Yahweh, because they do not keep the law given to the sons of Jacob. The duty of Jacob's descendants, their part in the covenant of v. 35, is then described

p. 64, who finds the division between source and Dtr2 composition between v. 34a and v. 34b.

44. The basic outline of this objection is heard in other places as well; cf. Hoffmann, *Reform*, p. 138, who notices that the ethnic identity of settlers in vv. 24-33 is at issue, whereas this is not the case at all in vv. 34-41.

45. M. Cogan, 'Israel in Exile: The View of a Josianic Historian', *JBL* 97 (1978), pp. 40-44 (40-41); cf. Cogan and Tadmor, *II Kings*, pp. 213-14. More support comes from Nelson, *Double Redaction*, p. 64, and McKenzie, *Trouble*, p. 142. Cf. contrary position of S. Talmon, 'Polemics'.

46. Ben Zvi, 'Inclusion', p. 102.

through the course of Unit 2. Instead, Israel have preserved their earlier traditions.[47] Rather than see the obligations specified in vv. 35-39 as directed at the settlers themselves, however, the inclusion of this elaboration may be merely for the edification of the reader as one of Jacob's offspring. The intent may be to ensure that the reader behaves better than the 'foreigners' who are denounced. Indeed, the commandments are specifically for Jacob's descendants, and so they are all the more culpable for their transgressions. There is nothing in 2 Kgs 17.24-41 to contradict the image that the northern territories were not stripped of the entire population of monarchic Israel. Verses 34-41, however, use the settlers as foils to establish the boundaries of true worship for greater Israel, the 'sons of Jacob'.[48] This worship is bound up in the ancestral covenant (vv. 34-35). Moreover, the object of reverence is the deity who brought the descendants of Israel out of Egypt (v. 36). The writing of the law is recalled, and the benefit of obedience is given as divine salvation from one's enemies (vv. 37-39). Verse 40 presents a problem as it reports that 'they' did not obey, which would at once suggest that the subjects are the Israelites. Verse 41, however, continues with mention of the foreigners. While this does give some evidence of expansions, if we are to read the passage holistically, it would seem that the 'foreigners' were obliged to follow the same religious obligations as Israel, but may be criticized because they failed. This failure only establishes the need for Israel's obedience and the special relationship between Israel and Yahweh.

The passage contrasts with, and complements, many other episodes in the book. Hiram of Tyre and the Queen of Sheba acknowledge the special relationship between Yahweh and greater Israel (1 Kgs 5.21 / 3 Kgdms 5.7; 10.9), and both call the deity by name. When Solomon prays, he asks Yahweh to heed the prayers of foreigners when they come to Jerusalem for the sake of the divine name. He hopes that all people will know of Yahweh's name and that Yahweh alone is god (1 Kgs 8.41-43, 60). The convert, the Aramean officer Naaman, is granted special leave to feign piety to another deity, to enable him to carry out his duties for his king (2 Kgs 5.15-19). Here there is a movement from the general's hope that some form of divine power may be localized in Israel to his realization that Yahweh is not only god in

47. Rudolph, 'Zur Text', pp. 213-14.
48. Hobbs, *2 Kings*, p. 227, observes that the unit compares what existed in the north after the exile with what should have existed there before it.

Israel, but is the ultimate power in the whole world (2 Kgs 5.15-17).

It is noteworthy, then, that in 2 Kings 17 neither the Assyrian king or his advisors refer to Yahweh by name; he is only the 'god of the land' (vv. 26-27). The narrator reports that the priest taught the religion of 'Yahweh' (vv. 28), but describes the settlers' recognition of this deity only after reporting their worship of Succoth-benoth, Nergal, Ashima, Nibhaz, Tartak, Adrammelech and Anamelech (2 Kgs 17.30-31). Yahweh's name is thus contrasted with those of the settlers' traditional gods. The settlers seem wanting, in view of the ideals of foreign recognition of Yahweh's divinity established elsewhere in Kings. Thus, 2 Kgs 17.24-41 does not actually forbid admission of foreigners into the body of worshipers of Yahweh, but establishes the extent to which reverence for Yahweh must supplant all other religious concerns.

There are other literary aspects to the episode. The Assyrians effect an inversion of the exodus; they have removed Israel and replaced them with others. Yahweh, however, sends lions to destroy the new settlers, because they do not worship him (2 Kgs 17.25). Ironically, because of the attempts to appease the angry god, the Assyrians are actually worthy of a better reputation than the Israelites they replaced, since there is no story of Israelite attempts to please Yahweh. Even so, the Assyrian king can think of no better teacher to send, other than a deported Israelite priest, and this man bases himself at the controversial shrine at Bethel.[49] There is, however, little in the way of condemnation for the priest. One may wonder if the settlers are to some extent exonerated for their polytheism, by the tradition of having a teacher who is himself of a suspect education in religious matters.[50] Even though the Assyrian king might be excused for not knowing any better in sending the priest, Assyrian royalty seem all the more misguided in 2 Kings 18–19 when Jerusalem is attacked, and an Assyrian officer taunts the Judaeans at the city walls. Yahweh cannot save Jerusalem, it is claimed, as the deity was offended by Hezekiah's reform. Moreover, the officer claims that Yahweh ordered the Assyrian attack. Yahweh

---

49. Hobbs, *2 Kings*, pp. 237-38, 240. See also M. Cogan, 'For We, like You, Worship your God: Three Biblical Portrayals of Samaritan Origins', *VT* 38 (1988), pp. 286-292 (290).

50. The lack of condemnation for the priest has led Gray, *Kings*, p. 650, to comment on the possibility that at least vv. 24-28 stemmed from a priest at the rejuvenated Bethel shrine. The proposal for such a provenance, however, is highly speculative.

did not save Samaria or any other nation, and so hope in Yahweh is in vain (2 Kgs 18.17-35). Yet the reader already knows how little the Assyrians understand about Yahweh. The Assyrians fall victim to their own hubris and the city is saved (2 Kgs 19.36-37). The reinvestiture of a heterodox cult in Samaria also gives added justification to Josiah's purge, which embraces all of greater Israel (cf. 2 Kgs 23.15-20, note the accent on Bethel and priests). As I will describe below, however, the actions of Josiah ensure that Babylon does not purge and purify Judah, but ravages her. So, too, is Assyria denied doing anything more positive in Israel than vanquishing its inhabitants. Assyria, like Babylon, is an instrument of punishment, not reconstruction. The concern for relating events in the territory of the former kingdom is itself noteworthy in view of the absence of any details of how the deportees fared. When Judah is vanquished, such details are also lacking, but at least there is the story of Jehoiachin's release to suggest that survival in exile, with a level of dignity, is possible (2 Kgs 25.27-30).

Even if 2 Kgs 17.24-41 is composite, which is highly probable in the very least, the episode is largely complementary to the book as a whole. The integration of the unit within Kings, however, makes identifying its actual role in the post-monarchic dialogue about who is or is not a member of Israel, or at least a true worshipper of Yahweh, not an easy matter to discern. Because the historical scope of Kings does not include any 'restoration' movements of Judaean exiles, it is hard to judge how Kings is related to the development of a relatively narrow Judah-ism, which saw itself as redeemed through the experience of the Judaean exile. It is likely that the writers held that 'true' Israelites or Judaeans lived in the lands of Israel and Judah, although they do not offer a reason as to how this became possible. In this sense, however, the notion of the 'empty land' in Kings is most likely an ideal, and, perhaps, has more to do with a spiritualization of history, politics and geography, than the actualities of mundane life. Within the interrelationships between the mundane and the spiritually valorized reality, however, the story of the settlers is a disturbing reminder that exile did not really solve all the problems of greater Israel. Occupation of the land may still be a goal but with the Assyrian actions, the land becomes, once again, 'Canaan', full of potential and yet full of snares. Any 'return' will confront Israel with foreign people and foreign ways, however well disguised. In its syncretistic disguise, the new Canaanite religion is deceptive, and inviting; and hence the polemic of the writers is directed not only at the content of the religion, but the 'foreignness' of its practitioners too. That the snare is planted in the north, and not Judah, may be a concession to a group of 'returned' exiles, or at least a way of preserving for a Judaean hierarchy a way of maintaining its own indigenous roots. What is different in the new 'Caanan', however, is that the 'Caananites' are not granted any status as the indigenous people. They are not even accorded the decency of a name which would reflect their new found home: they are the 'nations'.

That those who are not accorded Israelite descent, or who follow 'foreign' religious traditions, pose a threat to the integrity of the idea of Israel held by the writers of Kings is clear. Many scholars would also compare 2 Kgs 17.24-41 to Ezra 4, which offers a broadly comparable polemic against people claimed to have been brought into the land by the Assyrians.[51] Cogan, however, objects to this. Ezra 4.1-5 and 4.10 are the only texts which refer to the Assyrian kings by name, Esarhaddon and Osnappar/Ashurbanipal. The list of the original cities of the foreign settlers in Ezra 4.9-10 is different from that in 2 Kgs 17.24, 30-31. The confused religion in 2 Kings 17 is not at issue in Ezra. Idolatry is not the reason for Jerusalem's troubles with her neighbours anywhere in Ezra and Nehemiah. The problem is ethnic: priestly families permitted their sons to marry Samaritan women, cf. Neh. 13.28.[52] He concludes that Ezra 4 is not based on the information of 2 Kings 17 and originated in other circles.[53] Despite these objections, it seems clear to me that the two texts do offer a related historical claim, even if they handle it in very different ways. Such a plurality, however, should be expected, and there is no reason, simply on the disagreement on this point, that the two traditions are necessarily separated by any great length of time.[54] If there is any credence at all to my assertion that

51. E.g. Dexinger, 'Limits', pp. 90, 91; Talmon, 'Polemics', p. 67.

52. By way of contrast, however, it is worth pointing out that Neh. 13.26 does refer to the impropriety of Solomon's mixed marriages.

53. Cogan, 'Worship your God', pp. 288-90. He also argues that its is likely that the two texts have different dates.

54. This is especially so in view of Chronicles, which has the north populated with genuine Israelites after the kingdom's fall (cf. 2 Chron. 30.5-11, 18). Many have held Ezra and Nehemiah to have been composed by the author of Chronicles, but the different reactions to the fall of Israel is one of the many levels of argument that Williamson, *Chronicles*, pp. 66-67, uses to refute this view. He comments (pp. 1-3) that studies which are based on the theory of common authorship see

Kings is 'exilicist', then one should, perhaps, not expect too much agreement on a number of issues between Kings, Ezra and Nehemiah. Even if differences between them can be identified, these latter two books are usually considered primary texts in the expression of the ideology of returned exiles, who sought to uphold a notion of the true Israel as being those redeemed by the experience of deportation and repatriation.[55] Ezra and Kings do seem to agree, however, that at least some inhabitants of the north are not of 'Israel', even if they might disagree on whether 'Israel' is properly limited to the 'returnees' in Judah. An important aspect in understanding this point of agreement is that investigating the 'Israelite' opinions is only half of the equation. As Ben Zvi points out, political reasons would probably have prevented the post-monarchic northerners from accepting that Yahweh had a unique relationship with Zion. The response of the redeemed exiles in Judah would have been to exclude these northerners.[56] Exclusion is not simply a unilateral concept, as Dexinger writes concerning the Samaritans. The limits of tolerance of both parties need to be addressed.[57] A

Chronicles as offering an exclusionary view towards the Samarians (mentioning Torrey, Noth, von Rad), while those who see the works as distinct (Japhet, Willi) find a more inclusive attitude in Chronicles.

55. There is an increased shift in studies of Ezra and Nehemiah to appreciate the literary and ideological characteristics of these books to a greater extent, as noticed by Davies, 'Scenes', pp. 159-60. Davies is one of the scholars beginning to question the general integrity of the two biblical books as an originally single work. He suggests that the two represent rival conceptions of the founders of Judaism. See also, J.C. Vanderkam, 'Ezra–Nehemiah or Ezra and Nehemiah?', in E. Ulrich, *et al* (eds.), *Priests, Prophets and Scribes*, pp. 55-75; D. Kraemer, 'On the Relationship of the Books of Ezra and Nehemiah', *JSOT* 59 (1993), pp. 73-92. The implication of this work is that one should not simply assume that a 'post-exilic', 'restorationist' *Tendenz* in a book represents the product of an inherently unified social phenomenon. By extension, any other identified 'trend' in Israelite or Jewish religious thought should be seen, at least potentially, as the product of a diverse field of thought in that particular area, including the 'exilicist' perspective I identify in Kings. I have already issued a similar caveat in regard to the 'Deuteronomists' in the previous chapters.

56. Ben Zvi, 'Inclusion', pp. 239-40. He notes, however, that by this logic, had the northerners (given the name 'Samarians'), accepted teachings about this special relationship, they would have been admitted to the 'Israel' imagined by these thinkers. The relationship between Judah and Israel, however, would not have been egalitarian; Judah would have been the primary partner.

57. Dexinger, 'Limits', p. 89.

similar method is required regarding earlier time periods and groups. Because so little of the social and historical contexts of Kings is known, however, following up on these general observations to construct the specific ideological groups, is highly speculative, and will lead the present work too far afield. There is another pressing issue in 2 Kings 17, however, and one which has its echoes throughout the rest of the book.

3. *The Democratic Denouncement*

One of the most striking aspects of 2 Kgs 17.7-41 is its accent on the sins and obligations of the people as a whole, as opposed to the actions and injunctions placed on the monarchs. There is little talk of Israelite kings anywhere in the long passage. Even Hoshea, in most versions, is far less a villain than his predecessors (2 Kgs 17.2), while the ambiguous 'kings of Israel' do appear in v. 8. None of the actions of Jeroboam, Ahaz or Manasseh, implied in the section, are actually attributed to any other actors than the 'sons of Israel' (בני ישראל), or Judah and Israel. Only in vv. 21-23 is Jeroboam introduced by name, but the exile is blamed on the Israelites following his example. Some commentators have noted this shift to a 'democratic' emphasis, and use it to point to a change in authorship.[58] For Lyle Eslinger, 2 Kgs 17.2 is especially odd, as it contradicts v. 7-23 as to the reasons for the demise of Israel. The thematic and vocabulary linkages between 2 Kgs 17.7-23 and the preceding narratives invite the reader to investigate the connections and contradictions. The reader must choose either to accept the evaluation of 2 Kgs 17.7-23 and reject the narrative description, or to subsume a qualified evaluation within a larger unity of vision.[59] Eslinger finds through most of Kings that the narrator is not really concerned with the sins of the people, while there are numerous references to kings leading Israel into sin. In 1 Kgs 12.30; 13.33-34, Jeroboam's sins ensnare the people, yet Israel is only a pawn whose fate depends on the actions of the kings. In 1 Kgs 14.22-24, where the sins of Judah are mentioned, it is questioned whether this is the narrative confirmation of the claims of 2 Kgs 17.7-23. 1 Kings 14.22-24, however, needs to be related to 1 Kgs 14.15, in which Ahijah predicts that Israel will be vanquished for its sins (although this is found in the MT only). This prophecy, however,

---

58. E.g. Cogan and Tadmor, *II Kings*, pp. 206-207; McKenzie, *Trouble*, p. 141.
59. Eslinger, *Living God*, pp. 184-85.

also relates the sin of the people to those of Jeroboam. Eslinger claims that the parallelism between the reign of Jeroboam and that of Rehoboam in 1 Kings 13–14 (which, in my view, is not all that strong) suggests that the sins of the Judaeans in 1 Kgs 14.22-24 should also be attributed to monarchic leadership, as in the case of Israel. The lesser blame heaped on Rehoboam is a product of Jeroboam's standing as the paradigmatic wayward leader. Even though there are some references to the people sinning throughout 1 and 2 Kings, it is the kings who lead them into it.[60] There are many instances in which this is stated outright.[61] Eslinger contends that the narrator seeks to exculpate the Israelite people:[62]

> Here, in 1 Kgs 17.7-23 a subsidiary purpose is to expose the shallow, wrong-headedness of the traditional theodicy that placed all the blame for the exile on an incredibly obstinate, foolish Israel.[63]

In my view, Eslinger overstates the irony implicit in the disjunction between 2 Kgs 17.7-23 and the rest of the book, even if he is right in noting that there is little support for the claims of v. 13 that Judah and Israel were warned by prophets and seers.[64] In my view, 2 Kgs 17.7-23 renders ironic the persistent accusations against the kings themselves. In this long diatribe, the kings are not the convenient scapegoats they might seem to be elsewhere in the book. They may have led Israel to sin, but Israel is still culpable.[65] Moreover, the conflation of royal and public sins in 1 and 2 Kings is actually stronger than Eslinger will allow. In 1 Kings 8, of course, Solomon makes a number of references

---

60. Eslinger, *Living God*, pp. 196-200. He treats Kings as an integral part of the DtrH, and so makes much of a comparison between Judg. 2 and 2 Kgs 17. He also points out that, in the other books of the DtrH there are some references to the people's sin: Josh 7.11; Judg. 10.10, 15; 1 Sam. 7.6; 12.10; 14.33 (pp. 193-206).

61. 1 Kgs 14.16; 15.26, 30, 34; 16.2, 13, 19, 26; 21.22; 22.53; 2 Kgs 3.3; 10.29, 31; 13.2, 6, 11; 14.24; 15.9, 18, 24, 28.

62. Eslinger, *Living God*, p. 206.

63. Eslinger, *Living God*, p. 217.

64. Eslinger, *Living God*, p. 212, and n. 45. On the other hand, Eslinger makes no mention of Elijah's challenge to the Israelites on Mount Carmel to choose between Yahweh and Baal (1 Kgs 18.30-39). Admittedly, this passage does not offer a complete refutation of his claims.

65. Compare how Solomon's foreign wives turn his heart from Yahweh in 1 Kgs 11.4. Yet, in v. 8, he himself is to blame. A similar logic holds for the relationship between the kings and Israel as a whole.

to the sins of the people, which form a major theme in his prayers (vv. 31, 33, 35, 46).[66] The next chapter offers an ominous warning to Solomon which recalls a number of earlier passages. As I have already pointed out, in 1 Kgs 9.4-5 Solomon is encouraged to follow the example of David; if he obeys Yahweh, David's line will always sit on the throne of Israel (MT), or rule the nation (LXX). 1 Kings 9.6-7 speaks of Solomon and his sons, with implications for the whole of Israel. In vv. 8-9, however, recollection of the exodus seems to impart the sense that the sins of Israel as a whole are responsible for the destruction of Israel and its temple. Even if these verses are composite, there is a movement from the sins of the kings and the repercussions for them, to the sins of the people and the consequences for the nation as a whole. Likewise in the MT, when Yahweh's plan to tear the kingdom from Solomon is recapitulated in the prophecy to Jeroboam (1 Kgs 11.31-32) the reason provided is the popular sins (v. 33), even though in 1 Kgs 11.1-13, only Solomon's failings are in view. The Hebrew in 1 Kgs 11.33 is difficult. The verbs speaking of sins are in the plural עזבוני וישתחוו...ולא־הלכו, but, at the end of the list of offences, it is added that this apostasy was uncharacteristic of David, 'his father' כדוד אביו. In contrast, LXX and other versions feature singular verbs consistently.[67] In a similar vein, there is an implication of public culpability in the MT of 1 Kings 14. Appended to the condemnation of Jeroboam is the prophecy that Israel will be uprooted from its ancestral land because it has provoked Yahweh. Israel will be forsaken for the sins of Jeroboam and the sins he caused Israel to commit (1 Kgs 14.15-16). In 1 Kgs 14.22-24 apostasy in Judah is at issue, but again there is a discrepancy about who was at fault. In the MT, 'Judah' does evil (sing.); while 'they' exceeded all the sins their fathers committed (plural). The following list of specific infractions are formed in the plural. In the

66. I am equally unhappy with Eslinger's handling of 1 Kgs 8 in *Living God*, as I will outline in the chapter on the prayers of Solomon.

67. This is differently explained. Noth, *Könige*, I, p. 243, held that the MT was original, as it was the more difficult passage, and that the discrepancy is to be explained on literary-critical (i.e. conflation of sources) as opposed to text-critical grounds. Gray, *Kings*, p. 291, and McKenzie, *Trouble*, pp. 151-52, think the plural verbs are later glosses. De Vries, *1 Kings*, p. 146 reads the first two verbs in the plural with MT, making the references to the corporate actions an aside (placed in brackets). He reads the subject of the third verb, '(has not) walked' with the LXX in the singular, to agree with the reference to David.

LXX, however, 'Rehoboam' does evil, and provokes Yahweh with the same sins committed by 'his fathers'. Verses 22-24 then continue with plural verbs.[68] Even if we read 'Rehoboam' with the LXX, however, there remains a movement from royal to public sins.

In the following narratives, the northern kings are, in most cases, criticized for following the sins of Jeroboam, which he caused Israel to commit. Even though these do not develop the notion of corporate apostasy very far, the implication is made that the northern kingdom was sinful. The persistence of this motif raises expectations that something will be done about Israel's gullibility. Therefore, one might question whether these passages exonerate the people, or whether their sinful nature, having fallen victim to Jeroboam's influence, was at least partly to blame for the sins of the kings. Elijah conducts his challenge to the priests of Baal and Asherah as a public demonstration, partly intended to turn the people of the north from their apostasy (1 Kgs 18), and he refers to the sins of the people in 1 Kgs 19.14, 15. In 2 Kgs 13.2-3 Jehoahaz of Israel follows in the sins which Jeroboam caused Israel to commit. Yahweh is, therefore, angry with Israel. After the plea of the king, Israel is spared, but they do not turn from their errant ways (v. 6). In Judah, the people maintained worship at high places, to the discredit of otherwise commendable kings (1 Kgs 15.14; 22.43-44; 2 Kgs 12.3-4; 14.3-4; 15.3-4; 34-35). By the time the reader gets to 2 Kings 17, therefore, one could well expect some divine reaction to the corporate guilt.

Eslinger's understanding of the irony of 2 Kings 17 depends upon seeing a fundamental distinction between the people and the person of the king. Instead, I would argue that the fate of both are intimately related throughout the monarchic history. The split comes only with the loss of the kingdoms themselves, but even then, the very existence of Kings preserves the memory of the kings. After 2 Kings 17, the people's guilt is highlighted again. Hezekiah purges Judah of heterodox worship (2 Kgs 18.3-4; v. 12 returns to the collective sins of Israel). More significantly, in the condemnation of Manasseh, discussion of the

---

68. Besides the variants mentioned here, there are others in these verses, and so the situation is quite complex. Gray, *Kings*, p. 341, and De Vries, *1 Kings*, p. 183, read v. 22 with LXX[BL], 'Rehoboam', preferring the more difficult reading as original. Based on 2 Chron. 12.14, Noth, *Könige*, pp. 323-24, feels that originally no subject was mentioned after ויעש, but LXX rightly interpreted the intent. The MT was based on the following plural verbs.

sins of the king (2 Kgs 21.2-8) soon turns to the collective infractions (vv. 9-15). Even though this, for the most part, is construed as a recollection of a prophecy of doom, the narrator in v. 9 clearly associates the collective sin with the influence of the king. Here, the culpability of the two parties is conjoined; the people are guilty because of the influence of the kings. In the prophecy of Huldah to Josiah's courtiers, the prophetess begins by stating that Judah is doomed for its own transgressions. (2 Kgs 22.16-17). In 2 Kgs 23.26, however, the narrator does report that Yahweh did not turn from his wrath against Judah because of the sins of Manasseh. This may be taken as evidence of some comment on Yahweh's stubbornness, but, in my opinion, the association between people and king has been clear from the early stages of the book. Even though most of the references to the sins of the people are portrayed through the voice of Yahweh, or prophets speaking for him, I fail to see why this is fundamentally at odds with the narratorial voice. Each has its own view of events, but the two actually work as much together as against each other. The story of Judah and Israel is told through the biographies of the kings, and so the actions of the kings are only representative of the actions of the whole. Rather than cast a sarcastic light on the theology of collective retribution, 2 Kings 17 stands as a warning that blindly following the example of leaders can be rather dangerous.

Part III
DESTRUCTION AND ETERNITY

Chapter 8

JOSIAH'S PURGE: EXILE AND TRANSFORMATION

1. *The End of the Line*

One of the most important episodes in the book of Kings is that of the reign of Josiah (2 Kgs 22–23.30). It follows soon after the reign of Manasseh (2 Kgs 21.1-18), who so compromised Judah that its destruction was inevitable (vv. 11-15). Manasseh made Judah like the dispossessed and destroyed nations (vv. 2, 9, 11) and so, in a manner of speaking, had caused Judah to cease to exist. Josiah, however, 'recreates' Judah by reconstituting its national identity.[1] This 'recreation', however, is not in itself the turning back of the clock. Rather, it is the temporary reaffirmation of monarchic 'Israel' (at least in its 'Judaean' guise) as a brief prelude to a radical transformation. This prelude, however, allows for the re-establishment of core elements in Israel's identity against the fact of historical progression. In this sense, it is one of the 'sacred moments' that takes the place of a well-developed 'golden age' in biblical literature. Josiah's story becomes, at once, a part of the history of the entropy that cast Israel from its land, and a means of finding the timeless values that make Israel indestructible. In its mix of the ideal and contingent, it provides not only a welcome illumination of many thorny issues, but also another constellation in an inherently problematic symbolic universe.

Josiah's episode is well known. In the process of temple repairs, a piece of writing, ספר, is found, which Josiah apparently recognizes as indicative of the destruction of Judah for its sins (2 Kgs 22.8-11).[2] This

---

1. Mullen, *Narrative History*, pp. 78-79.
2. At its discovery, it is the 'Torah scroll' (ספר התורה) (2 Kgs 22.8, 11, cf. vv. 9, 10, 11, 13, 16; and 2 Kgs 14.6, also 2 Kgs 23.24, where its contents are described as 'words of the Torah' (דברי התורה). In 2 Kgs 23.2, 21 it is 'Covenant Scroll' (ספר הברית) (cf. v. 3). A definitive translation of ספר in these instances is difficult to determine. As to the physical medium, a scroll need not be specified

is confirmed by the prophetess Huldah, even though she says that Josiah will be spared having to experience this himself (2 Kg 22.12-20). Nonetheless, Josiah reaffirms the covenant between the people and Yahweh, engages in a sweeping purge of all that is not apparently orthodox across Judah and the northern territory, and then celebrates Passover in grand style (2 Kgs 23.1-25). Josiah is finally killed upon meeting Pharaoh Necho at Megiddo (2 Kgs 23.28-30). In the following episodes, no hint is given of Josiah's reforms having lasted. All subsequent kings are given a poor assessment, although none is actually described as undoing the work of Josiah.[3] Needless to say, the scholarly bibliography on the Josiah episode is massive, as its implications for other topics in biblical studies is great.[4] The development of the Josiah

since the root ספר can, in Ugaritic, refer to documents written on clay tablets (my thanks to N. Wyatt for this point). Moreover, in Isa. 30.8, לוח and ספר are used in parallel. The frequently offered translation 'book', therefore, appears quite reasonable. On the other hand, the English word 'book' may carry connotations of length, comprehensiveness, and manner of presentation which may read too much into the story in 2 Kings. This is in view of the frequent claims (themselves not at all unreasonable) that some part of Deuteronomy is clearly intended. How much of Deuteronomy, if any at all, however, remains an open question. In 1 Kgs 8.9, the contents of the ark are described as the 'tablets of stone' (להות האבנים). In Deut. 9.9, 11, this construction is used of Moses' tablets along with the further description of them as the 'tablets of the covenant' (לחות הברית). In 2 Kgs 22, however, it is not specified that these tablets were discovered (as this would require opening the ark, cf. 1 Kgs 8.9). E.W. Conrad, 'Heard but not Seen: The Representation of "Books" in the Old Testament', *JSOT* 54 (1992), pp. 45-59 (52), observes that ספר may mean 'legal document', 'letter', or 'register' in addition to 'book', although he himself does speak of Josiah's Book of the Law. He also argues that to identify this, or references to the words of prophets, with Hebrew Bible texts mistakes a rhetorical feature for information. I will maintain my translation of 'scroll', trading possible inaccuracy in terms of the physical medium for a more neutral stance regarding the document's contents, length and manner of presentation. Conrad also points out that the narrator in Genesis–2 Kings is empowered through the motif of the lost and then found document. The discovery report in 2 Kgs 22 parallels the readers' re-discovery of it in their own experiences (cf. Exod. 24.4-7). He comments that, after the Josiah episode it is lost to the reader again.

3. 2 Kgs 23.32, 37; 24.9, 19.

4. For a recent discussion of work on the episode, see B. Gieselmann, 'Die sogenannten josianische Reform in der gegenwärtigen Forschung', *ZAW* 106 (1994), pp. 223-42. A recent book-length treatment of 2 Kgs 22–23 is that of Eynikel, *The Reform*. A linguistic and structural study has been offered by P. Tagliacarne, *'Keiner war wie er' Untersuchung zur Struktur von 2 Könige 22–23*

traditions has been traced into later biblical books.[5] Three main points characterize the vast diversity of research into this episode, although many aspects of these are now subject to increasingly confident critiques:[6]

1. At least one 'deuteronomistic' writer is responsible for the present text of 2 Kings 22–23.[7]
2. The discovered scroll was intended to be thought of as Deuteronomy (or some early form thereof, an *Urdeuteronomium*).[8]

(ATSAT, 31; St Ottilien: EOS Verlag, 1989). See also Knoppers's lengthy treatment, *Two Nations*, II, pp. 121-228.

5. See especially A. Laato, *Josiah and David Redivivus: The Historical Josiah and the Messianic Expectations of Exilic and Postexilic Times* (ConBot, 33; Stockholm: Almqvist & Wiksell, 1992). Many scholars compare various stories of Josiah, i.e., in Kings, Chronicles, 1 Esdras, and Josephus: C.T. Begg, 'The Death of Josiah: Josephus and the Bible', *ETL* 64 (1988), pp. 157-63; *idem*, 'The Death of Josiah in Chronicles: Another View', *VT* 37 (1987), pp. 1-8; L. Eslinger, 'Josiah and the Torah Book: Comparison of 2 Kgs 22:1–23:28 and 2 Chron. 34:1-35:19', *HAR* 10 (1986), pp. 37-62; D.A. Glatt-Gilad, 'The Role of Huldah's Prophecy in the Chronicle's Portrayal of Josiah's Reform', *Bib* 77 (1996), pp. 16-31; Z. Talshir, 'The Three Deaths of Josiah and the Strata of Biblical Historiography (2 Kgs XXIII 29-30; 2 Chronicles XXXV 20:5; 1 Esdras I 23-31)', *VT* 46 (1996), pp. 213-36.

6. Gieselmann, 'Die Reform', pp. 241-42.

7. This is probably the least contested point, but C. Levin, 'Joschija im deuteronomistichen Geschichtswerk', *ZAW* 96 (1984), pp. 351-71, sees only a few verses in 2 Kgs 22–23 stemming from an exilic DtrH. The rest is postexilic, with important sections post-deuteronomistic.

8. This view is ancient, traceable to Athanasius, Jerome and others, according to E.W. Nicholson, *Deuteronomy and Tradition* (Philadelphia: Fortress Press, 1967), p. 1 n. 2, although modern critical thought on the subject stems from the similar position taken by De Wette. On the antecedents of his views, see M.J. Paul, 'Hilkiah and the Law (2 Kings 22) in the 17th and 18th Centuries: Some Influences on W.M.L. de Wette', in N. Lohfink (ed.), *Das Deuteronomium: Entstehung, Gestalt und Botschaft* (Leuven: Leuven University Press, 1985), pp. 9-12. Others take the view that very little of what is now Deuteronomy (Deut. 32) was the work to which Josiah's biographers referred; see J.R. Lundbom, 'The Lawbook of the Josianic Reform', *CBQ* 38 (1976), pp. 293-302. Others look to parts of Exodus. See the discussion in Nicholson, *Deuteronomy*, p. 4 nn. 1-2. Levin, 'Joschija', p. 369, thinks the document referred to is the whole of the *Torah*, in approximately its present form. L.K. Handy, 'The Role of Huldah in Josiah's Cult Reform', *ZAW* 106 (1994), pp. 40-53 (49-50 n. 23), needs mention here as he cautions against the standard association between the scroll and Deuteronomy. He notes that there is no indication that the content of the book is anything other than a prediction of the

3. Under the historical Josiah, actual religious reforms were undertaken, even if the motives, chronology, content and geographical expanse of this programme are matters of dispute.[9]

There is, however, little to be gained in rehearsing the various arguments here.[10] For the present purposes, it is not so important how, or if, the historical Josiah used any part of Deuteronomy or other document, but how the authors of Kings *used the character of Josiah* in their advancement of particular ideas and particular literature (much of which I do not doubt is also reflected in Deuteronomy). I begin by attending to some of the very features which many take as evidence of a Josianic edition.[11]

destruction of Judah. There is nothing in Huldah's words about a law code.

9. See the review and discussion in R.H. Lowery, *The Reforming Kings: Cult and Society in First Temple Judah* (JSOTSup, 120; Sheffield: JSOT, 1991), pp. 190-209. Sceptical of much of 2 Kgs 22–23, but still according some level of historicity to at least select parts of it, are: N. Lohfink, 'The Cult Reform of Josiah of Judah: 2 Kings 22–23 as a Source for the History of Israelite Religion', in P.D. Miller, P.D. Hanson and S.D. McBride (eds.), *Ancient Israelite Religion: Essays in Honor of Frank Moore Cross* (Philadelphia: Fortress Press, 1987), pp. 459-75; E. Würthwein, 'Die Josianische Reform und das Deuteronomium', in E. Würthwein, *Studien zum deuteronomistischen Geschichtswerk* (BZAW, 227; Berlin: W. de Gruyter, 1994), pp. 188-216 (reprinted from *ZTK* 73 [1976], pp. 395-423); H. Hollenstein, 'Literarkritische Erwägungen zum Bericht über die Reformmassnahmen Josias 2 Kön. XXIII 4ff.', *VT* 27 (1977), pp. 321-36; W. Dietrich, 'Josia und das Gesetzbuch (2 Reg. XXII)', *VT* 27 (1977), pp. 13-35; M. Rose, 'Bemerkungen zum historischen Fundament des Josia-Bildes in II Reg 22f.', *ZAW* 89 (1977), pp. 50-63. Some contest the scroll discovery account, thinking it is legitimizing legend, but see some kernel of truth in the story of the purge; cf. Diebner and Nauerth, 'Die Inventio'. Long, *2 Kings*, pp. 250-56, highlights the ambiguities of evidence. Among those rejecting virtually all of the story as fictitious are Davies, *'Ancient Israel'*, pp. 40-41; Handy, 'Historical Probability'; Hoffmann, *Reform*, pp. 264-270.

10. Due to the highly polarized debates, some recognize a need for meta-critical reflection, C. Conroy, 'Reflections on the Exegetical Task: Apropos of Recent Studies on 2 Kings 22–23', in C. Breckelmans and J. Lust (eds.), *Pentateuchal and Deuteronomistic Studies: Papers Read at the XIIIth IOSOT Congress, Leuven 1989* (Leuven: Leuven University Press, 1990), pp. 255-68 (256-57).

11. Among those already cited in this regard are Cross, 'Themes'; Nelson, *Double Redaction*; McKenzie, *Trouble*; Friedman, *Exile*; Knoppers, *Two Nations*. The exact cut-off point between the editions in 2 Kgs 23 is variously given, see the reviews listed in the notes above. Some, of course, like Provan, *Hezekiah*, see an original DtrH which culminated with Hezekiah.

The story in Kings seems to build up to Josiah's reign; many themes already familiar to the reader come to a head in this episode. After 2 Kings 23, there is no more talk of cultic centralization, or of David; post-Josianic kings are not even compared to the founder of their dynasty: they are rated according to their 'fathers'. The use of the plural in this regard in 2 Kgs 23.32, 37 is curious, since the writer had just described Josiah in such glowing terms.[12] The rich cultic terminology found in the story of Josiah is greatly decreased after 2 Kgs 23.24.[13] Josiah is set apart by detailing his actions at length, and portraying them as definitive and comprehensive. He pre-empts the use of heterodox cultic objects and places, such as the במות and מצבות (2 Kgs 23.14), by breaking them down and defiling them. Cultic personnel are brought to Jerusalem, co-opting their institutional sanction (2 Kgs 23.8). The zealous king goes beyond stopping child sacrifice, he defiles the sites as well (2 Kgs 23.14). He exceeds the requirement merely to burn the Asherah-icon (2 Kgs 23.4, 6; cf. Deut. 12.3, 7.5). Josiah is the only king to dare to touch the high places of Solomon (2 Kgs 23.13). Sins committed by other kings are also redressed (2 Kgs 25.3; cf. the 'horse' symbol, 2 Kgs 23.11).[14] The extremely positive and detailed depiction of Josiah's life, however, is in sharp contrast to the lack of commentary on his demise. He not only does 'right' in the eyes of Yahweh (2 Kgs 22.2), but is incomparable to any other king in his obedience (2 Kgs 23.24-25). This seems incongruent with the fact that his pious deeds do not save the nation (2 Kgs 22.16-17; 23.26-27), and

12. As noted by Friedman, *Exile*, pp. 6-7, regarding Kings Jehoahaz and Jehoiakim. On the other hand, one might think 'fathers' is a reference to a generally apostate dynasty. Manasseh is blamed in 2 Kgs 24.2-4. Jerusalem and Judah displeased Yahweh, and so were cast from the divine presence (2 Kgs 24.20). Of the other post-Josianic kings, Jehoiachin sins as did his father (2 Kgs 23.10), and Zedekiah follows him (2 Kgs 24.19). One could use the same features to argue the reverse of Friedman. The story of Josiah might be seen as a late development in a book which rather simply traced the succession of occasionally 'righteous' but mostly 'evil' kings from David to the exile.

13. G. Vanoni, 'Beobachtungen zur deuteronomistischen Terminologie in 2 Kön 23,25–25,30', in Lohfink (ed.), *Das Deuteronomium*, pp. 357-62 (358).

14. Knoppers, *Two Nations*, II, pp. 183-91. See references to Solomon, 2 Kgs 23.13; Manasseh, 2 Kgs 23.12; kings of Judah, 2 Kgs 23.5, 11, 12; kings of Israel, 23.19.

that his puzzling death is left without theological explanation (cf. 2 Kgs 23.29-30). Many scholars see the final sections of the book as displaying a marked change in pace; it 'suddenly begins to sputter' and 'it simply runs out of fuel altogether,' as one scholar writes.[15] The absence of many familiar themes after the reign of Josiah is not an argument from silence but a 'full-fledged change of perspective and manner of presentation of history'.[16] It is often concluded that Josiah's episode was the capstone to a history which was written to support the religious programme of this king. The history work advertized this programme as the proper way to avoid learning the lessons of the northern kingdom's history the hard way: that an apostate monarchy and nation is doomed to destruction. As the end-point of history, the purge expresses the return to a pious, davidic reign over greater Israel, which will bring back the glory of the past.[17]

Here I restate my objections to such a compositional history.[18] A lengthy discussion on the fall of both Israel and Judah is to be found in 2 Kings 17. Many scholars, with diverse opinions as to the compositional history of Kings, do see the Josiah episode as the 'climax' to the book, if the use of such a term is not completely anachronistic regarding ancient literature.[19] Paratactic compositional style means that such a high point need not be at the very end of the book.[20] There is little if

15. Lowery, *The Reforming Kings*, pp. 25.

16. Friedman, *Exile*, p. 7.

17. Knoppers, *Two Nations*, II, pp. 174-75. See also Cross, 'Themes', pp. 283-84; Nelson, *Double Redaction*, p. 122. De Vries, *1 Kings*, pp. xlviii-xlvix. An exception is McKenzie, *Trouble*, p. 150, who does not see the Josianic DtrH as propaganda for Josiah (despite some deference to him). He follows Van Seter's generic view of the DtrH as a history intended to render an account of Israel's national traditions, perhaps as part of a search for national identity after the fall of the northern kingdom. Eynikel, *The Reform*, pp. 358-59, sees Dtr1 writing immediately after the death of Josiah, yet still developing Josiah's image in view of the traditions about Moses.

18. See Chapter 2.

19. Hoffmann, *Reform*, pp. 169-263, treats Josiah's story at length, relating it to all other episodes of cultic 'reform' (both those deemed positive and negative). He sees the story of Josiah as the event to which the whole cultic history is building.

20. Van Seters, *In Search of History*, pp. 320-21; Long, *1 Kings*, pp. 17-18. Some claim that the climactic points of other biblical literature occur at some distance from the conclusion of the writings: cf. Lundbom, 'The Lawbook', p. 301, referring to his *Jeremiah: A Study in Ancient Hebrew Rhetoric* (SBLDS, 18; Missoula, MT: Scholars Press, 1975), pp. 69, 86, 89, 95 and to N.K. Gottwald,

any indication in the present versions of Kings that such a hypothetical Josianic edition held any possibility that Judah could have been saved. Certainly no remnant of a promise of national salvation remains in Huldah's oracle (2 Kgs 22.15-20). She only affirms what Josiah himself had concluded upon learning what the scroll said (2 Kgs 22.13): Judah was doomed, although, for his piety, Josiah could expect some manner of comfort.[21] There is also nothing in the descriptions of the covenant ceremonies of Josiah that suggests any hope that Judah would be spared (2 Kgs 23.1-3, 21-22). Even though Josiah is immediately aware of the threat against his kingdom upon hearing the words of the scroll (2 Kgs 22.11-13), he makes no further mention of the salvation of the nation. In view of the consistent trajectory towards the ostensible failure of the purge to have any lasting effect, emending the text and construing Josiah as a potential national saviour is rather drastic surgery.

Monarchic history in Kings does come to a head in the story of Josiah; all else that follows is, in some way, only the realization of the inevitable, and yet, a realization which seems integral to the book as a whole.[22] After the Josiah episode, little elaboration may have been necessary, as the end of Judah was already largely revealed and so much of the purpose of the book fulfilled. This, however, begs the question of how the purpose could be achieved before narration of the eventual fall, and why Josiah's reign was such a watershed point in an 'exilicist' world-view. Moreover, regardless of the preferred compositional history, the post-monarchic writers had, in Josiah, a 'failed' hero. Halpern

---

'Lamentations', *Int* 9 (1955), pp. 320-38 (330).

21. M.J. Paul, 'King Josiah's Renewal of the Covenant (2 Kings 22–23)', in Breckelmans and Lust (eds.), *Pentateuchal and Deuteronomistic Studies*, pp. 269-76 (269-72), contests the opinion of N. Lohfink, who considers 2 Kgs 22.19-20 to be a 'salvation oracle'. Paul observes that it is incorrect to call Huldah's prophecy an oracle of destruction, it is a prophetic clarification of the situation, with limited comfort for the king. The articles by Lohfink, cited by Paul, are 'Die Bundesurkunde des Königs Josias (eine Frage an die Deuteronomiumsforschung)', *Bib* 44 (1963), pp. 261-88, 461-98; and 'Die Gattung der "Historischen Kurzgeschichte" in den letzten Jahren von Judah und in der zeit des babylonischen Exils', *ZAW* 90 (1978), pp. 319-47. See also his 'Zur neueren Diskussion über 2 Kön 22-23', in N. Lohfink (ed.), *Das Deuteronomium*, pp. 24-48.

22. Mullen, *Narrative History*, p. 281, despite the anticipation of this conclusion by Cross, 'Themes', p. 288.

and Vanderhooft, maintaining an original DtrH, state a popular conception of the problems facing the post-monarchic historians, albeit with unusual drama:

> Josiah failed. Doom rode up the hilltops of Judah in Egyptian and Babylonian colors. The end overtook the Davidic state, sending most of its elite to Mesopotamia. How does one explain the death of a savior, a messiah?[23]

For Hobbs, the reform of Josiah fits the previously-established pattern of positive cult reforms: it was doomed to fail. This includes even Hezekiah's, as the prophecy concerning his display of wealth to the Babylonian emissaries indicates (2 Kgs 20.16-18).[24] J.G. McConville writes of Kings: 'Far from leading the reader consistently to expect salvation for Judah through a davidic king, it leads him rather to expect the opposite'.[25]

Josiah is the last king that the book offers to greater Israel as a positive role model, and his story seems to emphasize a transition to a post-monarchic world. That a major change in the nature of leadership symbolically takes place is indicated by the manner of reporting the accession of Josiah's successor, Jehoahaz (2 Kgs 23.30). Not only is he anointed, but his accession is due to his selection by the 'people of the land', עם־הארץ. Nelson would take as evidence of a second redactor the fact that, here, the people of the land, for the first time in the book, place an 'evil' king on the throne.[26] This view, however, fails to convince. There is a thematic development that has the 'people of the land' consistently associated with righteous kings until after Josiah: Joash of

---

23. Halpern and Vanderhooft, 'Editions', pp. 243-44. See too, Cogan and Tadmor, *II Kings*, pp. 301-302; O'Brien, *Deuteronomistic History*, pp. 272-74.

24. Hobbs, *2 Kings*, p. 343. On the 'exilic' reading of the prophecy to Hezekiah, see P.R. Ackroyd, 'An Interpretation of the Babylonian Exile: A Study of II Kings 20 and Isaiah 38–39', in P.R. Ackroyd, *Studies in the Religious Tradition of the Old Testament* (London: SCM Press, 1987), pp. 152-71, 282-85, originally in *SJT* 27 (1974), pp. 329-52. For a contrary position, see R. Nelson, '*Realpolitik* in Judah (687–609 B.C.E.)', in W.W. Hallo, J.C. Moyer and L.G. Perdue (eds.), *Scripture in Context. II. More Essays on the Comparative Method* (Winona Lake, IN: Eisenbrauns, 1983), pp. 177-89 (186).

25. McConville, 'Narrative and Meaning', p. 45. Cf. Hobbs, *2 Kings*, p. 343, who sees a pattern in presenting reforms. Repetition in 2 Kgs 18.5; 22.2; 23.24-25 establishes order. Reforms end in loss, or potential loss, the history of reform was intended to be a history of failure of such efforts (cf. 2 Kgs 14; 16).

26. Nelson, *Double Redaction*, pp. 41-42.

Judah (2 Kgs 11.14-20; 12.3), Azariah / Uzziah and Jotham (2 Kgs 15.5, 34),[27] and Josiah himself (2 Kgs 21.23-24). The change after Josiah, then, is marked. On the other hand, the people of the land not only choose an inappropriate king in Jehoahaz, but they also anoint him. In Kings, only Jehoahaz, Solomon, Jehu, and Joash of Judah are anointed monarch over one of the Israelite kingdoms. In Solomon's case, davidic succession is at issue; and while the legitimacy of Solomon is not marked by an oracle from Yahweh, at least a priest performs the ceremony (1 Kgs 1.34-39). In Jehu's case, a dynastic change in the north is the matter at hand, brought about by Yahweh's plan. Jehu is anointed by Elijah's assistant (2 Kgs 9.1-10). Joash's anointing is in the presence of the priest Jehoiada, even if it is not said he actually performed it (2 Kgs 11.12). The king's legitimacy, however, is not at all in question. In Jehoahaz's case, however, no proper cultic specialist is even noted as present. This does not suggest to me a change in writers. Instead, I see their anointing of an inappropriate king as suggestive of the extent to which Josiah's death is portrayed as symbolic of the complete collapse of the institutions supporting the ideal of a pious monarchy. Even the agency that supported Joash and Josiah is now unable to make a proper choice, and its blindness is only further highlighted by the extreme confidence in anointing its candidate. Jehoahaz, however, is little more than a slight annoyance to Egypt, and soon Pharaoh replaces him with Jehoiakim (2 Kgs 23.34). Pharaoh recalls Jehoahaz to Egypt (2 Kgs 23.33), but Yahweh had already withdrawn his sanction for the monarchy.

After Josiah's biography, the reader confronts a laconic, open-ended text. The narrative relating the collapse of Judah is but a necessary appendix to the far more detailed earlier chapters. When the Babylonians plunder the city, the temple and its accoutrements are not ascribed to any king other than Solomon, the original builder (2 Kgs 24.13; 25.8-17; on Solomon, 24.13; 25.16): Josiah had restored the temple to its former state. With his cleansed temple and the renewed covenant, the 'centre of the earth' is refounded in Israel's sacred history, if not in political fact. The exile, portrayed as inevitable since Manasseh, if not Hezekiah, or even Solomon himself (cf. 2 Kgs 21.11-15; 20.16-18;

---

27. Azariah was selected by the 'people of Judah', 2 Kgs 14.21. Nelson, *Double Redaction*, p. 41, speculates unnecessarily that the 'people of the land', are also to be associated with the episode of Amaziah's succession (2 Kgs 12.21-22; 14.3), as he merely suspects that the historical Amaziah received help from this group.

1 Kgs 9.6-9), becomes an expulsion and transformation, not an execution. Josiah remains the one who has led Judah back to Yahweh, and
becomes an example of piety to all. For their part, the Babylonians do
not seem particularly concerned with desecrating the sanctuary; rather,
they are portrayed as more interested in the gold, silver, and bronze. No
direct mention of the altar or the ark (or scroll, for that matter) is made.
Unlike Josiah (2 Kgs 23.20), the Babylonians do not burn priests on the
altar. Death comes to a selected group, including priests, but this is
after they are taken to Riblah (2 Kgs 25.18-21). The narrator has, in a
sense, preserved some sense of the sanctuary's inherent sacrality.
Moreover, the Babylonians have not purged the land of its heterodoxy.
They are instruments of punishment, not 'restoration'. They have completed the destruction of the outward, political sphere of greater Israel,
but the last commendable king has already averted the destruction of
the inner, spiritual life of the people. That he dies long before the
Babylonians reached Judah only highlights how the true monarchy had
been withdrawn from greater Israel without their assistance. Yet, Josiah
is spared the sight of his kingdom and people being vanquished, if only
at the cost of his own life. The portrait of Josiah remains a troubling
puzzle.

2. *The Priest-King*

For many scholars, Josiah is portrayed as the new David.[28] In my view,
however, the centrality of the davidic dynasty to the Josiah episode is
often overestimated. The status of the institution of the monarchy in
2 Kings 22–23 is a particularly difficult issue for those scholars who
emphasize Deuteronomy as the document referred to in the episode.
Deuteronomy does not espouse an overtly 'monarchist' political structure, although the institution is permitted, with some serious limitations on royal prerogative, in Deut. 17.14-20.[29] This is, of course, less

---

28. Josiah is David *redivivus*, according to Laato, *Josiah and David*, pp. 58-59;
cf. Knoppers, *Two Nations*, II, p. 245.

29. On the discrepancy, see for instance, J. Levenson, 'Who Inserted the Book',
pp. 227-28. Knoppers, *Two Nations*, II, pp. 123-24, holds that Josiah's royalist
agenda forced qualification of some deuteronomic standards, while the force of
Deuteronomy added impetus to Josiah's reforms. In seeing compromise and modi-
fication, Knoppers has offered what would be a reasonable resolution of the problem, if a monarchic edition could be isolated with confidence.

troublesome if post-monarchic dates are accepted, and Kings is seen as something less than explicit monarchist propaganda. This is especially so since the monarchy is depicted as failing due to neglect of injunctions similar to those preserved in Deuteronomy's standards. Although Manasseh receives the lion's share of the blame, few monarchs are completely free from criticism. Josiah is a glowing exception to the rule and, therefore, has earned his stellar reputation (the other is Hezekiah). In fact, Josiah may be the exception which proves the rule. Although Josiah is initially compared favourably with David (2 Kgs 22.2), there is little else in the chapter that particularly legitimizes or even accentuates Josiah's davidic lineage or the status of the dynasty.[30] Only 2 Kgs 23.25, which has Josiah compared to all the other kings, is suggestive of his being a paragon of virtue who reclaims honour for the dynasty. That 'there was no king' like Josiah, in fact, seems to indicate he even surpassed David.[31] In this same verse, however, Josiah fulfils, not the standards of David, but those of the 'teaching of Moses'. His biography, therefore, seems to move from a general interest in Josiah as part of the davidic dynasty to a greater interest in associating Josiah with a more formative character in Israelite history, Moses.

Friedman is among those who notice how Josiah compares with Deuteronomy's Moses. Josiah is the only king to inquire through a priest, in keeping with the injunctions of Deut 17.8-12. He is, also, the only king to obey the command to read the law publicly (Deut 31.11; 2 Kgs 23.2). Josiah is said not to have turned from the path of David 'to the right or left' (2 Kgs 22.2). Such a phrase is familiar, for example, from Deut. 5.32; 17.11, 20; Josh. 23.6, but nowhere else in 2 Kings. As there was no other like Moses (Deut. 34.10), so there is no other king like Josiah (2 Kgs 23.25) who obeys Yahweh with all his 'heart, soul and strength' (cf. Deut. 6.5). Josiah's actions against idols recall Moses' actions against the golden calf and the commandments to destroy heterodox cultic paraphernalia (cf. Deut. 9.21, 12.3; 2 Kgs

---

30. Josiah is 'king' in 2 Kgs 22.1, 3, 9, 10, 11, 12, 16, 18, 20; 23.1, 3, 4, 12, 13, 21, 23, 29.

31. This verse is sometimes held as incompatible with 2 Kgs 18.5, concerning Hezekiah and so is taken as evidence of multiple editions: e.g. Provan *Hezekiah*, p. 153. On the other hand, some see no contradiction because each king was 'greatest' in a different way: G.N. Knoppers, '"There was none like Him": Incomparability in the Books of Kings', *CBQ* 54 (1992), pp. 411-31. See too, McKenzie, *Trouble*, p. 102; Gerbrandt, *Kingship*, pp. 52-53.

23.15; 23.6, 12).[32] In 2 Kgs 23.2-3 Josiah affirms 'the covenant', הברית, implicitly the one originally made with Yahweh through Moses. Deuteronomy 28.69 and 29.9-19 depict the setting of this book as a covenant renewal on the plains of Moab.[33] These associations with the pre-monarchic covenant almost totally supersede any emphasis on Josiah's royal status, and, as noted above, he undoes the shameful work of previous kings of both Judah and Israel. Josiah's Passover was greater than those celebrated by the judges of Israel, or the kings of Judah or Israel (2 Kgs 23.21-23).[34] Despite this, however, Josiah does not lead Israel into a new phase of political piety. He can neither supplant the kingship with a new political entity or repair all the damage of earlier kings. The sins of Manasseh are left unatoned (2 Kgs 23.26-27). I commented above how Josiah is never mentioned as occupying the 'throne of Israel' and is never granted the title נגיד. To this may be added the fact that there is no speech in Josiah's episode celebrating a divine promise of rule over Israel to the line of David, or to Josiah personally (however conditional), as there was when Solomon dedicated the temple (1 Kgs 8.16, 19, 25-26; cf. other contexts, 1 Kgs 2.4; 9.5).[35] In 1 Kgs 13.2, Josiah's actions at Bethel are predicted, and reference is made there to his davidic lineage, but this point is not taken up when the prediction finds its fulfilment (2 Kgs 23.15-18). Rather than salvage something of a theocracy within a monarchy, Josiah's story highlights the need for a theocracy based on the *Torah*, while accepting that the monarchy is doomed to fail. Even so, Josiah's story preserves for posterity some level of respect for the memory of the monarchy, and hence allows the easier accommodation of the monarchic experience within Israel's other historical memories.

The lack of emphasis on the monarchy in Josiah's story can be illustrated by comparison with another episode in Kings.[36] Parallels

32. Friedman, *Exile*, pp. 6-11. J.C. Nohrnberg, *Like unto Moses: The Constituting of an Interruption* (ISBL; Bloomington: Indiana University Press, 1995), pp. 316-18, also develops the relationship between Josiah and Moses.

33. McKenzie, *Trouble*, p. 130, and Paul, 'Josiah's Renewal', p. 273.

34. Long, *2 Kings*, p. 263, considers that when Josiah comments on the sins of 'our fathers', אבתינו, in 2 Kgs 22.13, he is probably referring to previous kings, but I wonder if the plural suffix 'our' does not specify the 'ancestors' of the nation as a whole.

35. If one is to see an abridged book of Kings maintain Josiah's right to salvage the monarchy over greater Israel, I find this lack very curious.

36. It would be impossible to cover here all the ways in which 2 Kgs 22–23

between 2 Kings 11–12 and 22–23 might be taken as evidence of the primacy of the theme of monarchic rule in Josiah's story, but such a conclusion is not at all necessary.[37] Josiah's orders concerning temple repairs in 2 Kgs 22.3-7 echo Joash's on the same matter in 2 Kgs 12.5-16. One could point, in particular, to the similar orders given to the priests about money collections, and the motif of the honest workers. Moreover, Joash was once hidden away in the temple by a priest, whereas Josiah's priest found the book of the *Torah* there (cf. 2 Kgs 11.1-3; 22.8-10).[38] It is not necessary to follow Eynikel's overstatement of the inconsistency in having the covenant in 2 Kgs 23.1-3 precede the reporting of the purification of the temple. A similar course of events occur in 2 Kgs 11.4-20, which tells of the events surrounding Joash's rise to the throne and the overthrow of Athaliah.[39] Prior to the coup, the priest Jehoiada brings the young claimant to the throne out of hiding in the temple, and the boy is anointed king (2 Kgs 11.12). The queen is then executed (vv. 13-16). At this point, covenants between Yahweh and the people with their new king, and between the people and the king are made (v. 17). Only then does the destruction of Athaliah's Baal cult occur, after which a procession sees Joash to the royal throne, which is the ultimate resolution to the drama (v. 19). There are contrasts between the episodes, as well. In 2 Kings 22–23, it is the realization of a crisis, and not its resolution, that is produced from the temple. As in 2 Kings 11, however, a woman is confronted, although in 2 Kings 22 she only confirms that there can be no resolution.[40] At this point, Josiah reaffirms the covenant (2 Kgs 23.1-3), and this leads into the purge, which is then followed by another ceremony, Passover (2 Kgs 23.21-23). In both cases, ceremonies mark the beginning and end of violent purges, and these highlight the social significance of the events narrated.[41] In Joash's story, a break in the davidic line is

reflects different episodes in the book, e.g., the story of Jehu, 2 Kgs 9–10.

37. 2 Kings 11 has recently attracted much scholarly attention for its relating of the recovery of the throne of Judah to the davidic dynasty. See Mullen, *Narrative History*, pp. 21-54; Dutcher-Walls, *Narrative Art*.

38. See especially Hoffmann, *Reform*, pp. 193-97, also Hobbs, *2 Kings*, pp. 323-25.

39. Eynikel, *The Reform*, p. 320.

40. She predicts the death of Josiah, rather than dying herself, as did Athaliah.

41. See Mullen, *Narrative History*, pp. 50-52, for the ritual resolution in 2 Kgs 11.

obviously the matter at hand, whereas this is hardly the case in 2 Kings 22–23. Rather, a repeated plot structure (ceremony / cultic purge / ceremony) has a new focus. Concern with the legitimacy of the dynasty in the earlier episode, valid while much of its history is yet to unfold, is supplanted on the eve of the dynasty's very destruction. In the later episode, the writers focus on the covenant links between greater Israel and Yahweh and on the purge, motivated not by dynastic concerns, but by the *Torah*-scroll itself.[42]

If the concern for the dynasty is lessened in Josiah's case, Josiah's role is at least accorded some priestly, or perhaps better, cultic nuances. This is evident in 2 Kgs 23.1-3, with the renewal of the covenant before all the people, the priests and the prophets, and the great Passover celebration in 2 Kgs 23.21-23.[43] Similar imagery surrounds Solomon in 1 Kings 8. Handy contends that in the post-monarchic period, the high priest was not the ruler of Judah, and so the political and religious spheres were divided. This *status quo* is read anachronistically into the past in the production of Kings, and so the monarchs are excluded from any priestly activities. Handy observes how Josiah never enters the temple, dealing with it only through subordinates and priests. On the other hand, acting against all illicit religious behaviour is Josiah's prerogative, since the rulers are held responsible for leading the people astray.[44] I object to this on the grounds that, even though there is no mention of where in Jerusalem Josiah celebrated Passover (cf. 2 Kgs 23.23), the setting of the covenant ceremony in 2 Kgs 23.1-3 is the temple (cf. v. 2, ויעל המלך בית־יהוה). Solomon is granted access not only to the temple, but to the priestly activities of offering sacrifices (cf. 1 Kgs 8.5, 64-65). Priests play a role in the installation of the ark (1 Kgs 8.3-11), but then disappear from the story. It seems a more valid

---

42. Compare the extent of text granted the purge in 2 Kgs 11, only v. 18, with that of Josiah, 2 Kgs 23.4-20. Eslinger, 'Josiah', p. 59, comments that the structure of the Josiah episode calls attention to the law scroll. Gerbrandt, *Kingship*, p. 99, holds that the ideal king was a 'covenant administrator'. It is interesting that with the convocation of Judah and Jerusalem in 2 Kgs 23.1-3, talk of the 'Torah scroll' (ספר התורה) (2 Kgs 22.8, 11, cf. 23.24) is interrupted by a concern for the 'Covenant scroll' (ספר הברית) (2 Kgs 23.2, 21).

43. Long, *2 Kings*, pp. 267, 69; Hoffmann, *Reform*, pp. 200-203.

44. Handy, 'Role', p. 47.

line of questioning to relate the post-monarchic division of authority to the problem of why the role of kings, at a time of a defunct monarchy, with no direct counterpart in the writer's own world, could be upheld over that of an ostensibly reinstated 'ancient' priesthood (if the temple was, in fact, rebuilt by this time). One possible explanation is simply that the characters of Josiah and Solomon were loaded with as many important symbolic functions as possible, reflecting their importance to the story being told. Given the post-monarchic situation, and that no contemporary Israelite kings rivalled the status of the priesthood (although political figures may have challenged or influenced it), the ascription of priestly roles to the ancient monarchs at key points in history may not actually have threatened the security of the contemporary priesthood. Indeed, priestly claims to status could have been legitimized by a tradition whereby their function was occasionally performed by famous kings, the priests' status increasing through a closer association with the ancient political institution. Their priesthood might, therefore, be portrayed not only as the continuation of the monarchic era priesthood, but, in a manner of speaking, of the monarchy itself.

On the other hand, the minimal role granted priests in the book, and the absence of a post-monarchic temple restoration episode suggests that the legitimacy of a specific priesthood was not the primary concern of the writers. In this regard, another comparison between Josiah's episode and 2 Kings 11–12 can be made. Both episodes seem to display a less than high regard for priests, even if Jehoiada and Hilkiah are not in any way vilified. Their subservient role may, in fact, have served the purposes of a post-monarchic priesthood's claims to status, if not outright political power. To re-instate a davidic king, a figure who represents the continuity of the religious order upholding the dynasty is needed to legitimize the boy-king, and the priest Jehoiada fills this role in 2 Kings 11. In the repair episode, however, the priest takes only a supporting role, and seems actually called to account by the king in 2 Kgs 12.7 (cf. v. 10). Jehoiada has instructed the king to do right in the eyes of Yahweh, but the high places are not removed, indicating that Joash's education was somewhat wanting (2 Kgs 12.3-4). In 2 Kings 22, again it is the king who orders the priests and other officials to perform certain tasks in a certain way (vv. 4, 12, and, in the purge narrative, 23.4). Josiah's purge, of course, admits of no compromise. Moreover, Josiah's accession does not mark a reinstatement of the dynasty. His right to perform a central religious function has been established by his reaction to the scroll and the oracle of Huldah in 2 Kgs 22.11-20. The high priest sends the scroll to the king, but he himself is not accorded the legitimacy to interpret it (it is actually the scribe Shaphan who reads it, 2 Kgs 22.8). Instead, he obeys Josiah's order to inquire of Yahweh through the prophetess (2 Kgs 22.8-20). Hilkiah is not even given an important role in the covenant ceremony (2 Kgs 23.1-3), or one at all in the Passover (vv. 21-23).

The memories of a royal 'priest' and a subservient monarchic priesthood may also have served the legitimization of political leaders with little, if any, connection with the actual temple in Jerusalem, by providing a model of a political leader empowered to perform ritual functions. It is logical that this model in Kings be based upon the supreme political leader in the narrative world, the king himself. It is not necessary to propose that any post-monarchic leaders subscribing to such a model would necessarily have claimed royal status themselves, although this is possible. As a balance to this model, one should consider the emphasis on Elijah and other prophets as the true defenders of Yahwism in the episodes relating the history of the north, where even relatively pious kings are in precious short supply. Elijah himself offers sacrifices in 1 Kings 18.[45] In this clash of probably complementary, but potentially rival paradigmatic leadership models, the past may be constructed so as to legitimize the present, with no necessity that the present be made identical to the past. Josiah, then, as a priest-king, may have empowered diverse forms of political and religious leaderships, on a variety of regional, local, or sectarian levels.

3. *Yahweh's 'Gathering' of Josiah*

One of the most perplexing issues pertaining to Josiah is the manner of his death and its relation to the oracle of Huldah. Handy demonstrates that this episode has formal similarities with other near eastern texts dealing with the legitimacy of religious reforms. Based on these parallels, he argues that Josiah's motive in consulting a prophet (2 Kgs 22.9) was to obtain a legitimate interpretation of a divine communication.

---

45. A recent opinion, however, holds that in the DtrH the prophets are almost always portrayed in a way that does not usurp royal power, although cracks in this ideological facade appear; Bergen, 'The Prophetic Alternative'.

The biblical writers, however, could not use the more common 'normal channels' such as omens to deliver an initial word to the king, or such figures as diviners to confirm its contents. Instead, a document is confirmed by a prophetess. Peace for a king moved by a divine word is considered by Handy to be a standard motif in the ancient Near East. The biblical story differs from the Mesopotamian examples in that the king may be pardoned, but not the nation. That Josiah dies violently is claimed to be irrelevant to the generic prophecy of Huldah.[46] In my opinion, however, the writer should be thought of as potentially more in control of the material. I would, however, also relate the death of Josiah to the general pattern that shapes the illness and death reports of Jeroboam's son (1 Kgs 14.1-18; MT, 12.24g-n), Ahaziah (2 Kgs 1.1-17), Ben-Hadad (2 Kgs 8.7-15) and Hezekiah (2 Kgs 20.1-11).[47] The basic pattern sees a dying king send for an oracle from a deity. Although Josiah is not ill (cf. Jeroboam), he is physically upset by the words of the book, and seeks a prophet through intermediaries, as did Jeroboam, Ahaziah, and Ben-Hadad. In all of these cases, something very unexpected occurs. As the series progresses, however, these providential turns of fate become increasingly inexplicable. Jeroboam inquires after his son, and receives an oracle about his whole line. Ahaziah seeks Baal-Zebub, but his emissary receives an audience with a prophet of Yahweh. In both these cases, an 'evil' king receives an oracle of doom unexpectedly. Ben-Hadad, the Aramean king, is given a false prophecy and is assassinated by the one whom he trusted to obtain the prophetic word, who himself has received word that he will reign. This bizarre twist, with its deceitful prophecy, is overshadowed by the enigma surrounding the oracle given to Josiah's men, and the manner in which it is fulfilled. One can but wonder how to interpret the 'peace' he is promised, as he dies at the hand of Pharaoh Necho (cf. 2 Kgs 22.20; 23.29).

It is not an easy task to understand what motive Necho had in travelling to the Euphrates. The same may be said of Josiah's motive in going to Megiddo to meet him. Scholars debate whether 'he came up...to/against' (עלה...על) n v. 29 indicates that Necho confronted the king of Assyria in battle. Often this is denied on the strength of

---

46. Handy, 'Role'. The texts he compares the Josiah story to include Esarhaddon's 'Black Stone Inscription' and Nabonidus' 'Cylinder Inscription'.

47. R.L. Cohn, 'Convention and Creativity in the Book of Kings; The Case of the Dying Monarch', *CBQ* 47 (1985), pp. 603-16.

other information about the actual historical situation.[48] Yet, this
remains the more logical reading.[49] Regarding the other more pressing
issue of the construction 'and he went...to meet' (וַיֵּלֶךְ...לִקְרָאתוֹ),
which is used to describe Josiah's travels to meet Pharaoh (v. 29), one
also encounters a certain ambiguity as, elsewhere, it is used in both
confrontational and peaceful situations.[50] Many scholars prefer the
former alternative in interpreting the verse in question.[51] Talshir, however, asks whether the Kings passage would have been understood as
referring to a battle, had 2 Chron. 35.20-27 not included a reference to
such enmity. The verb combination found in Kings is rarely used to
indicate conflict, while the alternative 'he went out...to meet'
(יָצָא...לִקְרָאת) is frequently used to indicate a military confrontation
(e.g. Josh. 8.5, 14, 22). It is this combination that Chronicles employs
in regard to Josiah. The language used in the report about Josiah
resembles that used in 2 Kgs 16.10, in which Ahaz visits the Assyrian
king in order to affirm his subservience. Josiah is similarly depicted as

48. Tagliacarne, '*Keiner war wie er*', pp. 326-27, holds that the construction
implies enmity (cf. Judg. 18.9; 1 Kgs 15.17; 20.22; 2 Kgs 12.18; 17.3; 18.9, 13, 25;
Ezek. 38.11, 16). A 'neutral' meaning is found in Josh. 2.8. Hobbs, *2 Kings*, p. 340,
suggests this construction, at first glance, implies Pharaoh's enmity with Assyria,
but holds that the prepositions אֶל and עַל are largely interchangeable (cf. 2 Kgs
6.24; 12.18, 19). He concludes that Necho went 'on behalf of the king of Assyria'.
Cogan and Tadmor, *II Kings*, p. 291, suggest that Necho 'set out ... to the king of
Assyria'.

49. R.J. Coggins, '2 Kings 23.29: A Problem of Method in Translation', in
Breckelmans and Lust (eds.), *Pentateuchal and Deuteronomistic Studies*, pp. 278-
81. He offers some comments on the dangers of 'improving' the text.

50. Tagliacarne, '*Keiner war wie er*', pp. 327-28. As confrontational uses he
cites: Gen. 32.7; 1 Sam. 23.28; 1 Kgs 20.27. These may be compared to 1 Sam.
17.48, where, in a war situation, it seems to mean 'to draw near'. 'Neutral' uses are
Gen. 24.65; Exod. 4.27; Josh. 9.11; 2 Sam. 19.16; 1 Kgs 18.16; 2 Kgs 8.8, 9; 9.18;
16.10. Gray, *Kings*, p. 747, also avoids committing himself to a reading based
solely on the wording, employing historical reconstructions. Cogan and Tadmor,
II Kings, p. 301, consider the text here 'cryptic' and 'laconic', noting that warlike
actions on the part of Josiah are not necessarily implied. Yet, they translate 'confronted' (p. 29).

51. Hobbs, *2 Kings*, p. 330, understands the phrase as meaning 'to meet in
battle' citing the Chronicles passage. So too, Laato, *Josiah and David*, p. 78. For
his part, Noth, *Deuteronomistic History*, p. 67, 132 n. 18, writes that Josiah died in
battle, but Kings' author misunderstood his source, and expressed himself poorly,
resulting in an obscure text.

going to meet his overlord, who, for whatever reason, was in no mood to tolerate the Judaean.[52] I accept Talshir's reading, and view Kings as indicating that Josiah went to meet Pharaoh in peace. There is more irony than Halpern and Vanderhooft recognize in Josiah's death at the hands of an ally. Josiah seems to have done what Assyria, the implicit enemy of Egypt, once claimed was a very dangerous thing: to place trust in Egypt (2 Kgs 18.21).[53] No more is heard of Assyria in Kings, however, and so one might think that they had finally received their comeuppance at the hands of Pharaoh. Josiah's death, then, marks an important transition in the political sphere, Israel's independence is, once again, measured against Egyptian power, and once again, it falls short.

Huldah's prediction itself is rightly the centre of some controversy. 2 Kings 22.20 is constructed in a two-step parallel structure which has its consequences revealed in a third unit:[54]

α.   לכן הנני אספך על־אבתיך
β.   ונאספת אל־קברתיך בשלום
γ.   ולא־תראינה עיניך בכל הרעה
      אשר־אני מביא על־המקום הזה

Therefore, behold, I will gather you to your fathers,
And you will be gathered to your grave in peace
And your eyes, will not see all the evil which I am bringing upon this
    place

52. Talshir, 'The Three Deaths', pp. 215-18, speculates that Josiah's reforms may have upset Necho. In 1925, A.C. Welch, 'The Death of Josiah', *ZAW* 43 (1925), pp. 25-60, proposed that Josiah did not intend to meet Necho in conflict, and that the Chronicler's version of events is dependent upon the reports of the events at Ramoth-Gilead in 1 Kgs 22.29-38. Cf. H.G.M. Williamson, 'The Death of Josiah and the Continuing Development of the Deuteronomistic History', *VT* 32 (1982), pp. 242-48, develops the idea that Chronicles' report is based on the King's episode of the death of Ahab. See also Begg, 'The Death of Josiah: Josephus', p. 158.

53. Halpern and Vanderhooft, 'Editions', p. 228, write of the difficult passage: 'The obfuscation looks deliberate; its effect is to infer an ironic fulfilment of Huldah's oracle–Josiah met his death at the hand of one with whom he was *bšlm*, i.e., on a peaceable footing, even in collaboration, just as Joab's liege had been in a collaborative relationship with Abner and Amasa, whose warblood was spilled *bšlm*'.

54. Cf. Hoffmann, *Reform*, pp. 182-83.

The final word in line β, בשלום, seems ill-chosen to reflect the reported death of Josiah at the hands of Pharaoh Necho, which was hardly peaceful (2 Kgs 23.29). For some, אל־קברתיך בשלום refers not to the manner of Josiah's death itself, but to the political situation of the nation as a whole at that point in time, any conflict with Egypt perhaps overshadowed by the relative 'peace' prior to the Babylonian onslaught.[55] Other scholars maintain that there is little outright contradiction between 22.20 and 23.29, arguing that בשלום refers only to the king's actual burial, which might be seen as at least relatively peaceful, since the king seems to receive a proper funeral.[56] Recently, P.S.F. van Keulen has analysed נאספת אל־קברתיך in terms of the other attestations of 'gather' (אסף) which have to do with interment and which are followed by the root 'bury' (קבר). These either explicitly mention, or may be taken as elliptical references to, the 'gathering' of the bones of the slain (2 Sam. 21.13; Jer. 8.1, 2; Jer. 25.33; Ezek. 29.5). 2 Kings 22.20 may also be interpreted thus. Of the monarchs in Kings who are said to have been buried each 'in his (own) grave', all die violently (Ahaziah, 2 Kgs 9.27-28; Amon, 2 Kgs 21.23, 26; Josiah, 2 Kgs 23.29-30).[57] Van Keulen concludes that 2 Kgs 22.20 implies that Josiah will die violently, but be buried in peaceful circumstances.[58] While I do find much insight in van Keulen's argument, I still find it rather superficial to differentiate sharply between the actual slaying of Josiah and his funeral. To my mind, however, the parallelism between units α and β should, perhaps, be taken as more synonymous. Following the prediction that Yahweh will 'gather' Josiah to 'his fathers', the second unit uses the image of burial to restate the prediction of death.

This is the basic conclusion of a number of scholars. They, therefore,

55. Nicholson, *Deuteronomy*, p. 15. Hobbs, *2 Kings*, p. 328, objects that at Josiah's death, Judah was at war with Egypt.

56. Dietrich, *Prophetie*, pp. 57-58. Hoffmann, *Reform*, pp. 184-85; Provan, *Hezekiah*, p. 149. Long, *2 Kings*, pp. 254-55, says that Josiah's burial will be in peace, or honour.

57. There are some other similarities between the death of Ahaziah and Josiah. Both die in Megiddo, and both are carried to Jerusalem in a chariot by servants (2 Kgs 9.28-30; 23.29-30). Ironically, the death of Ahaziah is a part of the great purge of Jehu, while Josiah's death seems to mark the beginning of the end of his own line.

58. P.S.F. van Keulen, 'The Meaning of the Phrase *WN'SPT 'L-QBRTYK BšLWM* in 2 Kings XXII 20', *VT* 46 (1996), pp. 256-60.

maintain that there is a contradiction between 2 Kgs 22.20 and 23.29, and seek a diachronic solution, seeing 23.29 as part of the 'exilic' additions to a book originally written when Josiah was alive.[59] Knoppers observes that the writer of 2 Kgs 23.29-30 does not claim that Josiah's death meets the criteria of Huldah's prophecy. This is, therefore, an exception to the frequent notice that other prophecies have been fulfilled. See, for instance, 1 Kgs 12.15; 15.29; 16.12, 34; 17.16; 2 Kgs 1.17; 2.22; 4.44; 9.36-37. Moreover, 2 Kgs 23.30 does not add that they laid Josiah in his grave 'in peace'. The report of Josiah's death only fulfils the stipulation that he will not see the evil wrought against Judah.[60] Halpern and Vanderhooft observe that to be 'gathered' to one's 'kin' (עַם) is said of Abraham, Ishmael, Isaac, Jacob, Aaron, and Moses, none of whom die violently (Gen. 25.8, 17; 35.29; 49.29, 33; Num. 20.24, 26; 27.13; 31.2; Deut. 32.50). In Num. 20.26 the 'gathering' of Aaron is before his actual death. Genesis 25.8; 17; 35.29; 49.33; Deut. 32.50 are said to be 'Priestly' references to the time between death and burial. This compares favourably with Isa. 57.1 and Jer. 25.33. Huldah's oracle combines this 'P' expression with the DtrH/J idiom, 'to lie with the fathers', which marks a peaceful death. Genesis 15.15, anticipating the death of Abraham, is particularly echoed in Huldah's words, and so it is concluded that the prophetess assured Josiah of a peaceful end. An exilic editor was, therefore, confronted with a problem, and solved it by casting the words of the actual death report of the king to indicate (against the actual fact of the matter) that Josiah was in league with Necho against Assyria. Thus, 'in peace' is a heavy piece of irony, Josiah meeting his end at the hands of an ally, one with whom he was at peace. They conclude that the problems of accommodating the oracle and death report are so extensive that the exilic redactor would not have chosen such a strategy of irony had there been an alternative. It is claimed that the inclusion of the oracle as it now stands was necessitated by the fact that it was already enshrined in a monarchic era history.[61] While these scholars

---

59. For instance, Nelson, *Double Redaction*, p. 77; McKenzie, *Trouble*, p. 11. Cf. as well, Rose, 'Bemerkungen', pp. 58-59. On the other hand, Friedman, *Exile*, p. 25, does not commit to either of the 'peaceful death', or 'death in peacetime' alternatives, thinking the 'exilic' reworking too well integrated into the original document to allow solution to the problem.

60. Knoppers, *Two Nations*, II, pp. 150-51.

61. Halpern and Vanderhooft, 'Editions', pp. 221-29.

have uncovered a very insightful way of reading the extant text, I find no reason to maintain such a diachronic solution, and especially find no support whatsoever in the assertion that such irony could not be motivated by anything other than desperation at the thought of reconciling the irreconcilable. I see no reason why a post-monarchic author could not have completely constructed such an irony from choice, not compulsion, and capitalized on the resultant enigma by refraining to clarify Yahweh's involvement in the tragic events.[62]

I am also unconvinced that 2 Kgs 22.20 should be so closely linked to the Pentateuchal passages, although they are not wholly irrelevant. They add another layer to the irony. The Pentateuch actually offers no exact parallel to 2 Kgs 22.20. In each of the Pentateuchal verses cited above, as well as in Judg. 2.10, where 'be gathered' to one's 'fathers' is found, the verb אסף is in the *niphal*. In 2 Kgs 22.20, the verb in the first instance is in the *qal*; 'I (Yahweh) will gather you (Josiah)'. The second phrase is, as is more typical, in the *niphal*, 'You will be gathered'. In my estimation, the initial transitive verb is an important clue to the meaning of the whole. Huldah is not merely reporting that Josiah will die, but that Yahweh will actually bring it about. This suggests to me an intimation of Josiah's early death. The scholar is, therefore, actually presented with a three-way problem: reconciling Yahweh's 'gathering' of Josiah, his seemingly peaceful 'gathering' to his grave (2 Kgs 22.20), and the report of his murder (2 Kgs 23.29), in which the narrator does not actually implicate Yahweh. Halpern and Vanderhooft observe that Josiah's culture saw long life as a reward for piety.[63] Yet, he is not given the reward of long life that so many of the other 'culture-heroes' enjoyed. Abraham lives to old age (Gen. 25.8); Ishmael to 137 years (Gen. 25.17); Isaac, 180 (Gen. 35.28); Jacob, 147 (Gen. 47.28). Aaron dies at 123 (Num. 33.39), and Moses at 120 (Deut. 34.7). Josiah took the throne at age eight, and reigned 31 years (2 Kgs 22.1). At 39, he died young. Josiah is hardly portrayed as a minor character in the long list of major figures in the history of Israel, and, as he seems to recall no less a hero than Moses, his importance cannot be underestimated. Yet, the discrepancy between his early death and the long life of the Pentateuchal heroes is disturbing, especially since

---

62. In some ways, Halpern and Vanderhooft preserve the notion of an exilic redactor whose literary talents left something to be desired: cf. Cross, 'Themes', p. 288; Nelson, *Double Redaction*, p. 38.

63. Halpern and Vanderhooft, 'Editions', pp. 222-23.

Manasseh became king at 12, and reigned 55 years (2 Kgs 21.1). Even if the culture of the writers saw long life as a fitting reward for the pious, this belief could at least be suspended in certain cases.

Beside the moral question of Yahweh taking the life of Josiah as a reward for his piety, one is left to wrestle with how Josiah might go to his grave 'in peace'? On the one hand, there is great value placed on proper burial in the Hebrew Bible, and this may offer some resolution to the dilemma.[64] For instance, in the MT, Jeroboam's son, the only one of his clan who pleases Yahweh, is granted the decency of interment in a proper grave (1 Kgs 14.12-13; 3 Kgdms 12.24m does not offer a parallel).[65] Yet one can only reflect on the ending of 2 Samuel, where David is given the choice of falling into the hands of Yahweh or man. Trusting the mercy of Yahweh, David chooses not to be pursued for three months by his enemies. Yahweh then makes his own choice, sending pestilence for three days, rather than famine for seven years (2 Sam. 24.13-14). When Josiah meets Necho, has he fallen into the hands of man or of Yahweh? The deity is not mentioned at all when Josiah finally does meet his fate (2 Kgs 23.29-30). There is also no direct relating of Josiah's death to the notice that Yahweh had determined the sins of Manasseh were inexcusable, and that Judah could not be saved (2 Kgs 23.26-27; cf. 2 Kgs 22.15-17, 20). It would be wrong, however, to argue that the silence about Yahweh's role indicates that the death of Josiah was without theological significance to those who wrote about it. This silence only reflects a style found in other episodes as well. Most notable is the story of the murder of Gedaliah in 2 Kgs 25.22-26, who is portrayed as asking the Judaeans to submit to the Babylonians. Neither is there a reference to the deity in the book's concluding episode, the release of Jehoiachin (2 Kgs 25.27-30). Similarly, Pharaoh's attack on Rehoboam's Jerusalem is told with no explicit theological element, although it does follow closely on accusations of wrongdoing (1 Kgs 14.22-28). In 2 Kings 3 Elisha preserves the expedition against Moab in the face of a drought, yet neither he nor his god is even mentioned at the end of the chapter when the king of Moab sacrifices his son and a 'great wrath' comes upon Israel, who then

64. As noted by Hoffmann, *Reform*, pp. 184-85, cf. Gen. 47.30. On the horror of not being buried, see Deut. 28.26; 1 Sam. 17.44; 1 Kgs 16.4; 21.24; Prov. 30.17; Ezek. 29.5.

65. Cf. Hoffmann, *Reform*, p. 185. The absence of such a parallel in the LXX may undermine the strength of this somewhat.

withdraws (2 Kgs 3.27). Although a number of changes of dynasty in northern Israel are attributed to the divine will, later dynastic changes are related with no such explanation.[66] No reference to divine anger is found when the Judaean king Amaziah, who receives at least a qualified note of approval by the author (2 Kgs 14.3-4), is defeated by Israel's Jehoash, who plunders the temple riches (2 Kgs 14.14). This can hardly be considered of little import, as such plundering occurs throughout the book (1 Kgs 14.25-28; 2 Kgs 24.13; 25.13-15). While the moral or religious elements in many of these episodes may be determinable from the immediate context, the problems surrounding the deaths of Josiah and Gedaliah and the release of Jehoiachin are less easily solved.

The ironies and silences in this text remain troublesome, but leave the reader room to wonder about these events as representative of Yahweh's dealings with Israel. Yet, relating these events to other biblical traditions opens even more deeply unsettling questions. If Josiah went peacefully to visit Pharaoh, did he stop following the ways of David and mimic Solomon, who figuratively led Israel back to Egypt? As noted above, however, Josiah may also be likened to Moses. But, if he had already prepared his people to leave this 'Egypt', he himself had been forbidden to cross the sea. There are also no new plagues on Egypt to parallel the miracles in Moses' day, no clear vengeance for Necho's crimes. Still, Egypt's holdings in Palestine are eventually claimed by Babylon (2 Kgs 24.7), and so Israel has escaped. But they do not cross the parted sea or the Jordan river. They are carried across the Euphrates.

In view of these observations and speculations, it seems that the story of Josiah's 'failed' purge is in need of its own rehabilitation in the minds of modern scholars. Because Josiah seems to have received little in the way of personal benefit from his piety, the story is not a simple theodicy that shows how the pious receive divine protection.[67] Laato suggests that the death of the king was not the result of wickedness, but

66. Cf. Baasha over Jeroboam's dynasty (1 Kgs 15.27-29); Jehu over Ahab's dynasty (2 Kgs 9.1–10.17). Shallum destroys the dynasty of Jeroboam II (2 Kgs 15.10-11), while his own hopes are ended by Menahem's victory over Shallum (2 Kgs 15.14). In turn, his own son, Pekahiah, is ousted by Pekah, who is overthrown by Hoshea (2 Kgs 15.25, 30).

67. Eslinger, 'Josiah', pp. 46-47, comments on the impact of this on the usual notions of deuteronomistic theology.

of his suffering because of the sins of Manasseh.[68] This raises the question of whether the text hints that the death of the king was partially expiatory for these sins. Because there is no condemnation of Josiah, he certainly does not become a scapegoat. He is, instead, rather more of a martyr, even if an ambiguous one. He is martyred for his own humanity, which cannot overcome divine anger. As such, his life and death teaches the smallness of an individual, even a great king, in the greater movements of history. Josiah is the last 'good' king, and, like the whole idea of the monarchy as representative of Yahweh's theocracy, comes to a bitter end: so much potential unrealized. Yahweh has withdrawn the crown. Jonathan Z. Smith's understanding of the mythic type 'hero that failed' casts some light on King's enigmatic Josiah; such a hero

> ... was *not* successful in overcoming death or his humanity; rather through rebellion against order, he was initiated into, discovered and assumed his humanity. By his hard-won affirmation of both the human and cosmic structures of destiny, he became a model for his fellow men.[69]

How, then, should one think that Josiah found his 'peace' (if one insists that the prophecy should be fulfilled, without recourse only to painful ironies)? It seems to me that the key lies in a transformation in the nature of 'peace' within the narrative, from political stability and personal safety implied in the immediate literary context (and reader's expectations), to a concept having more to do with spiritual and emotional well-being. By seeing the 'peace' as internal, the 'failure' of the purge to alter history radically is undermined. Josiah acts because it is the right thing to do, despite Yahweh's resolution that the political state was not worth saving. In so doing, however, he has also made steps toward the reconciliation of Israel with Yahweh. His divinely-sanctioned death may have seemed untimely, but at least it was delayed until his work was done, and the new Moses led the people to some form of safety, illustrated graphically through the Passover ceremony (2 Kgs 23.21-23). In this, perhaps, Josiah finds the consolation for his spirit, so disturbed by the fateful discovery of Hilkiah.[70]

68. Laato, *Josiah and David*, pp. 40-41.

69. J.Z. Smith, *Map is not Territory: Studies in the History of Religions* (SJLA, 23; Leiden: E.J. Brill, 1978), p. 134.

70. Note how Josiah is depicted as extremely distressed at hearing the words of the scroll, tearing his clothes, and weeping (2 Kgs 22.11, 19).

4. *The Transformation of Israel*

Josiah's purge, as symbolically representing the transformation of Israel into its 'exilic' self, needs to be seen in the light of the two ceremonial actions which largely frame it, the covenant of 2 Kgs 23.1-3, and the Passover in 23.21-23. This frame marks the attempts at resolution of a social drama. Unlike the enigmatic ritualization of history in the case of the schism, or the upheaval of Jehu's carnival, there is a great sense of order to these proceedings. To Burke Long, the popular acceptance of the covenant results in a closure, that restores the ritual cosmos to its former order, although the king cannot alter the future (cf. 2 Kgs 22.17).[71] As noted above, this ceremony represents the renewal or restatement of the ancient, existing covenant, and not Yahweh's restoration of Israel by a wholly new one. There is no need for a new divine promise. Yet, in itself, this seems part of the progression towards exile. By reaffirming the existing covenant, there is no sense of a fresh start. What is accomplished, therefore, is not so much the disregarding of previous sins as the acceptance that their commission has brought dire consequences upon the nation. The renewed covenant looks not only to the future, but also to the past, linking both in a single continuum. The nation may be judged, but there is not an outright rejection of Yahweh's people. The covenant renewal and following purge, rather than interrupt the slide into exile, are integral parts of this historical trajectory. They never deny its outcome, but still reassert the fundamental link between Yahweh and Israel. Set on the very eve of exile, Josiah's 'failed' purge bridges the gap between a historian's condemnation of his people and a visionary's hope of reconciliation, even if it is not a bridge that the book leads its readers across. The readers in the post-monarchic world are transported to a narrative realm in which they are in a spiritually liminal, and so potentially transformative state. Somewhere betwixt and between the two ideals of retribution and salvation, they might reaffirm the covenant yet again and so have communion with the ancient god of Israel. The closure that Long envisages, therefore, cannot be complete. There seems to me to be a deliberate paradox: a mythic restoration of order tinged with an awareness that Israel is caught in an irrevocable historical progression. The combination of myth and historical progression results not in a

71. Long, *2 Kings*, p. 270.

nihilism but in a sense that history does not utterly destroy, nor does it produce fresh starts. It does, however, radically transform. The story of Josiah's reign depicts the transformation of monarchist greater Israel into 'exilic' Israel; transfiguring the political sphere of action into the model for an 'exilic' piety.

The liminality is highlighted by Josiah's Passover, and the silence about the cult in the newly purged temple. After the purge, there is no more talk of the temple at all, except for the notices that the Babylonians plundered it (2 Kgs 24.13; 25.9, 13-17). While this destruction certainly has an important place in the progression of the book, in a sense what the Babylonians do to the temple is not of ultimate significance. The restatement of the covenant is, implicitly, an affirmation not only of the continued relationship between Yahweh and Israel, but also of its obligations, and hence, the consequences of disobedience. Even if the covenant is not specified in 2 Kings 22, Josiah's realization that his kingdom was in jeopardy seems to imply his recognition of the consequences of breaking it.[72] By participating in the restatement of the covenant, then, the people have already implicitly accepted the punishment due their disobedience. This includes the destruction of the temple (1 Kgs 9.8-9). And by celebrating Passover, they have taken the first steps on a new, spiritual journey through the wilderness. Passover has a peculiar mix of the joy of victory, or at least protection, an air of transition, and most certainly of journey.[73] In Exodus 12, the Passover is celebrated on the eve of the exodus, and its participants are protected from the fate befalling the Egyptian households. Instructions for the rite's continued celebration are also given in Deuteronomy 16 (among other places). This Passover commandment also recalls the Egyptian experience (vv. 1, 3, 6). The escape from Egypt was a victory, but set Israel on an arduous journey into the wilderness. In Joshua, the actual conquest (itself sometimes a ritual event, cf. Josh. 6) and distribution of the land are framed by rituals and convocations, which include a

72. Deut. 27–28 establishes the consequences for breaking the *torah* which are the primary contents of the covenant. It is possible that Josiah's story may be reflecting this passage or something similar. Note how the temple document is alternately the 'scroll of the *torah*' (2 Kgs 22.8, 11; 23.24) and the scroll of the 'covenant' (2 Kgs 23.3).

73. Allusions to the exodus in 2 Kgs 22–23, however, are muted. There is no direct mention of the event in these chapters. Recollection of Moses in 2 Kgs 22–23 is not directed on the exodus itself, but the law (cf. 2 Kgs 23.25).

covenant agreement.[74] Major facets of the opening frame, of course, are the elaborate rituals of the crossing of the Jordan, and the circumcision of the male Israelites (Josh. 3.1-5.11), all of which culminate in the Passover. With it, Joshua declares the end of the Egyptian disgrace. This Passover marks a transition not from wilderness security, but to holy war, with success not to be taken for granted (cf. Josh. 7). At the conquest of the land (however partial) Joshua twice convenes the people, makes a covenant, and describes the necessity, as well as impossibility, of obeying every aspect of Yahweh's laws given through Moses (Josh. 23.1-24.28; the teaching of Moses, 23.6; cf. 2 Kgs 22.2; 23.25; and the covenant, Josh. 24.25).[75] This framework embodies the realization of the promise that Israel should have a land, but includes in it the recognition that control of it is conditional upon obedience. On a much smaller scale, the same sort of frame occurs in 2 Kings 23. The story moves from one ritual, involving a covenant, to a 'conquest' of greater Israel, and then to a new ritual series, the Passover, hinting at the inevitability of the exile. For Josiah, the purge meant a journey across the length and breadth of the land, but his Passover implies yet another trek for its adherents; this time outside the land, but Josiah himself would never leave. This is an inversion of the fate of Moses, who never sets foot in the promised land, and it has echoes of Joshua's campaign, which was less than completely successful (e.g. Deut. 32.49-52; Josh. 15.63; 16.10; 17.12-13). But still, Passover has connotations of divine protection, not only in the tradition of security from the terrors inflicted on Egypt, but in the image of the supernatural being who appeared to Joshua (Exod. 12; Josh. 5.13-15). Is there divine protection for Judah as they encounter the darkest side of Yahweh and his foreign agents of political destruction, the Babylonians? Will Judah find the 'peace' in political death that was promised to Josiah?

74. Cf. Hobbs, *2 Kings*, p. 332. R.D. Nelson, 'Josiah in the Book of Joshua', *JBL* 100 (1981), pp. 531-40; Nelson, *Double Redaction*, pp. 125-26, argues that Joshua is modelled as a prototype of Josiah. For a recent discussion of how these verses relate to the other mention of Passover in the Former Prophets, Josh. 5.10-12, see Eynikel, *The Reform*, pp. 288-95. He emphasizes that the Kings' passage does not really refer back far enough to equate its model of the Josianic Passover with Joshua's, and sees each book as the result of different compositional processes.

75. In Josh. 24.25-26, the protagonist also establishes his own instructions for Israel to follow.

Chapter 9

EGYPT, EXODUS AND EXILE

1. *The Mysteries of Egypt*

Israel's 'sojourn' in Egypt and the exodus occupy a primary place in the Pentateuch, and so have made an indelible stamp on the self-perception of anyone who traces their ethnic or religious heritage to the biblical 'Israel'. For a number of scholars, the recollection of the saving act of Yahweh in the exodus against the cruel Egyptian taskmaster was an integral part of the very essence of ancient Israelite worship and self-identity.[1] Egypt was a place of refuge when times were hard (e.g. Abram, Gen. 12.10; Jacob, Gen. 42.1-2). It was there that the offspring of the patriarchs became a great people (Gen. 47.27; Deut. 26.5). The result of this prosperity is, of course, discrimination and the oppressions that led to the exodus, but in some places in the Hebrew Bible, a very positive view of Egypt is still espoused. The time the ancestors spent in Egypt is sometimes used to ground an injunction against ill-will towards foreigners in Israel (cf. Exod. 22.20; 23.9; Lev. 19.34; Deut. 10.19). Isaiah 19.24 goes so far as to bless not only Israel, but Egypt and Assyria. Often, Egypt is seen as the source of military might and a lucrative trading partner for the Israelite and Judaean kings; but such dealings usually meet with the scorn of the biblical writers. Isaiah 31.1 and Hos. 12.2 may be cited as examples. Of great import, however, is Deut. 17.16-17 which specifies that the well-behaved Israelite king (LXX ἄρχων) should not 'cause the people to return' to Egypt in

1. Influential in this regard are M. Noth, *A History of Pentateuchal Traditions* (trans. B.W. Anderson; SPRS, 5; Chico, CA: Scholars Press, 1981), pp. 47-51, reprinted from the 1972 edition (Englewood Cliffs, NJ: Prentice–Hall), original: *Überlieferungsgeschichte des Pentateuch* (Stuttgart: W. Kohlhammer, 1948), and G. von Rad, 'The Form Critical Problem of the Hexateuch', (trans. E.W. Trueman Dicken; Edinburgh: Oliver & Boyd, 1965), pp. 4-8; original: *Das formgeschichtliche Problem des Hexateuch* (Munich: Chr. Kaiser Verlag, 1938).

order to obtain horses. Likewise, such a king should not value wealth and must abstain from at least *excessive* polygamy. But these are the sort of things which mark Solomon's reign. Deuteronomy also predicts that Israel will be removed back to Egypt should they ignore Yahweh's instructions (Deut. 28.68), and that they will suffer the afflictions of Egypt (Deut. 28.27, 60). This chapter links the idea of returning to Egypt with that of an exile to other nations (cf. Deut. 28.25, 32, 33, 36, 41, 49, 64). The oppression of Egypt at the hands of Judah is foreseen in Isa. 19.16-22, but it goes on to add that a temple to Yahweh will be built in Egypt and that there the deity will hear the Egyptian cries for help.

As with the rest of the Hebrew Bible, Kings' depiction of Egypt is ambivalent. It is a refuge and a place of tyranny. It opposes some of Israel's enemies and at other times is worthless as an ally. Often, the enemy itself is Egypt. Those responsible for Kings also paid a lot of attention to Egypt, both in the utilization of the symbol of Israel's origins in the exodus and in narrative episodes in which Egypt or Egyptians appear. Some of the episodes involving Egypt in Kings parallel and contrast with the role given to Assyria and Babylon. Most interestingly, the emphasis on the exodus in Kings is matched with a number of 'returns' to Egypt; Solomon, Jeroboam, Hoshea, and ultimately, refugees after the assassination of the Babylonian governor. It is this sense of closure, with the book leading the reader to where its oft-mentioned myth of origins begins, which makes Egypt's presence so mysterious.

Egypt's complex portrayal in biblical literature has been attended to by scholars.[2] Rather than a theory of relatively uniform change in attitudes toward Egypt to explain this complexity (as de Boer briefly posits), however, I find an explanation for this situation in the positing of a pluralistic and potentially highly-dispersed cultural entity attempting to come to grips with itself.[3] I think it possible that Kings is an Egyptian product, or something produced with a concern for the

2. See, for instance, P.A.H. de Boer, 'Egypt in the Old Testament: Some Aspects of an Ambivalent Assessment', in P.A.H. de Boer, *Selected Studies in Old Testament Exegesis* (OTS, 27; Leiden: E.J. Brill 1991), pp. 152-67; cf. Friedman, 'Egypt'.

3. De Boer, 'Egypt', pp. 166-67, suggests that a positive appreciation was later replaced by negative views, and these came to dominate Jewish and Christian thinking.

Diaspora in Egypt. Even if Egypt was not a 'true' home for Israel, life there was in need of some form of legitimizing expression. The ambivalent conflation of the 'exilic' sense of displacement (perhaps reinforced through suffering discrimination) and optimism stemming from the belief in the divine sanction for the Judah-ist way of life may ultimately explain the complexity of much of the Hebrew Bible's texts pertaining to Egypt.

2. *The Exodus*

As noted in a variety of places in the preceding chapters, the exodus is mentioned in many important contexts in Kings, and is utilized to make a number of different points. The construction of the temple is dated from the exodus at 1 Kgs 6.1. 1 Kings 8.9 recalls the exodus in describing the contents of the ark of the covenant. Similar recollections appear in 1 Kgs 8.16 and 21. These bracket Solomon's blessing of the people (vv. 15-21) and highlight the uniqueness of the divine selection of David and Jerusalem. 1 Kings 9.9 is a part of the second vision of Solomon (1 Kgs. 9.3-9), and specifies that the chosen lineage and consecrated house will be rejected, should Israel forsake the god of the exodus. In these places, the exodus functions to establish the primacy of the *Torah*, the temple and davidic dynasty within Israel. A closer look at this motif, then, is in order.

The closing statement of Solomon's prayer (1 Kgs 8.51-53) features no less than two mentions of the exodus, but these emphasize the uniqueness of Israel in relation to other nations. Already in vv. 41-43 Solomon prays that Yahweh will hear the prayer of the faithful foreigner, so that the name of the deity might be known world-wide. But Israel remains distinct; they alone are called the 'people of Yahweh'. In vv. 51-53, however, the special status of Israel is emphasized in a dramatic fashion. In v. 51 Yahweh is asked to heed the pleas of Israel *because* they are his 'inheritance' נחלה. In v. 53, Yahweh's response is expected *because* he has set Israel apart as his נחלה. Both of these latter verses make reference to the exodus to drive their point home. The section, then, reinforces the division between religion and ethnicity. Others may worship Yahweh, but they are not the people or inheritance of Yahweh, because they have no connection with the exodus. This may be compared to 2 Kgs 17.36. This verse has as its setting a divine speech addressed to the descendants of Jacob (vv. 34-40). They are enjoined to worship only Yahweh, who brought them out of Egypt. This passage follows the narration of the syncretic religion of the Assyrian settlers occupying the territory of the former northern kingdom (vv. 24-34). In the greater unit, it is implied that 'Israel' is not equal to the sum of the faithful, or those claiming to be. Rather, 'Israel' is a group descended from the patriarch, and saved by Yahweh from Egypt. There is no explicit commandment that non-Israelites should worship Yahweh; rather, devotion is required of Israel because of the ancestral covenant and the exodus. Foreigners, whose syncretistic religion is at issue in the larger context, are, nonetheless, criticized not only for their improper worship, but are also further distanced from the 'sons of Jacob', because of their heritage, which does not include ancestral participation in the exodus.

In turning to 2 Kgs 21, one finds that vv. 10-16 build on the theme of disobedience and specify that removal from the land is unavoidable. In v. 15 it is claimed that Yahweh's people had been sinning since the exodus. The 'separation' mentioned at the end of Solomon's prayer is, therefore, totally inverted in this section; the people are to be delivered into their enemy's hands. These passages are linked by the use of the noun נחלה to refer to the people as the 'inheritance' of Yahweh.[4] The two such uses in Solomon's prayer and one in the condemnation of Manasseh are the only uses of the term with such a meaning in Kings.[5] Furthermore, 2 Kgs 21.15 is the final exodus reference in Kings, and is the only one to trace the origins of the sin which ultimately spelled the end of Judah. Compare this with the first mention of the exodus, at 1 Kgs 6.1. Here, the exodus is the event from which the start of the temple's construction is dated. If the exodus tradition is used to establish primary institutions within the greater concept of Israel and its history, and plays a part in articulating the unique status of Israel over foreigners, it also has a role in expressing the relationship between the people of Judah and the northern kingdom, as I have demonstrated in reference to the schism in Chapter 5, above. 2 Kings 21.10-16, as has

---

4. This expression has been studied by S.E. Loewenstamm, 'נחלת ה'', in S. Japhet (ed.), *Scripta Hierosolymitana: Publications of the Hebrew University, Jerusalem. XXXI. Studies in Bible 1986* (Jerusalem: Magnes Press, 1986), pp. 155-92.

5. But, see 1 Kgs 8.36, in which the land is the inheritance for the people; 1 Kgs 12.16, the Israelites have no inheritance in David; 1 Kgs 21.3-4, Naboth's inheritance from his father.

been discussed already, traces the sin of the remnant of Yahweh's people back to a time before the monarchy. The passage also explicitly links the fate of Judah with that of Israel. Other passages imply this as well. As I have noted earlier, v. 7 of 2 Kgs 17.7-12 underscores the fall of the north as part payment of the sins committed by the 'sons of Israel' throughout history. Both kingdoms, of course, are named in v. 13. The exodus (v. 7, and conquest, vv. 8, 11) reinforces a central idea expressed in the passage, that the offence was by an 'Israel' greater than either kingdom. In 1 Kgs 12.28 Jeroboam claims that his golden calves represent the deities of the exodus. This passage is the only exodus reference in Kings used in discussing the division of the kingdom. What is presented here, however, is a radically different impression of the god of the exodus, an impression that seriously compromised Israel's relationship with Yahweh during the exodus itself (Exod. 32; Deut. 9.16-21), and it is important to note that it is made by one of the most vilified characters in the book.

In Kings, the historical experience of the exodus is a major determinative factor, not only for claims to the name Israel and certain geographical areas, but also to a unique relationship with the divine.[6] Differentiation is, of course, a major strategy in social identity. That the exodus is used in these contexts is significant as its recollection may have expressed a hope for a separation of the 'sons of Israel' from foreigners. If separation is advocated, however, does this recollection of the exodus serve as a model for post-monarchic behaviour, recommending physical relocation from Egypt or other lands to Judah? Or does it promote an isolationist lifestyle within foreign nations, or in the lands of Judah and Israel overrun by foreign powers? The dating of the sin of Israel to the exodus in 1 Kgs 21.15 suggests that, whereas the exodus is seen as the mythic origin of Israel, a new exodus will not merely re-create Israel as a pure nation; rather, the problem of apostasy is carried with them out of foreign captivity. As Graham Harvey points out, there is little sense in the Hebrew Bible of the name Israel being restricted to a pure people, even if the ideals of purity are incumbent

6. The memory of the patriarchs are used in this regard as well. This is plain in 2 Kgs 17.34-35 regarding Jacob, although the next verse also refers to the exodus. The patriarchs are referred to in 2 Kgs 13.23, where the salvation of the northern kingdom is predicated on the covenant with the ancestors. This verse maintains the membership of the north in greater Israel, the whole of the community of Yahweh's people.

upon all Israel. 1 Kings 6.1 and 1 Kings 8, with their accent on the temple, associate the exodus with a hope of reconciliation between a fallen people and their deity. One may be inclined to think that the biblical exodus as a historical tradition is but a temporal and geographical projection of the writers' hopes for a spiritual journey. As such, it embraces not only religious values, and recognizes the problems of human will, but includes the religious grounding for social and ethnic identity. That one exodus failed does not mean the ideal is rendered void. Indeed, the memory of failure, in terms of the political realization of the ideals, may be an incentive for greater efforts on a personal, or social level.

3. *Egypt and Israel's Kings*

When one turns to the narratives in which Egypt or Egyptians are involved, another series of provocative questions are raised. Solomon's relations with Egypt are mentioned in a number of places from 1 Kings 3–11. The MT and the Septuagint display different sequences of events. 1 Kgs 3.1, in the Hebrew, describes the alliance between Solomon and Pharaoh and his marriage to an Egyptian princess. This location places the marriage notice just prior to the description of the people's worship at the 'high-places', במות. In the Greek, the marriage report is distanced from the reference to the high places, being found at 3 Kgdms 5.14a, with some content also found at 3 Kgdms 2.35c. The Hebrew version of 1 Kgs 11.1 refers to the Egyptian woman again in the context of criticizing Solomon for forbidden marriages with foreign women. The Greek omits reference to the Egyptian woman at this place.[7] Another part of the Hebrew's harsher portrayal of Solomon is the different sequence in reporting the construction of the palace and other buildings. The MT interrupts the description of the temple's construction by that of the palace (1 Kgs 7.1-8).[8] The final phase of this secular building program is the construction of a house for Pharaoh's daughter. The different sequences may reflect different levels of concern that Solomon had broken the injunctions of Deut. 17.16-17. The reports of Solomon's military trading with Egypt (1 Kgs 10.28-29) also reflect

---

7. The LXX is also more strident in asserting that Solomon eventually moved his wife out of the city of David (cf. 3 Kgdms 9.9, but see 3 Kgdms 2.35c, f; 1 Kgs 3.1, 7.8).

8. Auld, *Privilege*, pp. 24-34, considers the MT order secondary.

Solomon's infractions in this regard. The marriage and weapons-dealing attest to a trust in Egypt that is surprising. This is reinforced by the report that Gezer was gifted to Solomon's bride as a dowry from her father (1 Kgs 9.16; 3 Kgdms 5.14b). As I pointed out in Chapter 5, it seems as though Israel is transformed into a kind of Egypt.[9] On the other hand, two of Solomon's enemies find sanctuary from Solomon in Egypt (1 Kgs 11.17-22; 40). After the division of the United Monarchy, during the apostate reign of Rehoboam, Pharaoh Shishak invades Judah and confiscates the golden shields made by Solomon (1 Kgs 14.22-28). These shields may be taken to represent the imperial power wielded in Jerusalem. Depending on which text is read, Rehoboam or Judah itself is named as the sinful party; but neither the Septuagint or MT openly justify the invasion by reference to the misdeeds.[10] A similar situation is repeated towards the end of the book, and it is to the fall of Israel and Judah that I now turn. Egypt's presence in the intervening text is minor. In 2 Kgs 7.6, Samaria was saved from an Aramean siege by Yahweh, who made the attackers hear sounds which were mistaken for the noise of advancing Egyptian and Hittite forces. In 2 Kgs 19.8-9 rumours about the Cushite king interrupt Assyria's menacing of Jerusalem, although there is no mention that Hezekiah had hired them.[11]

The story of the fall of Israel in 2 Kgs 17.3-6 reports that, after becoming a vassal to the Assyrian king Shalmaneser, Hoshea is caught withholding tribute and sending envoys to Egypt. Hoshea is then imprisoned. The Assyrian subsequently attacks and besieges Samaria for three years. The eventual fall of the city is dated to the ninth year of Hoshea. As observed in Chapter 7, interpreters have proposed different sources for vv. 3-4 and 5-6, and have wrestled with difficult historical problems. Moreover, the dating formula that dates the fall to the ninth year of a king deposed three years earlier is held to be suspicious. In my view, the text of 2 Kgs 17.1-6 (whatever its composite origins) may have been the result of literary goals concerned with thematic development throughout the book.

9. On the other hand, there is no mention in Kings of the illicit worship of Egyptian gods.

10. MT at v. 22 reads 'Judah' and the LXX 'Rehoboam'.

11. On the Cushite rule of Egypt at the time of the historical Hezekiah, see the reconstruction and bibliography in G.W. Ahlström, *The History of Ancient Palestine from the Palaeolithic Period to Alexander's Conquest* (JSOTSup, 146; Sheffield: JSOT Press, 1993), pp. 708-13.

2 Kings 17.4, which tells of Hoshea's envoys to Egypt, is noteworthy as it is the first mention of voluntary dealings between a reigning monarch of Israel or Judah and Egypt since the time of Solomon. Solomon's relations were suspicious and, ironically, turning to Egypt is the ostensible reason for Hoshea's downfall. Moreover, Jeroboam had come out of sanctuary in Egypt to become the first king of a newly independent Israel (1 Kgs 12). The final king of Israel relies on Egypt to free himself from Assyria. But he only precedes his people into captivity. The failure of Hoshea contrasts with the later success of Hezekiah against the same Assyrian enemy. Hezekiah is accused of reliance on Egyptian power by Assyria in 2 Kgs 18.21, 24, but chs. 18–20 do not offer any narrative to suggest that these accusations are well-founded. 2 Kings 19.6-9 reports how the Assyrian king put a brave face on the distraction caused by news of activities of the Cushite king. The lack of clear association between Cush and Egypt in our text, however, is telling. More important is that Hezekiah is not said to ask the Cushites for help. There is, therefore, no support for the Assyrian's mocking of Hezekiah for his trust in Egypt. Indeed, in Isaiah's oracle denouncing the hubris of the Assyrian, Egypt is one of the victims of Yahweh's demonstration of power (2 Kgs 19.24). Hoshea, in his attempt to bolster his military potential by going to Egypt, has recalled Solomon. Hezekiah, on the other hand, is explicitly compared to David (2 Kgs 18.3).

There are also parallels between Israel's fate and Judah's. Already, just after the schism, Egypt plunders Jerusalem (1 Kgs 14.25-28), and 2 Kgs 17.7-18 discusses the sins of both Israel and Judah. This is a clue that, perhaps, the story of Samaria's fall told in 2 Kgs 17.1-6 parallels that of Judah's collapse in chs. 24–25. The difficult sequence of events in 2 Kgs 17.3-6 is, in fact, understandable in view of the final stages of the Judaean monarchy. Certainly, there is no attempt to produce a direct parallel of the fates of the three final Judaean kings by the reign of a single Israelite monarch, but there are some interesting correspondences. 2 Kings 17.3 tells how Hoshea became a vassal when Shalmaneser 'came up' against him, עליו עלה. In 2 Kgs 24.1, Nebuchadnezzar makes Jehoiakim a vassal. In both instances, the vassals soon rebel (2 Kgs 17.4; 24.1). In Hoshea's case, this is with the aid of Egypt, while 2 Kgs 24.7 reports that Pharaoh did not dare make an appearance outside his own country, as Babylon had taken their whole empire. In this respect, then, the stories of Israel and Judah differ. Furthermore,

Hoshea is imprisoned for his intrigue, while Jehoiakim seems to die naturally, although Judah is punished by raiding bands (2 Kgs 17.4; 24.2-6). With Hoshea deposed, Assyria attacks Israel again, for reasons which are unstated, but it takes three years for Samaria to fall (2 Kgs 17.5-6). Similarly, the fall of Judah is a protracted affair, and this begins with an apparently unprovoked attack by Nebuchadnezzar, which sees King Jehoiachin give himself and his family up. He is the Babylonians' counterpart to Assyria's imprisoned Hoshea. The Babylonians plunder the city and exile its inhabitants (2 Kgs 24.10-16), but this is not the end of Judah. Zedekiah is installed as king (v. 17). He proves unfaithful to his masters, and his unsuccessful rebellion finally fails under the weight of siege (2 Kgs 25.1-4). The destruction of the kingdom is completed: Zedekiah is bound and carried into captivity (vv. 5-7). The final episode of Kings, however (2 Kgs 25.27-30), does tell of the release of Jehoiachin, but, as with Hoshea, no word on the ultimate fate of the final Judaean king is given.[12] The events described in Hoshea's reign, that some find illogical as a simple sequence, appear to me as an anticipation of the series of attacks that spelt the doom of Judah. The anticipation suggests that Egypt will be involved in Judah's

---

12. There are a variety of traditions recorded in the Hebrew Bible about the fates or destinies of the final kings. Jehoahaz is said to have died in Egypt (2 Kgs 23.34). This is in general agreement with the prediction in Jer. 22.11-12. 2 Chron. 36.4 includes his removal to Egypt, but not his death. The MT of 2 Kgs 24.6 tells us that Jehoiakim 'slept with his fathers', but the expected burial notice is not given. The LXX[A] adds that he was buried with his fathers in the Garden of Uza. On the other hand, Jer. 22.19 says that this king will be given the burial of an ass, dragged out and left lying outside of Jerusalem. 2 Chron. 36.6 says that Jehoiakim was taken to Babylon, but no death notice is given. 2 Chron. 36.10 agrees with 2 Kgs 24.12 that Jehoiachin was taken to Babylon, but unlike the last verses of Kings and Jer. 52, there is no notice that he was ever released. On the other hand Jer. 22.24-30 predicts that Jehoiachin would die in Babylon. No mention is made of his release, but he is to be without succession; none of his children will be acceptable for the davidic throne. Neither Chronicles or Kings tell of what happened to Zedekiah after he was taken captive by the Babylonians. 2 Kgs 25.7 finds its echo in Jer. 39.7, which reads as does Kings, but Jer. 52.11 adds a note that Zedekiah died in Babylon. Jer. 21.7 says that Zedekiah is doomed to die by the sword, although in Jer. 34.4-5 Jeremiah is to tell the king that he will not die by the sword but will die in peace. Jer. 32.5 says that the king will remain in Babylon until God takes note of him.

final hour. These expectations are not misplaced, even if their discarded mantle is eventually picked up by Babylon.[13]

4. *Egypt, Babylon and Judah's Curtain Call*

Egypt explodes onto the Judaean political scene in 2 Kgs 23.29-30, when it is reported that Pharaoh Necho went up to the Euphrates, apparently to confront the Assyrians. He meets Josiah at Megiddo and kills the Judaean reformer. The meeting of Josiah and Necho may be read against the earlier stories of the intrigue of Hoshea and Egypt, or even the Egyptian dealings of Solomon. Josiah is not immediately faced with domination by Assyria, although the fact that Necho feels compelled to march to the Euphrates to meet the Assyrian king suggests that the contrast can be drawn. Josiah turns to meet Necho, but, as the Assyrian officer once warned Hezekiah (2 Kgs 18.21), Egypt has proven dangerous. Necho does not immediately install a successor to Josiah. The people of the land place Jehoahaz on the vacant throne, but he lasts only three months. When Necho finally acts, Jehoahaz is transported to Riblah, and then on to Egypt (2 Kgs 23.30-33). Necho sets up Eliakim as king, affirming his dominion over the Judaean by changing his name to Jehoiakim, and imposing a tax on the people (2 Kgs 23.33-35). Necho's control over Judah may be seen as a part of the divine punishment against Judah pronounced in 2 Kgs 23.26-27, but the announcement of punishment says nothing explicit about the Egyptian actions. Rather, the exile of Judah under Babylon is anticipated. This situation recalls the placing of the report of Rehoboam's or Judah's sins right before the episode of the invasion of Shishak in 1 Kings 14. There is no mention of a future destruction of Judah in this place. On the other hand, neither is there an explanation that the Egyptian campaign was a punishment, although the implication is too strong to be ignored. Such implications are also present for Egypt's actions at the end of Kings, but nothing is made explicit, and these suggestions are qualified a great deal by the emphasis on Babylon.

For its part, Babylon appears in 2 Kgs 24.1, where it is reported that Jehoiakim became Nebuchadnezzar's vassal, although he proved rebellious. Judaean intrigue with Egypt, however, is not reported. After reporting that Judah was severely punished for their rebellion (2 Kgs

13. Long, *2 Kings*, pp. 286-87.

24.2-4), 2 Kgs 24.7 claims that Nebuchadnezzar had taken all that belonged to Pharaoh, and that the Egyptian king did not venture out of his land.[14] With this, Kings marks the end of Egypt's rule over Judah, and the end of her potential influence as an ally. Zedekiah rebels in 2 Kgs 25.1, but there is no mention of Egypt.[15] The notice that Babylon had taken Egypt's possessions is also interesting because of the wording employed. These territories are said to extend from the Wadi of Egypt to the river Euphrates. Such terms are similar, although not identical, to those used to describe the realm of Solomon in 1 Kgs 5.1 and 8.65. While the allusion back to Solomon may be understandable, as a similar geographical area is intended, the irony is worth noting, especially since this notice also recalls the description of the land promised to Abraham in Gen. 15.18. What had become Nebuchadnezzar's was taken from Pharaoh, not one of Solomon's descendants.[16]

With Judah in Babylonian hands, the history of the kingdom is in its final stages. The time of Babylonian hegemony, however, has numerous parallels with the previous period of Egyptian domination. Little is reported of Jehoiakim, other than his death and that his son, Jehoiachin, succeeds him (2 Kgs 24.6). As in the case of Jehoahaz, however, there is no imperial role reported in the succession. Jehoahaz is made king by the choice of the people of the land, while Jehoiachin is merely said to have reigned in the place of his father (2 Kgs 23.30; 24.6). Both these kings reign but three months (2 Kgs 23.31; 24.8). Both of these monarchs, however, are deposed. Necho eventually removes Jehoahaz to Egypt, where he dies (2 Kgs 23.33-34), while Jehoiachin surrenders to Nebuchadnezzar and is taken to Babylon (2 Kgs 24.12, 15). The parallels between the time of Egyptian and Babylonian dominance continue. Jehoiakim, who succeeded Jehoahaz, and Zedekiah, who followed Jehoiachin, each reign for eleven years, and their successions are each deliberate exercises of imperial fiat.[17] This includes new names for the

---

14. There is an interesting variant at 2 Kgs 24.2. The Hebrew makes Yahweh the one who sent the raiding parties, while the LXX implies that Nebuchadnezzar did. Both, however, later explain these events as reflecting the punishment of Yahweh (vv. 3-4).

15. But cf. Jer. 37.5-7, 11, and Ezek. 17.11-18.

16. See the earlier discussions on Solomon's Israel as a kind of Egypt.

17. The repetition of reign lengths and other formulaic descriptions of the reigns of these final kings are sometimes taken as evidence of the poor attempts at updating a book originally ending somewhere in 2 Kgs 23. There is no point

puppet kings (Eliakim becomes Jehoiakim, 2 Kgs 23.34; while Matta-niah becomes Zedekiah, 24.17). The repetition of the act of renaming symbolizes not only power over Judah, but, in the Babylonian case, the transfer of power from Egypt. Another parallel can be highlighted. In 2 Kgs 23.33-34 it is reported that Jehoahaz is taken to 'Riblah in the land of Hamath' by the Egyptians, before being transferred to Egypt. Similarly, Riblah is where Zedekiah is taken to be punished before being sent on to Babylon (2 Kgs 25.6-7).[18] That it was important to note that both Egypt and Babylon sent a Judaean king there suggests that the two imperial powers are being contrasted and compared. I sus-pect that Riblah, whatever historical events unfolded there at Judah's fall, offered the writers of Kings a common setting for the Judaean kings to meet their respective overlords and, therefore, to suggest a comparison between these overlords in a history that repeats itself. The absence of a theological justification for the actions of Pharaoh, and the presence of such for those of Babylon, makes the comparison all the more poignant. Egypt is a 'false' Babylon. They inflict suffering, but not Yahweh's chastisement. Another pattern can be illuminated in this regard. Both Jehoahaz and Jehoiakim, the two Egyptian vassals, are said to have done the sort of evil their fathers had done (2 Kgs 23.32, 37). The use of the plural 'fathers', in each case, seems to enrol Josiah along with the evil-doers, but this conclusion may be avoided by understanding the plural as making a general statement about the mon-archic period. Yet, while the judgments on these kings look back over the course of Judaean history, the judgments on the following two kings are differently formulated. Jehoiachin is compared only with his father and, therefore, Jehoiakim is identified again. The evil of Zede-kiah is also likened to that of Jehoiakim. No mention of Manasseh is made after the reign of Jehoiakim is reported (cf. 2 Kgs 24.3-4).

discussing this in detail here. There are so many parallels between the Egyptian and Babylonian phases that the patterning is best seen as a deliberate literary device, although certainly this may have developed through expansions on earlier, less rep-etitious versions.

18. Other notables of Judah are later killed by the Babylonians at Riblah (2 Kgs 25.20-21). There are textual difficulties at 2 Kgs 24.6 which affect the exact nuances of the verse, but these need not detain the present study. Cf. the *Ketib* במלך בירושלם v. *Qere*, ... ממלך. See Cogan and Tadmor, *II Kings*, pp. 303-304. Burney, *Notes*, p. 364, finds the reference to Riblah in the LXX could hardly be original, given the verb employed, advising a comparison with 2 Chron. 36.3.

2 Kings 24.20 merely mentions the anger of Yahweh at the actions of Jerusalem and Judah. Jehoiakim's reign, of course, marks the transition from Egyptian power to Babylonian. By associating the sins of Jehoiachin and Zedekiah with those of Jehoiakim, the model for 'Babylonian era' transgressions is found in the last king who served Egypt.

The narratives describing the looting of the treasuries and the payment of tribute or bribes from these resources also illustrate how Babylon has taken over from Egypt on a theological as well as a political level. Of the three times in which the temple and palace treasuries are plundered, some special features are to be noted. 1 Kings 14.21-28 describes the first plundering of the treasuries by Shishak. The next time sees the Israelite king, Jehoash, capture Jerusalem in the time of Amaziah, as described in 2 Kgs 14.11-14. This is the only time in which a Judaean king, who receives a qualified good judgment from the author, suffers such an embarrassment. The final pillaging of the treasuries occurs in 2 Kgs 24.10-13, when the Babylonians help themselves. The other mentions of the treasuries do not entail their violent plundering; rather the money is surrendered by the Judaean king.[19] The taking of the treasuries by Babylon represents the completion of a cycle. No references to the despoliation of the treasuries specify that gold items manufactured by Solomon were taken or handed over, except the first time by Shishak, and the final time by Nebuchadnezzar. If, in the minds of the writers of the text, it was evidence of divine punishment to lose the riches from the storehouses, and in particular to lose Solomon's gold, then by the end of the monarchic period, Egypt is no longer entitled to deliver the sentence. When Necho imposes a fine on Judah at the deposition of Jehoahaz, the fee is lodged against the people as a whole. Jehoiakim does not pay out from the royal or temple funds, but from the proceeds of a special tax (2 Kgs 23.33-35). Egypt, through their vassal, again burdens the people as a whole, as they did in Moses' day. At the close of the monarchic period, however, the legitimate recipient of Judah's state wealth is Babylon, and this seems a fitting fulfilment of Isaiah's prophecy to Hezekiah in 2 Kgs 20.16-18 even if

---

19. 1 Kgs 15.16-19, Asa; 2 Kgs 12.18-19, Joash; 2 Kgs 16.7-9, Ahaz; 2 Kgs 18.13-16, Hezekiah. See the discussion in E.T. Mullen, Jr, 'Crime and Punishment; The Sins of the King and the Despoliation of the Treasuries', *CBQ* 54 (1992), pp. 231-48.

the connections are not specifically spelt out (cf. 2 Kgs 24.13).[20] The final sacking of the temple (2 Kgs 25.13-17) does not mention the storehouses, but it does specify Solomon as the builder of the many items destroyed or confiscated in the attack. The references and allusions back to Solomon raise, again, the question of the extravagance of his temple and lifestyle, particularly in view of Deut. 17.16-17. This text, likewise, forbids a king to bolster his military power by causing people to return to Egypt. This certainly does not cast Solomon in a complimentary light, and Hoshea seems to have fallen foul of the injunction as well. When all of this is viewed alongside the display of imperial power by Egypt in the closing chapters of Kings, a display which killed and deposed kings, and taxed the people, a great irony is found. It is only when the Israelites (as represented by Judah) have been given into the hand of the king of Babylon that they have finally been brought out from under the hand of Pharaoh.

Whatever else the final few kings of Judah were supposed to have done to earn their poor reputations with the writers of Kings, it seems not to have been the contravention of the injunction of returning to Egypt. But these writers do tell of some people who did go back.

20. C.T. Begg, 'The Reading at 2 Kings XX 13', *VT* 36 (1986), pp. 339-40, argues that the wording of 2 Kgs 20.13 indicates that Hezekiah had 'hearkened', שׁמע, to the diplomatic overtures of Babylon, (cf. 1 Kgs 15.16-20, Aram accepting Asa's bribe for support; 2 Kgs 16.5-9, Ahaz gaining the support of Assyria). At issue in Begg's paper is the discrepancy between the majority of Hebrew manuscripts at 2 Kgs 20.13 and the Targum of Jonathan on the one hand, and a minority of Hebrew manuscripts along with the LXX, Syriac, and Vugate texts which, like the parallel in MT's Isa. 39.2, read, or presuppose, 'rejoice' (שׂמח). Begg draws few conclusions beyond maintaining MT's originality here, but the repeated use of the 'hearkening' formulae may then be seen to link Hezekiah's display of his wealth to the payment of foreign powers expressed elsewhere in the book. Some scholars would excise the apparent notice of the fulfilment of Isaiah's prediction about Hezekiah's foolish actions, 2 Kgs 24.13, as a later addition (e.g. Nelson, *Double Redaction*, p. 88). The fulfilment notice makes clear that the temple itself is plundered, while 2 Kgs 20.13, 17 make no mention of the temple treasures at all. This indicates to some that the two verses have little to do with each other, and that 2 Kgs 20.17 is not necessarily a prediction '*vaticinium ex eventu*', cf. Nelson, *Double Redaction*, pp. 129-32, followed by C.T. Begg, '2 Kings 20.12-19 as an Element of the Deuteronomistic History', *CBQ* 48 (1986), pp. 27-38 (29). Even so, Begg (pp. 31-34) associates the 2 Kgs 20 episode with the writers' condemnation of monarchs for relying on their money, instead of their god.

5. *The Exodus to Egypt*

The story of this return is told in 2 Kgs 25.22-26. It is set in Mizpah, where those Judaeans who were not deported, including some military forces, gather before the new governor, Gedaliah. He promises that if they serve the Babylonians, it will go well with them. But Ishmael, one of the army commanders, who is also of the royal house, assassinates the governor. Out of fear of reprisals, all the people, including the commanders, flee to Egypt. A number of scholars have interpreted this story in tandem with the following episode, which tells of the release of Jehoiachin (2 Kgs 25.27-30). They argue that the murder of Gedaliah illustrates that there is no hope for the future, except in the exile, the savagery of which has passed with the mercy shown to Jehoiachin, who, even after 37 years of captivity, is called the 'King of Judah' (2 Kgs 25.27, 30). Christopher Begg argues that vv. 22-30 are a 'Babylonian apologetic', and that the Gedaliah story sums up numerous themes in both the DtrH and the Tetrateuch. Gedaliah's short speech uses expressions like 'do not fear', 'dwell in the land', 'serve' and 'it will be well with you', which are common in deuteronomistic literature, although sometimes with different formulations. If great things are expected at the outset of the story, these expectations are dashed with the murder. Begg suggests that the role of Ishmael in Kings is a 'negative recapitulation' of the rejection of Abraham's similarly named first-born in Genesis. Both the mother and wife of the first Ishmael were Egyptian (Gen. 16.3-4; 21.9, 21). At the end of Kings, 'Ishmael' finally returns from exile to wreak vengeance on the usurper of his prerogatives.[21] Because of the negative treatment of Egypt in the DtrH, and because Egypt is portrayed as deceitful in the Joseph story, Begg claims that the return to Egypt is an act of 'unfathomly perverse' disrespect for the lessons of history.[22]

While a negative view of the assassination and escape makes a great deal of sense, some questions can still be raised. Why is 'deuteronomistic' language used to gain willing obedience to Babylon, if there is no mention of Yahweh? If the monarchy fell because the people would not 'serve' the deity, why should Babylon usurp Yahweh's

21. C.T. Begg, 'The Interpretation of the Gedaliah Episode (2 Kgs 25,22-26) in Context', *Ant* 62 (1987), pp. 3-11. Note that in Gen. 37.25-27; 39.1, Ishmaelites take Joseph to Egypt.

22. Begg, 'The Interpretation', p. 8.

rights? It is an important point that the story of Gedaliah and Ishmael follows closely on the narration of the bloody deaths of the priests, officials, and 60 others at Riblah, at the hands of a Babylonian officer. Does this story, told with no explicit editorial, imply that Babylon was too harsh, and therefore, the events at Mizpah were at least understandable, if not completely commendable? No editorial is attached to the Mizpah episode either. While not specifying it, Kings suggests that Ishmael, who is not the perfect figure of the outcast son of Abraham since he is still a member of the Judaean royal family, went to Egypt with the other escapees. Thus, the land is emptied, but in the two lands to which the 'children of Israel' traced their ancestry, Mesopotamia and Egypt, surviving populations live with members of the dynasty.

The confrontation between Gedaliah and Ishmael is not the only episode which biblical literature has set in Mizpah. Of the few different places with this name mentioned in the Hebrew Bible, this site in Benjamin may be considered a symbolic place, as much as has been suggested above for Shechem. Often, it is associated with references to questions of power, recollections of the exodus and relations with Ammon. If the Benjaminite Mizpah is in view in Judges 11, Jephthah's bargain over the leadership of Gilead seems to be ratified there, although perhaps this is not the same Mizpah to where he returns from the battle against Ammon (vv. 11, 34).[23] In the negotiations before the battle, however, reference is made to Israel's flight from Egypt (Judg. 11.13-16). In Judges 19–21, Mizpah figures in the dispute of the tribes with the Benjaminites (cf. Judg. 20.1-8; 21.1). They seek to avenge a rape and murder so shocking, the like of which, they exclaim, had not been heard of since the exodus (Judg. 19.30). Mizpah is also the scene of an assembly before Samuel, and one of that prophet's seats of office as judge of Israel (1 Sam. 7.5-7, 16). In 1 Sam. 10.17, however, Mizpah is the place where Samuel tells the Israelites of their rejection of Yahweh in demanding a king: yet their demands are heeded, and Saul becomes king. The next chapter tells of Saul's campaign against Ammon.

---

23. P. Arnold, 'Mizpah', *ABD* IV (6 vols.; New York: Doubleday, 1992), pp. 879-81, thinks that perhaps two places called Mizpah are mentioned in the Judges story, cf. Judg. 10.17 with those references mentioned already. Begg, 'The Interpretation', p. 6, has no problem linking the Jephthah story to the Benjaminite Mizpah, and that the associations of the place raise expectations of something important about to transpire in 2 Kgs 25.22-26.

Mizpah's image as a place associated with problems of leadership is also reinforced in Gedaliah's story. Kings does not specify whether Gedaliah or Ishmael was in the wrong. But, if it is disturbingly silent about the moral implications of the incident, the disgruntled reader could find some consolation in the much longer version of the story in Jeremiah, which runs from 40.7 to the end of ch. 44. Here the flight to Egypt is described as contrary to Yahweh's wishes, and Jeremiah criticizes the Judaean-Egyptian communities. The Kings' version, spanning only five verses, is sometimes seen as an abridgment of the Jeremiah story.[24] This is hardly the place to examine the Jeremiah story in detail. A comparison does, however, reveal a few interesting points about Kings. In Jeremiah, the episode does not follow the detailing of the bloody deeds at Riblah, but follows the report that Jeremiah was permitted to remain with Gedaliah, rather than go into exile (Jer. 40.1-6). The presence of the prophet Jeremiah, therefore, legitimizes the Mizpah community. The assassination plot is also more complex, with the Ammonites implicated by those who warn Gedaliah. Ishmael actually attempts to take the Judaeans to Ammon before he is frightened off by Johanan and flees to Ammon (Jer. 40.13-41.15). The Judaeans then choose to go to Egypt, despite Jeremiah's threats that this course of action will invoke the wrath of god. Yahweh, he says, promises prosperity if they stay in Judah (Jer. 41.16-43.7). After Jeremiah ends up in Egypt with the Judaeans, he soundly denounces them, and predicts their near-complete annihilation, and the defeat of Egypt at the hands of Babylon (Jer. 43.7-44.29).

Unlike Kings, the Jeremiah story vilifies Ishmael, and makes a hero of Johanan. The hero, however, proves false, he is instrumental in the rejection of Yahweh's word and he leads the people to Egypt. In Jeremiah, then, the Egyptian community is left in the command of Johanan and other leaders, who are clearly in disobedience to Yahweh. The community has no connection with the royal house, as Ishmael has fled. In Kings, no prophet remains with Gedaliah at Mizpah to legitimize his governorship, nor harass the refugees in Egypt with denouncements and predictions of doom. What the enigmatic episode in Kings accomplishes is the placement of a Judaean community, along

24. E.g. Jones, *Kings* II, p. 646; Begg, 'The Interpretation', pp. 4-5, notes the consensus, but suggests that the Kings passage may be the source behind Jeremiah; cf. the similar comment by R.P. Carroll, *Jeremiah: A Commentary* (London: SCM Press, 1986), p. 708.

with a member of the royal house, Ishmael, in Egypt, with no indication that their presence there is undesirable. But, even if we see Ishmael as making a regrettable choice, his decision leads to a situation similar to that in Genesis 42–50, where the family of Jacob establishes itself in Egypt. In view of the most likely pluralistic and dispersed cultural setting of Kings' origins, the ambivalence regarding Egypt may be understood as an admission that the Egyptian Judah-ist community belonged to greater Israel. On the other hand, the accent on the exodus would suggest that Egypt still retained the symbolism associated with slavery, even though the Babylonians seem hardly less severe. This might be taken as an indication that the Babylonians' successors, the Persians, had some level of support from the writers, but since the text does not say anything at all about the Persians directly, such an evaluation is conjectural.

Chapter 10

THE ETERNAL TEMPLE

1. *Sacred in the 'Right' and the 'Wrong' Way*

The notion of the emptied land, with which Kings ends, expresses not only a geographical displacement from a 'homeland' for those living outside of the lands of Judah and Israel, but a certain level of estrangement from Yahweh for the readership as a whole. Geography and demography, therefore, become spiritualized at the end of Kings, as much as Deuteronomy's setting in the plains of Moab does. The temporal and spatial aspects of Deuteronomy have led J.G. Millar and J.G. McConville to write of the wilderness journeys of Israel as a metaphor for spiritual development. Millar writes:

> Yesterday, Today and Tomorrow, wherever the nation finds itself—in the land or outside it—a simple decision faces Israel: to live for Yahweh or not—to move further into the land with Yahweh, or to go back to Egypt. There can be no standing still.[1]

The spritualization of displacement, however, only calls attention to the lost land, its central locales and sacred centres, especially Jerusalem and its temple. As cited above, A.D. Smith comments how a 'land of dreams' is more significant than the possession of actual terrain.[2] This is so, even if that land's holy places are defiled or otherwise 'out of bounds' for their former purposes. Indeed, Kings seems to deny sanction to the re-established cult in Jerusalem or anywhere else.[3] This ban

---

1. J.G. Millar, 'Living at the Place of Decision: Time and Place in the Framework of Deuteronomy', in J.G. Millar and J.G. McConville, *Time and Place in Deuteronomy* (JSOTSup, 179; Sheffield: Sheffield Academic Press, 1994), pp. 15-88 (88).

2. Smith, *Ethnic Origins*, p. 28.

3. E. Ben Zvi, 'The Account of the Reign of Manasseh in II Reg 21, 1-18 and the Redactional History of the Book of Kings', *ZAW* 103 (1991), pp. 355-74

is certainly explicable in terms of a belief in the temple site being *profaned* by the actions of the conquering armies as Yahweh's punitive measures against Israel. Yet the actual desecration of the temple is not a primary theme in the descriptions of how the Babylonians plundered it (2 Kgs 24.13-14; 25.13-17). The purification of the temple under Josiah, in fact, preserves for the temple some level of its sacrality, even if it is doomed to destruction. In view of this, I suspect that the force behind the ban on a return to a sacrificial cult was that the temple's 'ruins' (or at least 'illegitimate' restored structure) evoked for the writers feelings of estrangement and punishment alongside a sense of awe at Yahweh's continuing relationship with Israel (accepting that such feelings may have had some basis in the ulterior motives of political posturing).[4] These evocations come, not from an impression of the site's desecration, but from exiled Israel's unsuitability. Because the site of revelation has become a symbol of judgment, it remains sacred, or, if you will, its positive sacrality has been inverted, it is now 'sacred in the wrong way'. For this phrase, I am indebted to Jonathan Z. Smith, who, admittedly, uses it in a somewhat different sense, to describe the way chaos is never equivalent to the profane, citing as an example the biblical traditions of the wilderness:[5]

(367-68), observes that the ban on sacrificial cults outside the temple is underscored by Manasseh's reversal of Hezekiah's actions against the high places. This is the only case in the book of the resumption of such a cult once it had been abolished, and Manasseh commits the mortal sin. The result is a blunt message to the post-monarchic community. One could add that 1 Kgs 9.1-9, Yahweh's response to Solomon's temple dedication, already anticipates this conclusion.

4. D.L. Petersen, 'The Temple in Persian Period Prophetic Texts', in Davies (ed.), *Second Temple Studies*, I, pp. 125-44 (130), calls attention to the fact that the temple had a religio-social function which expressed structures of power and status, and was not simply 'sacred space'. On the matter of the 'ruined' temple, Jer. 41.5 tells of mourning pilgrims coming to the 'House of Yahweh' to make an offering, מנחה. Arnold, 'Mizpah', p. 879, maintains that the destination of these men was a temple at Mizpah. Most commentators, however, see this as a sojourn to Jerusalem to mourn the loss of the temple or the exile, or perhaps pilgrims on a more regular trek to the holy city: cf. Carroll, *Jeremiah*, p. 709-10; W. McKane, *A Critical and Exegetical Commentary on Jeremiah. II. Commentary on Jeremiah XXVI–LII* (ICC; Edinburgh: T. & T. Clark, 1996), p. 1019; W.L. Holladay, *Jeremiah. II. A Commentary on the Book of the Prophet Jeremiah Chapters 26–52* (Hermeneia; Minneapolis: Fortress Press, 1989), p. 297.

5. Smith, *Map*, pp. 97, 109.

> The desert or wilderness is a place of strange, demonic, secret powers. It
> is a sacred land, a holy land in that it is a demonic realm; but it is not a
> place for ordinary men. It is not a place which is a homeland, a world
> where men may dwell.[6]

The temple site, of course, was not the centre of a wilderness or a
demonic realm, but neither was it really a place for humans; it was the
place where the divine name dwelt. Even the priests could not minister
when the presence of Yahweh first manifested itself there (1 Kgs 8.10-
11). Yet, no greater sign that the territories of Israel were a homeland
could be given. With the rejection of the temple and exile, however,
that presence, manifested at the temple dedication as the final conclusion to the exodus, is gone. In concert with this, the land itself becomes
like a wilderness; a wasteland devoid of any people.[7] The temple site,
however, may be thought of as the emptiest of all: in 1 Kgs 9.7-9 its
ruins are the symbol of divine judgment. It can never be neutral or
irrelevant: it has become sacred in the most frightening way possible.

Because of this, the site of the Jerusalem temple becomes the chief
axis in a sacred geography. The orientation it provides, however, is not
only spatial, but also historical. Preservation of this frightening symbol
of the requirements of Israel's god grants continuity, preventing a feeling of oblivion by preserving the memory of radical change. Since the
temple is not described as part of the original creation of the physical
world, however, this historicality is two-fold. Not only has there been a
withdrawal of divine sanction from the temple, but there was a time
before such sanction was ever granted. A limited expanse of time,
therefore, becomes marked as special, and its two end points are particularly sacred moments. They mark moments of divine intervention
into the human realm, highlighting the approach and withdrawal of the
deity.[8] Hayden White comments that a narrative's plot imposes a
structure which is revealed at the conclusion but 'was immanent in the

6.   Smith, *Map*, p. 109.
7.   For discussion of the theology of the 'empty land' in a number of Hebrew
Bible texts as a strategy for the control of land by the Persian imposed elites of
Jerusalem, see R.P. Carroll, 'Textual Strategies and Ideology in the Second Temple
Period', in Davies (ed.), *Second Temple Studies*, I, pp. 108-24.
8.   Indeed, according to 2 Sam. 5–6, Jerusalem was not even in Israelite hands
until David had been made king of all Israel, and its capture seems to celebrate his
accession; see above, Chapter 4. Its full transformation to a holy site, however, is
not made until Solomon dedicates his temple.

events *all along*.[9] If so, then the temple's 'sacrality of (divine) absence' should be implicit in the texts that mark its original 'sacrality of (divine) presence' (to coin a few expressions of my own). Orientation and estrangement merge at the consecration of Solomon's temple, in another of Kings' frequent paradoxes. For these reasons, the portrayal of the consecration of the temple is a fitting subject with which to conclude this study of Kings.

As should be expected, the history of research into this chapter is complex, and conclusions very diverse. One issue scholars have attended to is that the chapter posits the temple as a house of prayer, not the centre of a sacrificial cult. This attention is certainly well founded. I, too, will address this issue, although I must refrain from commenting on the variety of diachronic conclusions stemming from this interest, or from the study of a number of other features of the episode.[10] Most scholars who study 1 Kings 8 find in Solomon's words an example of one of the tell-tale 'deuteronomistic orations', which Noth held organized and unified the DtrH. These orations, whether by a character or narrator, are held to be explicit revelations of the author's own thoughts on the subject at hand.[11] De Vries finds that 1 Kings 8 is crucial to Dtr's purposes, as advantage has been taken of the opportunity to put Dtr's own theology in the mouth of Solomon.[12] As noted above, however, Eslinger disputes this approach, and finds differing motives between the narrator and characters. The wording of

9. H. White, 'The Value of Narrativity in the Representation of Reality', in W.J.T. Mitchell (ed.), *On Narrative* (Chicago: University of Chicago Press, 1981), pp. 1-23 (19).

10. N. Knoppers, 'Prayer and Propaganda: Solomon's Dedication of the Temple and the Deuteronomist's Program', *CBQ* 57 (1995), pp. 229-55 (229-33), attends to some of the issues raised by others, but argues convincingly against explanations that the emphasis on prayer reflected a devaluation of the temple, or a turn from the 'mythical' thought which is part of sacrificial religion. He dates the bulk of the chapter to a Josianic edition, and finds the call to prayer an expansion of the role of the temple. For a dating proposal of 597-87 BCE for 1 Kgs 6–8, see R. Tomes, '"Our Holy and Beautiful House": When and Why was 1 Kings 6–8 Written', *JSOT* 70 (1996), pp. 33-50. Others find a great extent of 'exilic' material in the words given to Solomon: J. Levenson, 'Temple to Synagogue'. Greater distribution of material between editors is proposed by Brettler, 'Interpretation'; Talstra, *Solomon's Prayer*, pp. 171-256.

11. Noth, *Deuteronomistic History*, pp. 5-6.

12. De Vries, *1 Kings*, p. 121.

Solomon's prayer, then, is down to the way the author wished to depict Solomon, and does not form a programmatic statement by the author on 'proper' religion.[13] In fact, Eslinger finds no greater discontinuity between the narrator and character, or between one of the great orations and its literary context, than in the case of Solomon's temple dedication. He prefers to see Solomon as attempting to force Yahweh to restore the unconditional dynastic sanction which was once offered David, but had since been revoked. Solomon uses a spectacular and patronizing ritual to shame the deity into complying to this, and to what amounts to the effective withdrawal of the covenantal curses of Deuteronomy 28. Solomon's 'deuteronomistic language' is finally countered by Yahweh's own in 1 Kgs 9.3-9, while the narrator reports the proceedings from a more detached position, concealing ironic criticisms of the bold king.[14] Even Talstra's analysis finds that Solomon's 'deuteronomistic' orations do not develop the same themes or use the same range of 'deuteronomistic' terminology as the others.[15] While I will build on Eslinger's reading of the chapter, it is not clear to me that the writer has totally abandoned the potentially fruitful strategy of legitimizing a personal perspective by attributing it to a famous person from the past. Certainly, the character's version of the author's 'truth' may be mediated by the personality and experiences described for that character, but to rule such a strategy out of hand is excessive. Solomon's expression of hope that the temple would be the locus of reconciliation does stand as an antithesis to the rejection of the temple in 2 Kgs 23.27, and actually seems quite pathetic in view of Yahweh's threats in 1 Kgs 9.3-9. Eslinger's line of questioning is, therefore, valid: how can Solomon be held to represent the views of the author about the temple? Yet I question the uniformity of Solomon's selfish ambitions that Eslinger finds in the king's speeches. I will demonstrate a progression in Solomon's thought, in which the king slowly comes to realize the limitations of his temple, limitations justified by the narrator's exposition as well. It is this transformation, however incomplete or temporary, which salvages the episode, and makes of it another way to 'imagine' Israel's existence vis-à-vis its deity.

It is clear to me, therefore, that the episode is interpretable as the story of a social drama, even if there is not a particular breach and

---

13. Eslinger addresses 1 Kgs 8 directly in *Living God*, pp. 123-81.
14. Eslinger, *Living God*, p. 123.
15. Talstra, *Solomon's Prayer*, pp. 169-70.

crisis with which Israel is faced.[16] On the other hand, the installation of the ark in the temple is a dangerous undertaking (cf. 1 Sam. 6.1-20; 2 Sam. 6.6-8) which upsets the *status quo* and seeks to establish a new symbol of Yahweh's presence amongst Israel. Resolution of such dramas may be either reintegration or recognition of schism, but here the two possibilities are held in tension. Potential reconstitution of order is found in the acknowledgment of the demand for obedience (cf. 1 Kgs 8.23-25, 58-61) and in the pleas for Yahweh to hear prayers (vv. 31-52). The ark is installed, and the temple dedicated, but Solomon himself looks ahead to the failure of the drama, with the rise of a new crisis, exile. Yet it is in this crisis that the true efficacy of the drama is found. Reintegration and recognition of schism merge.

The drama's relevance is demonstrable in a number of ways. First of all, it is highly ritualistic, with Solomon convening the whole of Israel (v. 1) and offering sacrifices and celebrating a feast (vv. 5, 62-65). The actual transference of the ark itself is a ritualized action (vv. 3-9), which accesses the metaphor of Israel as the people of the exodus. The presence of Yahweh (vv. 10-11) guarantees the event's social relevance, not only within the narrative world, but to the reader as well. Although Eslinger makes some valid points, I prefer to agree with the other scholars who find the episode paradigmatic. Long considers the dedication ceremony to be 'both climax and paradigmatic center'. Its literary architecture centres on the prayers which take the most space. 'It is as though one buffers the prayer with speeches all round, like the outer courts which surround the holy of holies (ch. 6), defining and protecting at once the sacred center.'[17] Long concludes that the exilic deuteronomist offered the episode as a paradigmatic moment 'from which the past and future, especially that longed for by the temple-shorn and landless exiles, derived its value and significance'.[18] He and Levenson note the prominence of the number seven: seven petitions, seven shifts in perspective in the wordplays on 'repent', שׁוּב, and 'captivity', שׁבה, the prayer is offered in the seventh month (1 Kgs 8.2),

16. cf. Turner, 'Social Dramas', p. 145. Mullen, *Narrative History*, makes only relatively infrequent, and mostly passing references to 1 Kgs 8. It becomes plain that he has not really appreciated the importance of 1 Kgs 8. For the most part, his handling of the chapter surrounds the matter of the conditional promises to David and the deuteronomistic views on Jerusalem as the place of Yahweh's choosing.

17. Long, *1 Kings*, pp. 94-95.

18. Long, *1 Kings*, p. 104.

the festival lasts for (twice) seven days (v. 65). Construction of the temple lasts seven years (1 Kgs 6.38).[19] A seven-fold framing structure in the chapter is identified by Knoppers.[20] Levenson would link the prominence of the number seven in the temple descriptions (cf. 1 Kgs 6.38; 8.2) with the seven days of creation (Gen. 1.1–2.4).[21] George Savran observes that the temple construction is ringed by two visionary encounters, and this establishes the temple as a sacred centre. He takes the position that Solomon is a prototypical figure, in both positive and negative senses, and his speeches express optimism and foreboding.[22]

The narrator puts a great accent on the presence of the collective of the people and the direct manifestation of Yahweh's presence, which makes something more of the episode than a staged production by Solomon to serve his dynastic ambitions.[23] Even though the narrator reports that Solomon 'convened' יקהל Israel (v.1), there is little in the narrator's words in vv. 1-11 that hint at Solomon's attention to the dynastic or monarchic institution (cf. 'City of David' v. 1). Israel attends the king without respect to the divisions imposed in 1 Kings 4, for instance. Solomon has little role in the actual installation of the ark, other than to offer sacrifices with Israel.[24] The priests are those who perform the real task. The ceremonial gathering is striking in its comprehensiveness and harmony within Israel, even if there are hints that all is not right between Israel and Yahweh.

The opening section of the chapter, 1 Kgs 8.1-5, stresses the gathering of all Israel before Solomon. The Greek is significantly briefer in its description of this convocation, although the emphasis the MT places on the communal aspects of the meeting are not in any way denied in the LXX. The collective is also a unified body, ignoring the divisions implied in earlier episodes. None of the tribes is mentioned by name, except for the 'Levites' in v. 4 of the MT (LXX only has 'priests').[25]

19. Long, *1 Kings*, p. 104; Levenson, 'Temple', p. 154.

20. Knoppers, 'Prayer', pp. 233-35.

21. J.D. Levenson, 'The Temple and the World', *JR* 64 (1984), pp. 275-98 (288).

22. Savran, 'Kings', pp. 155-59.

23. Eslinger, *Living God*, pp. 157-58. Cf. Knoppers, 'Prayer', pp. 240-41.

24. On the other hand, he doesn't engage in anything as controversial as David did with his dance in 2 Sam. 6.14-16, 20-23 when the ark was moved into the City of David.

25. The Levites are rather conspicuous by their absence from most of Kings, elsewhere, see only 1 Kgs 12.31.

This relatively small concession to the traditions of a tribe with a special status is only slightly strengthened, however, by the MT's unique
references to the 'tribal heads' and leaders of 'ancestral houses'
כל־ראשי המטות נשיאי האבות (1 Kgs 8.1). On the other hand, the
intended effect of the implicit divisions within the MT's view of greater
Israel seems to me to be more of an assertion that the collective acted
in unison than an admission of notable internal disparity. The collective
audience is affirmed by the narrator prior to Solomon's major
speeches.[26] 1 Kings 8.5 refers to 'all the congregation' (עדה) of Israel
(LXX has 'all Israel').[27] All the 'assembly' (קהל) of Israel are Solomon's audience in 1 Kgs 8.14, 22, 55.[28] At the close of Solomon's
speeches, he and 'all Israel' (vv. 62, 63, 65) offer sacrifices. In 1 Kgs
8.65, the Israelites comprise a 'great assembly' (קהל גדול) coming
from 'Lebo-hamath to the Wadi of Egypt' (v. 65). They celebrate a
feast for twice seven days. The group participation at the close of the
ceremony gives a sense of social relevance to the meeting, which may
have allowed the intended readership to imagine themselves as participants. There is no hint of the schism in the narrator's words. Neither
are there in the words of Yahweh in 1 Kgs 9.3-9.

As I have indicated in earlier chapters, reflections of other historical
traditions of the origins of Israel as a nation often impart a sense of
integrity to the fractious history told in Kings. In 1 Kings 8, these historical reflections are not only accomplished through the affirmation of
the ancestral houses and elders in vv. 1-5. The ark itself has irrefutable
connections with the exodus traditions. Its contents are described as
being nothing but the tablets of Moses placed in it at Horeb (v. 9). The
whole scene in vv. 1-13 (LXX, vv. 1-11) seems infused with a sense
that the dedication of the temple is not so much a singular event, but
rather marks the ultimate end to the exodus itself. 1 Kings 6.1 goes so
far as to date the completion of the temple to the 480th (MT) or 440th
(LXX) year after the flight from Egypt. Either system arguably locates
the completion of the temple at an important chronological milestone in

26. The initial declaration in MT 1 Kgs 8.11-12 and its differently positioned
Greek counterpart are exceptions.

27. This expression appears only here.

28. Cf. ἐκκλησία in the LXX, cf. minor variant in vs. 14. Elsewhere, cf. 1 Kgs
12.3, where the Israelites confront Rehoboam. The verbal form is used in 1 Kgs 8.1
and 12.21.

Israel's history from the life of Abraham to the exile, if not beyond.[29] Rather than Solomon's own vocal self-assertiveness, the real 'presence' of character in 1 Kgs 8.1-11 is that of Yahweh himself, already intimated by the descriptions of the cultic paraphernalia and processions. As the final moment in the exodus, the installation of the ark sees the return of the cloud, עָנָן, signifying Yahweh's presence. With this event, then, the transition from the wilderness to the land is complete. The god who led Israel from Egypt has left the tent of meeting אֹהֶל־מוֹעֵד (1 Kgs 8.4) which was once filled with his glory (Exod. 40.34-38), and moved into the house built for his name.

There is a sense of ominous foreboding, however, as the ark is certainly not to be trifled with (1 Sam. 6.1-20; 2 Sam. 6.6-8). The presence of Yahweh is such that not even the priests can minister before the 'glory' of the deity, כְּבוֹד־יְהוָה (vv. 10-11).[30] At its own dedication, the cult of the temple has proven inadequate. This is reinforced by Solomon's own admission in v. 27 that even the heavens cannot contain Yahweh, let alone the building he has made. Moreover, the altar proves too small at the very consecration of the temple that contains it (v. 64). The routinization of the formal, cultic worship of Yahweh at the end of the exodus is immediately rendered problematic, superficial and, perhaps, unnecessary. Ironically, the site of this routinized cult becomes symbolic, not only of the divine presence and the divine judgment, but of the transcendence of Yahweh. It also perhaps hints at the transience of Israel as an autonomous geo-political entity: Yahweh,

---

29. That both chronological references are part of differently formulated historical periodization schemes is discussed in Hughes, *Secrets*, pp. 36-39 and *passim*. The MT figure at 1 Kgs 6.1 places the completion of the temple equidistant between the exodus and restoration of the temple as dated in Ezra 3.8. Hughes considers the MT original at 1 Kgs 6.1, but, as he demonstrates, the differences are related to other textual variants throughout Kings and in other books. The difficulties with the Greek are compounded by the complex history of the Greek versions themselves and the likelihood of secondary manipulations within the chronological data themselves. The original chronology of Kings, and the historical regnal chronology of Judah and Israel are topics of much dispute, and Hughes gives good discussions and bibliography. This may be updated by G. Galil, *Chronology*, pp. 1-11, who considers it improper to find chronological periodization schemes in Kings' figures which rely on the restoration which, in any case, is not narrated in the book. This objection is quite valid, but 1 Kgs 6.1, which dates the temple by reference to the exodus, still marks the building as a major episode in history.

30. For the cloud in the Pentateuch, cf. Exod. 40.34-38.

the basis of its stability, is too powerful to be contained.

Solomon's behaviour in this episode is central, since his words take up so much of the text. It is, therefore, important to note that the strength of the narrator's affirmation of the unity of Israel is exceeded by Solomon's own. Perhaps the most significant element of Solomon's terminology, highlighting the collective perception of Israel, is the frequent references to Israel as the people of Yahweh in vv. 16 (2×), 30, 32 (LXX only, MT has 'servants'), 33, 34, 36, 38, 41, 43, 52, 56, 59. This is reinforced by the handful of times in which Yahweh is called the 'god of Israel' (vv. 15, 17, 20, 23, 25, 26, 28 [LXX only, MT has 'my god']).[31] Not even in 1 Kgs 8.16, in which Solomon affirms the status of the davidic dynasty, does he imply any disunity within Israel. In the Hebrew version of this verse Solomon recalls Yahweh's words that, ever since the exodus, he had not chosen a city from all the 'tribes' (שבטים) of Israel in which a temple to the divine name might be built.[32] David, Solomon continues, was chosen to rule Israel. As the speech unfolds, however, it is clear that Solomon intends his temple to be seen as Yahweh's choice of place (vv. 20-21). No mention of 'Judah' is made at all, even if the Greek does add in v. 16 that Jerusalem was the eventual chosen city. The positive emphasis on the city and temple in the Greek, matched with a higher reputation for Solomon, do contrast with the MT, but in terms of the eventual destruction of the temple and the critique of Solomon, the two texts differ in degree, not kind.[33] There is in the MT a tendency to highlight

31. Solomon also refers to Yahweh's 'servants', which should be taken as indicating Israel. The textual situation here is complex, as the noun also occurs in the singular, indicating David, Moses or Solomon himself. The MT and LXX differ in a number of cases as to the singular and plural.

32. For other uses of שבט see also 1 Kgs 11.13, 31, 35, 36; 12.20, 21 where it is translated by σκῆπτρον. In 1 Kgs 11.32, שבט is translated by φυλή, as is also the case in 1 Kgs 14.21; 18.31; 2 Kgs 17.18; and 21.7. 3 Kgdms 12.24o also uses φυλή to speak of the tribes mustered by Jeroboam. In 1 Kgs 18.31, φυλῶν τοῦ Ισραηλ is the Greek counterpart to שבטי בני־יעקב.

33. The LXX, however, does refer to the selection of Jerusalem. 4QKings (4Q54), of the proto-Masoretic tradition, nonetheless mentions both the selection of David and Jerusalem, thus comparing favourably to the parallel in 2 Chron. 6.5-6. J. Trebolle Barrera, 'A Preliminary Edition of 4QKings (4Q54)', in J. Trebolle Barrera and L. Vegas Montarer (eds.), *The Madrid Qumran Congress: Proceedings of the International Congress on the Dead Sea Scrolls, Madrid 18-21 March 1991*, I (2 vols.; STDJ, 11; Leiden: E.J. Brill, 1992), pp. 229-46, explains the short MT text

Solomon's inadequacies as an ideal ruler, and even if it is mediated to some degree, it can still be found in the LXX.[34] It suffices here just to note that 1 Kgs 8.16 in the MT does not legitimize a tribal division within Israel, while the Greek does so only if Jerusalem is seen as strictly a Judaean city, and not one important to greater Israel. This, however, is to be resisted, given the setting of 1 Kings 8 in the time of the United Monarchy, and the absence of any specific reference to Judah anywhere in the chapter.

One of the primary matters at issue in 1 Kings 8 is Solomon's affirmation that his temple is a divinely-sanctioned locus for Yahweh's actual presence, or at least that of his 'name', as symbolic of his concern.[35] In 1 Kgs 8.12-13 (LXX, after v. 53) Solomon declares how

as the result of a scribal error, the original being only partially preserved in the LXX. This is plausible, except that the *partial* preservation requires explanation. W.M. Schniedewind, 'Notes and Observations: Textual Criticism and Theological Interpretation: The Pro-Temple *Tendenz* in the Greek Text of Samuel-Kings', *HTR* 87 (1994), pp. 107-16, considers that the LXX reading reflects the pro-temple bias in Samuel and Kings. Variants in 2 Kgdms 7.5, 11, 16 emphasize the temple in the context of the dynastic promise. 2 Kgdms 24.25 has Solomon expand David's altar, thus linking that structure to Solomon's temple.

34. The Greek also reveals another variant. Solomon's first Hebrew oration (vv. 12-13) contains Solomon's comments about his building an 'exalted house', בית זבל, for the god who chose to abide in 'darkness', בערפל , to establish his dwelling 'forever'. It follows the reporting of the priests' inability to minister before the divine cloud of glory (vv. 10-11). In the LXX, it is found only after v. 53, after Solomon's petitions. It is also significantly longer here, prefacing the common statements with the additional comment that Yahweh had manifested the sun in the heavens, and concluding the brief section with a rhetorical question, implying that Solomon's words were taken from another document, the 'book of the song', βιβλίῳ τῆς ᾠδῆς. Jones, *Kings*, I, p. 196, is among those who hold that the most probable *Vorlage* is שיר, which could reasonably be emended to ישר, to produce 'Book of Yashar'; cf. Josh. 10.13 and 2 Sam. 1.18. For different reasons, scholars have tended to prefer the version recorded in the Greek, but the MT has its advocates as well, even if the LXX is not attributable to error, but its intent to undertake an extensive rehabilitation of Solomon. This includes using his speech as a new prayer formulae, reinforced by the reference to the book of Jashar, according to V. Peterca, 'Ein Midraschartiges Auslegungsbeispiel zugunsten Salomos 1 Kön 8,12-13–3 Reg 8,53a', *BZ* 31 (1987), pp. 270-75.

35. Many scholars juxtapose the apparent different conceptions in this regard as evidence of compositional layering. A very recent example is Brettler, 'Interpretation', pp. 17-35. There may be some validity in this, but a literary explanation of the changes in focus is equally not out of order, as I will describe below.

Yahweh will dwell in the house built for him. In vv. 16-21 Solomon advertizes his fulfilment of the divine will in building a house for Yahweh, and setting within it the ark of the covenant. Later he affirms that the temple is the place where Yahweh's name will dwell, even if the heavens cannot contain him (1 Kgs 8.27-9). In Solomon's petitions the temple or 'place', מָקוֹם, that Yahweh chose, בָּחַר, is offered as the focal point for prayers (1 Kgs 8.31, 33, 35, 38, 42, 43; 'choice' is specified in vv. 44, 48). This, however, is radically altered in Solomon's final oration, in which the temple does not figure at all in the reference to the prayers of those seeking to worship Yahweh (vv. 56-61).[36] This change of affairs, coupled with the seemingly deliberate avoidance of the issue of the schism throughout 1 Kgs 8.1–9.9, seems to foreshadow the way the 'choice' of Jerusalem and the temple's acceptability is handled in later episodes, in which the schism and eventual exile of greater Israel are played out.[37]

In 1 Kgs 11.13, 32 Yahweh reports that for the sake of David and the chosen city, one tribe, שֵׁבֶט, will be retained for Solomon's son. In 1 Kgs 11.36, David's heirs will have their 'fief' (נִיר), one tribe, before Yahweh in Jerusalem, the city Yahweh chose. In Chapter 5 I suggested that this implies that Judah, as a davidic property, will be represented in the divinely chosen city where *all* the tribes of Israel are at least ostensibly represented.[38] Rehoboam, who provided the political incentive to the schism, is said to have ruled in Jerusalem, the city chosen from all the tribes of Israel (1 Kgs 14.21). There is no sense here, however, that Judah is a chosen tribe. Rather, it emphasizes the shameful rule of the apostate Judaean king, who, in any case, was the product of one of Solomon's illicit marriages (1 Kgs 14.21-24). The report of Manasseh's defiling of the temple includes the narrator's concern for Yahweh's selection of Jerusalem from among the tribes (2 Kgs 21.7; cf. v. 4).

---

36. Talstra, *Solomon's Prayer*, p. 163.

37. Solomon's failure to foresee it might be explained by the author painting Solomon as ignorant of the consequences of his actions, but since both the narrator and Yahweh also refrain from speaking of Judah and Israel, far more seems to be going on here.

38. Of the other נִיר references, 1 Kgs 15.4 (MT and LXX[L]) refer to the fief 'in Jerusalem' although all do later associate the establishment of the city with the rise of the dynasty. No mention of the 'choice' of the city is made, however. In 2 Kgs 8.19, 'Jerusalem' does not appear at all. As I argued in Chapter 5, however, both these verses develop contrasts between Judah and Israel.

Here, again, Manasseh's transgressions seem all the more serious for the importance granted Jerusalem. On the other hand, the mention of the special status of the city implicitly links Judah with the rest of greater Israel. This is reinforced by 2 Kgs 21.3, 11-15, where Judah's behaviour and destiny are likened to those of Israel. It is noteworthy, therefore, that, despite all the seemingly pro-Jerusalem actions of Josiah, there is absolutely no mention of Yahweh's 'choice' of the city in the narratives of the temple repair or the purge. Yet when the narrator reports that all of the king's efforts could not appease Yahweh, the deity's vow that he would reject the city which he chose (2 Kgs 23.27), and the temple where his name abides, is recalled. The banishment of Judah is also compared to that of Israel. This final reference not only inverts the divine action of selection, but marks the completion of divine judgment against the whole. The 'sacrality of absence' has macabre connotations of reintegration, as exile becomes the 'great equalizer' between Judah and Israel. Seemingly in anticipation of this, at the dedication of the temple there is only greater Israel. That Jerusalem has, indeed, been chosen is evident from the trouble-free and highly ritualized installation of the ark and the way in which Yahweh's presence fills the temple (1 Kgs 8.1-11). Moreover, in 1 Kgs 9.1-9, Yahweh appears to Solomon directly, indicating his acceptance of the temple and Solomon's prayers, while warning of the exile. Selection and rejection converge, even at the initial moment of Israel's history of urbanized, cultic religion, and the nation as a whole is addressed as a unity.

The convening of all Israel marks not only the start of the consecration of the temple as holy space (and in geographical terms, of holy place), but also of the start of a sacred time. At the close of the chapter, more sacrifices mark the transition back to the narrative, sequential world, and the close of this sacred moment. The narrative, therefore, stands both within and outside the sequence of events leading up to the exile. On the one hand, the temple dedication is a part of the monarchic glory which Solomon's apostasy will squander; on the other, it is a commentary on the whole course of Israelite history, from the exodus to the exile, and it stands as another of the 'social metaphors' by which Israel might identity itself, entrenching both the 'right' ways and 'wrong' ways in which Jerusalem and its temple are sacred axes of a spiritualized history and geography.

2. *Solomon's Finest Hour: In Spite of Himself*

Eslinger sees 1 Kings 8 as Solomon's attempt to coerce from Yahweh an unconditional sanction for his reign, and the neutralization of Deuteronomy's curses, while 1 Kgs 6.11-13 are Yahweh's warning that such plans are in vain.[39] While Solomon does force the divine hand, it is only to his own downfall. He does not win the hoped-for concessions, as 1 Kgs 9.3-9 reveal.[40] For Eslinger, 1 Kings 1–11 shows how the temple was the breaking point between God and Israel, and that Yahweh won by virtue of strength.[41] It is clear from 1 Kgs 9.1-9 that Solomon fails to win a restatement of the 'unconditional' divine promise, but Yahweh still accepts the temple, at least conditionally. If the temple was the 'breaking point', however, one can only wonder why, in 1 Kgs 11.1-13 and vv. 31-33, which present Yahweh's case against Solomon, no mention of the inappropriateness of the temple is made. Moreover, the care with which Josiah is described as purging the temple (in which virtually all details are given by the narrator) suggests that the author still held some concern for the place. If it was an edifice only to Solomon's miscalculations about Yahweh, then it should have been reported destroyed along with the other symbols of Solomon's impiety, such as the shrines to other gods (2 Kgs 23.13-14). It is the continued presence of the 'high places', and not the temple, which the narrator considers the grounds for qualifying the good reputation of some Judaean monarchs (1 Kgs 15.11-14; 22.43; 2 Kgs 12.3-4; 14.3; 15.3-4, 34-35). Defiling the temple is the cause of much narratorial disgust. Josiah destroys what is heterodox, but purifies what Yahweh knows he will one day reject. The temple is not the breaking point, but rather a very exceptional case which, actually, might bridge the gap between Israel and Yahweh.

---

39. 1 Kgs 6.11-14 is absent in the Greek. Many scholars are convinced of these verses' 'deuteronomistic' origins, and some seem, therefore, to conclude that they are integral to the book, and so the omission in Greek requires no comment: cf. Gray, *Kings*, p. 167; De Vries, *1 Kings*, pp. 86-95. For De Vries, *1 Kings*, p. 93, 1 Kgs 6.11-13 is an intrusive, and 'noticeably irrelevant admonition' interrupting the temple construction report.

40. Eslinger, *Living God*, pp. 145, 157.

41. Eslinger, *Living God*, pp. 178-80. Solomon's rhetoric is more polished than Yahweh's, and Eslinger wonders if this is not the reason why commentators have tended to find the narrator's voice in Solomon's words, and not Yahweh's.

In my view, Eslinger offers too restricted a view of Solomon in
1 Kings 8. While Eslinger has a valid point about the dispute between
Solomon and Yahweh, I think that the manipulative king is being mani-
pulated himself. Rather than see a single-minded strategy designed to
win dynastic and covenantal benefits for Solomon and Israel, I see a
development in Solomon's thought in which concern for the dynasty
is *replaced* by other themes. This proposal is already intimated in
Eslinger's handling of Solomon's judgment concerning the two women
(1 Kgs 3.16-28). The narrator reports that the people recognize that
Solomon had the wisdom of God to judge. The people (and most readers) assume that Solomon planned the judgment in the way it worked
out, but the narrator does not confirm such suspicions:[42]

> The people do indeed see the wisdom of God operating, but it is not a
> wisdom controlled by Solomon. Rather, the divine wisdom that resolves
> this difficult case is accidental to Solomon's own wisdom; it appears in
> the events more through the intercession of the mother of the live child
> than through Solomon's decree.[43]

Similarly, Solomon is placed in a precarious situation in 1 Kings 8.
While he may have had a lucky escape in 1 Kings 3, in which 'justice'
suddenly dawned on him, in ch. 8 he is subsumed by the monumental
events unfolding around him. It is these events, cast as a social drama,
that come to control Solomon, who, ironically, orchestrated them in the
first place. Slowly Solomon manages to make something of the situation. He turns his attention from the dynasty to the need for reconciliation. At this moment, however, he never truly rises above the level of a
pious fool, whose understanding of the true mind of God is always
inadequate and who eventually proves himself incapable of even taking
his own advice about repenting. Even so, the fool has his uses: Yahweh
accepts the temple, and the place where it stands is, therefore, marked
as holy for all time; but in a manner which Solomon can imagine in
only the most naive of ways. Armed with the hindsight of history, however, the reader may attain a bitter wisdom that even Solomon could
not fathom.

In Solomon's opening words (MT, 1 Kgs 8.12-21; LXX, 14-21), the
king's main theme is that the temple and his own person are the fulfilment of God's promise to David. Eslinger rightly points out that

---

42. Eslinger, *Living God*, pp. 138-40.
43. Eslinger, *Living God*, p. 139.

Solomon mentions only the propitious divine acts, omitting not only reference to the conditions on the davidic dynasty, but also to the Sinai covenant, in his review of Israel's history (vv. 15-20).[44] One should note, however, that Solomon does close his blessing with a reference to the exodus covenant (v. 21). Because of this recollection, Talstra sees vv. 14-21 as affirming that the temple is not only in the dynasty's interests, but the people's, and this is, in my view, a superior way of reading the unit.[45] Eslinger finds that, in vv. 23-26, Solomon finally addresses the real problem facing his temple project, the conditional qualification of the original dynastic promise to David. Solomon tries to undercut the original, conditional Sinai covenant and concentrates on the divine promises and obligations to David (vv. 23-26). In v. 25, the conditions attached to davidic rule are recalled, but Solomon's choice of wording still serves his purposes. He only mentions that the conditions could be met by following David's example (ignoring David's emphasis on whole-hearted virtue, in 1 Kgs 2.4), which, given the less than perfect image of David in the books of Samuel and 1 Kings 1–2, should be far easier to follow than Yahweh's 'laws and commandments' (cf. 1 Kgs 3.14; 6.11-13). Solomon's selectivity in quoting the conditions is matched by the selectivity in quoting what is to be gained. He fails to refer to 3.13, where God promises only lengthened days (and 2.4, where David refers to the obedient king's enduring success). Rather, Solomon develops the thought of 6.13, in which God vows not to renege on the promise to David; that is, not to forsake Israel.[46]

Eslinger recognizes a major shift occurring in 1 Kings 27 and sees vv. 27-30 as an introduction to the petitions beginning in v. 31. Solomon's repeated calls for Yahweh to 'hear and forgive' (vv. 30, 32, 34, 36, 39, 43, 45, 49-50) are the keynote of his prayer and the main front against the provisos to the davidic covenant.[47] While vv. 27-30 do serve as such an introduction, I would also relate the passage back to vv. 22-26, as does Talstra. He sees vv. 22-30 as marking a transition

---

44. Eslinger, *Living God*, pp. 158-59. Eslinger also sarcastically praises Solomon's graciousness at providing Yahweh with a dwelling he does not want, and, in 2 Sam. 7.6-7, forbade. Eslinger, however, does not observe that later in 2 Sam. 7 (vv. 12-13), not only will Yahweh build a 'house' for David's son, but will have a 'house' built for himself as well.

45. Talstra, *Solomon's Prayer*, pp. 151-52.

46. Eslinger, *Living God*, pp. 159-62.

47. Eslinger, *Living God*, p. 163.

from an admittedly strong concern for the dynastic promise (he does not notice that the conditions are 'watered-down') to a concern for the temple, and from praying *for* the dynasty to discussion of the prayers *of* the king and his people. Moreover, the legitimacy of the temple is not challenged, but its role as a 'house' for Yahweh is played down by the assertion that God is in heaven (vv. 30).[48] It is between vv. 22-26 and 27-30 that one can see Solomon change his mind about some key issues. Solomon prepares for his speech by spreading his arms toward heaven and declaring that Yahweh is unique in heaven and earth (v. 22). In v. 27, however, he asks whether God really can dwell on earth; indeed, the heavens and earth cannot contain him. Solomon's request that the promise of a dynasty be fulfilled (vv. 25-26) is replaced with a hope that Yahweh will attend to the prayers made in the place he himself had chosen (v. 29). The conditions on dynastic rule in v. 25 are all the more poignant by the admission of human sin in vv. 29-30. Claims to the receipt of a promise are abandoned in favour of a plea to forgive (vv. 26, 29-30). The shift from emphasis on the dynasty undertaken in this unit is never reversed in the rest of Solomon's words. Solomon's admission that not even heaven can contain Yahweh seems to reflect the earlier scene of the priests retreating from the divine cloud (vv. 10-11). Is Solomon attempting to coerce through flattery, or seriously rethinking what he had already said and trying to start again? Is Yahweh turning the event to his own purposes?

In his petitions, Solomon presents seven hypothetical cases in which Yahweh should 'hear in heaven' and judge or forgive the penitent people who offer prayers in or towards the temple. In the first petition, he prays for Yahweh's judgment in legal matters (1 Kgs 8.31-32), in the second, for restoration after defeat (vv. 33-34). The third and fourth foresee drought and plagues (vv. 35-40). The fifth concerns the pious foreigner (vv. 41-43). The sixth, again, deals with Israel at war, and the seventh prays for mercy in captivity (vv. 44-50). Eslinger maintains that Solomon's strategy is to lull Yahweh into thinking that he is genuine in his piety, by building on an innocuous opening petition, while positing the temple as the proper place for judgment (vv. 31-32). This is reinforced, in the subsequent petitions, with repeated pleas that

---

48. Talstra, *Solomon's Prayer*, p. 155. More properly, the text is quite ambivalent about Yahweh's location. Solomon spreads his arms to heaven (v. 22), states that Yahweh is unequalled in heaven or earth (v. 23), and that the heavens or earth cannot contain him (v. 27).

Yahweh 'hear' from his heavenly vantage point (vv. 32, 34, 36, 39, 43, 45, 49). These are incessant reminders that the temple cannot contain Yahweh, while establishing Solomon's building as the 'mechanism for repentance'.[49] Eslinger writes that Solomon's emphasis on Yahweh's ownership of Israel and the land (with such phrases as 'your servants', 'your people, Israel') in the petitions is designed to assert that Yahweh is obliged to Israel, because of the covenantal agreement. Yet, with the temple, 'God and man need never again face the harsh finality proposed by Moses in the book of Deuteronomy'.[50] Indeed, Yahweh should hear the prayers of Israel because they remain the people whom Yahweh once saved from Egypt (vv. 51-53).[51] This obligation to Israel, however, is asserted without mention of the davidic dynasty, as were all seven petitions. This is not surprising to Talstra, since Solomon's words after vv. 27-30 are effectively transformed into a paradigm of the prayers which the king, the people, or the foreigner will offer in or towards the temple.[52] Solomon seems to have forgotten the dynasty as he recognizes human frailty. In the first petition, Solomon affirms that Yahweh knows how to deliver a fair judgment (vv. 31-32). In this petition, he ignores his own God-given wisdom in granting judgment (cf. 1 Kgs 3.4-28). In the third petition, the ability to follow the proper path is, itself, a gift of Yahweh, granted upon repentance (v. 36). A similar thought is expressed in v. 58. The fourth petition asks Yahweh to hear the personal pleas of individuals whose problems only Yahweh himself may appreciate (vv. 38-39). Most importantly, the final petition, which looks ahead to the exile, implies that sin is inevitable, since there is no one who does not sin (v. 46). McConville writes that

---

49. Eslinger, *Living God*, pp. 163-64.

50. Eslinger, *Living God*, p. 167. For another view on the relationship between 1 Kgs 8 and the curses of Deuteronomy, see J.G. McConville, '1 Kings VIII'.

51. Eslinger, *Living God*, pp. 166-73.

52. Talstra, *Solomon's Prayer*, pp. 160-61. In the LXX at v. 36, there is a reference to a singular 'servant', which refers to Solomon. In the MT, however, the term is plural, kings in general are referred to. Talstra recognizes that the prayer offerer can be the collective Israel, a single Israelite, or even a foreigner, which complicates the issue. There are only three references to the speaker (vv. 43, 44, 48; cf. *Qere*), in which Solomon asserts that he is the temple builder. While these may be taken as indicative of Solomon's sense of self-importance, they still do not constitute a major monarchic theme in the unit.

The most prominent individual-corporate relationship in the books of Kings is between king and people. The words, 'there is no man who does not sin', in the mouth of Solomon, are pregnant, foreshadowing their egregious fulfilment in himself, and hinting at the momentous consequences for the nation of the sin of the king in particular.[53]

The strongest call for Yahweh actually to heed penitent prayers comes in the concluding verses to his prayer, vv. 51-53. The incentive Solomon provides is that Israel is Yahweh's people and 'inheritance', נחלה, whom he once saved from Egypt (v. 51). In v. 53, Solomon claims that Yahweh separated Israel 'as his own inheritance' (הבדלתם לך לנחלה) from all the other nations, something he told Moses that he would do during the exodus. If there is coercion here, the restatement of the exodus event still marks a dramatic shift in Solomon. Here the selected party is *Israel*, not David (cf. v. 16). Solomon seems no longer interested in his own destiny. As Talstra points out, Moses is the 'servant' of Yahweh in v. 53, in replacement of David, who was the 'servant' of vv. 24-25. Something else has changed between these verses. Solomon recalls that Yahweh spoke directly to David about his dynasty, but Moses is only an intermediary for a message to Israel. Thus, both the identity and role of the 'servant' changes.[54] However much the temple was posited as the mechanism for repentance in the petitions, the role of the temple disappears in vv. 51-53, and Yahweh is asked to hear supplications directly.[55] The closing of the speech on the note about Moses and the exodus also recalls v. 9, where the narrator reminds the reader of the contents of the ark of the covenant. Solomon has changed his mind again.

Another change in emphasis is taken in Solomon's subsequent blessing of Israel (1 Kgs 8.54-61). Here, the narrator takes time to reset the scene, indicating that Solomon repeats the actions he used to mark the opening of his prayers. Solomon stands near the altar, and spreads his arms to the heavens before the 'assembly' (קהל) of Israel (1 Kgs 8.22, 54-55). Solomon's orations conclude with another blessing of Israel (vv. 54-61). Eslinger sees Solomon as trying to win Yahweh's favour through obsequious and rather inaccurate rewriting of history.

---

53. McConville, '1 Kings VIII', p. 73.

54. Solomon is sometimes the 'servant' in his prayers. MT and LXX sometimes differ in their construal of the term 'servant' in singular or plural form. Verses 23, 36, are plural in the MT, singular in the LXX.

55. Talstra, *Solomon's Prayer*, p. 163.

By cataloguing uncompromised success and unmitigated divine loyalty to Israel, he throws the burden of proof of fidelity onto Yahweh, not Israel. Solomon's words ring hollow, however, since they reflect the narrator's 'ironic', and Joshua's 'dramatically ironic', assessments of the success of the conquest in Josh. 21.43-45, and Joshua's assertions that Yahweh has lived up to his word (Josh. 23.14); assertions which Eslinger holds are 'always incorrect'. Solomon argues that only through providing for Israel will Yahweh achieve the greater purpose of the exodus universal acknowledgment of himself. It is only in his closing words that Solomon actually calls for action from Israel, but the onus on action, overall, is still weighed heavily on Yahweh's side, therefore inverting the overbalance in Deut. 28.15-68, the curses Solomon seeks to undermine.[56] Talstra, however, compares vv. 54-61 with vv. 22-30. There, obedience (using the verbs הלך 'walk' and שמר 'keep', vv. 23, 25) is prior to the prayer being answered. In the final oration, however, obedience (note same verbs, vv. 58, 61) is the result of the answer to the prayer.[57] This again reveals the transition in the thought of Solomon. He is far removed from his original goal of asserting what he feels are the rights to an unconditional divine sanction. Solomon has come to claim that everything, even the ability to fulfil Yahweh's own commandments, is ultimately dependent upon Yahweh. His temple has become a locus for those seeking piety, not for dynastic grandeur.

After Solomon's speeches, the king and the people offer sacrifices before travelling home (vv. 62-66). As before, the narrator makes no mention of the role of the dynasty. For Eslinger, the sacrifices are the 'crowning glory' of Solomon's rhetoric (1 Kgs 8.62-66).[58] In the final verse of the chapter, however, the narrator reintroduces the name of David; as it is reported that the people were rejoicing over the goodness Yahweh had shown to his servant, David, and his people, Israel. This

56. Eslinger, *Living God*, pp. 174-76.

57. Talstra, *Solomon's Prayer*, p. 165. Talstra concludes that diachronic analysis is needed to explain these shifts in the text (pp. 169-70). While the text does have a 'history', diachronic analysis is not the end of interpretation. Moreover, it can be questioned whether, at this point, Talstra has arrived at the proper place to begin an in-depth diachronic study. He has too readily accepted the association between the writer and the speaker of Dtr language in the text to undertake a rigorous examination of the narratological features of the episode.

58. Eslinger, *Living God*, pp. 173-76.

brings the dedication ceremony full circle. Once again, the servant is David. One needs to ask, however, why the writer did not have the Israelites be glad of the goodness shown Solomon. Perhaps the trans-formations that led to Solomon's abandonment of the theme of dynasty and his own role within it are shown as having had its effect on his audience. It has made him invisible; David remains the paradigmatic figure. More ominously, it intimates that Yahweh may still show something other than goodness to Solomon. Even so, the thrust of Solomon's final speech seems to be taken in hand: Israel recognizes that 'David' is a co-recipient, and not the deliverer, of Yahweh's bene-ficence. With this, however, the sacred moment passes, and the course of history resumes. The leading actors in this drama, however, have their curtain call, as Yahweh appears to Solomon in 1 Kgs 9.1-9, and offers a different view of the house of prayer after the fall of the chosen place. This vision, however, stands outside of the drama itself, as it provides the prelude to the greater epic of the fall of monarchic Israel.

In Yahweh's response to Solomon (1 Kgs 9.1-9), the temple is accepted (v. 3). Yahweh reasserts that obedience to the divine com-mandments is necessary, and that the example of David should be fol-lowed. Here Yahweh affirms that the reward for obedience will be a secure dynasty; the punishment for failure, however, will be exile. This warning (1 Kgs 9.3-9) seems to follow the same progression displayed in Solomon's speeches. Concern for the acceptance of the house, and the eternal sanction for the dynasty are mentioned first (vv. 3-5), fol-lowed by the consequences for all Israel should the conditions not be met (vv. 6-9). As in Solomon's petitions, there is no indication that the dynasty itself will be eradicated; rather, the punishment is directed towards the people themselves and the temple. The destruction of the temple, of course, is also not foreseen by Solomon, and equally impor-tantly, Yahweh does mention room for penitence and forgiveness. Eslinger observes how the narrator neither offers support for Yahweh's response to Solomon nor chastises him for reneging on the uncondi-tional support once offered David:[59]

> God is not presented as immoral for having changed the terms of the Davidic covenant. He is, rather, amoral. The divine end justifies the divine means. Or does it? The result is a narrative presentation of divine action in human history that is very much like that of the exodus

59. Eslinger, *Living God*, pp. 178-80.

narratives, in which God does things that would be reprehensible if performed by a human and yet comes away with clean, amoral hands.[60]

The amoral deity Eslinger discovers in these chapters is also easy to find in 2 Kings 22–23, with the 'gathering' of the pious Josiah. The result, in both cases, is a sense of the incomprehensibility of Yahweh. Yet, against such a God, what can anyone do but what Solomon actually ends up doing in his final words to Israel, asking Yahweh to remain true to his own history. His argument, however selfish and manipulative, must speak for Israel. Once Yahweh chose them, he should keep them forever.

If Solomon has ended up highlighting how one might pray for forgiveness, it is noteworthy how little impact his words seem to have in the book and how little of the offences detailed in Kings are actually reflected in his words. Josiah does not pray for forgiveness, and it is in his reign that the city and temple are rejected (2 Kgs 23.27).[61] Talstra observes that the words Solomon uses to describe sin and forgiveness (e.g. 'forgive' (סלח), vv. 30, 33, 39, 50; 'rebel' (פשׁע), v. 50; 'act wickedly' (רשׁע), vv. 32, 47; 'commit iniquity' (עוה), v. 47) are not found in the other Dtr orations. Moreover, Solomon says nothing of the 'other gods' and idols, which mark other 'deuteronomistic' speeches such as Joshua 23, Judg. 2.11-13 and 2 Kgs 17.7-18.[62] Neither does Solomon compare the temple to the high places.[63] These sorts of sins mark the evaluations of the kings in the book. Even most 'good' kings fail by tolerating the 'high places'(1 Kgs 15.14; 22.43-44; 2 Kgs 12.3-4; 14.3-4; 15.3-4, 34-35), and the reigns of 'evil' kings are full of provocation of Yahweh (e.g., 1 Kgs 16.26, 33; 2 Kgs 21.6, 15, 17). For his part, Yahweh introduces the notion of the worship of 'other gods' in 1 Kgs 9.6, 9. Solomon's silence about these injunctions suggests how ignorant he is of the sort of sins that are endemic to Israel, and this seems to call into question everything he had prayed for.

60. Eslinger, *Living God*, p. 179.

61. On the other hand, McKenzie, *Trouble*, p. 108, points to formal similarities between the prayer of Solomon and that of Hezekiah (2 Kgs. 19.15-19).

62. These terms include expressions such as 'other gods' אלהים + אחר, 'provoke' כעס (2 Kgs 21.6) 'to do evil' עשׂה + רע, to 'break'(i.e. covenant) עבר, 'serve' (idols) עבד.

63. Talstra, *Solomon's Prayer*, pp. 105-106, 168. Talstra offers appendices of the Dtr expressions in Solomon's prayer and in the other Dtr orations, including a list of the words used in these other texts which are not used in 1 Kgs 8, pp. 267-87.

Yet, Solomon does not really offer the temple as a mechanism for undoing the exile. He does not pray for the end of the exile, he merely prays for mercy *within* exile (1 Kgs 8.46-50).[64] Punishment for the monarchic idolatry may be beyond the prayers given to Solomon, and yet, in communities that still see themselves as part of an Israel still exiled and estranged from Yahweh, the temple prayer of Solomon may provide a focus for their more immediate concerns. Indeed, Yahweh does accept this 'lesser' penitence in 1 Kgs. 9.3, as he hears Solomon's supplication and prayer. The following threats concerning the worship of 'other gods', however, seem to prevent this impression, but this is not really the case. Yahweh acknowledges his salvation of Israel from Egypt (v. 9), in the course of explaining his anger. This acknowledgment at least confirms acceptance of Israel as the inheritance of Yahweh (cf. Solomon's words in 1 Kgs 8.51-53). Exile is the punishment due Israel because of its relationship with Yahweh, not the cancellation of the relationship itself. For the readership, the punishment of exile has already been delivered; and, even if the temple is in ruins, may they yet pray to 'this place' and win the attention of Yahweh in heaven? Rather than make such prayers pointless, the temple's ruins make any such prayer necessarily fervent, as the petitioner must concentrate on the fact that Yahweh will not withhold judgment.

Rather than see the narrator coldly showing how Solomon's ill-conceived plan was finally defeated by its own selfishness and Yahweh's stubbornness, I prefer to see the author breaking Solomon down to the point where he can but pray for a merciful god. Solomon's temporary wisdom soon passes as his great celebration comes to an end. Solomon proves forgetful of his own lesson, and in any case he has not moved

---

64. In his second petition Solomon asks that a defeated Israel be 'restored to the land', אל־האדמה והשבתם (1 Kgs 8.34), should they repent and entreat Yahweh 'in this house', בבית הזה (v. 33). No report of the temple's post-conquest restoration is included in Kings, even though its destruction seems evident in 2 Kgs 25.9, 13-17, and so this request is hard to interpret. This may be a plea for an end to the Diaspora / exile, or, perhaps, merely to the return of the remnants of a defeated army. Such a scenario is plausible within the narrative world of monarchic Israel, but also may have some relevance in the post-monarchic world of the readers, as one might think of Israelite forces in the imperial military. The exile, however, is implied in the final petition, 1 Kgs 46–50, although here Yahweh is asked only to grant Israel mercy in the eyes of their captors. Moreover, the prayers are directed 'in the direction of the land', to the city and the temple. In these petitions, the temple is not imagined as destroyed.

the stern Yahweh to toleration of any such short-sightedness. 1 Kings 8, as much as it highlights the weakness of Solomon and plays a part in the chain of events leading to exile, remains as a moment out of time, which assimilates the entropy of Israel's religious history to a greater sense of eternity. Two opposite poles, of human hope for the perpetual divine presence and of fears of a divine wrath and absence, come together within it. Israel's integrity is reasserted, their origins in the grace of God affirmed. In this moment, Solomon enjoys his finest hour, if only in spite of himself. Moreover, it is an hour that somehow endures, despite the inexorable movement of time, and the disasters that have befallen Solomon's kingdom. The narrator seems convinced that Solomon had achieved something of a lasting significance when, in v. 65, it is reported that Solomon and Israel had celebrated the feast before 'Yahweh, *our* God', יהוה אלהינו / κυρίου θεοῦ ἡμῶν.[65] The narrator's self-assertion and assimilation to the 'Israel' of the reader brings a renewed relevance to the proceedings, especially since it is *'the* feast' החג that is celebrated, implying familiarity with the readers.[66] Moreover the narrative's contemporary significance is all the more mysteriously intimated by v. 8. Here the narrator tells the reader that the poles of the ark, בדים, are still in place, 'unto this day'.[67] The poles, which facilitated human contact with the holy relic, however, remain unseen. Is the ark still in the rubble somewhere? Will Yahweh still hear in heaven?

3. *Postscript: Solomon, Josiah and 'Exilic' Israel*

Israel went home from Jerusalem rejoicing in 1 Kgs 8.66, but there is an ominous sense that the moment cannot last and that everything will be swept away. There is no report of rejoicing at the end of Josiah's purge, despite the great Passover (2 Kgs 23.21-23): the temple is purified, but Judah is doomed. If anything, these two episodes are different sides of the same melancholy outlook on history. The Passover marks not only protection, but the start of a painful journey. Yet exile is the beginning of reintegration. The greatest relevance of Solomon's new innovation is to be found in the time of Israel's greatest shame

65. Twice in LXX. Long, *1 Kings*, pp. 94, comments that such a shift in perspective is rare in biblical literature.

66. Some hold that this is meant to be the Feast of Booths, cf. Lev. 23.34, e.g. Provan, *Kings*, p. 75.

67. Cf. Exod. 25.13-15.

when its structure is itself destroyed. As White has suggested, the end of a book is implicit from its outset. Yet, the early episode of 1 Kings 8 offers more than an intimation of the end of 2 Kings.[68] Solomon's greatest accomplishment suggests a strategy of accommodating the exile. The distance between the pre-arranged answer to the crisis of exile and the narration of that event itself preserves for that tragic story its full measure of horror. The proper response, therefore, is not hinted at too obviously. It is as if the reader is challenged by the reporting of the debacle to decide whether the past is among the casualties of Babylon or not. Is a 'new' religion and a new identity necessary, or merely the re-articulation of the 'true religion' of old and the deliberate promulgation of greater Israel as the people whom Yahweh has been concerned with since time immemorial? If the reader chooses the latter, the example of Josiah, who purged a doomed land and restored the covenant, is close at hand. Josiah's restoration of the sacred axis through Jerusalem (of which Kings only plays a part in a greater body of tradition) means that the city has become a beacon for an Israel that has transcended its own former (real or imagined) political borders. More daring or, perhaps, optimistic readers, however, may push their searching back even further into the monarchic history just read. At the very founding of the temporary temple cult, the symbols of the eternal union between Israel and Yahweh are affirmed against the certainty of exile. In this light, 1 Kings 8 has a role not only within the story-line of the book as a whole, but also as an event whose relevance is not confined by these temporal bounds. Like a myth, it records a moment out of time, whose transformative power is instantly accessible to the adherent. It is, therefore, the dedication of a sacred site which, however geographically defined, finds its true sacrality in the past, not the present. With such a focal point, both spatially and temporally, the whole of the world is given a sacred orientation. Wherever Israel may be scattered, there is a line of communion with the god of the sacred land, and sacred past.

Jerusalem, however, is a problematic centre. Claims and counter-claims to political power and prestige would have necessarily been part of Jerusalem's (and its rivals') articulation as a focal point in Judah-ist thought. With the great accent on the temple in 1 Kings 8, and 2 Kings 22–23, one may be inclined to suggest that Kings serves to legitimize a

---

68. White, 'Narrativity', p. 19.

post-monarchic Jerusalem cult as the only legitimate Yahwistic cult. On the other hand, so little is spoken in the book about specific cultic practices (indeed, 1 Kgs 8 seems to affirm the inadequacy of the temple), that what such a cult would have entailed is hard to determine. I would, in fact, make a distinction between the legitimization of a particular cult (or temple construction) on the one hand, and the legitimization of the temple site on the other. The persistent sacrality of the site, of course, could inspire any number of claims that any new or refurbished building on the site has direct continuity with the ancient ideal, or that any particular cult is the one Yahweh demands.[69] Increasing the number of claims, however, would only prove (at least to those involved in the dialogues) that the site is inherently sacred. On the other hand, the stories of Solomon's temple need not be in the service of one proposed cult in particular. One might speculate that adherents to other Yahwistic centres, perhaps in Samaria, or outside the lands of Judah and Israel, would have some sense of an ideal temple in whose sacrality their own installation could participate in some, perhaps limited, way. If one accepts the received wisdom that the LXX is a product of Egyptian translators, then perhaps that text's higher reputation for Solomon and its pro-temple bias was due to the need for a prototype for their own temple or sanctuary.[70] Here, I have in mind a similar situation to that proposed by Joan R. Branham, in regard to the later rise of the synagogue. According to her, the ancient synagogue was constantly involved in a dialectic between the assertion of its own legitimacy and viability, on the one hand, and acknowledgment of the bonds which tied it to the Jerusalem temple tradition, on the other. There was a tentative transference of the sanctity of the temple tradition to the synagogue, which introduced into the synagogue an endowment of what may be labelled 'vicarious sacrality'.[71] The synagogue appropriated the ritual and ontological importance of the temple. In so doing, however, the constructed temple model is both rivalled and

69. R.P. Carroll, 'What Do We *Know* about the Temple?', pp. 49-50.

70. See Schniedewind, 'Notes and Observations'. Of course, some of these features may be due to the Hebrew *Vorlage*, which does raise a number of other questions.

71. J.R. Branham, 'Vicarious Sacrality: Temple Space in Ancient Synagogues', in D. Urman and P.V.M. Fletcher (eds.), *Ancient Synagogues: Historical Analysis and Archaeological Discovery* (2 vols.; Leiden, E.J. Brill, 1995), II, pp. 319-45 (320).

threatened by the new institution.[72] The conflict escalates as the new institution comes to resemble more closely its ideal model; and that soon forbids imitation. This results in a double bind: Imitation is mandatory, and forbidden.[73] The double bind could be seen as part of the dialogues about Egyptian and other temples or shines in the post-monarchic world. Strategies, or perhaps better, structures, of legitimacy are probably too complex to reduce to a simple 'us' versus 'them' mentality. Multiple identities result in multiple self-images presented to the world. Temples, and other sacred installations, are not simply buildings; they are, themselves, images of the world and cosmos, repositories of the symbolic universe.[74]

On the other hand, duplication of an ideal need not entail duplication of every feature. Ronald E. Clements reports that rabbinic literature offers a number of five-point lists of features of the first temple which were absent from the second. *Midrash Num. R.* 15.10 lists the ark, the candlestick, fire, the holy spirit, and the cherubim. Talmud *Yom.* 21B lists the ark, its cover and the cherubim together, and the fire, Shekinah, holy spirit, and the Umim and Thummim, whereas *Yom.* 52B speaks of the ark, manna, water, Aaron's rod, and the chest of the Philistines. Figuring large in these lists are the absence of the Shekinah, the divine presence, and the holy spirit. The most vital features of the first temple were lacking in the second. Although this literature is relatively late, Clements holds that the perception of the absence of Yahweh dated from the construction of that second temple. The view eventually arose, in some circles, that the ideal temple, and indeed, city of Jerusalem, were in heaven, and not on earth at all.[75] The sense of a heavenly ideal, which may have been latent in any ancient Near Eastern perception of temples, therefore, relativizes the inviolability of the Solomonic temple. Regardless of what happened on earth, the ideal might still exist in heaven. But Yahweh could not actually dwell in *that* temple either, at least by Solomon's admission, since the whole heavens and earth could not contain him (1 Kgs 8.27).[76] Yet, by its connection with

---

72. Branham, 'Vicarious Sacrality', p. 335.

73. Branham, 'Vicarious Sacrality', p. 339.

74. Cf. Levenson, 'The Temple and the World'.

75. R.E. Clements, *God and Temple* (Oxford: Basil Blackwell, 1965), pp. 126-27. Petersen, 'The Temple', p. 128, also raises the question of the early date of the views expressed in the Rabbinic writings.

76. Levenson, 'The Temple', p. 289, writes that this disclaimer renounces the

that ideal, Solomon's temple, and by extension the real estate upon which it sat, marked the centre of the world.[77]

In my view, Kings' accent on Jerusalem reflects the imperative for accepting its uniqueness, and the desire to recreate, or perhaps better, to access, its sacrality in the exilic world that the writers saw themselves inhabiting. This recreation could easily offer power to whatever authorities were in control of the city. On the other hand, the ability of Solomon's temple to legitimize rival shrines meant that these authorities would potentially have had to negotiate rather carefully their own situation vis-à-vis the Solomonic prototype. Claims to the exclusive primacy of Jerusalem as a cultic site seems more of the problem faced by the writers than it is their proposed solution to questions of religious identity in the exile. Their logic seems to hold that, when Jerusalem was the sanctioned place, worship had to be exclusive, as was implied regarding Jeroboam's heterodox cult, and the polemic against the high places, found throughout Kings. This is despite some exceptions, that is, Elijah's sacrifices on Mt Carmel in 1 Kings 18. With the fall of Judah, however, Jerusalem's status is significantly altered. Jerusalem, however, is not the only sacred site that the biblical literature knows of. In Deuteronomy, there are numerous references to a site of Yahweh's choosing, which has numerous claims to exclusivity, but nowhere is there specific mention that this is Jerusalem.[78] J.G. McConville observes that in Joshua, the chosen place seems to be Shiloh. There stands the Tent of Meeting when Joshua convenes with all Israel, and there the land is apportioned. Other texts, such as Jer. 7.12 and Ps. 78.60 acknowledge the selection of Shiloh. He sees Zion not as the end point or dénouement of the story of the Hebrew Bible, but as a problem still in need of a solution:[79]

notion that Yahweh is physically present in the temple, as so many other scholars have noticed. Yet, 'The disclaimer distinguishes Temple from cosmos only by placing the same limitation on both. The Temple is less infinite, so to speak, than the world. Since the latter cannot contain God, a fortiori the former cannot. The distinction seems to be speaking in the context of a cosmology in which world and temple were thought to be comparable.'

77. Levenson, 'The Temple' offers an excellent analysis of this from biblical to Rabbinic literature.

78. Cf. Deut. 12.5, 11, 18, 21, 26; 14.23, 24, 25; 15.20; 16.2, 6, 7, 11, 15, 16; 17.8, 10; 18.6; 26.2; 31.11.

79. J.G. McConville, 'Time, Place and the Deuteronomic Altar-Law', in J.G. McConville and J.G. Millar, *Time and Place in Deuteronomy* (JSOTSup, 179;

> That problem arises sharply from the tension between, on the one hand, the 'givenness' of city and temple—a givenness implied in the symbolism of the temple itself, and perhaps of the city as political capital, and on the other, the liability of an errant covenant people to judgment.[80]

In my view, Kings does display a theme of cultic centralization while the affirmation of this centrality may actually be a strategy by which various other installations in other places are legitimized. This openness is effected not simply by the exile and rejection of the city and temple, but by the refusal to describe the rehabilitation of the temple. This strategy is not simply fatalistic, anti-Jerusalem, or bitterly ironic. Rather, it is a method of preservation (or construction) of symbols. I suspect that for the writers of Kings, sacrality per se was not found in specific institutions like the temple, priesthood, or political agencies, most of which may have been remote to the dispersed readership or, perhaps, not always accommodating to an 'Israel' that imagined itself still in exile. Rather, these institutions made manifest the sacrality of the cultural symbols preserved in stories and images of the past. The articulation of these symbols within such traditions not only provided means of legitimizing specific institutions, but also described the transformation of 'Israel' from its ancient to its contemporary situation, while preserving the sense of a timeless essence not totally dependent upon the contemporary institutions. In my view, the past imagined in Kings, therefore, does not so much offer unqualified legitimization for particular institutions as it does show their relative inadequacy or imply their impermanence. Even so, this past, however, remained a repository of symbols and ideals upon which the contemporary world was based.[81] The symbols and ideals offered routes to legitimization and to judgment. With the appearance of immunity to the transience of the mundane world, they were always accessible through ritual, prayer or the retelling and exegesis of the sacred history or myth by respected elders, other specialists, or even society's own critics. Whether Kings was deliberately produced as a part of the exegesis of earlier tradition or was produced for less 'serious' reasons, and only subsequently assimilated to the corpus of 'sacred' tradition and interpretation remains an open question. The ideals which seem implicit in the book, however,

Sheffield: Sheffield Academic Press, 1994), pp. 89-139 (91-96).

80. McConville, 'Time and Place', p. 96.

81. McConville, 'Time and Place', p. 123, writes, 'History with Israel's God cannot end in an institution dedicated to the status quo'.

have every right to be taken seriously as reflecting some level of serious social commentary.

Kings presented the ancient reader with a vast number of tools for imagining an essentially unified, if practically pluralistic, greater Israel as a single people of Yahweh. The book affirms that behind their rivalry, Judah and Israel are unified through history. The story of the monarchy is presented in the light of a unified exodus and other allusions to the pre-monarchic period, as well as that of the glory which was the United Monarchy. Symbols of theocratic leadership alternate between the south and north; the 'throne of Israel' carries with it more obligations than privileges while Israel and Judah share similar fates. Israel and Judah are more than siblings, they are different sides of the same coin. Kings does not smooth over their differences, but takes the harder road of accommodating them within a history in which there are no invulnerable heroes, no simple right and wrong. The two high points of this history, of course, are the exchange of 'houses' between the davidic dynasty and Yahweh, which culminates in Solomon's grand celebration in Jerusalem, and Josiah's reform which purifies the land whose promise has been withdrawn. How this dynamic history corresponded to social debates of the writer's own day is a question which must be asked, even if only to illustrate how it must be left unanswered. It is with a deliberate reluctance that I have addressed issues of provenance and historical context, and this only speculatively. The potential complexity of any representation of the past prevents confidence in this matter, especially since there is so little extra-textual data upon which to build. Yet the future may hold the promise of new data, and so some of the gaps in our knowledge may be filled. New approaches are also opening new doors, and these may lead to knowledge in areas only rarely explored at present. Perhaps these doors may lead even to some of the old questions taking on a new significance, with a renewed hope of reliable answers.

BIBLIOGRAPHY

Aberbach, M., and L. Smolar, 'Jeroboam's Rise to Power', *JBL* 88 (1969), pp. 69-72.

Ackroyd, P.R., 'An Interpretation of the Babylonian Exile: A Study of II Kings 20 and Isaiah 38–39', in P.R. Ackroyd, *Studies in the Religious Tradition of the Old Testament* (London: SCM Press, 1987), pp. 152-71, 282-85, originally in *SJT* 27 (1974), pp. 329-52.

Ahituv, S., 'Suzerain or Vassal? Notes on the Aramaic Inscription from Tel Dan', *IEJ* 43 (1993), pp. 246-47.

Ahlström, G.W., *The History of Ancient Palestine from the Palaeolithic Period to Alexander's Conquest* (JSOTSup, 146; Sheffield: Sheffield Academic Press, 1993).

Alt, A., 'The Formation of the Israelite State in Palestine', in A. Alt, *Essays on Old Testament History and Religion* (trans. R.A. Wilson; BibSem; Sheffield: Sheffield Academic Press, 1989), pp. 171-237, originally, 'Die Staatenbildung der Israeliten in Palästina', in A. Alt, *Reformationsprogramm der Universität Leipzig, 1930*, reprinted in A. Alt, *Kleine Schriften zur Geschichte des Volkes Israel* II (3 vols.; Munich: Beck, 1953), II, pp. 1-65.

Alter, R., *The Art of Biblical Narrative* (London: George Allen & Unwin, 1981).

Anderson, B., *Imagined Communities: Reflections on the Origin and Spread of Nationalism* (London: Verso, 1983).

Arnold, P., 'Mizpah', *ABD* 4, pp. 879-81.

Aronoff, M.J., 'Myths, Symbols, and Rituals of the Emerging State', in L.J. Silberstein (ed.), *New Perspectives on Israeli History: The Early Years of the State* (New York: New York University Press, 1991) pp. 175-92.

Ash, P.S., 'Solomon's? District? List', *JSOT* 67 (1995), pp. 67-86.

Auld, A.G., *Kings without Privilege: David and Moses in the Story of the Bible's Kings* (Edinburgh: T. & T. Clark, 1994).

—'Reading Joshua after Kings', in J. Davies, G. Harvey and W.G.E. Watson (eds.), *Words Remembered, Texts Renewed: Essays in Honour of John F.A. Sawyer* (JSOTSup, 195; Sheffield: Sheffield Academic Press, 1995), pp. 167-81.

Barr, J., 'The Synchronic, the Diachronic and the Historical: A Triangular Relationship?', in J.C. de Moor (ed.), *Synchronic or Diachronic? A Debate on Method in Old Testament Exegesis* (OTS, 34; Leiden: E.J. Brill, 1995), pp. 1-14.

Barth, F., 'Ethnic Groups and Boundaries', in F. Barth, *Process and Form in Social Life: Selected Essays of Fredrik Barth* (London: Routledge & Kegan Paul, 1981), I, pp. 198-227, originally: 'Introduction', in F. Barth (ed.), *Ethnic Groups and Boundaries* (Boston: Little, Brown & Co., 1969).

Begg, C.T., 'The Death of Josiah in Chronicles: Another View', *VT* 37 (1987), pp. 1-8.

—'The Death of Josiah: Josephus and the Bible', *ETL* 64 (1988), pp. 157-63.

—'The Interpretation of the Gedaliah Episode (2 Kgs 25,22-26) in Context', *Ant* 62 (1987), pp. 3-11.

—'2 Kings 20.12-19 as an Element of the Deuteronomistic History', *CBQ* 48 (1986), pp. 27-38.

—'The Reading at 2 Kings XX 13', *VT* 36 (1986), pp. 339-40.

—'The Significance of Jehoiachin's Release: A New Proposal', *JSOT* 36 (1986), pp. 49-56.

Beit-Hallami, B., 'Religion as Art and Identity', *Rel* 16 (1986), pp. 1-17.

Ben Zvi, E., 'The Account of the Reign of Manasseh in II Reg 21, 1-18 and the Redactional History of the Book of Kings', *ZAW* 103 (1991), pp. 355-74.

—'Inclusion in and Exclusion from Israel as Conveyed by the Use of the Term "Israel" in Post-Monarchic Biblical Texts', in E.W. Holloway and L.K. Handy (eds.), *The Pitcher is Broken: Memorial Essays for Gösta W. Ahlström* (JSOTSup, 190; Sheffield: Sheffield Academic Press, 1995), pp. 95-149.

—'Once the Lamp has been Kindled...: Reconsideration of the Meaning of the MT *Nîr* in 1 Kgs 11.36; 15.4; 2 Kgs 8.19; 2 Chr 21.7', *AusBR* 39 (1991), pp. 19-30.

—'Prophets and Prophecy in the Compositional and Redactional Notes in I–II Kings', *ZAW* 105 (1993), pp. 331-51.

Bergen, W.J., 'The Prophetic Alternative: Elisha and the Israelite Monarchy', in R.B. Coote (ed.), *Elijah and Elisha in Socioliterary Perspective* (SemS; Atlanta: Scholars Press, 1992), pp. 127-37.

Berger, P.L., and T. Luckmann, *The Social Construction of Reality: A Treatise in the Sociology of Knowledge* (Harmondsworth: Penguin Books, 1967).

Biran, A., and J. Naveh, 'An Aramaic Stele Fragment from Tel Dan', *IEJ* 43 (1993), pp. 81-98.

Bloch, M., 'Introduction', in M. Bloch (ed.), *Political Language and Oratory in Traditional Society* (London: Academic Press, 1975), pp. 1-28.

Block, D.I., '"Israel"–"Sons of Israel": A Study in Hebrew Eponymic Usage', *SR* 13 (1984), pp. 302-26.

Boer, R., *Jameson and Jeroboam* (SemS; Atlanta: Scholars Press, 1996).

Boer, P.A.H. de, 'Egypt in the Old Testament: Some Aspects of an Ambivalent Assessment', in P.A.H. de Boer, *Selected Studies in Old Testament Exegesis* (OTS, 27; Leiden: E.J. Brill, 1991), pp. 152-67.

Bolin, T.M., 'When the End is the Beginning: The Persian Period and the Origins of the Biblical Tradition', *SJOT* 10 (1996), pp. 3-15.

Bond, G.C., and A. Gilliam, 'Introduction', in G.C. Bond and A. Gilliam (eds.), *Social Construction of the Past: Representation as Power* (OWA, 24; London: Routledge, 1994), pp. 1-22.

Boon, J.A., *Other Tribes, Other Scribes: Symbolic Anthropology in the Comparative Study of Cultures, Histories, Religions and Texts* (Cambridge: Cambridge University Press, 1982).

Borowski, O., 'Hezekiah's Reform and the Revolt against Assyria', *BA* 58 (1995), pp. 148-55.

Brass, P.R., *Ethnicity and Nationalism: Theory and Comparison* (New Delhi: Sage, 1991).

Brenner A. (ed.), *A Feminist Companion to Samuel and Kings* (The Feminist Companion to the Bible, 5; Sheffield: Sheffield Academic Press, 1994).

Brettler, M., *God is King: Understanding an Israelite Metaphor* (JSOTSup, 79; Sheffield: Sheffield Academic Press, 1989).

—Review of *The First Historians: The Hebrew Bible and History* (San Franciso: Harper & Row, 1988), by B. Halpern, in *JRel* 70 (1990), pp. 83-84.

—'Ideology, History, and Theology in 2 Kings XVII 7-23', *VT* 39 (1989), pp. 268-82.

—'Interpretation and Prayer: Notes on the Composition of 1 Kgs 8.15-53', in M. Brettler and M. Fishbane (eds.) *Minhah le-Nahum: Biblical and Other Studies Presented to Nahum M. Sarna in Honour of his 70th Birthday* (JSOTSup, 154; Sheffield: JSOT Press, 1993), pp. 17-35.

—'The Structure of 1 Kings 1–11', *JSOT* 49 (1991), pp. 87-97.

Burney, C.F., *Notes on the Hebrew Text of the Book of Kings* (Oxford: Clarendon Press, 1903).

Calhoun, C., 'Social Theory and the Politics of Identity', in C. Calhoun (ed.), *Social Theory and the Politics of Identity* (Oxford: Basil Blackwell, 1994), pp. 9-36.

Campbell, A.F., 'Martin Noth and the Deuteronomistic History', in S.L. McKenzie and M.P. Graham (eds.), *The History of Israel's Traditions* (JSOTSup, 182; Sheffield: Sheffield Academic Press, 1994), pp. 31-62.

—*Of Prophets and Kings: A Late Ninth-Century Document (1 Samuel–2 Kings 10)* (CBQMS, 17; Washington, DC: Catholic Biblical Association, 1986).

Carlson, R.A., *David, the Chosen King: A Traditio-Historical Approach to the Second Book of Samuel* (Stockholm: Almqvist & Wiksell, 1964).

Carroll, R.P., *Jeremiah: A Commentary* (London: SCM Press, 1986).

—'So What Do We *Know* about the Temple? The Temple in the Prophets', in T.C. Eskenazi and K.H. Richards (eds.), *Second Temple Studies. II. Temple Community in the Persian Period* (JSOTSup, 175; Sheffield: Sheffield Academic Press, 1994), pp. 34-51.

—'Textual Strategies and Ideology in the Second Temple Period', in P.R. Davies (ed.), *Second Temple Studies. I. The Persian Period* (JSOTSup, 117; Sheffield: Sheffield Academic Press, 1991), pp. 108-24.

Clements, R.E., *God and Temple* (Oxford: Basil Blackwell, 1965).

Cogan, M., 'For We, Like You, Worship your God: Three Biblical Portrayals of Samaritan Origins', *VT* 38 (1988), pp. 286-92.

—'Israel in Exile: The View of a Josianic Historian', *JBL* 97 (1978), pp. 40-44.

Cogan, M., and H. Tadmor, *II Kings* (AB, 11; New York: Doubleday, 1984).

Coggins, R., '2 Kings 23:29: A Problem of Method in Translation', in C. Breckelmans and J. Lust (eds.), *Pentateuchal and Deuteronomistic Studies: Papers Read at the XIIIth IOSOT Congress Leuven 1989* (Leuven: Leuven University Press, 1990), pp. 278-81.

—'What Does "Deuteronomistic" Mean?', in J. Davies, G. Harvey and W.G.E. Watson (eds.), *Words Remembered, Texts Renewed: Essays in Honour of John F.A. Sawyer* (JSOTSup, 195; Sheffield: Sheffield Academic Press, 1995), pp. 135-48.

Cohen, A.P., *The Symbolic Construction of Community* (KIS; Open University, London: Routledge, 1985).

Cohn, R.L., 'Convention and Creativity in the Book of Kings: The Case of the Dying Monarch', *CBQ* 47 (1985), pp. 603-16.

—'Literary Technique in the Jeroboam Narrative', *ZAW* 97 (1985), pp. 23-35.

Conrad, E.W., 'Heard but not Seen: The Representation of "Books" in the Old Testament', *JSOT* 54 (1992), pp. 45-59.

Conroy, C., 'Reflections on the Exegetical Task: Apropos of Recent Studies on 2 Kings 22–23', in C. Breckelmans and J. Lust (eds.), *Pentateuchal and Deuteronomistic*

Studies: Papers Read at the XIIIth IOSOT Congress, Leuven 1989 (Leuven: Leuven University Press, 1990), pp. 255-68.

Cook, A., 'Fiction and History in Samuel and Kings', *JSOT* 36 (1986), pp. 27-48.

Cortese, E., 'Theories Concerning Dtr: A Possible Rapprochement', in C. Breckelmans and J. Lust (eds.) *Pentateuchal and Deuteronomistic Studies: Papers Read at the XIIIth IOSOT Congress, Leuven 1989* (Leuven: Leuven University Press, 1990), pp. 179-90.

Cowley, R.W., 'Technical Terms in Biblical Hebrew?', *TynBul* 37 (1986), pp. 21-28.

Cross, F.M., 'The Themes of the Book of Kings and the Structure of the Deuteronomistic History', in F.M. Cross, *Canaanite Myth and Hebrew Epic: Essays in the History of the Religion of Israel* (Cambridge, MA: Harvard University Press, 1973), pp. 274-87, originally, 'The Structure of the Deuteronomistic History', in J.M. Rosenthal (ed.), *Perspectives in Jewish Learning* (Chicago: College of Jewish Studies, 1967), pp. 9-24.

Danell, G.A., *Studies in the Name Israel in the Old Testament* (Uppsala: Appelbergs Boktryckeri, 1946).

Davies, P.R., 'God of Cyrus, God of Israel', in J. Davies, G. Harvey and W.G.E. Watson (eds.), *Words Remembered, Texts Renewed: Essays in Honour of John F.A. Sawyer* (JSOTSup, 195; Sheffield: Sheffield Academic Press, 1995), pp. 207-25.

—*In Search of 'Ancient Israel'* (JSOTSup, 148; Sheffield: Sheffield Academic Press, 2nd edn, 1992).

—'Method and Madness: Some Remarks on Doing History with the Bible', *JBL* 114 (1995), pp. 699-705.

—'Scenes from the Early History of Judaism', in D.V. Edelman (ed.) *The Triumph of Elohim: From Jahwisms to Judaisms* (CBET, 13; Kampen: Kok, 1995), pp. 145-82.

—(ed.), *Second Temple Studies. I. The Persian Period* (JSOTSup, 117; Sheffield: JSOT Press, 1991).

Dearman, J.A., review of *Narrative History and Ethnic Boundaries: The Deuteronomistic Historian and the Creation of Israelite National Identity* (SBLSS; Atlanta: Scholars Press, 1993), by E. Theodore Mullen, Jr, in *JBL* 114 (1995), pp. 301-302.

DeNora, T., and H. Mehan, 'Genius: A Social Construction, The Case of Beethoven's Initial Recognition', in T.H. Sarbin and J.I. Kitusse (eds.), *Constructing the Social* (London: Sage, 1994), pp. 157-73.

Deurloo, K.A., 'The King's Wisdom in Judgment: Narration as Example (I Kings iii)', in A.S. van der Woude (ed.), *New Avenues in the Study of the Old Testament* (OTS, 25; Leiden: E.J. Brill, 1989), pp. 11-21.

De Vries, S.J., *1 Kings* (WBC, 12; Waco, TX: Word Books, 1985).

Dexinger, F., 'Limits of Tolerance in Judaism: The Samaritan Example', in E.P. Sanders, A.I. Baumgarten and A. Mendelson (eds.), *Jewish and Christian Self-Definition: Aspects of Judaism in the Graeco-Roman Period* (Philadelphia: Fortress Press, 1981), II, pp. 88-114.

Diebner, B.J., and C. Nauerth, 'Die Inventio des ה35ה ספר in 2 Kön 22. Struktur, Intention und Funktion von Auffindungslegenden', *DBAT* 18 (1984), pp. 95-118.

Dietrich, W., 'Josia und das Gesetzbuch (2 Reg. XXII)', *VT* 27 (1977), pp. 13-35.

—'Martin Noth and the Future of the Deuteronomistic History', in S.L. McKenzie and M.P. Graham (eds.), *The History of Israel's Traditions: The Heritage of Martin Noth* (JSOTSup, 182; Sheffield: Sheffield Academic Press, 1994), pp. 153-75.

—*Prophetie und Geschichte: Eine redaktionsgeschichtliche Untersuchung zum deuterono-mistischen Geschichtswerk* (FRLANT, 108; Göttingen: Vandenhoek & Ruprecht, 1972).

Dutcher-Walls, P., *Narrative Art, Political Rhetoric: The Case of Athaliah and Joash* (JSOTSup, 209; Sheffield, Sheffield Academic Press, 1996).

—'The Social Location of the Deuteronomists: A Sociological Study of Factional Politics in Late Pre-Exilic Judah', *JSOT* 52 (1991), pp. 77-94.

Edelman, D.V., 'Solomon's Adversaries Hadad, Rezon and Jeroboam: A Trio of 'Bad Guy' Characters Illustrating the Theology of Immediate Retribution', in S.W. Holloway and L.K. Handy (eds.), *The Pitcher is Broken: Memorial Essays for Gösta W. Ahlström* (JSOTSup, 190; Sheffield: Sheffield Academic Press, 1995), pp. 166-91.

Eskenazi, T.C., 'Current Perspectives on Ezra–Nehemiah and the Persian Period', *CRBS* 1 (1993), pp. 59-86.

Eskenazi, T.C., and E.P. Judd, 'Marriage to a Stranger in Ezra 9–10', in T.C. Eskenazi and K.H. Richards (eds.), *Second Temple Studies. II. Temple Community in the Persian Period* (JSOTSup, 175; Sheffield: JSOT Press, 1994), pp. 267-85.

Eskenazi, T.C., and K.H. Richards (eds.), *Second Temple Studies. II. Temple Community in the Persian Period* (JSOTSup, 175; Sheffield: JSOT Press, 1994).

Eslinger, L., *House of God or House of David: The Rhetoric of 2 Samuel 7* (JSOTSup, 164; Sheffield: JSOT Press, 1994).

—*Into the Hands of the Living God* (JSOTSup, 84; Sheffield: Almond Press, 1989).

—'Josiah and the Torah Book: Comparison of 2 Kgs 22.1–23.28 and 2 Chr 34.1–35.19', *HAR* 10 (1986), pp. 37-62.

—*Kingship of God in Crisis: A Close Reading of 1 Samuel 1–12* (BLS, 10; Sheffield, Almond Press, 1985), pp. 307-309.

Evans, C.D., 'Naram-Sin and Jeroboam: The Archetypal *Unheilsherrscher* in Mesopotamia and Biblical Historiography', in W. Hallo, J. Moyer and L. Perdue (eds.), *Scripture in Context: More Essays on the Comparative Method* (Bloomington: Indiana University Press, 1983), II, pp. 97-125.

Eynikel, E., *The Reform of King Josiah and the Composition of the Deuteronomistic History* (OTS, 33; Leiden: E.J. Brill, 1996).

Finnegan, R., *Literacy and Orality: Studies in the Technology of Communication* (Oxford: Basil Blackwell, 1988).

Flanagan, J.W., 'The Deuteronomic Meaning of the Phrase "kol yisra'el"', *SR* 6 (1976–77), pp. 159-68.

—'Judah in All Israel', in J.W. Flanagan and A.W. Robinson (eds.), *No Famine in the Land: Studies in Honor of John L. McKenzie* (Missoula, MT: Scholars Press, 1975), pp. 101-16.

Fohrer, G., *Introduction to the Old Testament* (trans. D.E. Green; Nashville: Abingdon Press, 1968), p. 194. German original, *Einleitung in das Alte Testament* (Heidelberg: Quelle & Meyer, 1965).

Frevel, C., 'Vom Schreiben Gottes Literarkritik, Komposition und Auslesung von 2 Kön 17, 34-40', *Bib* 72 (1991), pp. 23-48.

Friedman, J., 'Myth, History and Political Identity', *CulAnth* 7 (1992), pp. 194-210.

—'Notes on Culture and Identity in Imperial Worlds', in P. Bilde, T. Engberg-Pedersen, L. Hannestad and J. Zahle (eds.), *Religion and Religious Practice in the Selucid Kingdom* (SHC; Aarhus: Aarhus University Press, 1990) pp. 14-39.

Friedman, R.E., *The Exile and Biblical Narrative: The Formation of the Deuteronomistic and Priestly Works* (HSM, 22; Chico, CA: Scholars Press, 1981).

—'From Egypt to Egypt: Dtr1 and Dtr2', in B. Halpern and J.D. Levenson (eds.), *Traditions in Transformation* (Winona Lake, IN: Eisenbrauns, 1981), pp. 167-92.

Frisch, A., 'The Narrative of Solomon's Reign: A Rejoinder', *JSOT* 51 (1991), pp. 22-24.

—'Shemaiah the Prophet versus King Rehoboam: Two Opposed Interpretations of the Schism (I Kings xii 21-4)', *VT* 38 (1988), pp. 466-68.

—'Structure and its Significance: The Narrative of Solomon's Reign (1 Kings 1–12.24)', *JSOT* 51 (1991), pp. 3-14.

Galil, G., *The Chronology of the Kings of Israel and Judah* (SHCANE, 9; Leiden: E.J. Brill, 1996).

Garbini, G., 'Hebrew Literature in the Persian Period', in T.C. Eskenazi and K.H. Richards (eds.), *Second Temple Studies*. II. *Temple Community in the Persian Period* (JSOTSup, 175; Sheffield: JSOT Press, 1994), pp. 180-88.

García-Treto, F.O., 'The Fall of the House: A Carnivalesque Reading of 2 Kings 9 and 10', *JSOT* 46 (1990), pp. 47-65.

Gieselmann, B., 'Die sogenannten josianische Reform in der gegenwärtigen Forschung', *ZAW* 106 (1994), pp. 223-42.

Gilhus, I.S., 'Carnival in Religion: The Feast of Fools in France', *Numen* 37 (1990), pp. 24-52.

—'Religion, Laughter and the Ludicrous', *Rel* 21 (1991), pp. 257-77.

Gelinas, M.M., 'United Monarchy–Divided Monarchy: Fact or Fiction?', in S.W. Holloway and L.K. Handy (eds.), *The Pitcher is Broken: Memorial Essays for Gösta W. Ahlström* (JSOTSup, 190; Sheffield: Sheffield Academic Press, 1995), pp. 227-37.

Gerbrandt, G.E., *Kingship According to the Deuteronomistic History* (SBLDS, 87; Atlanta: Scholars Press, 1986).

Glatt-Gilad, D.A., 'The Role of Huldah's Prophecy in the Chronicle's Portrayal of Josiah's Reform', *Bib* 77 (1996), pp. 16-31.

Glück, J.J., 'Nagid-Shepherd', *VT* 13 (1963), pp. 144-50.

Gooding, D.W., 'Pedantic Timetabling in the 3rd Book of Reigns', *VT* 15 (1965), pp. 153-66.

—'The Septuagint's Rival Versions of Jeroboam's Rise to Power', *VT* 17 (1967), pp. 173-89.

Goodman, L.E., 'Mythic Discourse', in S. Biderman and B.-A. Scharfstein (eds.), *Myths and Fictions* (Leiden: E.J. Brill, 1993), pp. 51-112.

Gordon, R.P., 'The Second Septuagint Account of Jeroboam: History or Midrash?', *VT* 25 (1975), pp. 368-93.

Grabbe, L.L., *Judaism from Cyrus to Hadrian*. I. *The Persian and Greek Periods* (Minneapolis: Fortress Press, 1992).

Gray, J., *I and II Kings* (OTL; Philadelphia: Westminster Press, 2nd edn, 1970).

Hall, R.G., *Revealed Histories: Techniques for Ancient Jewish and Christian Historiography* (JSPSup, 6; Sheffield: JSOT Press, 1991).

Halpern, B., *The Constitution of the Monarchy in Israel* (Chico, CA: Scholars Press, 1981).

—Review of *In Search of History: Historiography in the Ancient World and the Origins of Biblical History* (New Haven & London: Yale University Press, 1983), by John Van Seters, in *JBL* 104 (1985), pp. 506-509.

—*The First Historians: The Hebrew Bible and History* (San Francisco: Harper & Row, 1988).

Halpern, B., and D.S. Vanderhooft, 'The Editions of Kings in the 7th–6th Centuries B.C.E.', *HUCA* 62 (1991), pp. 179-244.

Hamilton, M.W., 'Who Was a Jew?: Jewish Ethnicity During the Achaemenid Period', *ResQ* 37 (1995), pp. 102-17.

Handy, L.K., 'Hezekiah's Unlikely Reform', *ZAW* 100 (1988), pp. 111-15.

—'Historical Probability and the Narrative of Josiah's Reform in 2 Kings', in S.W. Holloway and L.K. Handy (eds.), *The Pitcher is Broken: Memorial Essays for Gösta W. Ahlström* (JSOTSup, 190; Sheffield: Sheffield Academic, 1995), pp. 252-75.

—'The Role of Huldah in Josiah's Cult Reform', *ZAW* 106 (1994), pp. 40-53.

Harvey, G. *The True Israel: Uses of the Names Jew, Hebrew and Israel in Ancient Jewish and Early Christian Literature* (AGJU, 35; Leiden: E.J. Brill, 1996).

Hastrup, K., 'Establishing an Ethnicity: The Emergence of the "Icelanders" in the Early Middle Ages', in D. Parkin (ed.), *Semantic Anthropology* (ASAM, 22; London: Academic Press, 1982), pp. 146-60.

Hobbs, T.R., *2 Kings* (WBC, 13; Waco, TX: Word Books, 1985).

Hobsbawm, E., and T. Ranger (eds.), *The Invention of Tradition* (Cambridge: Cambridge University Press, 1983).

Hoffman, Y., 'The Deuteronomist and the Exile', in D.P. Wright, D.N. Freedman and A. Hurvitz (eds.), *Pomegranates and Golden Bells: Studies in Biblical, Jewish, and Near Eastern Ritual, Law, and Literature in Honor of Jacob Milgrom* (Winona Lake, IN: Eisenbrauns, 1995), pp. 659-75.

Hoffmann, H.-D., *Reform und Reformen* (ATANT, 66; Zürich: Theologischer Verlag, 1980).

Hogland, K., *Achaemenid Imperial Administration in Syria-Palestine and the Missions of Ezra and Nehemiah* (SBLDS, 125; Atlanta: Scholars Press, 1992).

Holder, J., 'The Presuppositions, Accusations, and Threats of 1 Kings 14:1-18', *JBL* 107 (1988), pp. 27-38.

Holladay, W.L., *Jeremiah. II. A Commentary on the Book of the Prophet Jeremiah Chapters 26-52* (Hermeneia; Minneapolis: Fortress Press, 1989).

Hollenstein, H., 'Literarkritische Erwägungen zum Bericht über die Reformmassnahmen Josias 2 Kön. XXIII 4ff.', *VT* 27 (1977), pp. 321-36.

Holt, E. K., '" ... urged on by his wife Jezebel": A Literary Reading of 1 Kgs 18 in Context', *SJOT* 9 (1995), pp. 83-96.

Hughes, J., *Secrets of the Times: Myth and History in Biblical Chronology* (JSOTSup, 66; Sheffield: JSOT Press, 1990).

Huizinga, J., 'A Definition of the Concept of History', in R. Klibansky and H.J. Paton (eds.), *Philosophy and History: Essays Presented to Ernst Cassirer* (Oxford: Clarendon Press, 1963), pp. 1-10.

Ishida, T., *The Royal Dynasties in Ancient Israel: A Study on the Formation and Development of Royal-Dynastic Ideology* (BZAW, 142; New York: W. de Gruyter, 1977).

Jamieson-Drake, D.W., *Scribes and Schools in Monarchic Judah: A Socio-Archeological Approach* (JSOTSup, 109; Sheffield: Almond Press, 1991).

Jensen, H.J.L., 'The Fall of the King', *SJOT* 1 (1991), pp. 121-47.

Jobling, D., '"Forced Labor": Solomon's Golden Age and the Question of Literary Representation', *Sem* 54 (1991), pp. 59-76.

Johnson, W.M., 'Ethnicity in Persian Yehud: Between Anthropological Analysis and Ideological Criticism', *SBL 1995 Seminar Papers* (Atlanta: Scholars Press, 1995), pp. 177-86.

Jones, G.H., *1 and 2 Kings* (2 vols.; NCBC; London: Marshall, Morgan & Scott, 1984).

Kertzer, D.I., *Ritual, Politics and Power* (New Haven: Yale University Press, 1988).

Keulen, P.S.F. van., 'The Meaning of the Phrase *WN'SPT 'L-QBRTYK BŠLWM* in 2 Kings XXII 20', *VT* 46 (1996), pp. 256-60.

Knibb, M.A., 'The Exile in the Literature of the Intertestamental Period', *HeyJ* 17 (1976), pp. 253-72.

Knoppers, G.N., 'The Deuteronomist and the Deuteronomic Law of the King: A Reexamination of a Relationship', *ZAW* 108 (1996), pp. 329-46.

—'Prayer and Propaganda: Solomon's Dedication of the Temple and the Deuteronomist's Program', *CBQ* 57 (1995), pp. 229-54.

—'"There was none like Him": Incomparability in the Books of Kings', *CBQ* 54 (1992), pp. 411-31.

—*Two Nations Under God: The Deuteronomistic History of Solomon and the Dual Monarchies. I. The Reign of Solomon and the Rise of Jeroboam* (HSM, 52; Atlanta: Scholars Press, 1993).

—*Two Nations Under God: The Deuteronomistic History of Solomon and the Dual Monarchies. II. The Reign of Jeroboam, the Fall of Israel, and the Reign of Josiah* (HSM, 53; Atlanta: Scholars Press, 1994).

Kraemer, D., 'On the Relationship of the Books of Ezra and Nehemiah', *JSOT* 59 (1993), pp. 73-92.

Kristeva, J., 'Word, Dialogue and Novel', in J. Kristeva, *The Kristeva Reader* (ed. T. Moi; New York: Columbia University Press, 1986), pp. 35-61. French original in *Séméiotiké*, 1969.

Landy, F., *Hosea* (Readings; Sheffield: Sheffield Academic Press, 1995).

Laato, A., *Josiah and David Redivivus: The Historical Josiah and the Messianic Expectations of Exilic and Postexilic Times* (ConB, 33; Stockholm: Almqvist & Wiksell, 1992).

Lemche, N.P., *Ancient Israel: A New History of Israelite Society* (BibSem; Sheffield: Sheffield Academic Press, 1988).

—*The Canaanites and their Land: The Tradition of the Canaanites* (JSOTSup, 110; Sheffield: JSOT Press, 1991).

—'Clio is also among the Muses' Keith W. Whitelam and the History of Palestine: A Review and Commentary', *SJOT* 10 (1996), pp. 88-114.

—'Is it still Possible to Write a History of Ancient Israel?', *SJOT* 8 (1994), pp. 165-90.

—'The Old Testament: A Hellenistic Book?', *SJOT* 7 (1993), pp. 163-93.

Lemche, N.P., and T.L. Thompson, 'Did Biran Kill David?: The Bible in the Light of Archaeology', *JSOT* 64 (1994), pp. 3-22.

Levenson, J.D., 'Who Inserted the Book of the Torah?', *HTR* 68 (1975), pp. 203-33.

—'The Last Four Verses in Kings', *JBL* 103 (1984), pp. 353-61.

—'From Temple to Synagogue: 1 Kings 8', in B. Halpern and J.D. Levenson (eds.) *Traditions in Transformation* (Winona Lake, IN: Eisenbrauns, 1981), pp. 143-66.

—'The Temple and the World', *JR* 64 (1984), pp. 275-98.

Lévi-Strauss, C. 'From Mythical Possibility to Social Existence', in *The View from Afar* (trans. J. Neugroschcel and P. Hoss; Oxford: Basil Blackwell, 1985), pp. 157-74.

Levin, C., 'Joschija im deuteronomistichen Geschichtswerk', *ZAW* 96 (1984), pp. 351-71.

Lincoln, B., *Discourse and the Construction of Society: Comparative Studies of Myth, Ritual, and Classification* (Oxford: Oxford University Press, 1989).

Linville, J.R., 'Rethinking the "Exilic" Book of Kings', (forthcoming, *JSOT*).

Lipiński, E., 'NAGID, der Kronprinz', *VT* 24 (1974), pp. 497-99.

Loewenstamm, S.E., "נחלת ה", in S. Japhet (ed.) *Scripta Hierosolymitana: Publications of the Hebrew University, Jerusalem:* XXXI *Studies in Bible 1986* (Jerusalem: Magnes Press, 1986), pp. 155-92.

Lohfink, N., 'The Cult Reform of Josiah of Judah: 2 Kings 22–23 as a Source for the History of Israelite Religion', in P.D. Miller, P.D. Hanson and S.D. McBride (eds.), *Ancient Israelite Religion: Essays in Honor of Frank Moore Cross* (Philadelphia: Fortress Press, 1987), pp. 459-75.

—'Kerygmata des deuteronomistischen Geschichtswerks', in J. Jeremias and L. Perlitt (eds.) *Die Botschaft und die Boten: Festschrift für Hans Walter Wolff zum 70. Geburtstag* (Neukirchen–Vluyn: Neukirchener Verlag, 1981), pp. 87-100.

—'Zur neueren Diskussion über 2 Kön 22-23', in N. Lohfink (ed.), *Das Deuteronomium: Entstehung, Gestalt und Botschaft* (BETL, 68; Leuven: Leuven University Press, 1985), pp. 24-48.

Long, B.O., 'Historical Narrative and the Fictionalizing Imagination', *VT* 35 (1985), pp. 405-16.

—*1 Kings, with an Introduction to Historical Literature* (FOTL, 9; Grand Rapids: Eerdmans, 1984).

—*2 Kings* (FOTL, 10; Grand Rapids: Eerdmans, 1991).

Long, V.P., *The Art of Biblical History* (FCI, 5; Grand Rapids: Zondervan, 1994).

Lowery, R.H., *The Reforming Kings: Cult and Society in First Temple Judah* (JSOTSup, 120; Sheffield: JSOT Press, 1991).

Lundbom, J.R., 'The Lawbook of the Josianic Reform', *CBQ* 38 (1976), pp. 293-302.

Macdonald, J., 'The Structure of II Kings xvii', *GUOST* 23 (1969), pp. 29-41.

Macholz, G.C., 'NAGID–der Statthalter, "praefectus"', *DBAT* 1 (1975), pp. 59-72.

Mandell, S., 'Religion, Politics, and the Social Order: The Creation of the History of Ancient Israel', in J. Neusner (ed.), *Religion and the Political Order: Politics in Classical and Contemporary Christianity, Islam and Judaism* (SRSO, 15; Atlanta: Scholars Press, 1996), pp. 33-47.

McCarter, P.K. Jr, *II Samuel* (AB, 9; Garden City, NY: Doubleday, 1984).

McCarthy, D.J., 'II Samuel 7 and the Structure of the Deuteronomic History', *JBL* 84 (1965), pp. 131-38.

McConville, J.G., '1 Kings VIII 46–53 and the Deuteronomic Hope', *VT* 42 (1992), pp. 67-79.

—'Narrative and Meaning in the Books of Kings', *Bib* 70 (1989), pp. 31-49.

—'Time, Place and the Deuteronomic Altar-Law', in J.G. McConville and J.G. Millar, *Time and Place in Deuteronomy* (JSOTSup, 179; Sheffield: Sheffield Academic Press, 1994), pp. 89-139.

McKane, W., *A Critical and Exegetical Commentary on Jeremiah.* II. *Commentary on Jeremiah XXVI-LII* (ICC; Edinburgh: T. & T. Clark, 1996).

McKenzie, S.L., 'The Prophetic Record in Kings', *HAR* 10 (1985), pp. 203-20.

—*The Trouble with Kings: The Composition of the Book of Kings in the Deuteronomistic History* (VTSup, 42; Leiden: E.J. Brill, 1991).

—'The Source for Jeroboam's Role at Shechem (I Kgs 11:43–12:3, 12, 20)', *JBL* 106 (1987), pp. 297-300.

McKenzie, S.L., and M.P. Graham (eds.), *The History of Israel's Traditions: The Heritage of Martin Noth* (JSOTSup, 182; Sheffield: Sheffield Academic Press, 1994).

Mettinger, T.N.D., *King and Messiah: The Civil and Sacral Legitimation of the Israelite Kings* (Lund: C.W.K. Gleerup, 1976).

Meyers, E.C., 'Second Temple Studies in the Light of Recent Archaeology. I. The Persian and Hellenistic Periods', *CRBS* 2 (1994), pp. 25-42.

Millar, J.G., 'Living at the Place of Decision: Time and Place in the Framework of Deuteronomy', in J.G. Millar and J.G. McConville, *Time and Place in Deuteronomy* (JSOTSup, 179; Sheffield: Sheffield Academic Press, 1994), pp. 15-88.

Millard, A.R., J.K. Hoffmeier and D.W. Baker, *Faith, Tradition and History: Old Testament Historiography in its Near Eastern Context* (Winona Lake, IN: Eisenbrauns, 1994).

Miller, J.M., 'Is it Possible to Write a History of Israel without Relying on the Hebrew Bible?', in D.V. Edelman (ed.), *The Fabric of History, Text, Artefact and Israel's Past* (JSOTSup, 127; Sheffield: JSOT Press, 1991), pp. 93-102.

Miscall, P.D., Review of *Narrative History and Ethnic Boundaries: The Deuteronomistic Historian and the Creation of Israelite National Identity* (SBLSS; Atlanta: Scholars Press, 1993), by E.T. Mullen Jr, in *CBQ* 57 (1995), pp. 151-52.

—*1 Samuel: A Literary Reading* (ISBL; Bloomington: Indiana University Press, 1986).

Montgomery, J.A., 'Archival Data in the Book of Kings', *JBL* 53 (1934), pp. 46-52.

—*A Critical and Exegetical Commentary on the Books of Kings* (ed. H.S. Gehman; ICC; Edinburgh: T. & T. Clark, 1951).

Moore, S.F., 'Epilogue: Uncertainties in Situations, Indeterminacies in Culture', in S.F. Moore and B.G. Myerhoff (eds.), *Symbol and Politics in Communal Ideology* (Ithaca: Cornell University Press, 1975), pp. 210-39.

Mullen, E.T., Jr, 'Crime and Punishment; The Sins of the King and the Despoliation of the Treasuries', *CBQ* 54 (1992), pp. 231-48.

—*Narrative History and Ethnic Boundaries: The Deuteronomistic History and the Creation of Israelite National Identity* (SBLSS; Atlanta: Scholars Press, 1993).

—'The Royal Dynastic Grant to Jehu and the Structure of the Book of Kings', *JBL* 107 (1988), pp. 193-206.

Na'aman, N., 'The Debated Historicity of Hezekiah's Reform in the Light of Archaeological Research', *ZAW* 107 (1995), pp. 179-95.

Nelson, R.D., 'The Anatomy of the Book of Kings', *JSOT* 40 (1988), pp. 39-48.

—*The Double Redaction of the Deuteronomistic History* (JSOTSup, 18; Sheffield: JSOT Press, 1981).

—*First and Second Kings* (IntCom; Atlanta: John Knox, 1987).

—'*Realpolitik* in Judah (687–609 B.C.E.)', in W.W. Hallo, J.C. Moyer and L.G. Perdue (eds.) *Scripture in Context: More Essays on the Comparative Method* (Winona Lake, IN: Eisenbrauns, 1983), II, pp. 177-89.

Neusner, J., *The Foundations of the Theology of Judaism: An Anthology. III. Israel* (SHJ, 48; Atlanta: Scholars Press, 1992).

—*Judaism and its Social Metaphors: Israel in the History and Jewish Thought* (Cambridge: Cambridge University Press, 1989).

Nicholson, E.W., *Deuteronomy and Tradition* (Philadelphia: Fortress Press, 1967).

—'Story and History in the Old Testament', in S.E. Balentine and J. Barton (eds.) *Language, Theology and the Bible: Essays in Honour of James Barr* (Oxford: Clarendon Press, 1994), pp. 135-50.

Nohrnberg, J.C., *Like unto Moses: The Constituting of an Interruption* (ISBL; Bloomington: Indiana University Press, 1995).

Noth, M., *The Deuteronomistic History* (trans. J. Doull, J. Barton, M.D. Rutter and D.R. Ap-Thomas; JSOTSup, 15; Sheffield: JSOT Press, 1981), original: *Überlieferungsgeschichtliche Studien* (Tübingen: M. Niemeyer, 1943).

—*A History of Pentateuchal Traditions* (trans. B.W. Anderson; SPRS, 5; Chico, CA: Scholars Press, 1981), pp. 47-51, reprinted from the 1972 edition (Englewood Cliffs, NJ: Prentice–Hall), original: *Überlieferungsgeschichte des Pentateuch* (Stuttgart: Kohlhammer Verlag, 1948).

—*Könige. I Könige 1–16* (BKAT, 9.1; Neukirchen–Vluyn: Neukirchener Verlag, 1968).

O'Brien, M.A., *The Deuteronomistic History Hypothesis: A Reassessment* (OBO, 92; Göttingen: Vandenhoeck & Ruprecht, 1989).

Parker, K.I., 'The Limits to Solomon's Reign: A Response to Amos Frisch', *JSOT* 51 (1991), pp. 15-21.

—'Repetition as a Structuring Device in I Kings 1–11', *JSOT* 42 (1988), pp. 19-27.

—'Solomon as Philosopher King?: The Nexus of Law and Wisdom in I Kings 1–11', *JSOT* 53 (1992), pp. 75-91.

Paul, M.J., 'Hilkiah and the Law (2 Kings 22) in the 17th and 18th Centuries: Some Influences on W.M.L. de Wette', in N. Lohfink (ed.) *Das Deuteronomium: Entstehung, Gestalt und Botschaft* (BETL, 68; Leuven: Leuven University Press, 1985), pp. 9-12.

—'King Josiah's Renewal of the Covenant (2 Kings 22–23)', in C. Breckelmans and J. Lust (eds.), *Pentateuchal and Deuteronomistic Studies: Papers Read at the XIIIth IOSOT Congress, Leuven 1989* (Leuven: Leuven University Press, 1990), pp. 269-76.

Perlitt, L., 'Hebraismus-Deuteronomismus-Judaismus', in L. Perlitt, *Deuteronomium-Studien* (Tübingen: J.C.B. Mohr, 1994), pp. 247-60.

Person, R.F., *Second Zechariah and the Deuteronomic School* (JSOTSup, 167; Sheffield: JSOT Press, 1993).

Peterca, V., 'Ein midraschartiges Auslegungsbeispiel zugunsten Salomos 1 Kön 8,12-13–3 Reg 8,53a', *BZ* 31 (1987), pp. 270-75.

Petersen, D.L., 'The Temple in Persian Period Prophetic Texts', in P.R. Davies (ed.), *Second Temple Studies. I. The Persian Period* (JSOTSup, 117; Sheffield: JSOT, 1991), pp. 125-44.

Polzin, R., *David and the Deuteronomist* (Bloomington: Indiana University Press 1993).

—*Moses and the Deuteronomist: A Literary Study of the Deuteronomistic History. I. Deuteronomy, Joshua, Judges* (New York: Seabury, 1980).

—*Samuel and the Deuteronomist. II. 1 Samuel* (New York: Harper & Row, 1989).

Preuß, H.D., 'Zum deuteronomistischen Geschichtswerk', *TRu* 58 (1993), pp. 229-64, 341-95.

Provan, I.W., *Hezekiah and the Books of Kings: A Contribution to the Debate about the Composition of the Deuteronomistic History* (BZAW, 172; Berlin: W. de Gruyter, 1988).

—'Ideologies, Literary and Critical: Reflections on Recent Writing of the History of Israel', *JBL* 114 (1995), pp. 585-606.

—*1 and 2 Kings* (NIBC; Peabody, MA: Hendrickson, 1995).

Rad, G. von, 'The Deuteronomic Theology of History in I and II Kings', in *The Problem of the Hexateuch and other Essays* (trans. and ed. E.W. Trueman; Edinburgh: Oliver & Boyd, 1966), pp. 205-21, original: 'Das deuteronomistische Geschichtstheologie in den Königsbücher', in *Deuteronomium Studien* Part B (FRLANT, 40; Göttingen: Vandenhoek & Ruprecht, 1947), pp. 52-64.

—'The Form Critical Problem of the Hexateuch', (trans. E.W.T. Dicken; Edinburgh: Oliver & Boyd, 1965), original: *Das formgeschichtliche Problem des Hexateuch* (Munich: Chr. Kaiser Verlag, 1938).

Reinhartz, A., 'Anonymous Women and the Collapse of the Monarchy: A Study in Narrative Technique', in A. Brenner (ed.), *A Feminist Companion to Samuel and Kings* (FCB, 5; Sheffield: Sheffield Academic Press, 1994), pp. 43-65.

Richter, W., 'Die *nagid*-Formel: Ein Beitrag zur Erhellung des *nagid*-Problems', *BZ* 9 (1965), pp. 71-84.

Robinson, B.P., 'Elijah at Horeb, 1 Kings 19.1-18: A Coherent Narrative?', *RB* 98 (1991), pp. 513-36.

Rofé, A., 'The Vineyard of Naboth: The Origin and Message of the Story', *VT* 38 (1988), pp. 89-104.

Rogers, J.S., 'Narrative Stock and Deuteronomistic Elaboration in 1 Kings 2', *CBQ* 50 (1988), pp. 398-413.

Rogerson, J.W., Review of *In Search of History: Historiography in the Ancient World and the Origins of Biblical History* (New Haven and London: Yale University Press, 1983), by John Van Seters, in *JTS* 37 (1986), pp. 451-54.

Römer, T.C., 'Transformations in Deuteronomistic and Biblical Historiography: On "Book-Finding" and other Literary Strategies', *ZAW* 107 (1997), pp. 1-11.

Rose, M., 'Bemerkungen zum historischen Fundament des Josia-Bildes in II Reg 22f.', *ZAW* 89 (1977), pp. 50-63.

Rost, L., *The Succession to the Throne of David* (trans. M.D. Rutter and D.M. Gunn; HTIBS, 1; Sheffield: Almond Press, 1982), original: *Die Überlieferung von der Thronnachfolge Davids* (BWANT, 42; Stuttgart: W. Kohlhammer, 1926).

Rudolph, W., 'Zum Text der Königsbücher', *ZAW* 61 (1951), pp. 201-15.

Rütersworden, U., *Die Beamten der israelitischen Königzeit* (BWANT, 117; Stuttgart: W. Kohlhammer, 1985).

Salzman, P.C., 'Culture as Enhabilmentis', in L. Holy and M. Stuchlik (eds.), *The Structure of Folk Models* (ASAM, 20; London: Academic Press, 1981), pp. 233-56.

Sarbin, T.H., and J.I. Kitusse, 'A Prologue to *Constructing the Social*', in T.H. Sarbin and J.I. Kitusse (eds.), *Constructing the Social* (London: Sage, 1994), pp. 1-18.

Savran, G., '1 and 2 Kings', in R. Alter and F. Kermode (eds.), *The Literary Guide to the Bible* (London: Fontana, 1987), pp. 146-64.

Scheff, T.J., 'Emotions and Identity: A Theory of Ethnic Nationalism', in C. Calhoun (ed.), *Social Theory and the Politics of Identity* (Oxford: Basil Blackwell, 1994), pp. 277-303.

Schmidt, L., *Menschlicher Erfolg und Jahwes Initiative: Studien zu Tradition, Interpretation und Historie in Überlieferungen von Gideon, Saul und David* (Neukirchen–Vluyn: Neukirchener Verlag, 1970).

Schneider, T.J., 'Rethinking Jehu', *Bib* 77 (1996), pp. 100-107.

Schniedewind, W.M., 'Notes and Observations: Textual Criticism and Theological Interpretation: The Pro-Temple *Tendenz* in the Greek Text of Samuel–Kings', *HTR* 87 (1994), pp. 107-16.

Scott, J.M., 'Philo and the Restoration of Israel', in *SBL 1995 Seminar Papers* (Atlanta: Scholars Press, 1995), pp. 553-75.

Shaviv, S., 'Nabi and Nagid in I Samuel IX 1–X 16', *VT* 34 (1984), pp. 108-13.

Shanks, H., 'David Found at Dan', *BARev* 20 (1994), pp. 26-39.

Shenkel, J.D., *Chronology and Recensional Development in the Greek Text of Kings* (Cambridge, MA: Harvard University Press, 1968).

Smend, R., *Die Entstehung des Alten Testaments* (Stuttgart: W. Kohlhammer, 1978).

—'Das Gesetz und die Völker', in H.W. Wolff (ed.), *Probleme biblischer Theologie* (Munich: Chr. Kaiser Verlag, 1971), pp. 494-509.

Smith, A.D., *The Ethnic Origins of Nations* (Oxford: Basil Blackwell, 1986).

Smith, D.L., *The Religion of the Landless: The Social Context of the Babylonian Exile* (Bloomington, IN: Meyer Stone, 1989).

Smith, J.Z., *Map is not Territory: Studies in the History of Religions* (SJLA, 23; Leiden: E.J. Brill, 1978).

Smith, M., *Palestinian Parties and Politics that Shaped the Old Testament* (London: SCM Press, 2nd edn, 1987).

Smith-Christopher, D.L., 'The Mixed Marriage Crisis in Ezra 9–10 and Nehemiah 13: A Study of the Sociology of the Post-Exilic Judaean Community', in T.C. Eskenazi and K.H. Richards (eds.), *Second Temple Studies. II. Temple Community in the Persian Period* (JSOTSup, 175; Sheffield: JSOT Press, 1994), pp. 243-65.

Somers, M.R., and G.D. Gibson, 'Reclaiming the Epistemological "Other": Narrative and the Social Construction of Identity', in C. Calhoun (ed.), *Social Theory and the Politics of Identity* (Oxford: Basil Blackwell, 1994), pp. 37-99.

Sperber, D., *Rethinking Symbolism* (trans. A.L. Morton; CSSA; Cambridge: Cambridge University Press, 1975).

Spina, F.A., 'Eli's Seat: The Transition from Priest to Prophet', *JSOT* 62 (1994), pp. 67-75.

Stahl, R., Summary of R. Stahl, 'Aspekte der Geschichte deuteronomistischer Theologie: Zur Traditionsgeschichte der Terminologie und zur Redaktionsgeschichte der Redekomposition' (Diss. B., Jena, 1982), *TLZ* 108 (1983), pp. 74-75.

Strange, J., 'Joram, King of Israel and Judah', *VT* 25 (1975), pp. 191-201.

Strange, J.F., 'Reading Archaeological and Literary Evidence: A Response to Sara Mandell', in J. Neusner (ed.), *Religion and the Political Order: Politics in Classical and Contemporary Christianity, Islam and Judaism* (SRSO, 15; Atlanta: Scholars Press, 1996), pp. 49-58.

Tagliacarne, P., *'Keiner war wie er' Untersuchung zur Struktur von 2 Könige 22–23* (ATSAT, 31; St Ottilien: EOS Verlag, 1989).

Talmon, S., 'Polemics and Apology in Biblical Historiography: 2 Kings 17:24-41', in R.E. Friedman (ed.), *The Creation of Sacred Literature* (NES, 22; Berkeley: University of California Press, 1981), pp. 57-68.

Talshir, Z., *The Alternative Story of the Division of the Kingdom (3 Kingdoms 12:24 q-z)* (Jerusalem: Simor, 1993).

—'The Contribution of Diverging Traditions Preserved in the Septuagint to Literary Criticism of the Bible', in L. Greenspoon and O. Munnich (eds.), *VIIIth Congress of the IOSCS, Paris 1992* (SCSS, 41; Atlanta: Scholars Press, 1995), pp. 21-41.

—'Is the Alternative Tradition of the Division of the Kingdom (3 Kgdms 12:2a-z) Non-Deuteronomistic?', in G.J. Brooke and B. Lindars (eds.), *Septuagint, Scrolls and Cognate Writings: Papers Presented to the International Symposium on the Septuagint and its Relations to the Dead Sea Scrolls and Other Writings, Manchester 1990* (SCSS, 33; Atlanta: Scholars Press, 1992), pp. 599-621.

—'The Three Deaths of Josiah and the Strata of Biblical Historiography (2 Kgs XXIII 29-30; 2 Chronicles XXXV 20:5; 1 Esdras I 23-31)', *VT* 46 (1996), pp. 213-36.

Talstra, E., *Solomon's Prayer: Synchrony and Diachrony in the Composition of I Kings 8, 14-61* (CBET, 3; Kampen: Kok Pharaos, 1993).

Thackeray, J.S., 'The Greek Translators of the Four Books of Kings', *JTS* 8 (1907), pp. 262-78.

Thompson, T.L., *Early History of the Israelite People: From the Written and Archaeological Sources* (SHANE, 4; Leiden, E.J. Brill, 1992).

—'The Intellectual Matrix of Early Biblical Narrative: Exclusive Monotheism in Persian Period Palestine', in D.V. Edelman (ed.), *The Triumph of Elohim: From Jahwisms to Judaisms* (CBET, 13; Kampen: Kok Pharos, 1995), pp. 107-24.

—'A Neo-Albrightean School in History and Biblical Scholarship', *JBL* 114 (1995), pp. 683-98.

Tov, E. 'The LXX Additions (Miscellanies) in 1 Kings 2 (3 Reigns 2)', *Textus* 11 (1984), pp. 90-117.

Trebolle Barrera, J., 'A Preliminary Edition of 4QKings (4Q54)', in J. Trebolle Barrera and L. Vegas Montarer (eds.), *The Madrid Qumran Congress: Proceedings of the International Congress on the Dead Sea Scrolls, Madrid 18-21 March 1991* (2 vols.; STDJ, 11; Leiden: E.J. Brill, 1992), I, pp. 229-246.

—'Redaction, Recension, and Midrash in the Books of Kings', *BIOSCS* 15 (1982), pp. 12-35.

—'The Text-Critical Use of the Septuagint in the Books of Kings', in C. Cox (ed.), *VIIth Congress of the IOSCS, Leuven 1989* (SCSS, 31; Atlanta: Scholars Press, 1991), pp. 285-99.

Turner, V., 'Social Dramas and Stories about Them', in W.J.T. Mitchell (ed.), *On Narrative* (Chicago: University of Chicago Press, 1981), pp. 137-64.

Ulrich, E., J.W. Wright, R.P. Carroll and P.R. Davies (eds.), *Priests, Prophets and Scribes: Essays on the Formation and Heritage of Second Temple Judaism in Honour of Joseph Blenkinsopp* (JSOTSup, 149; Sheffield JSOT Press, 1992).

Valeri, V., 'Constitutive History: Genealogy and Narrative in the Legitimation of Hawaiian Kingship', in E. Ohnuki-Tierney (ed.), *Culture through Time: Anthropological Approaches* (Stanford: Stanford University Press, 1990), pp. 154-92.

VanderKam, J.C., 'Ezra-Nehemiah or Ezra and Nehemiah?', in E. Ulrich *et al.* (eds.), *Priests, Prophets and Scribes: Essays on the Formation and Heritage of Second Temple Judaism in Honour of Joseph Blenkinsopp* (JSOTSup, 149; Sheffield: JSOT Press, 1992), pp. 55-75.

Vanoni, G., 'Beobachtungen zur deuteronomistischen Terminologie in 2 Kön 23,25–25:30', in N. Lohfink (ed.), *Das Deuteronomium Entstehung: Gestalt und Botschaft* (BETL, 68; Leuven, Leuven University Press, 1985), pp. 357-62.

Van Seters, J., *In Search of History: Historiography in the Ancient World and the Origins of Biblical History* (New Haven and London: Yale University Press, 1983).

Van Winkle, D.W., '1 Kings XII–XIII 34: Jeroboam's Cultic Innovations and the Man of God from Judah', *VT* 46 (1996), pp. 101-14.

Viviano, P.A., '2 Kings 17: A Rhetorical and Form-Critical Analysis', *CBQ* 49 (1987), pp. 548-59.

Walsh, J.T., 'The Characterization of Solomon in First Kings 1-5', *CBQ* 57 (1995), pp. 471-93.

—'The Contexts of 1 Kings XIII', *VT* 39 (1989), pp. 354-70.

—*1 Kings* (Berit; Collegeville, MN: Liturgical Press, 1996).

—'Methods and Meanings: Multiple Studies of I Kings 21', *JBL* 111 (1992), pp. 193-211.

Washington, H.C., 'The Strange Woman (אשה זרה/נכריה) of Proverbs 1–9 and Post Exilic Judaean Society', in T.C. Eskenazi and K.H. Richards (eds.), *Second Temple Studies. II. Temple Community in the Persian Period* (JSOTSup, 175; Sheffield: JSOT Press, 1994), pp. 217-42.

Weinfeld, M., *Deuteronomy and the Deuteronomic School* (Oxford: Clarendon Press, 1972).

Weippert, H., 'Die "deuteronomistischen" Beurteilung der Könige von Israel und Juda und das Problem der Redaktion der Königsbücher', *Bib* 53 (1972), pp. 301-39.

—'Das deuteronomistische Geschichtswerk: Sein Ziel und Ende in der neueren Forschung', *TRu 50* (1985), pp. 213-49.

Welch, A.C., 'The Death of Josiah', *ZAW* 43 (1925), pp. 25-60.

White, H., 'The Value of Narrativity in the Representation of Reality', in W.J.T. Mitchell (ed.), *On Narrative* (Chicago: University of Chicago Press, 1981), pp. 1-23.

Whitelam, K.W., 'Sociology or History: Towards a (Human) History of Ancient Palestine?', in J. Davies, G. Harvey and W.G.E. Watson (eds.), *Words Remembered, Texts Renewed: Essays in Honour of John F.A. Sawyer* (JSOTSup, 195; Sheffield: Sheffield Academic Press, 1995), pp. 148-66.

Williamson, H.G.M., *Israel in the Book of Chronicles* (Cambridge University Press, 1977).

—'The Death of Josiah and the Continuing Development of the Deuteronomistic History', *VT* 32 (1982), pp. 242-48.

Willis, T.M., 'The Text of 1 Kings 11:43–12:3', *CBQ* 53 (1991), pp. 37-44.

Wolff, H.W., 'Das Kerygma des deuteronomistischen Geschichtswerks', *ZAW* 73 (1961), pp. 171-86.

Würthwein, E., *Die Bücher der Könige: 1 Könige 1–16* (Göttingen: Vandenhoek & Ruprecht, 2nd edn, 1985).

—*Die Bücher der Könige: 1 Könige 17–2 Kön. 25* (Göttingen: Vandenhoek & Ruprecht, 1984).

—'Erwägungen zum sog. deuteronomistichen Geschichtswerk: Eine Skizze', in E. Würthwein, *Studien zum deuteronomistischen Geschichtswerk* (BZAW, 227; Berlin: W. de Gruyter, 1994), pp. 1-11.

—'Die Josianische Reform und das Deuteronomium', in E. Würthwein, *Studien zum deuteronomistischen Geschichtswerk* (BZAW, 227; Berlin: W. de Gruyter, 1994), pp. 188-216, reprinted from *ZTK* 73 (1976), pp. 395-423.

Younger, K.L., 'A Critical Review of John Van Seters, *In Search of History*', *JSOT* 40 (1988), pp. 110-17.

Zakovitch, Y., 'Story versus History', in D.C. Kron (ed.), *Proceedings of the Eighth World Congress of Jewish Studies: Panel Sessions: Bible Studies and Hebrew Language; Jerusalem August 16-21, 1981* (Jerusalem: World Union of Jewish Studies, 1983), pp. 47-60.

Zöbel, H.-J., ישראל *yisra'el'*, *TDOT*, VI, pp. 307-420; original in *ThWAT*, III, pp. 986-1011.

INDEXES

INDEX OF REFERENCES

OLD TESTAMENT

OTHER ANCIENT LITERATURE

INDEX OF AUTHORS

JOURNAL FOR THE STUDY OF THE OLD TESTAMENT
SUPPLEMENT SERIES